Shepsle

Congress Reconsidered

Congress Reconsidered

edited by

Lawrence C. Dodd
University of Texas at Austin

and

Bruce I. Oppenheimer
Brandeis University

PRAEGER PUBLISHERS · New York

COPYRIGHT ACKNOWLEDGMENTS

"The Conservative Coalition in Congress," by John F. Manley, is reprinted from *American Behavioral Scientist*, Vol. 17, no. 2 (Nov./Dec. 1973), pp. 223–247, by permission of the Publisher, Sage Publications, Inc.

"Congress and the President: Enemies or Partners?," by James L. Sundquist, has been condensed, with minor modifications, from the author's chapter 13 in *Setting National Priorities: The Next Ten Years*, edited by Henry Owen and Charles L. Schultze. © 1976 by The Brookings Institution. Used by permission of The Brookings Institution.

"Will Reform Change Congress?," by Charles O. Jones, was originally prepared for a seminar on "The Role of Congress II, A Study of the Legislative Branch." © 1975 by Time Inc. and Charles O. Jones. Reprinted by permission.

"Strengthening a Congressional Strength," by Richard F. Fenno, Jr., was originally prepared for a seminar on "The Role of Congress II, A Study of the Legislative Branch," © 1975 by Time Inc. and Richard F. Fenno, Jr. Reprinted by permission.

Published in the United States of America in 1977
by Praeger Publishers,
200 Park Avenue, New York, N.Y. 10017

© 1977 by Praeger Publishers,
A Division of Holt, Rinehart and Winston, Publishers
All rights reserved

Library of Congress Cataloging in Publication Data
Main entry under title:

Congress reconsidered.

Bibliography: p. 308
1. United States. Congress—Addresses, essays,
lectures.   I. Dodd, Lawrence C.   II. Oppenheimer,
Bruce Ian.
JK1061.C587   328.73   76-17249
ISBN 0-275-23410-X
ISBN 0-275-64640-8 pbk.

789 074 987654321

Printed in the United States of America

Preface

Why reconsider Congress? It is a logical question to ask. After all, there exists a substantial body of literature on Congress. Why another book? Why this book?

Those are the very questions we might have asked in November 1974. Both of us had been teaching courses on Congress at our respective universities—a small, private one in the Northeast and a large, public one in the Southwest. We were just starting a year's stint in Washington as American Political Science Association Congressional Fellows. And it did not take us long to discover the need for a book like *Congress Reconsidered*. The Congress we observed and worked in ourselves was indeed substantially different from the one about which we had read and taught.

From the waning days of the 93rd Congress through much of the first session of the 94th Congress, we witnessed a period of great activity and change. The separate events in and of themselves were fascinating—the fall of Wilbur Mills, the overthrow of three House committee chairpersons, the start of the new congressional budget process, the modification of the Senate filibuster rule, the activities of the select intelligence committees, the increasingly active party caucuses, and many other events. Taken together, these events possessed far greater meaning. What we witnessed, in fact, was the culmination

of a substantial period of congressional reform and a consequent creation of a new structure of congressional power. That in itself makes
reconsideration of Congress a worthy venture, particularly since the
new power structure has been justified as a means of strengthening
the role of Congress in the American political system.

A reassessment of Congress must occur at several levels. The first
level is in terms of players and organizational processes. Congress is
not now the home of a few powerful conservatives who possess substantial power as chairs of standing committees. Instead, a relatively
large number of members share power as chairs of standing subcommittees; in addition, moderates and liberals rather than conservatives
tend to be dominant. Congress today no longer features what Harry
McPherson, a former aide to Lyndon Johnson and now a Washington
lawyer, described in *A Political Education* as the Senate's "whales"—
members who had "the negative power to stop legislation" and without whom a "controversial proposal could not pass." The existing
members of Congress are only shadows of individuals such as Richard
Russell, Robert Kerr, and Clinton Anderson in the Senate, or Wilbur
Mills, Howard Smith, and Carl Vinson in the House. Strangely, however, the "minnows"—those with little or no influence—are also a
disappearing species. As McPherson himself phrased it in a recent informal discussion of congressional change, the members of Congress
today are mostly "speckled trout." This leveling in status and influence in the House and Senate has resulted from reforms that distributed many of the requisite resources for influence among a wide
number of members, both within standing committees and within
party caucuses. In turn, as several of the essays in this collection demonstrate, the leveling and spreading of political resources has had
profound effects on the way the congressional process operates.

A second level at which to reconsider Congress involves specifying and evaluating the consequences of reform for congressional policy making. One of the outgrowths of the Vietnam war, Watergate,
and a general mistrust of presidential power has been the cry from the
public and from within Congress for Congress to reassert itself in the
making of public policy. Congress has responded with the War Powers Act, the Budget and Impoundment Control Act, investigations of
the CIA and FBI, and beefed-up professional staffing and information
services. Is the new budget process giving Congress better control
over federal spending and forcing it to set policy priorities? Did its investigations of the intelligence community produce useful results? Can
we expect Congress to spend time overseeing the federal bureaucracy?
Can Congress usefully play a role independent of the president in the
making of domestic and foreign policy? These are the types of questions to which a second set of essays in this collection is addressed.

On a final level, reconsideration of Congress requires looking at the changes in a broader perspective. Congress is intended to play an integral part in our constitutional system as our most democratic institution, the institution that can speak authoritatively for the citizenry and yet be responsive to and representative of their numerous and varied policy demands. Most political observers believe that Congress has been in decline during the twentieth century, that it increasingly has lacked the capacity and willingness to fulfill its constitutional responsibilities. The decline of Congress is seen as one element in the rise of an imperial presidency. A third set of essays in this volume inquires into the ability of recent reforms to change the overall functioning of Congress and to assist Congress in reasserting its constitutional roles. These essays focus not on particular dimensions of congressional change or process but rather on the general viability of Congress as an institution and the direction we can expect of it in the future.

For purposes of organization, this book is divided into four sections. Part I is designed to give general accountings of the changes and continuities that characterize the new Congress. The first two essays discuss the internal organization and procedures of the Senate and the House, stressing the ways in which recent reforms include moves toward both decentralization and centralization of congressional power. The third essay provides an overview of key patterns of electoral change that underlie these broader organizational transformations. The other three parts of the book correspond to the three levels of analysis described above. Part II includes three essays that highlight specific internal areas of congressional change: the conservative coalition, the revenue committees, and party control of the Rules Committee. These three essays were selected to illustrate changes at the individual, committee, and party levels. Part II concludes with an essay that provides a theoretical framework for the discussion of congressional structure, process, and change. Part III focuses on the changing nature of congressional-executive relations and the potential impact of these changes on the policy process. The first three essays are (1) a systematic discussion and evaluation of the new budgetary process, (2) a firsthand account of the recent House and Senate investigations into the intelligence community, and (3) a discussion of the possibility for and constraints on congressional oversight of the bureaucracy. The fourth essay delves into the changing relations between the Congress and the president, with regard to both domestic and foreign policy.

The final part provides a broad perspective on Congress and its future. The first essay considers the potential impact of recent reforms on party government and the factors that should shape the future direction of congressional parties. The second essay assesses reforms from the perspective of the individual representative and committee decision making and suggests directions for future changes within committees. The concluding essay places the reforms of the 1970s, and the essays in this book, in a broader historical and theoretical perspective; it argues that a long-term strengthening of Congress may require alterations of the constitutional structure itself.

There is a necessary overlap between the various sections of this collection and the various essays. The general overview essays do discuss specific internal patterns of continuity and change. Essays on internal dynamics contain substantial material relevant to policy processes. Material on congressional-executive relations also presents assessment of the future of those relations. And so forth. The division between sections is thus a bit arbitrary. We have tried to group the essays according to their primary focus and in a manner that would best assist the reader in comprehending and assessing the nature of the current Congress. As an aid in ensuring both the accuracy of the essays and their utility, we have chosen essays by individuals who, in virtually every case, combine firsthand experience in Congress with experience in teaching about Congress in the college classroom. Moreover, to ensure timeliness, most of the essays were commissioned specifically for this collection. Two essays were recently written but not yet published; two others were previously published. These four were selected because of the important contributions they offer to the reconsideration theme and because they are contemporaneous in content and focus.

This collection constitutes an effort to engender in others our own fascination with and appreciation of Congress. We hope that the essays presented here will better enable students of Congress to assess its new emerging structure and to reconsider its position in American politics. Although confident that *Congress Reconsidered* does fulfill these goals, we are firm believers that the proof of the pudding is in the eating. We invite our readers to take a taste and judge for themselves.

L.C.D.
B.I.O.

Acknowledgments

We would be remiss if we did not extend our warmest appreciation to the many individuals who fostered us in putting together this
collection. Without the American Political Science Association Congressional Fellowship Program, *Congress Reconsidered* would not have
been conceived or possible. The Fellowship experience provided us
with the inspiration, the time, and the access to pull our ideas
together. Moreover, it is important to point out that many of the contributors have also been Congressional Fellows, while others have
benefited from the program indirectly. Tom Mann, director of the
Fellowship, put together a first-rate year for us and offered excellent
comments on many of our ideas. The other program participants in
1974–75, especially John Ellwood, Eve Lubelin, Michael Lyons, Cathy
Rudder, and Marcia Whicker Taylor, were major sources of insight
and careful critics of our ideas.

The offices in which we worked during the program were unusually conducive to our own reconsiderations of Congress. In Bruce
Oppenheimer's case, Congressman Gillis W. Long (D-La.) and his
staff offered insights, openness, encouragement, and personal friendship that cannot easily be repaid, and the Rules Committee members
and staff were unusually cooperative with his research efforts. For
Lawrence Dodd, Congressman John McFall (D-Calif.), his administra-

tive assistant, Irv Sprague, and the staff of the House Majority Whip Office provided excellent help in understanding the rebirth of party leadership. Congressman Bob Eckhardt (D-Tex.) and his staff provided Dodd with their invaluable insight into the many demands placed on a member daily engaged in committee struggles and deeply devoted to serving the public interest. In addition, we both benefited immensely from observing and conversing with Congressman Richard Bolling (D-Mo.), who probably has given more thought to the House, its workings, and its place in American government than any other member.

Others helped us in a variety of ways. Bob Peabody provided critical help in getting this book off the ground. Sheliah Koeppen allowed us to try out some of our ideas in essays for the *DEA News* and discussed them with us. Terry Sullivan, Paul Lenchner, James Thurber, and Arthur Stevens offered important comments and assistance. We are also grateful to our students for helping to sustain our interest once we returned to our respective campuses. Our contributors deserve much praise for producing such fine essays under serious time constraints. Denise Rathbun, our editor at Praeger, has played an important part in molding this project and has been extremely patient in responding to our questions.

Our moves to and from Washington, our unpredictable schedules on Capitol Hill, and our junketing between Boston and Austin as we completed the manuscript have not made us easy people to live with. Despite this, Kim, Cheryl, and Meredith have been understanding and supportive throughout the project. Finally, we must each acknowledge his tremendous debt to the other. From start to finish this has been a joint project with equally shared tasks. The experience has underscored for us both the personal joys and friendship that can derive from a truly cooperative venture such as this.

Contents

xi

I

PATTERNS OF CONGRESSIONAL CHANGE

1. The Changing Senate: From the 1950s to the 1970s

Norman J. Ornstein, Robert L. Peabody,
and David W. Rohde

Few political institutions have captured the attention of the American public as the United States Senate has. From televised hearings on crime, communism, and Watergate, from media attention focused on Senate-based presidential contenders, and from movies like *Mr. Smith Goes to Washington* and *Advise and Consent*, the public is much more aware of the Senate than it is of "the other body," the House of Representatives. Curiously, though, the public's awareness of the Senate has not been matched by a comprehensive and systematic analysis of how the Senate operates and how senators behave. We have broad knowledge of the Senate of the 1950s, thanks primarily to the efforts of two outstanding political scientists, Ralph K. Huitt and Donald R. Matthews.[1] But, like the rest of the American political system, the Senate has changed a good deal in the past two decades—in the nature of its membership, in its formal and informal leadership, in its internal processes and structures, and in its policy directions. This essay attempts to show how the Senate has changed, to what extent it has remained relatively stable, and why.[2]

The Membership

It will come as no surprise that the membership of the Senate has changed substantially since the mid-1950s. Only nineteen of the senators serving in the 94th Congress (1975–77) were also members of the 85th Congress (1957–59). The change, however, has meant more than simply substituting one man for another. With respect to a variety of criteria and categories, different *kinds* of senators have replaced those who served earlier, and this has had an effect on the operation of the Senate and on the policies it has produced. We will consider three aspects of this change: partisan division, ideology, and sectional party affiliation.

The most obvious of the changes has been in party affiliation of the membership. From the end of World War II through most of the 1950s, the partisan division of the Senate was unusually close. Neither party ever controlled the body by more than a few votes. However, in the election of 1958, the Democratic membership of the Senate jumped from 49 to 64. From that time until today, the number of Democrats has usually been in the 60s, and has never fallen below 55. In the 94th Congress, Democrats held 62 seats. Thus, the close partisan division of the 1950s has been followed by two decades of Democratic dominance.

A second aspect of change relates to the regional character of the two parties. Through the 1950s, Democratic membership was concentrated in the South and West, while Republicans came primarily from the East and Midwest. For example, in 1957 the Democrats held every Senate seat from the South and 13 of the 22 seats from the West, but they had only 5 of the 20 eastern seats and 3 of the 22 midwestern seats. During the intervening years these regional patterns have changed markedly. In the 94th Congress the Democrats held a majority of the seats from every region of the country. However, dramatic gains by Democrats in the East and Midwest have been somewhat offset by losses in the South. In 1975 Democrats held 16 of the 22 southern seats.

These two changes—the increase in the number of Democrats and the altered regional character of the parties—have combined to alter substantially the relative power of various groups within the Senate. Until the 1960s southern Democrats dominated the Democratic party in the Senate, and through that dominance and frequent alliance with conservative Republican members, they were able to control the Senate. With the narrow partisan division of the 1950s, southerners accounted for more than 40 percent of the Democratic membership. With the large influx of northern Democrats after the 1958 election, the percentage fell to 34. This was followed by a fairly continuous decline as the Republicans began winning seats in the South. In 1975 south-erners accounted for only 26 percent of Senate Democrats.

The partisan and regional changes also partially caused a third aspect of Senate change, which relates to the ideological character of the membership. Table 1 shows the proportions of liberals, moderates, and conservatives among various groups of senators in 1957–58 and in 1975.[3]

Democrats in the 85th Congress were divided almost evenly be-tween liberals and conservatives, whereas the Republicans were over-whelmingly conservative. This produced a conservative majority in the Senate in 1957–58. The subsequent sharp increase in the number of Democrats and almost matching decline in the number of Republi-cans produced a liberal plurality by 1975.

It should also be noted from the table, however, that not all of the ideological change is due to these numerical shifts. On the contrary, there have also been shifts in the make-up of various subgroups in the Senate. For example, in the 85th Congress, while northern and south-ern Democrats had their distinct ideological character, there was also substantial heterogeneity within each group. By the 94th Congress this was no longer true; there were no northern conservatives and no southern liberals, and the proportion of moderates in each group had also declined. Over the same period, moreover, the Republicans in the Senate became a good deal more heterogeneous.

Thus, through these changes, the Senate has become more Demo-

Table 1. Ideological Divisions in the Senate, 85th Congress (1957–58) and 94th Congress (1975)

	85TH CONGRESS (1957–58)				
	Northern Democrats	*Southern Democrats*	*All Democrats*	*Republicans*	*All Members*
Liberals	67%	9%	41%	2%	22%
Moderates	19	27	22	26	24
Conservatives	15	64	37	72	54
	(N = 27)	(N = 22)	(N = 49)	(N = 47)	(N = 96)

	94TH CONGRESS (1975)				
	Northern Democrats	*Southern Democrats*	*All Democrats*	*Republicans*	*All Members*
Liberals	85%	—	63%	16%	45%
Moderates	15	19%	16	26	20
Conservatives	—	81	21	58	35
	(N = 46)	(N = 16)	(N = 62)	(N = 38)	(N = 100)

cratic, more liberal, and less dominated by southerners than was the case in the 1950s. These changes have had substantial impact on the Senate, the most important of which are suggested below.

Norms and Rules

The Senate is a continuing decision-making institution, and as such it has a set of formal rules that regulate its operations. It is also a group of individuals, and "just as any other group of human beings, has its unwritten rules of the game, its norms of conduct, its approved manner of behavior." [4] The Senate has both formal and informal rules, and while there has been a great deal of continuity in both categories during the past two decades, there have also been some significant changes.

The "unwritten rules" or norms of the Senate describe expectations about how a senator ought to behave and ought not to behave in his capacity as a senator, expectations that are shared by a large number of members. They indicate what patterns of behavior are expected of senators by other senators. In his study of the Senate in the mid-1950s, Donald Matthews cited six norms, or "folkways," as he termed them. The first was that new senators were expected to serve a period of *apprenticeship*. A freshman senator was expected to wait a substantial amount of time before participating fully in the work of the Senate. During this time freshmen were expected to learn about the Senate and seek the advice of senior members. A second norm required that members devote a major portion of their time to the *legislative work* that fell to them. A senator was to do his work in committee and on the floor and not seek personal publicity at the expense of his obligations. The third folkway was *specialization:* a senator was expected to concentrate his attention and activity on matters within the jurisdiction of his committees or those which particularly affected his constituents. The norm of *courtesy* required that the political conflicts within the body should not become personal conflicts. References to colleagues in legislative situations were formal and indirect, and personal attacks were deemed unacceptable. The fifth folkway was *reciprocity*. Members were expected to help colleagues when possible and to avoid pressing their formal powers too far (e.g., by systematically objecting to unanimous consent agreements). A member was to understand and appreciate the problems of his colleagues and to keep his bargains once they were struck. Finally, there was the norm of *institutional patriotism*, which required that a member protect the Senate as an institution, avoiding behavior that would bring it or its members into disrepute.

Many of these folkways, assuming that they are observed, provide substantial benefits to the collective membership, and it is not surprising that most of them have endured and are still recognized in the Senate today. For example, the norms of legislative work and specialization clearly persist. The Senate, like the House, is characterized by division of labor through the committee system. This system allocates legislative responsibilities to members, and these responsibilities have grown substantially since the 1950s. The Senate's ability to make policy depends in large measure upon each member's living up to the responsibilities allocated to him, and the norms of legislative work and specialization express the expectations of members that each of them ought to do so. One senator said that the way to have influence in the Senate was "just year after year of patience—willingness to carry at least your fair share of the work." Another said, on the same point, "I believe the principle could be stated very simply—that is, keep up with your work." When asked about specialization, a third senator commented:

> I believe that senators do specialize in their activities as far as their committee . . . that doesn't mean that they can't learn a lot about other things . . . but you are expected to know in greater detail and greater accuracy about the things that your committee has jurisdiction over. That is an obligation.

While legislative work and specialization still exist as norms—as *expectations*—we should note that these norms are observed less frequently today than they were in the 1950s. The increasing focus on the Senate as a presidential breeding ground has meant extended absences from the Senate while presidential campaigns are explored or promoted. To enhance their presidential possibilities, senators will often turn to the mass media, rather than their committees or the floor, as a forum for their policy ideas and get involved in a wide spectrum of policy areas extending beyond their committee assignments.

The folkways of courtesy, reciprocity, and institutional patriotism continue almost unabated in the Senate. Courtesy permits political conflict to remain depersonalized, allowing yesterday's opponent to be tomorrow's ally. (As one Republican senator said, "It's the catalyst that maintains a semblance of order.") Reciprocity, and particularly its aspect of individual integrity, continues to be important in an institution which operates informally and in which virtually all agreements are verbal. Finally, institutional patriotism tends to be reinforced by the increase in competition between Congress and the executive branch for control over policy outcomes in matters like foreign policy and the budget.

Thus, five of the folkways that were operative in the Senate two decades ago apparently still describe expected behavior within the body today. This is not true, however, of the sixth norm, apprenticeship. Unlike the other folkways, it is difficult to discern what benefits apprenticeship provided to the membership in general or collectively. Although, as Matthews noted,[5] it clearly had its roots very early in the Senate's history, by the 1950s the only group that could be seen to benefit from the observance of this norm were the senior conservatives in both parties who dominated the positions of power in the Senate at that time. Beginning with the 1958 election, as more and more liberal northern Democrats entered the Senate, the conservative dominance began to break down [6] and junior members had less incentive to observe the norm. Gradually, as these junior senators of the early 1960s became senior members, the expectations regarding the norm became less widely shared. Today, not only do junior members not want or feel the need to serve an apprenticeship, but also the senior members do not expect them to do so, as these statements from senators indicate:

> All the communications suggest "get involved, offer amendments, make speeches. The Senate has changed, we're all equals, you should act accordingly." [A junior Democrat]

> Well, that [apprenticeship] doesn't exist at all in the Senate. The senior Senators have made that very clear, both Democrats and Republicans. [A junior Republican]

> We now hope and expect and encourage the younger guys to dive right into the middle of it. [A senior conservative Republican]

Thus, the Senate of the 1970s is a more egalitarian institution when considered along seniority lines. Junior members have come to play a more important role within the Senate, and this change in the informal rule structure of the body has been one of the causes of some important changes in the formal rules.

One fairly direct result has been the adoption of certain rules that have placed direct limits on the importance of seniority. For example, in 1970 a rule was adopted which limited members to service on only one of the Senate's four top committees (Appropriations, Armed Services, Finance, and Foreign Relations). This rule restricted the centralization among senior members of assignments to these committees and facilitated the appointment of relatively junior senators much earlier in their careers than would have otherwise been possible. Also, both parties adopted rules that limited the role of seniority in the selection of committee chairmen. In 1973 the Republican caucus agreed to a system under which the Republican members of each committee would elect the ranking member. In 1975 the Democratic caucus adopted a proposal by Senator Dick Clark of Iowa (who had served only two years in the Senate), which permits secret ballot votes by the caucus on any committee chairman if one-fifth of the Democratic senators request it.

Another consequence of the enlargement of the role of junior members came from the fact that as they increased their activity, they began to feel more intensely the disparity of resources between themselves and the senior senators. This was particularly true with regard to staff. Therefore, the junior members sponsored and aggressively pushed a plan, S. Res. 60, which permitted them to hire additional legislative staff to assist in their committee duties. The Senate adopted S. Res. 60 in June 1975.

The Senate has also recently adopted a number of reforms that were not directly concerned with the interests of newer senators vis-à-vis their more senior colleagues. Certainly the most publicized of these was the 1975 change in the Senate's rule for cutting off debate. Liberals had been seeking to alter the rule for ending "filibusters" (which required the vote of two-thirds of the members present and voting) since the late 1950s. The new provision required the affirmative vote of three-fifths of the entire Senate membership. If almost all members voted, cloture (the technical term for ending debate) would be easier to achieve under the new rule.

A final set of reforms dealt with the openness of the Senate's conduct of its business. In 1975, almost three years after a similar action by the House, the Senate adopted rules requiring that most mark-up (i.e., bill-drafting) sessions be open to the press and the public. This set of rules also required open conference committee meetings, a change that the House, too, adopted in 1975.

Thus, since the 1950s, junior members have come to play an increasingly important role in Senate activity, and the expectations of senior members have gradually changed so that this is acceptable behavior. Partially as a consequence of this, the Senate has altered a number of its formal rules. The overall effect of these changes is that the Senate of the 1970s is a much more egalitarian and open institution in which each senator's ability to affect policy is less dependent on what formal position he holds or where he ranks in the seniority hierarchy.

Leadership

The evolution in Senate leadership patterns from the 1950s to the mid-1970s has both contributed to and been reflective of changes in

Senate membership, committee structure, norms, and rules. That such organizational variables should be closely related is hardly surprising. But if anything, the relatively small size of the Senate, the lengthy tenure of its membership, and its pervasive collegial atmosphere have all tended to reinforce their interconnected aspects, with enhanced consequences for decentralizing and power-sharing trends in the Senate.

Our task of assessing Senate practices and modifications in majority and minority party leadership over the first quarter of a century is facilitated by three factors. First, as already indicated, the writings of Huitt, Matthews, and others have provided a refined portrait of majority leader Lyndon Johnson and a well-developed sense of what the Senate was like under his direction in the 1950s.[7] Second, the lengthy tenure of his successor, Mike Mansfield, extends from 1961 until his retirement in 1976. For the first eight of his unprecedented sixteen years as majority leader, Mansfield worked closely with Democratic presidents Kennedy and Johnson; for the remaining eight years Republican presidents Nixon and Ford were in the White House. Thus, his tenure in office provides an unusually rich opportunity to analyze the role of a majority leader under both united and divided party control of the national government. Third, by a combination of circumstances, especially the announced retirements of both Mansfield and minority leader Hugh Scott (R-Pa.), 1976 promises to be a bench-mark year in party leadership change.[8]

In contrast, evaluation of Senate minority leadership patterns is somewhat complicated by the fact that four Republicans served as floor leaders for their party—Robert Taft (R-Ohio, 1953), William Knowland (R-Calif., 1953–58), Everett Dirksen (R-Ill., 1959–69), and Hugh Scott (R-Pa., 1969–76). Given Democratic dominance of the Senate over most of the past two decades, coupled with the more formally decentralized nature of Senate Republican leadership for most of this period, treatment of its role will be justifiably abbreviated here. With the major exception of Dirksen, Republican leadership continued to be "more formalized, institutionalized, and decentralized" than its Democratic counterpart.[9]

There is little need here to outline, let alone develop, the stark contrasts in the personalities and leadership styles of Johnson and Mansfield.[10] Suffice to conclude that whereas Johnson sought to centralize control over organizational and policy outcomes in himself, Mansfield's objective was to serve the Senate, to create and maintain a body that "permitted individual, coequal senators the opportunity to conduct their affairs in whatever ways they deemed appropriate."[11] One Democrat who served with both majority leaders summarizes these contrasts as follows:

Johnson was aggressive and Mansfield is more the organizer, manager. I think he senses his primary duty is to insure the Senate moves in the conduct of its business in the most orderly fashion that we can. The result of our actions, while I'm sure he feels strongly on a lot of issues, he leaves up to each individual. Lyndon Johnson wanted to influence the outcome of every decision—not just to insure that we acted, but acted in a certain way.[12]

The contrasting leadership styles of Johnson and Mansfield are starkly revealed by their attitudes toward—and, even more important, by their uses of—the several Democratic party instruments that they chaired: the Steering Committee (which makes committee assignments), the Policy Committee (which discusses issues and helps to set legislative agendas), and the Conference (the organizing body composed of all Democratic senators).

As leader, Johnson carefully controlled the appointment of members to both the Steering and Policy committees and then made every effort to dominate their deliberations. As one liberal Democrat on the Steering Committee recalled, Johnson "would come into the Steering Committee with his list, and that would be it. He'd just tell the Steering Committee who would be on [the committees]. [We] had no function at all."

In keeping with his general style of low-keyed, nondirective leadership, Mansfield approached the Steering Committee and the Policy Committee far differently. He seldom attempted to control their deliberations but rather permitted them to work their will. During his tenure as leader, most committee vacancies were filled primarily by accommodating the preferences of requesters. When there was competition for a vacancy—as was frequently the case in the most prestigious committees—the contest was settled by secret ballot.

Mansfield had, however, a profound, if more indirect, impact on Steering Committee outcomes. As leader, with control over appointments to the committee, he sought to liberalize its membership, and with notable effect. During his tenure, the membership of the committee became more and more representative of Senate Democrats in general, and thus increasingly liberal.[13] As a consequence, moderate and liberal Democratic strength on such important Senate committees as Appropriations, Armed Services, Finance, and Foreign Relations substantially increased.[14]

For Johnson, the seven-member Democratic Policy Committee in the 1950s served mainly as an advisory council charged with deciding what legislation should come to the floor and when. Its membership consisted mainly of senior, independent power holders, southerners like Richard Russell of Georgia, Lister Hill of Alabama, and Robert

Kerr of Oklahoma, plus a scattering of northern moderates. When Mansfield took over the chairmanship in 1961, he expanded the size of the committee, added more junior and liberal members, and generally sought to "democratize" its activities.

Under Johnson's reign, the Democratic Conference only infrequently met after its organizing session at the beginning of each new Congress. Under Mansfield's leadership, the party conference met more frequently and became a more significant party forum. Many of the reforms—staffing, open meetings, filibuster change, party leadership selection, committee jurisdictions—have been either initiated or preliminarily discussed in the Mansfield-run conference.

What can be concluded about the relative success of Johnson and Mansfield as Senate majority leaders? In his careful study of the last two Congresses under Johnson's direction and the first two Congresses under Mansfield's direction, John Stewart concludes:

> Despite the dispersal of many tasks of party leadership and the generally permissive if not at times passive attitude displayed by the majority leader [Mansfield] in managing the legislative program, the senatorial party in the Eighty-seventh and Eighty-eighth Congresses [1961–64] functioned effectively, and its performance compared favorably with and often surpassed the record compiled by the Eighty-fifth and Eighty-sixth Congresses [1957–60] under the driving and centralized leadership of Lyndon Johnson.[15]

Although greater historical perspective is needed to evaluate fully the relative effectiveness of these two leaders, they clearly illustrate the wide range of style, given different environmental settings, allowable in effective Senate leadership. Mansfield's relaxed style and his conscious attempts to bring junior members into Senate decision making have, however, clearly contributed to the diffusion of power and the opening of procedures and opportunities that have characterized the Senate in the 1970s.

Republicans have not been in the majority in the Senate since the 83rd Congress (1953–54). Unlike the Democratic party leadership, which is largely concentrated in the floor leader and whip, the Republicans elect different senators as floor leader, assistant floor leader or whip, chairman of the Republican Policy Committee, chairman of the Committee on Committees, and chairman of the Republican Conference. From the late 1950s through the 1960s, Dirksen's leadership style more nearly approximated Johnson's, especially in terms of its centralizing tendencies. Scott, his successor, in keeping with the changing membership and power structure of both Senate parties, more closely paralleled Mansfield's lower-keyed, shared leadership style.[16] The more open and relaxed leadership of both Scott and Mansfield was an important factor in the Senate's movement toward an egalitarian, decentralized form of decision making.

Committees

From its earliest days, the U.S. Senate, like the House of Representatives, has used a division of labor into a committee system to organize its work. The committee system is the single most important feature affecting legislative outcomes in the Senate; not surprisingly, the committee system has changed as other aspects of the Senate—work load, membership, power—have themselves been altered in the 1960s and 1970s.

Committee Assignments

Every senator is assigned to committees shortly after being sworn in. In addition, senators can and do switch assignments on occasion, when a vacancy occurs on a more attractive committee. Overall, the committee assignment process is crucial to the Senate, for it can determine the policy orientation and activity of each committee. Each party handles its own members' assignments; Democrats use a nineteen-member Steering Committee, chaired by the majority leader, while Republicans have a thirteen-member Committee on Committees, with an elected chairman. In the 1940s and early 1950s, committee assignments reflected the norm of apprenticeship: freshmen senators were assigned only to minor committees, and senior members dominated "prestige" committees like Foreign Relations, Appropriations, Finance, and Armed Services.

Lyndon Johnson changed these procedures when he became majority leader, instituting the "Johnson rule," which guaranteed every Democrat, no matter how junior, a major committee assignment. However, as we have noted, Johnson ran the Steering Committee as a one-man show, and he continued to parcel out choice assignments very selectively. Senior, more conservative members continued to dominate the prestige committees. Under Mike Mansfield, the Steering Committee has operated more democratically, and assignments to all committees have become more open to junior and liberal Democratic senators. Table 2 shows that, for the four most important Senate

Table 2.   Seniority at Time of Appointment to Prestigious Standing Committees

Committee	MEAN SENIORITY AT TIME OF APPOINTMENT (YEARS)	
	80th–84th Congresses *	*94th Congress*
Foreign Relations	8.1	4.0
Appropriations	5.8	2.0
Finance	3.0	2.7
Armed Services	2.1	1.2

* Figures taken from Donald R. Matthews, *U.S. Senators and Their World* (New York: Vintage, 1960), p. 153.

committees, junior members now have greater access to assignments. Indeed, in the 94th Congress, liberals Dick Clark and Joe Biden (D-Del.), in the Senate only two years, were assigned to the Foreign Relations Committee; two-year liberals Bill Hathaway (D-Me.) and Floyd Haskell (D-Colo.) were assigned to Finance; and freshmen John Culver (D-Iowa), Gary Hart (D-Colo.), and Patrick Leahy (D-Vt.), with no service at all in the Senate, were assigned to Armed Services. Gradually, the important Senate committees are beginning to reflect more accurately the Senate as a whole—in the process, they are becoming more junior and more liberal.

For the past several decades, committee chairmanships have been selected through the process of seniority, though, as we have noted, some modifications in this procedure have recently been implemented. But because of the operation of the seniority system, the overall decline of the South in the Democratic party has been reflected only partially in committee chairmanships. In 1975, as we have mentioned, southerners accounted for only 26 percent of Senate Democrats; however, they made up 39 percent of committee chairmanships, including the leadership of such powerful committees as Appropriations, Finance, Armed Services, Foreign Relations, and Judiciary. Northern liberals have made gains in the past few Congresses, though, and by 1975 they controlled seven committee chairmanships, including Budget, Government Operations, Banking, Housing and Urban Affairs, Labor and Public Welfare, and Commerce. With the likely departure in the near future of such senior southern Democrats as James Eastland and John Stennis of Mississippi, John McClellan of Arkansas, and John Sparkman of Alabama, northern liberals will ascend to the chairmanships of several more prestige committees, including Appropriations and Foreign Relations.

Committees and Work Load

An ever-increasing legislative work load has had a major impact on the Senate. There were five times as many roll calls on the Senate floor in the 93rd Congress as there were in the 84th, and the more than 1,000 roll calls were paralleled by increases in bills introduced and hearings held. As policy making has increased in number of decisions and in complexity, the Senate has responded in part by expanding the number of its committees and subcommittees. In 1957 there were 15 standing committees with 113 subcommittees in the Senate. By 1975 there were 18 committees and 140 subcommittees.

More important, perhaps, is that the Senate has increased the *sizes* of many committees and subcommittees. Since the size of the Senate has grown only by four members in the past several decades (with the addition of Hawaii and Alaska as states), this has meant more assignments for individual members. In 1957 each senator averaged 2.8 committee assignments and 6.3 subcommittee assignments, whereas by 1973 senators on the average served on 3.9 committees and 11.9 subcommittees.

As the number of committees and subcommittees has expanded, the number of available chairmanships and ranking minority memberships has grown correspondingly. With the turnover of the 1960s and 1970s, and the laissez-faire leadership of Mike Mansfield, many of the chairmanships have been assumed by junior members. Indeed, in the 94th Congress, first-term Democrats in the Senate averaged 1.9 subcommittee chairmanships; nearly all majority party senators receive at least one chairmanship the day they enter the body. Chairmanships mean influence; the ability to hold hearings, investigate problems, oversee executive branch activities, and report legislation is highly significant in the policy process. And the prestige of wielding a gavel can do much to overcome the stigma of inexperience. Thus, the expansion of subcommittees, to cope with work load, has enhanced the role of junior members and has contributed to the decline of the norm of apprenticeship. Since most of the junior Democrats are liberal, the expansion of subcommittees has also meant an expansion of power to the liberal forces.

More assignments per member also mean, of course, that each senator is spread thinner and has less time and attention to devote to any individual area. This has resulted in lessened expertise among senators and within committees. One response to this problem by legislators and committees has been to expand their staffs. We have already mentioned S. Res. 60, a 1975 device to expand the number of legislative assistants available to senators. Committee staffs have also grown, from roughly 300 in the 85th Congress to over 1,000 by the 94th.[17] The expansion of staffs has allowed senators to cope more easily with more work and greater responsibilities. It has also spread resources further in the Senate, to junior as well as senior senators. In recent years, staffs have been allocated increasingly through subcommittees rather than full committees. This has accentuated the spread of power to junior senators and has correspondingly reduced the relative power of committee chairmen. Writing of the Senate in the 1950s, Donald Matthews commented, "Within certain limits, the [committee] chairman appoints and controls the committee staff." [18] In the 1970s far more staff are appointed by subcommittee chairmen than by committee chairmen. The ability of committee chairmen to maintain monopoly control over expertise and to command unchallenged loyalty from staff, which had been emphasized by Matthews, no longer exists. Expertise and staff are now widely dispersed throughout the Senate.

Along with expanding subcommittee chairmanships and expanding staffs, there has also been more openness in committee deliberations in recent years. All of these factors together have loosened the control that committee leaders once maintained over the products of their committees. Junior senators on a committee now have subcommittee bases from which to challenge the policy recommendations of the committee chairman; moreover, senators who do not serve on a committee will have enough access to information to enable them to offer successful amendments on the floor to the committee's bills. Thus, in recent years committees have become less cohesive internally and have had their bills more open to challenge on the Senate floor. With the appearance of these trends, committees themselves, along with the chairmen, have had their influence in the Senate lessened. More frequently, in the 1970s, legislating in the Senate has shifted from the committee rooms to the Senate floor, while the functions of agenda setting and legislative oversight have moved from the committees to the subcommittees. Committees remain highly important; all legislation is referred to them, as are all executive and judicial nominations, and they retain the authority either to kill or to report out the bills and nominations. But the Senate is a more open and fluid and more decentralized body now than it was in the 1950s. Power, resources, and decision-making authority have become more diffuse. Changes in membership, norms, leadership, work load, and committees have, in interaction, produced a markedly different Senate in the 1970s.

The Senate as a Presidential Incubator

So far we have focused mainly on internal changes in Senate structures and behavior. But the Senate has not operated in a vacuum; it has been greatly affected by trends in the society and the broader political system, and it has in turn had its own impact on American politics. Nowhere is this more true than in the area of presidential nominations. Though senators actively contested for presidential nominations in past decades, in the period from 1960 to 1972 senators were dominant. During that twelve-year span, the two parties relied exclusively upon either senators (Kennedy, Goldwater, and McGovern) or former senators who became vice-presidents (Nixon, Johnson, and Humphrey) before obtaining their party's presidential nod.

There are numerous reasons for this remarkable string of successes by senatorial contenders. Because of several factors, governors of large states, who formerly were rivals in presidential nominating politics, have not been in a position, since 1960, to be serious contenders for nominations. The near-revolutionary growth in media influence over politics, especially that of television, has focused public attention on Washington and on the Senate. Television has contributed to, and been affected by, the increasing nationalization of party politics. A national attentiveness to foreign affairs has heightened the importance of the Senate with its well-defined constitutional role in foreign policy.

As the Senate has opened up its proceedings, spread its resources, and decentralized its power, it has become more attractive to potential presidential contenders. Nearly one-third of the members of the Senate were formerly governors, who now receive much more public attention from their Washington base.

The effects upon the Senate of this remarkable presidential focus extend beyond those few legislators who obtain party nominations.[19] Many more senators consider themselves presidential possibilities, or are mentioned as such on television networks and in the polls, and tailor their behavior accordingly, spreading out their legislative interests beyond the concerns of their individual states, increasing their legislative activity and public visibility, and emphasizing media coverage over legislative craftsmanship. As we commented earlier, this has contributed to violations of the norms of specialization and legislative work. It has also increased the pressure within the Senate to spread out resources and power to junior members.

Conclusion

As we have seen, the Senate has changed in varied and interrelated ways in the past two decades. The nature of the membership of the Senate, its internal norms and rules, its leadership styles and effects, its committees, and the role of the Senate as a breeding ground for presidential candidates have all evolved to make the Senate quite a different legislative institution in the 1970s from what it was in the 1950s.

The Senate has gone from close partisan balance to dominant Democratic party control. A powerful southern Democratic wing, which once maintained great power through the seniority system and a coalition with like-minded Republicans, has gradually diminished in size and influence,[20] while, beginning with the 1958 election, liberal northeastern and midwestern Democratic senators have experienced a corresponding growth in numbers and power. Junior senators, once relegated to a position of apprenticeship and subservience, have found their importance enhanced in the contemporary Senate. With the active assistance of Majority Leader Mike Mansfield, junior senators have developed access to prestigious committee assignments and to legislative staff resources and have carved out a highly significant role in the legislative process.

Through these and other trends, the Senate has become more open, more liberal, more decentralized, and more equal in its distribution of power. In the meantime, the Senate work load has increased markedly, senators' obligations and time commitments have also grown, and thus the ability of the Senate and its members to deal with complex problems in an in-depth fashion has been diminished. In 1976 the Senate launched two efforts—a Commission on the Operation of the Senate and a Select Committee to Study the Senate Committee System—to cope with its ever-increasing responsibilities. With the additional factor of the retirements of Majority Leader Mansfield and Minority Leader Scott, and thus the ascension of a whole new generation of leaders, it is clear that major change in the Senate has not been concluded. The Senate of the 1980s will likely be as different from the Senate of today as today's is from the Senate of the 1950s.

NOTES

1.	See the collection of articles by Huitt in Ralph K. Huitt and Robert L. Peabody, *Congress: Two Decades of Analysis* (New York:

Harper & Row, 1969); and Donald R. Matthews, *U.S. Senators and Their World* (New York: Vintage, 1960).

2. This article is part of a broader study of the Senate, conducted since 1973 by the authors, with the help of a grant from the Russell Sage Foundation. In addition to legislative and electoral data, our broader analysis rests upon more than fifty semistructured, taped interviews conducted with incumbent and former senators in 1973–76.

3. The classification is based on a variation of the conservative coalition support score published annually by Congressional Quarterly, Inc. The variation employed is produced by dividing the support score of a member by the sum of his support and opposition scores. This removes the effect of absences on the scores, and we call it the conservative coalition support ratio. We classified members whose scores were 0–30 as liberals, 31–70 as moderates, and 71–100 as conservatives. The scores for 1957–58 were calculated from the appropriate roll calls listed in the *Congressional Quarterly Almanac* for those years. The scores for 1975 were taken from Congressional Quarterly *Weekly Report,* January 24, 1976, p. 174.

4. Matthews, op. cit., p. 92.

5. Ibid., pp. 116–17.

6. For a discussion of the changes during the 1960s, see Randall B. Ripley, *Power in the Senate* (New York: St. Martin's, 1969), especially chap. 3.

7. In addition to the works of Huitt and Matthews, see Rowland Evans and Robert Novak, *Lyndon B. Johnson: The Exercise of Power* (New York: New American Library, 1966); Randall B. Ripley, *Majority Party Leadership in Congress* (Boston: Little, Brown, 1969); and John G. Stewart, "Two Strategies of Leadership: Johnson and Mansfield," in Nelson W. Polsby, ed., *Congressional Behavior* (New York: Random House, 1971), pp. 61–92.

8. Robert L. Peabody, *Leadership in Congress: Stability, Succession and Change* (Boston: Little, Brown, 1976).

9. Matthews, op. cit., p. 124.

10. Stewart, op. cit., and Peabody, op. cit., pp. 333–45.

11. Stewart, op. cit., p. 69.

12. See our "Political Change and Legislative Norms in the United States Senate," a revised version of a paper delivered at the 1974 annual meeting of the American Political Science Association, Chicago, September 1974, p. 26.

13. Ibid., p. 30.

14. Ibid., pp. 31–33.

15. Stewart, op. cit., p. 87.

16. See Neil MacNeil, *Dirksen: Portrait of a Public Man* (New York: World, 1970); Jean Torcom Cronin, "Minority Leadership in the United States Senate: The Role and Style of Everett Dirksen," Ph.D. dissertation, Johns Hopkins University, 1973; and Charles O. Jones, *The Minority Party in Congress* (Boston: Little, Brown, 1970).
17. This includes both permanent and investigative staff.
18. Matthews, op. cit., p. 160.
19. For an extended treatment of the causes and impact of the Senate's role in presidential nominations, see our "The United States Senate as a Presidential Incubator: Many Are Called but Few Are Chosen," *Political Science Quarterly*, Summer 1976.
20. One should not conclude from this that southern conservatives are now powerless. They still retain several important committee chairmanships. Moreover, a single dedicated senator, with knowledge of the rules, can have a tremendous impact on the legislative process. Senator James Allen of Alabama is one whose use of the filibuster and other techniques of parliamentary procedure has delayed, killed, or significantly changed several pieces of major legislation in the past few years.

2. *The House in Transition*

Lawrence C. Dodd and Bruce I. Oppenheimer

Most people view the House of Representatives as a decrepit, unchanging institution, ruled by ancient, arch-conservative, mossback chairmen who were themselves selected by that most undemocratic process—seniority. Although in constitutional theory the House is supposed to be our nation's most representative collection of decision makers, in the popular mind it is considered unresponsive to the people, with members insulated from the popular will by a complex maze of committees and subcommittees. The House should be the one national arena in which an individual from "back home" can debate public policy openly and unite with like-minded members to make laws that will serve the real interests and desires of the people. Too often, however, the House has been seen not as an open institution but as a secret society in which hearings, debates, and votes were held in private, closed meetings. Throughout much of the twentieth century, the House has been viewed not as a chamber in which a majority, united behind party principle, could govern with the people's mandate, but as an obstacle course so cluttered by legislative hurdles as to make majority decision making practically impossible.

These widespread conceptions of the House owe much of their basis in reality to a reform movement that occurred around 1910. Up until 1910 a system of party government had prevailed in the House;

power had resided in a Speaker of the House who was selected by and served as the leader for the majority party. While the era of strong Speakers did have some notable problems—the chief of which was the arbitrariness of some Speakers—the system did allow for majority government on the major questions of public policy. In 1910 insurgent Republicans united with Democrats in the House to strip the Speakership of its power, removing the threat of arbitrariness; in the process, they destroyed the system of party government that had relied on a strong Speakership. After a short flirtation with rule by party caucus, the House turned to a system of committee government which dispersed power among a set of autonomous committees. Appointment to committees, particularly the major committees, came to be determined within parties largely by seniority in the House; selection to chair one's committee came to depend entirely on committee seniority among members of the majority party. Each committee was left to fashion public policy in its own jurisdiction; the fate of public policy came to depend largely on the composition of committees and thus, by indirection, on patterns of seniority within the House and within committees.

In 1946 two events occurred that further helped to mold the postwar perceptions of the House. First, Congress passed a Legislative Reorganization Act that was designed to strengthen Congress in its relations with the executive branch. This act "streamlined" the committee system by reducing the number of standing House committees from 48 to 19 and by removing many subcommittees and special committees. At the same time, moves to strengthen the potential for party leadership were defeated. The 1946 Reorganization Act thus concentrated power further in the hands of a small number of committees and, more precisely, in the chairs of those committees. These chairs were left autonomous and uncoordinated by party leaders in party caucus. Second, the 1946 elections produced a Republican defeat of many northern Democrats, wiping out years of seniority and placing southern Democrats at the head of the Democratic party's seniority rankings. The 1946 election thus assured that Democratic majorities in the House would be led by southern conservatives.

In the years from 1946 to 1970 Democrats organized the House for twenty of twenty-four years. Power in the House rested in committee chairs, who maintained the authority to choose committee staffs, create subcommittees and select their chairs, control committee agendas and parliamentary procedure, schedule committee proceedings, report committee legislation to the full House, and serve as floor managers for committee bills. The committee meetings themselves, particularly important meetings, often were held in closed session. The individuals who chaired the meetings were conservative, southern, and elderly. Throughout much of this time, the House was precisely what the public perceived it to be: an insulated, closed, and largely unresponsive institution.[1]

During the 1970s the House has undergone changes that are altering it more fundamentally than at any time since 1910. These changes are occurring both through the steady influx of new members who differ in their attributes from an earlier generation of representatives and through reforms of the norms and procedures of the House. Since many of the norms and procedures that actually govern House deliberations are not explicit rules of the House but informal modes of behavior within the governing caucus, reform of the House has come largely through reforms within the Democratic caucus, which has continued to maintain control during the 1970s. These reforms are altering considerably the distribution of power at the committee level, the roles of the House parties, and the overall characteristics of the legislative process in the House. This essay attempts to delineate the changes and continuities in the House with the hope that a better understanding of them may contribute to a clearer and more accurate conception of the new emerging House.

Membership Change

For a legislative body which at the start of the 92nd Congress could boast that a record 20 percent of its membership had been elected to at least ten terms, the House in recent years has undergone significant membership turnover. House "careerism," as Charles Bullock III has called this condition, has declined significantly.[2] By the start of the second session of the 94th Congress in 1976 only 14 percent of House members met the ten-term criterion (the lowest since 1955), and projections for the 95th Congress anticipate a further decline. Perhaps more significant than the decline in "careerists" is the fact that over one-third of House members at the start of the 94th Congress were beginning either their first or second term, and the middle House members in terms of seniority was beginning his fourth term. The House, which Samuel Huntington criticized in the 1960s for operating in isolation because it lacked, among other things, "biennial infusion of new blood," has been provided with recent transfusions.[3]

The change in House membership means more than just new faces replacing old. There have been changes in the partisan, ideological, and sectional make-up of the institution as well as the age, sex, and racial composition of the membership. Although the Democrats have had a majority continuously since 1955, the size of that majority has changed considerably. In the 84th and 85th Congresses they possessed only a 30-seat margin over the Republicans, and control of the House was still in the hands of a conservative coalition of Republicans and southern Democrats. The 1958 landslide boosted the Democratic seat total from 234 to 283, but, as will be seen shortly, conservatives were still able to hold their own. After small losses of House seats in both the 1960 and 1962 elections, the Goldwater debacle provided a 295–149 margin for the Democrats. And the famed 89th Congress enacted many of the liberal policies in the Johnson legislative program. From the 90th to the 93rd Congress the Democratic House membership ranged from 243 to 255. With the Republican administrations during the last six of these eight years, the ability of liberal Democrats to enact programs or to prevent the dismantling of programs enacted during the 89th Congress was severely undercut. Only after the 1974 election did House Democrats again reach majorities of the size they held in the 86th and 89th Congresses.

During this time the ideological make-up of the House has also changed. A comparison of the ideological composition of the House during the first session of the 86th and of the 94th Congress, as presented in Table 1, provides some insights into the nature of this change.[4] First, while a smaller percentage of northern Democrats are classified as liberals in the 94th Congress than in the 86th (74 percent versus 82 percent), the number of northern Democratic liberals is nearly the same (148 versus 150). This is due to the fact that, despite

Table 1. Ideological Divisions in the House of Representatives

	Northern Democrats	Southern Democrats	All Democrats	All Republicans	All Members
86TH CONGRESS, 1ST SESSION					
Liberal	82% (140)	2% (2)	51% (142)	4% (6)	34% (148)
Moderate	13% (23)	13% (14)	13% (37)	15% (23)	14% (60)
Conservative	5% (8)	85% (94)	36% (102)	81% (124)	52% (226)
	(N = 171)	(N = 110)	(N = 281)	(N = 153)	(N = 434)
94TH CONGRESS, 1ST SESSION					
Liberal	74% (148)	11% (10)	55% (158)	1% (2)	37% (160)
Moderate	24% (47)	30% (27)	26% (74)	19% (28)	23% (102)
Conservative	2% (4)	59% (53)	20% (57)	79% (115)	40% (172)
	(N = 199)	(N = 90)	(N = 289)	(N = 145)	(N = 434)

similar Democratic majorities in both Congresses, the number of
northern Democrats is substantially greater in the 94th Congress. Second, there is a sizable decrease in the percentage of southern Democrats classified as conservative and a corresponding increase in the
moderate and liberal grouping between the two Congresses. Third,
the ideological composition of Republicans in the two Congresses is
relatively unchanged. Taken together, these figures indicate that the
House in the 94th Congress is substantially less conservative than it
was in the 86th Congress. This can be readily seen by comparing the
total number of liberals, moderates, and conservatives in the two sessions. Conservatives are a House majority in the 86th Congress,
whereas in the 94th there are nearly as many liberals as conservatives,
with moderates holding the balance of power.

There are two significant facets to this change. The southern Democratic membership has become significantly more liberal than in the
past. Liberals and moderates in the 94th Congress comprise a substantial segment, albeit a minority, of southern Democratic membership.
New southern Democrats in the House are very different from the
members they are replacing. Several southern liberals and moderates
attribute the change directly to the Voting Rights Act that has brought
substantial numbers of southern blacks into the electorate. In addition, with the decrease in the number of southern Democrats in the
House, the influence of conservatives within the House Democratic
party has dropped markedly, and liberals are now in firm control.

While Republican membership has remained conservative, there
is one change that the data in Table 1 do not reveal. This is the growth
in the number of southern Republicans in the House. In 1974, 27
southern Republicans were elected to the House. Although this is a
decrease from the 34 elected in 1972, it is still a marked gain from 1960,
when only 7 southern Republicans were elected.[5] It should further be
noted that unlike their southern Democratic colleagues, every one of
the southern Republicans fell into the conservative classification.

There are other changes in the membership of the House. It
should not be surprising, given the high turnover rate in recent years,
to find that the average age of House members has dropped. At the
start of the 94th Congress the average age of a House member was less
than fifty for the first time since World War II, and 87 of the members
were forty years old or under, a 50 percent increase over the 93rd
Congress. There have also been changes in the racial and sex composition of the House. In 1975 there were 16 black members of the House,
including 2 from the South. By comparison, in 1962 there were only 5
blacks, a figure only topped previously in 1874 when the South sent 7
blacks to the House. Corresponding to the increased activity of
women in politics, there has also been an increase in the number of

women elected to the House. In 1974 all 12 women incumbents who sought reelection to the House—10 Democrats and 2 Republicans—were successful, and 6 other women won seats for the first time. The presence of 18 women in the House was an all-time record for that chamber.[6]

Certainly these figures do not come close to being proportional to the size of these groups in the population, but, as with the growth in southern liberals, they do show some trends in the House toward membership diversification. Moreover, they demonstrate how the House, with narrower, more homogeneous constituencies, has a better capacity than the Senate to include southern liberals, northern conservatives, blacks, and women in its membership. These changes in the House membership, especially those related to the size and composition of the Democratic majority, are of great significance in understanding the reforms and changes that have occurred in the operation of the House of Representatives.

Rules and Procedures

Since the House is a much larger institution than the Senate—435 members as compared to 100 members—the House must rely more on formal rules and explicit procedures than on norms. The House does have norms such as reciprocity, courtesy, hard work, and expertise, as the work of Herbert Asher has shown.[7] And practice in the House has long honored that most hallowed of norms, seniority. Nevertheless, the rules of the party caucuses, the rules of committees, and the rules of the House itself are primary guides to member behavior and are the center of contention in struggles over power. The shifts in the partisan, ideological, and regional make-up of the House, together with a diversification in the personal attributes of its members, brought to the House throughout the 1960s and early 1970s a new breed of members who wanted power at least commensurate with their numbers. The older members of the House used the existing rules to protect themselves from the effects of these changing tides; the newer members sought to alter rules as a way to gain power for themselves.

In many ways the movement toward reform of the rules started in the late 1950s with the creation of the Democratic Study Group (DSG).[8] That group, an organization of Democratic liberals committed to liberal legislation and liberal control of the House, pushed throughout the 1960s for changes in House procedures and party practice. During much of that time, liberals sought formal changes in House rules, and their efforts resulted in the 1970 Legislative Reorganization Act. This act, passed by a coalition of two groups of outsiders (House Republicans and liberal Democrats), primarily served to liberalize and formalize parliamentary procedure in committees and on the floor of the House. Provisions of the act that affected committee behavior included the requirement that committees make public all roll call committee votes, the requirement that committee members be given three days to file minority or supplementary reports on committee legislation, provisions for advance notice of committee meetings, provisions to allow committee members to call up a bill that had been cleared for floor action but was being withheld by the committee chair, and encouragement of open committee sessions. The act altered floor procedure by permitting recorded teller votes during the amending process and debates on recommital motions, requiring legislation passed by committees to lay over for three days before its consideration on the floor, guaranteeing time for floor debate on amendments, and dividing debate on a conference report between majority and minority positions.[9]

In the late 1960s, just at the time that these formal rules changes were approaching ratification, liberal Democrats changed their strategy in a fundamental fashion. The liberals seemed increasingly to constitute the dominant faction of the House Democratic party in size, yet they did not dominate the positions of congressional power that are derived from party membership, particularly the assignments on the key committees and the chairs of key committees. The formal changes in House rules could not alter the distribution of power positions, since those positions derive from the majority party. Formal changes in House rules also could not ensure the procedural protection of House liberals (or Republicans), since the only real way to enforce the changes was through discipline of committee chairpersons and party leaders within the majority party; lacking mechanisms of party discipline, no real way existed to make congressional leaders abide by the changes. Liberals thus decided to shift their immediate attention away from reforms of House rules and to focus on reforms of the Democratic party. This decision entailed a revitalization of the Democratic party caucus.

Throughout most of the twentieth century, the Democratic party caucus, the organization of all House Democrats, had been largely dormant. The caucus met only at the beginning of each new Congress to select party leaders and ratify the nominations of committee members and leaders made by the Democratic Committee on Committees. The existence of an inactive caucus in the late 1960s served the interests of the older and more conservative members, who were increasingly a minority of the caucus yet were in control of the key power positions (ratified *pro forma*) distributed by the caucus. The creation of a strong, active caucus, by contrast, offered liberals and newcomers a mechanism whereby they could both attack the distribution of congressional power among party members and influence public policy by forcing the caucus to take strong public stands on policy issues. At the beginning of the 91st Congress in January 1969, DSG members together with then Majority Leader Carl Albert were strong enough to convince Speaker John McCormack to support the activation of the party caucus. The result was the development of a party rule stating that a caucus meeting could be held each month if fifty members demanded the meeting in writing; the petition to the chair of the caucus would outline the proposed agenda.

The creation of the new party rule opened the door to reform-oriented Democrats and brought the caucus to the fore as an instrument of change in the House. In 1969 and 1970 liberal Democrats called several caucus meetings to discuss reform. In March 1970 these liberals proposed the creation of a caucus committee to study reform. The caucus approved the committee and then caucus chairman Dan Rostenkowski (Ill.) appointed a widely representative, respected group of members to compose the committee. Julia Butler Hansen (Wash.) became chairwoman of the committee, giving the committee its popular name, the Hansen Committee. Operating through the Hansen Committee, which itself was a vehicle of the Democratic caucus, reform-oriented members were able to bring a series of reforms to the attention of the Democratic caucus. The first Hansen reforms (Hansen I) came out of the committee in January 1971, were passed by the caucus, and were implemented in the 92nd Congress. These reforms limited legislative subcommittee chairs to one per member and specified that each subcommittee chair could select a professional staff member for the subcommittee, subject only to the approval of the Democratic members of the standing committee. In addition, Hansen I moved to restructure the process whereby the Democratic caucus made its selection of committee leaders.

As noted earlier, the House had followed seniority for sixty years in selecting its committee chairs. Seniority was a norm, an unwritten rule. The norm of seniority, however, was reinforced by rules that did exist in each party for selecting the party's ranking members on each committee. In the case of the Democratic party, the Democratic Committee on Committees made nominations of ranking committee members (the committee chairs during periods of Democratic majority); it was composed of all House Democrats on the Ways and Means Committee. The Committee on Committees always followed committee seniority in making these nominations. It then presented the nominations to the caucus as a slate, which the caucus voted either up or down in its entirety. No way existed to single out one nominee and defeat her or him. It was politically impractical to vote an entire slate down, since the nominating power for the second slate would rest with the Committee on Committees, and that slate, as well as any further slates, might still contain the objectionable nominee or nominees, with the Committee on Comittees removing the more favored candidates. In the end, the caucus, worn down by sheer exhaustion, might accept a final slate that was even worse than the first. Rather than undertake such a chance, initial slates were always ratified *pro forma*.

As part of Hansen I, House Democrats voted on January 20, 1971, to change the system for caucus votes on chair nominations. The new changes left nominating power for committee chairs and committee members with the Committee on Committees, though the rules explicitly stated that the committee need not follow seniority. Under the new system, however, the committee would present its nominations to the caucus one committee at a time. Upon the demand of ten or more members, any nomination could be debated and voted on. If the caucus rejected a nomination, the Committee on Committees would submit another nominee. On this same day, the House Republicans established a new procedure for selecting their ranking committee members; under their new procedure, all members of the House Republican caucus (or "conference," as they prefer to call it) were allowed to vote by secret ballot on each nomination made by their Committee on Committees. These rules changes in both the Democratic and Republican caucuses opened the possibility that committee seniority would no longer guarantee a chair or ranking position to a member and that the party caucuses might discipline specific members for past indiscretions.[10]

At the beginning of the 93rd Congress in January 1973, the Hansen Committee produced a second wave of reform proposals (Hansen II).[11] These proposals, which the Democratic caucus passed, refined the method of voting on chair nominations in such a way as to virtually guarantee secret ballots on each committee chair nomination; under the new rules, each nomination by the Committee on Committees would be voted on automatically and, if so demanded by 20 percent of the members, by secret ballot. The new Hansen reforms expanded the Democratic Committee on Committees to include not only Ways and Means Democrats but the Speaker, majority leader, and caucus chairperson, with the Speaker rather than the Ways and Means chairperson to chair the Committee on Committees. The reforms created a new Democratic Steering and Policy Committee chaired by the Speaker and composed of twenty-four members; its role was to direct the party's legislative strategy. Third, in reaction to the tendency of the Ways and Means Committee to introduce its legislation under a closed rule that disallowed floor amendments, the committee recommended and the caucus approved a procedure whereby requests for closed rules could be fought: (1) fifty or more Democrats could bring a proposed amendment to the caucus for its consideration; (2) the caucus could instruct Democratic members of the Rules Committee to allow that amendment to face a floor vote; (3) Ways and Means legislation could then be amended on the floor.

As part of Hansen II, the caucus also passed a series of reform proposals collectively known as the Subcommittee Bill of Rights.[12] Under the new provisions, the power to select subcommittee chairs was taken away from the chairperson of a committee and placed in the Democratic caucus of each standing committee; in the new system, Democratic committee members, ordered by committee or subcommittee seniority, would bid for subcommittee chair positions and the committee caucus would vote on the bids. The Subcommittee Bill of Rights also specified that subcommittees should have fixed jurisdictions, authorization to meet and hold hearings, adequate budgets, a staff selected by the subcommittee chair, and a ratio of Democrats to Republicans at least as favorable as that on the full committee. In addition, all committee legislation would be referred to the appropriate subcommittee for initial consideration unless the committee caucus voted to consider the measure in full committee. Each committee member was also given the right to at least one "choice subcommittee assignment." At the same time that the Subcommittee Bill of Rights came before the caucus, a third set of proposals was being pushed by Common Cause to open up committee meetings. The caucus went on record in support of this move, and on March 7, 1973, the House approved (370–27) a modified version of a resolution introduced by representatives Bob Eckhardt (D-Tex.) and Dante B. Fascell (D-Fla.).[13]

The final effort of the Hansen Committee (Hansen III) came in 1974. Throughout 1973 and 1974 a House Select Committee on Committees—the Bolling Committee—had been preparing a plan to restructure the House committee system.[14] The eventual Bolling plan alienated many conservative, moderate, and liberal Democrats, and they turned to the Hansen Committee to provide an alternative formulation. The Democratic caucus voted to delay the Bolling Committee plan until an alternative was drafted by the Hansen Committee. Both plans were then introduced to the House—the Bolling plan, which was a product of a bipartisan House select committee, and the Hansen plan, which was a product of the Democratic caucus. The Hansen plan won on the House floor, a victory of sorts for the Democratic caucus, though not a victory for hard-core reformers. The Hansen plan was far more moderate than the Bolling plan and left the committee system largely intact, while increasing somewhat the power of the Speaker by giving him considerable control over the referral of bills. Under the new role, the Speaker could send a bill to more than one committee, either simultaneously or sequentially, could split up a bill, or could send portions of it to different committees. In addition, Hansen III stipulated that standing committees composed of more than fifteen members were required to have at least four subcommittees; in effect, this required subcommittees for all committees except Rules and Standards of Official Conduct. The Hansen resolution also produced a change that further increased the role of the Democratic and Republican caucuses: it mandated Congress to return in December of each election year beginning in 1974 to organize the next Congress in advance (rather than one month later, after the start of Congress). This change allowed caucuses more time to conduct organizational business and thus increased the utility of the caucus to party reformers and activists.

In December 1974 and January 1975 the newly elected or reelected members of the House met and, building upon the caucus reforms of the preceding six years, moved to consolidate the prior reforms within the House Democratic party and to clearly assert the new power of the party caucus. First, the caucus stripped Ways and Means Democrats of their role as Committee on Committees, giving that power to the Steering and Policy Committee. This change meant that the power to nominate committee members and the committee chair no longer rested with Ways and Means Democrats but with the members of the Democratic Steering Committee. Second, the caucus adopted a rule that allowed nominations for committee chairpersons to be made from the floor of the caucus meetings in second-round votes where an initial Steering and Policy Committee nomination had been defeated and a new nomination by Steering and Policy was being considered. Third, the caucus adopted a rule requiring nominees for chairs of Appropriations subcommittees to be approved by the same procedures that applied to nominees for chairs of standing committees; this rule change seemed in order, since Appropriations subcommittees are in many cases more powerful than standing committees.

While the foregoing series of reform efforts were under way within the Democratic caucus, the House was also involved (along with the Senate) in a massive change in the congressional budgetary process. As part of the Budget and Impoundment Control Act of 1974, the House created a new 25-member House Budget Committee and, with the Senate, a Congressional Budget Office designed to serve both the House and Senate. The role of the new process, and the new House committee, was to produce a congressional budget that would serve to coordinate rationally the decisions made within the authorization, appropriations, and revenue committees of the House. Of the 25 members, 5 must come from the Appropriations Committee (3 Democrats, 2 Republicans), 5 must come from the Ways and Means Committee (3 Democrats and 2 Republicans), and 2 must come from the respective party leaderships. The tenure of members of the House Budget Committee is restricted in that no member may serve for more than four years out of any ten-year period. The power to select the director of the Congressional Budget Office was lodged in the Speaker of the House and the president pro tem of the Senate.

By the opening of the 94th Congress, the organizational structure and rules that governed the House of Representatives differed fundamentally from those in existence six to eight years earlier. In retrospect, the changes in rules and organization, although largely pushed by liberal reformers, were not uniform in the stimulus that produced them or in their effect on the House. Amid the bewildering array of changes, two definite trends existed. First, some reforms clearly served to decentralize power within committees. These reforms occurred largely from 1970 to 1973 and were justified on the grounds that they would democratize the House and give more members a piece of the pie; as a primary by-product, of course, liberals hoped that the changes would provide them with greater control over the policy-making apparatus within committees. This first stage of reforms thus constituted a very real attempt to alter the House committee system. The second trend evident in these changes is a move toward centralization of certain powers in the party caucuses, the Speaker, and a new budget committee. These reforms occurred largely from 1973 to 1975 and were justified by a desire to make the House a better-coordinated and more effective institution. This stage of the reforms altered fundamentally the role of the congressional parties, particularly the majority party, in the operations of the House.

The Rise of Decentralized Government

The decentralization of the House has occurred along two related but analytically distinct dimensions: a growth of subcommittee government and a corresponding decline in the power of committee chairpeople. Although, it is important to deal with them separately, it should be remembered that the growth of subcommittee power and the decline in the authority of committee chairs are very much interrelated. As the one gained in influence, the other lost, and vice versa.

The Growth of Subcommittees: Number,
Staffing, and Activity

Subcommittees in the House of Representatives in the past two decades have increased in their number, staff, activity, and independence. As Table 2 shows, at the start of the 84th Congress (1955–56), when the Democrats began their current streak as the majority party in the House, there were 83 standing subcommittees in the House. When the organization of the 94th Congress was completed, that number had grown to 139. Moreover, the chair and ranking minority member of each subcommittee were entitled to appoint at least one professional staff member to serve her/him. By comparison, in the 86th Congress, the first time the *Congressional Staff Directory* was published, only 57 of the 113 subcommittees were shown to have their own staffs. Not surprisingly, as subcommittees have grown in number and in

Table 2. Standing Subcommittees in the House of Representatives

84th Congress	83	90th Congress	108
86th Congress	113	92nd Congress	114
88th Congress	105	94th Congress	139

staff available to them, their activity has increased. In the 84th Congress only about one-third of the authorization committee hearings were held in subcommittee. Data computed through the 91st Congress indicate that this figure has increased to over 60 percent, and recent observations indicate that it continues to rise.[15]

It would be incorrect to assume that the changes and reforms mentioned earlier are the only causes for the growth of subcommittee government. As is apparent from the preceding data, subcommittee growth began prior to the reform wave of the 1970s. And although the relationship between those reforms and subcommittee growth will be presented in some detail, it is important to consider briefly two other factors that contributed to the growth of subcommittees. The first of these, for lack of a better term, we call the environmental factor. It includes a variety of changes in the political environment in which Congress operates that have had gradual, but increasing, influence on the growth of subcommittees. The increase in both the number and complexity of issues that are of federal concern created the need for higher levels of legislative specialization and naturally favored the growth in subcommittees. In some cases the work load just became too great for a committee to handle every issue within its jurisdiction without relying on subcommittees. At times, the creation for activation of subcommittees became the only way a committee was able to protect its jurisdiction against the encroachment of other committees and their subcommittees. One of the reasons the Ways and Means Committee members were willing to accept the provision of Hansen III that required it to establish subcommittees was the threat to its jurisdiction in the resolution by the Bolling Select Committee on Committees. The Bolling resolution called for Ways and Means to lose jurisdiction over trade legislation, nontax aspects of health and unemployment compensation, general revenue sharing, WIN, and renegotiation. The Bolling Committee justified these changes because Ways and Means, without subcommittees, was unable to deal with these important legislative areas simultaneously. In addition to preventing the jettisoning of much of its legislative jurisdiction by supporting Hansen III over Bolling, Ways and Means by creating subcommittees undercut the rationale for future attacks on that jurisdiction.

Another change in the political environment that fostered the growth of subcommittees was the steady increase in the number of House "careerists" from the 84th until the 93rd Congress. With an increasing number of careerists that reached a record 20 percent of the House in the 92nd Congress, there was pressure from the growing number of careerists who had not become committee chairmen to provide them with a "piece of the action." The creation and staffing of subcommittees became an effective way to meet this demand. Ironically, careerism has been on the decline since the start of the 93rd Congress. This decline may itself result in part from the success of careerists in gaining subcommittee positions that has given them greater visibility and made possible races for statewide or national office.

The second factor that contributed to the growth of subcommittees involves a series of ad hoc reforms or revolts within given committees. They differ from the changes and reforms that affected the entire House in that these changes and reforms occurred in individual committees. Thus, there had been revolts against particular committee chairpeople within their own committees that led to major changes in the operation of particular committees and subcommittees. For example, at the start of the 89th Congress, Tom Murray, a conservative Tennessee Democrat who, as chairman of the Post Office and Civil Service Committee since 1949 (with the exception of the 83rd Congress), only allowed one or two subcommittees to have staff and kept most legislation under the control of the full committee, found himself circumvented by the committee members. They adopted rules that limited his control of subcommittee chairs, referral of legislative matters, staff, and budget. During the 89th Congress all the committee's hearings were held by the subcommittees (in the 88th, 75 percent of the hearings were held by the full committee), and separate subcommittee staff were hired. Although cases exist in which power was recentralized after a period of increased subcommittee activity, such as on the Government Operations Committee during the chairmanship of Chet Holifield (D-Calif.), these countertendencies are usually short-lived.

Despite these long-run influences on the growth of subcommittees, the reforms of the 1970–75 period are the key in guaranteeing subcommittee influence in the House. As noted by Norman Ornstein, in limiting each member to chairing only one legislative subcommittee, Hansen I allowed for a minimum of sixteen new subcommittee chairmen. This added not to the number of subcommittees but to their activity. It provided sixteen members with new policy forums, and the beneficiaries of the slots tended to be liberal activists who used the forums.[16] In addition, while Hansen I left the final decision on subcommittee staffing for approval by the full committee caucus, it recognized that subcommittees would remain ineffective without minimal staff support.

Hansen II, which set forth the Subcommittee Bill of Rights, gave major impetus to further subcommittee activity. By providing subcommittees with a budget and their own staff, it ensured that subcommittees would have the necessary resources for operation. Moreover, the provisions for setting subcommittee jurisdictions and a process for referral of legislation gave subcommittees turf on which to operate. Prior to Hansen II it was possible for full committee chairs to withhold legislation from particular subcommittees either by keeping considerations at the full committee or by referring the legislation to another subcommittee. Finally, in setting up a process of bidding for subcommittee chairs, Hansen II encouraged subcommittee chairs to make active use of their subcommittees. What better way for members to ensure support for continuation in chairing a subcommittee than to show that the subcommittee was active under her or his leadership? With the adoption of Hansen II, subcommittee government was given the necessary resources, independence, and incentives for full operation. It is important, however, to note David Rohde's finding in his study of the Subcommittee Bill of Rights that compliance with the reforms varied during the 93rd Congress. Compliance was highest on the jurisdiction and referral matters and lowest on the selection of subcommittee chairmen and membership.[17]

The reforms during the 93rd and at the start of the 94th Congress gave additional incentives for subcommittee growth and reinforced the Subcommittee Bill of Rights. The resolution produced by the Bolling Committee and even the weakened package as adopted in the amended Hansen substitute (Hansen III) continued the established trend toward subcommittee activity. The provision of Hansen III requiring all committees with more than fifteen members to establish at least four subcommittees forced the Ways and Means Committee to decentralize its operations. When Ways and Means complied with the change, it created six subcommittees, instead of the minimum four, and six new chairs to be filled. Further, in response to the Hansen III provision allowing each committee to establish an oversight subcommittee or to require each of its subcommittees to conduct oversight in their separate areas of jurisdiction, several new subcommittees were created and others expanded oversight operations.

The organization meeting of the House Democratic caucus for the 94th Congress gave further backing to subcommittees. By allowing Democratic members of a committee to select all the subcommittee assignments instead of just one as originally provided for in Hansen II, the caucus established a mechanism likely to produce the most interested and active membership for subcommittees. Following the adoption of the final set of reforms, two subcommittee chairs, Harley Staggers (D-W.Va.) and Leonor Sullivan (D-Mo.), were defeated in attempts to retain their positions by votes of the majority caucuses of their respective committees. Both already chaired full committees, and their majority committee colleagues were persuaded to give the subcommittee chairs to other members. Moreover, the reforms meant that subcommittee chairs no longer automatically retained their positions through seniority. They can be challenged within their committee, and actions like the defeat of Staggers and Sullivan may do much to stimulate subcommittee chairs to build records of achievement within their subcommittees.

Overall, while these reforms of the 1970–75 period had a definite impact on the power of committee chairs, to be discussed shortly, they also added to the number and the importance of subcommittees. They moved them further from the control and influence of the committee chairs, and they gave subcommittees the staff, jurisdiction, and resources for independent operation. One measure of the impact of these changes is the growth in the number of members of the House who now chair a committee or subcommittee. As Table 3 indicates, the number of subcommittee chair positions grew from 113 to 126 between the 86th (1959–60) and 89th (1965–66) Congresses, but the number of different individuals chairing committees or subcommittees held constant at 102, with multiple chair assignments increasing from the 86th to the 89th Congresses. From the 89th to the 94th (1975–76) Congresses, subcommittees increased from 126 to 139, and two standing committees were added. In addition, between these two Congresses the caucus rules were passed that mandated the spread of subcommittee positions. In the 94th Congress, as a result, 137 different members chaired a committee or subcommittee, an increase of 35 from the 89th Congress in the number of individuals who had a "piece of the pie." This spread is all the more significant because the pie was much tastier in the 94th Congress, with the numerous subcommittee positions carrying far more significance than in the 89th Congress.

Table 3.   Distribution of Committee and Subcommittee Chairs

	Number of Standing Subcommittees	Number of Standing Committees	Number of Individuals Holding at Least One Chair
86th Congress	113	20	102
89th Congress	126	20	102
94th Congress	139	22	137

The Decline of Committee Chairs

A discussion of the growth of subcommittee government in the House and its contributions to trends to further decentralization of decision making in the House is incomplete without a parallel analysis of committee chairs. The two facets of the decentralization trend are mutually reinforcing. Depending on how one views the situation, as subcommittees grew in number, staff, and influence, they detracted from the power of the committee chairs, and as the chairpeople relinquished power (voluntarily or under pressure), subcommittees were among the decision-making components to gain.

One can analyze the decline of committee chairs with the same sets of explanations that were used to evaluate the growth of subcommittee influence. "Environmental" factors leading to an increase in the number and complexity of issues within a committee's jurisdiction not only fostered the growth of subcommittees but meant that a chairperson found it more difficult to keep a rein on it all. The ad hoc revolts and reforms that led to the growth of subcommittees were revolts against committee chairs. In some cases, the revolts did not involve the creation of subcommittees but only attacks on the chair's power. For example, the 1961 fight to expand the Rules Committee was an effort to diminish the control of Judge Howard Smith.

In addition to the above, other chairs relinquished power voluntarily or were unwilling or unable to use the power available to them. At times this happened immediately following the retirement of a particularly influential or arbitrary chairperson. Classic cases of this are to be found in the 1950s following the retirements of Will Whittington as chairman of Public Works and James Richards (D-S.C.) as chairman of Foreign Affairs. Whittington (D-Miss.), who ran his committee with an iron hand, was replaced by Charles Buckley (D-N.Y.), who was more interested in power in the Bronx than the House. Richards's successor, Thomas Gordon (D-Ill.), was incapable of running the committee or understanding foreign policy.[18] In both cases, and in others, power was never again recentralized under a strong chair. Even in cases where the successor has been neither weak nor disinterested, the new chair has at times been only a faint shadow of a prominent predecessor. F. Edward Hebert (D-La.), chairman of the Armed Services Committee until the start of the 94th Congress and reputed to be one of the remaining powerful House chairpeople (he reportedly once called the Joint Chiefs of Staff on the phone and announced, "This is God"), was viewed by most observers as less powerful than Mendel Rivers and a step further removed from Carl Vinson.

Thus, in discussing how the changes and reforms of the 1970–75 period diminished the influence of committee chairs, one should realize that the "powerful committee chairman" had already become an endangered species. The across-the-board reforms of recent Congresses certainly have contributed to that, but, more important, they prevented the rebirth of the species.

The first crack in the armor of the chairpeople came when House liberals, after a series of reform efforts, established a procedure for the Democratic caucus to elect the chairs of standing committees. It began with the adoption of the Hansen I provision by the caucus that allowed for ten members to demand a vote on a committee chair nomination. One month later, liberals used the provision to try to deny John McMillan (D-S.C.) continuation as chairman of the District of Columbia Committee. The vote, despite its failure to defeat McMillan, presented the committee with a major threat to all committee chairpeople in that it legitimized the right of the caucus to fill committee chairs on a basis other than seniority. The threat was strengthened in 1973 when the caucus adopted the requirement of voting on every committee chair. And again, although no senior committee Democrat was defeated, several received "no" votes in the 25–30 percent range. Among those in this category were F. Edward Hebert, Wright Patman, (D-Tex.), Bob Poage (D-Tex.), and Wayne Hays (D-Ohio), all of whom should have seen the vote as a significant warning. Two years later, in the January 1975 meetings of the House Democratic caucus, Poage, Patman, and Hebert were each defeated in attempts to retain their chairs, and Hays barely survived. This provided the proof of the pudding. While other changes removed certain duties from the total control of the chairmen, the automatic vote and the willingness of the caucus to use it to defeat chairpeople presented a different kind of threat. A chair who proved unresponsive to his party's majority was no longer faced just with losing control of the committee, like Tom Murray, but also with the loss of the chair position itself.

If the threat to the chair itself was not enough to undercut severely the power of committee chairpeople, when combined with the other reforms of the 1970–75 period, the effect was devastating. The chairpeople had lost the right to determine the number, size, and majority party membership of subcommittees. They no longer retained the power to appoint subcommittee chairs, to control referral of legislation to subcommittees, or to prevent their committees from meeting. Finally, as a result of the growth of subcommittee activity, many were forced to defer to their subcommittee chairpeople in the management of legislation.

It would be wrong to conclude from this analysis that committee chairs are totally devoid of power and that subcommittee government is all-encompassing. To varying degrees certain chairs remain influential, despite the loss of formal powers. They still retain substantial control over the staff of the full committees. To the degree that they do not abuse the power, many chairpeople maintain control over the agenda and the calling of meetings. Committee members still tend to defer to the judgment of the chair on questions about which the member is unfamiliar or undecided. But most important, the remaining influential chairs are ones who have substantial policy expertise and/or political skill. Although these two features were significant at an earlier time in separating out the more and less influential chairs, today they are prime. In John Manley's study of the Ways and Means Committee, he analyzed the basis of Wilbur Mills's influence. Manley found that expertise, legitimacy, deference, and rewards were important factors in Mills's influence, while the use or threat of sanctions was not. Today a chairperson has far fewer rewards to offer, and the acceptance of her/his actions as legitimate is more often brought into question. He or she simply has fewer resources with which to exert influence.[19]

It is important to note that seniority has not been totally overturned. The selections of all the remaining committee chairmen were in line with seniority, and, with the exception of the Sullivan and Staggers cases, the same held true for subcommittee chairs. Moreover, the influx of seventy-five new Democratic House members was a necessary catalyst to bringing about this occurrence at the start of the 94th Congress.

Finally, there is an amazing irony or paradox to these reinforcing trends. Now that many of the resources available to committee chairpeople have been removed, it is far less important who becomes chair-person of a full committee than it was at an earlier time. Or, to state it conversely, now that the caucus has the ability to select the individuals it feels are best qualified to lead House committees, it has left those individuals with fewer sources of influence.

Sunshine in the House

One additional reform in the 1970–75 period, separate yet related to the opening up of the House under subcommittee government, was the decision requiring open committee (and subcommittee) sessions. On March 7, 1973, the House passed H. Res. 259 by a vote of 370 to 27. That resolution requires that all committee sessions be open to the public unless a majority of the committee's members vote by roll call to close that particular meeting. Excepted from the requirement were meetings on internal committee matters such as budget and personnel. Moreover, the closing of hearings was restricted to those cases in which public disclosure would "endanger national security" or violate House rules.[20] The effect of this rule change was marked. In 1972, prior to the change, 44 percent of committee meetings were closed. In 1973 this dropped to 10 percent, in 1974 to 8 percent, and in 1975 to less than 3 percent. Only committees such as Armed Services, the Select Committee on Intelligence, and International Relations closed more than a handful of hearings in 1975, and those three closed 24 percent, 10 percent, and 8 percent, respectively. Even legislative mark-up sessions are normally open now, with only 2 percent closed in 1975.[21]

Effectively what this means is that the House not only has opened up internally to invite broader participation among its members but has also opened much of its operations to inspection by the press and the public. The problem remains for both members and the public to monitor committee action in the House because so much is going on at once. In 1975 a record 3,881 open meetings of House committees and subcommittees made the job of participant, reporter, or citizen most difficult.

The Emergence of Party Government

Throughout most of the postwar years, political parties in Congress have been weak, ineffectual organizations.[22] Power in Congress has rested in the committees or, increasingly, in the subcommittees. Although the party caucuses nominally have had the power to organize committees and select committee chairpeople, the norm of congressional or state delegation seniority has dominated the former (though not exclusively), while the norm of committee seniority has dominated the latter (exclusively). In reality, Congress has been governed by a conservative coalition of southern Democrats and Republicans; their strength has been particularly evident on the most powerful committees such as Appropriations, Ways and Means, and House Rules. Party leaders have existed primarily to assist in smoothing the flow of legislation and mediating conflict, not to provide policy leadership or coordination. The parties themselves—particularly the House Democratic party—have been loose coalitions of convenience, not programmatic, cohesive organizations dedicated to enacting a specified set of policies. In many ways, political parties in Congress during the postwar years, as one observer has written, have been "phantoms" of scholarly imagination that were perhaps best to be exorcised from attempts to explain congressional organization, behavior, and process.[23]

The changes in rules and procedures during the 1970s, particularly those from 1973 to 1975, have reinvigorated the House parties and thrust them into a new set of postwar roles. These changes have occurred primarily in the role of the Democratic party caucus and the Democratic party leadership. By the 94th Congress (1975–76) it was no longer true that the Democratic caucus was merely an ornament on the House organizational chart; it was becoming, rather, an integral part of the House decision-making process. The party leadership was no longer simply a handmaiden to committees but increasingly a central power in and an influence on decision making. The House Democratic party appeared not so much a phantom as a phoenix arising from the ashes.

The Party Caucus

The emergence of the party caucus came with the 1969 rule that allowed regular meetings of the caucus. The creation of the Hansen Committee and the success of that committee in producing acceptable reforms served to legitimize the caucus as a center of activity. In addition, some of the reforms themselves strengthened the caucus. The changes in Hansen I and Hansen II that altered the voting procedure for chair nominations increased the power of the caucus by making it a viable place in which to seek to challenge committee chairs and discipline obstinate chairpersons. The creation of the Steering and Policy Committee provided the caucus with a serious coordinating committee that could help give it direction and leadership. The decision to invest the Steering and Policy Committee with Committee on Committees power strengthened caucus control over committee nominations, since Steering and Policy members were selected, directly or indirectly, by the caucus and, unlike Ways and Means Democrats, were subject to alteration from Congress to Congress. The new rule allowing the caucus to bind Democratic members on the Rules Committee served notice that the caucus was final arbiter of its members' votes within a committee. Since committee membership comes from the party, the party caucus was asserting its right to control committee votes and thereby enforce a general direction to public policy, particularly in the case of the Rules Committee, which regulates the flow of all legislation. Finally, the rule produced by Hansen III that mandated each caucus to conduct organizational business prior to the opening of each Congress brought the caucuses clearly into the limelight as legitimate centers of institutional struggle and decision making. No longer was the caucus to be a *pro forma* stage in the approval of congressional leaders and decision makers.

The forceful role made possible for the party caucus by these reforms came to the fore in the 94th Congress and can be illustrated by three sets of decisions made within the caucus. The first example, and the most highly publicized reform of the 1970s, came at the start of the 94th Congress when the Democratic caucus violated seniority in the selection of three committee chairs, a clear and sharp break with the traditions of the House. In each case (Hebert of Armed Services, Patman of Banking, and Poage of Agriculture), the sitting committee chairperson was denied the position for the 94th Congress and was replaced by a person with less committee seniority. In overthrowing Hebert and Poage, the caucus went against the initial Steering and Policy Committee nominations of those two men; in overthrowing Patman, the caucus (after initial confusion) agreed with the initial rejection of his candidacy within Steering and Policy. In one case, that of Wayne Hays of House Administration, the caucus approved a candidate who had been defeated initially within the Steering and Policy Committee. The overthrow of these chairmen made national heroes out of seventy-five freshmen Democrats who were elected to the 94th Congress, the assumption being that they produced the overthrow. The new Democrats apparently did provide margins of victory in each case (although the use of secret ballots make absolute confirmation of this impossible). The departure from seniority was a culmination of six years of steady growth in caucus assertiveness and power, however, not an overnight revolution.

A second example of an activist party caucus is the role of the party in oil depletion legislation in 1975.[24] During the Ways and

Means Committee deliberations on the Tax Reduction Act of 1975, Ways and Means liberals attempted to add an amendment to the act severely limiting oil depletion provisions of the existing tax code. They were defeated by a coalition of Republicans and conservative and oil-state Democrats; the latter coalition also united in asking for a closed rule on the bill, thus making it impossible for the liberals to win their fight on the House floor. Normally, since the Rules Committee is composed of a majority of Republicans and conservative or oil-state Democrats together with a group of Democrats desirous of honoring committee rule requests if possible, the Ways and Means request would have been honored and oil depletion reform ended for this bill. This time, however, the liberals tried a new tack. They obtained fifty signatures on a petition that called for a Democratic caucus meeting to consider the matter. In the caucus meeting, they won a vote to bind Rules Committee Democrats to support a rule on the bill that would allow floor votes on the oil depletion amendments. The liberals, led by William Green (Pa.) and Sam Gibbons (Fla.), took their fight to the House floor and won, ultimately obtaining a (weakened) set of constraints on oil depletion tax write-offs.

This vote was a critical indication of the potential power of the party caucus. The conservative coalition has long been a bugaboo of House analysts, particularly at the committee level. This vote was a clear warning to conservative Democrats that the old coalition may not work under the new rules and that a protective alliance with fellow Democrats might be more fruitful. Second, this vote underscored the fundamental importance of the reforms in changing the actual power balance in the House. Some observers have argued that the closed rule and Rules Committee have no real effect on major legislation because real majorities do not exist that would have passed legislation previously bottled up by them. Few doubt, however, that the Rules Committee would have given the Tax Reduction Act a closed rule, except for the decision by the Democratic caucus to bind its members on the Rules Committee. It is equally clear that, without the Rules Committee and closed rule operating, a clear majority for oil depletion reform did exist. In other words, this example indicates that the party reforms seem to have removed hurdles that otherwise would have clearly stopped or undermined certain liberal proposals.

A third example of caucus activism is its reaction to the sex scandal involving Wayne Hays, who, while chair of the House Administration Committee, employed on the committee payroll a woman who later claimed to have served only as his mistress. The Hays scandal in June 1976, together with other publicized indiscretions by House members, created a press furor over the sexual appetites of House members and the use of public moneys by some members to satisfy their yearnings. The scandal did not stop with Hays's public confession and his request for understanding, however, and the Democratic caucus swiftly reacted. First, the members of the caucus made clear their intention to remove Hays from the key posts he held, thus forcing him to resign as chair of the Democratic Campaign Committee and chair of the House Administration Committee. The overthrow of the three committee chairs in January 1975 served as a necessary backdrop to Hays's forced resignation. Second, the caucus approved a package of changes in the House's administrative system; these changes were proposed by a Steering and Policy Committee task force that the Speaker created to design appropriate reforms. Overall, these reforms brought regulation of members' perquisites (that is, benefits and allowance given to representatives to run their offices and serve their constituents) under the control of the full House rather than just the House Administration Committee; established procedures for fuller disclosure of how House funds are spent; consolidated and reduced member spending allowances; and created a commission to study and recommend further changes. These reforms, together with the resignation of Hays, demonstrated the willingness of the caucus to react rapidly and publicly to a crisis, a stark contrast with prior years when internal House problems had been allowed to fester indefinitely and erode public confidence in the institution and the governing party. The ability of the caucus to react this swiftly also resulted from the existence of a stronger Speaker and the Steering and Policy Committee.[25]

Party Leadership

Throughout most of the twentieth century, parties in the House have been unwilling to vest power in their party leaders. This reticence stems from early in the century when Speaker "Uncle Joe" Cannon used the considerable authority that the Speaker possessed at that time to dominate House proceedings and relegate most members to a relatively insignificant status. After the 1910 insurgency against Cannon stripped the Speakership of all of its major powers except the constitutional role as presiding officer, members guarded their personal prerogatives and committee power assiduously against usurpation by the Speaker. Although the 1946 Legislative Reorganization Act attempted to resolve many problems of committee government, for example, it did not include reforms strengthening the Speakership or party leaders.

In the early 1970s liberals in the House were willing to turn to the Speakership for a variety of reasons. First of all, Carl Albert was Speaker. Albert supported, or at least did not oppose, much of the reform efforts of the caucus, including the strengthening of subcommittees and personal prerogative of members on the floor. Albert had liberal leanings, at least for an Oklahoman. And because of his mild demeanor and consensual politics, he did not seem a personal threat. A second factor, not to be underestimated, was the presence of Richard Bolling in the House and his strong personal influence on reformist liberals and on Albert. Bolling is a rarity among members of Congress, an individual who has studied the history and structure of the institution, contemplated the lessons of history, and developed reformist proposals based not so much on his immediate personal interests as on the perceived interests of the House and the country. As a result of his experience as a lieutenant to Sam Rayburn and of his study of the House, Bolling has become a staunch supporter of a strong Speakership and strong party leadership; he has continually pushed his views in the DSG and party meetings, keeping them alive and adding an element of legitimacy to them. A third factor, of course, was the existence of divided government and the presidency of Richard Nixon. As Nixon forced such issues as the Cambodia invasion and impoundment, Democrats needed some leadership and coherent strategy to thwart Nixon's efforts at undermining the role of Congress in public policy. A strong Speaker offered the possibility of leadership. Fourth, because the party caucus selected the Speaker by secret ballot, the Speaker should be more responsive to the caucus than committee chairs, protected by the seniority norm, had traditionally been. Finally, the party did not have to give the Speaker all of the power Cannon had possessed in order to strengthen the office. By specifying more clearly and liberally certain rules of procedure, such as three-day layover and electronic voting, the ability of the strengthened Speaker to arbitrarily control floor votes was limited. In addition, the central power of the party could be divided between the Speaker and a Steering Committee in such a fashion as to keep the Speaker in bounds.

The move toward a strong Speakership came in two waves. The first effort, which came with the Hansen reforms of 1973, placed the Speaker, as well as the majority leader and caucus chairperson, on the Committee on Committees. This was a curtailment of the Ways and Means power and the power of its chairperson, Wilbur Mills, who had chaired the Committee on Committees. Simultaneously it was a strengthening of the Speaker, giving him a role in the selection of committee members and committee chairs. The 1973 reforms also created a new Steering and Policy committee to replace the dormant Steering Committee. This new committee consisted of twenty-four members: the Speaker, the majority leader, the chairman of the caucus, the majority whip, the chief deputy whip, the three deputy whips, four members appointed by the Speaker, and twelve members elected by regional caucuses within the House Democratic party. The role of the new committee was to help devise and direct party strategy in the House. The Speaker was made the chairperson of the committee. In addition, the Speaker had a dominant role in selecting the members of the committee, since not only would the four members appointed by him owe service on the committee to him but also the five whips would be indebted, since they are appointed to their whip positions by the Speaker in conjunction with the majority leader.

The second wave in strengthening the Speaker came at the end of 1974 and early 1975, first with the Hansen substitute for the Bolling plan and second with the reform actions of the 94th Congress. The Hansen substitute plan strengthened the Speaker by giving him considerable control over the referral of bills. The early organizational caucuses of the 94th Congress strengthened the Speaker by giving him the power within the party to nominate the Democratic members and the chairperson of the House Rules Committee, thus bringing that committee more clearly into control of the Speaker and the party.[26] Second, the early caucus took the Committee on Committees power away from Ways and Means Democrats and placed it in the Steering and Policy Committee. This considerably increased the role of the party leadership, particularly the Speaker, in selecting committee members and committee chairs, since the Speaker personally selected four members of the Steering and Policy Committee and, with the majority leader, selected five others in the process of naming the party whips. Out of the committee of twenty-four, the Speaker thus had ten votes over which he should have considerable sway (his vote and those of his four appointees and the five whips).

While these two stages of party reforms were occurring, an additional set of changes took place that served to strengthen the Speaker. First, throughout the 1970s, the financial and staff resources of the party whip office were increased and the number of whips appointed by the party leadership was increased. The end product was a stronger and more active whip system at the disposal of the party leadership in efforts to pass legislation. Second, the creation of the new budgetary process provided mechanisms through which a skillful party leadership could control budgetary process and coordinate decision making by House committees. The Speaker's potential control of the House budgetary process resulted from his appointment (in conjunction with the Senate's president pro tem) of the director of the Congressional Budget Office, the leadership's appointment of one of its lieutenants to the House Budget Committee, and the ability of the Speaker, as chair of the Steering and Policy Committee, to oversee appointments of Democrats to the Budget Committee.

All of these changes, taken together, increased the prerogatives of the Speaker. For the first time in decades a Democratic Speaker now has a direct and significant formal role in committee nominations and the nominations of committee chairs. While he cannot make the decisions in a personal, arbitrary fashion (except in the case of Rules), the Speaker does chair the Committee on Committees and plays a dominant role in the selection of nine of the other twenty-three members. Members of the party seeking committee positions or leadership roles now have far more reason to listen to and follow the Speaker than in the past, since he, more than any other person, would seem critical to successful candidacies. Second, although the Speaker is not a member of the Rules Committee and does not chair it (as was the case in Cannon's day), the Speaker does choose the Democratic members of that committee, lessening thereby the likelihood that its Democratic members will delay or block the scheduling of legislation desired by the party leadership. Third, as chair of the Steering and Policy Committee, itself revitalized with real power, the Speaker now has greater legitimacy as a policy spokesperson of the party and greater opportunity to fashion and direct the party's legislative program. Fourth, with the new powers of the Speaker with regard to referral of bills, the Speaker has regained some of the ground lost by Cannon relative to control of legislation. Fifth, the Democratic Speaker now has a much strengthened whip system to use in passing Democratic legislation. Finally, the Steering and Policy Committee, together with the new budget process, provides tools that a Speaker can use to coordinate and direct major legislation. The one area in which Cannon lost ground and in which recent changes do not seem to significantly redress the loss of power is in the control of parliamentary procedures on the floor. If anything, recent changes allowing recorded votes on amendments and electronic voting (which has cut time of roll call votes considerably and reduced the leadership control over the pace of floor votes) have further reduced the Speaker's power as presiding officer and solidified the procedural protections of the average member. Nevertheless, the sum total of the changes seems to constitute a real resurgence of the Speakership and a move back toward the power of the era of Cannon. This movement is not uninhibited, however. It is constrained by the subcommittee bill of rights and other rules changes that protect members' rights within committees and subcommittees, by the specification of fairly clear-cut procedural roles on the floor, and by the existence of the Steering and Policy Committee. The last item is particularly important.

In many ways, the creation of the Steering and Policy Committee is the immediate key to the success of the overall move toward party government. For party government to be successful, to endure, the average member of the caucus must feel that it is a cooperative effort to fashion a widely accepted set of policies and strategies, not simply an ego trip by the one person who happens to be Speaker. The party caucus, although useful as an arena in which to generate certain decisions and legitimize reforms or policy positions, cannot operate on a daily and intimate basis to direct party strategy and constrain the Speaker. The Steering and Policy Committee, as a relatively small committee composed partly of the Speaker's appointees and partly of members selected by regional caucuses, provides the best arena in which the spirit of party cooperation and a representative direction to party efforts can be fashioned, while at the same time constraining and guiding the Speaker. In the best of situations, the Steering and Policy Committee will be a representative body, reflective of the dominant party majority, that keeps the Speaker in touch with the sentiments of the party generally, provides healthy debate and innovative directions on public policy, and spurs the party leadership into an articulate, persuasive policy role that reflects the dominant sentiment of the party. In the worst of situations, the Steering and Policy Committee may become the arena in which intense, fratricidal struggles occur, a highly visible symbol of a divided, polarized, immobilized party.

Whatever the long-term fate of the Steering and Policy Committee and the renewed powers of the Speakership, it is clear that they did transform House decision making at least for the 94th Congress. The overthrow of committee chairs at the beginning of the 94th Congress was precipitated in part by initial decisions within Steering and Policy to depose Patman and Hays. The swift reaction to the Hays sex scandal owed much to the efforts of the party leadership to activate the caucus and enact the reforms. In addition, many of the economic programs passed by the House in the 94th Congress owed their existence to the party leadership.

It is a truism of American politics that if they do not have a president in the White House, American congressional parties lack a program to provide policy coordination and guidance. In late 1974, as the country's recession continued to worsen, Speaker Albert tried to break with this tradition by creating a House Democratic Task Force on the Economy. This task force, chaired by Deputy Whip Jim Wright (D-Tex.), was an arm or committee of the Steering and Policy Committee, from which it gained its legitimacy. The ten-member committee was appointed by Albert to set program goals for the party. It was this committee that initially developed the idea of a tax cut in 1974 that formed the basis of the 1975 Tax Reduction Act. This committee also initiated a number of other proposals, with the support of Albert and the Steering and Policy Committee, including jobs and housing legislation.

The task force provided a significant departure from tradition for House Democrats. It acted as a central committee that initiated general ideas, publicized them, and kept an eye on their progress in committee. The creation of the task force allowed for policy direction to come from the party leadership and provided an opportunity to coordinate economic policy across committees and between the House and Senate (after the Senate Democrats later created a similar task force). The task force, as an arm of the party leadership, also provided a focal point for publicity about the effort of House Democrats to resolve the nation's economic problems, and several widely publicized news conferences were held with Albert and Wright presenting the task force proposals and defending them. Were the House Democratic party (and the Senate party) to solidify the task force approach, it could herald a new day for broad, overt, publicized policy leadership by the congressional party.

Conclusion

It is difficult enough to catalog and interpret the changes that have occurred in the House in the 1970s. Perhaps a broader-based analysis of the full implications of these alterations will have to wait a few years until the impact is digested.[27] Nevertheless, there are several important themes that deserve comment now in evaluating the effect of the changes on the House.

One is the idea that the House, because of the changes, operates with greater equality among its members. The large number of subcommittees gives more members a piece of the action and an outlet for their policy interests. The new process for the selection of subcommittee members allows even first-term members to obtain high-ranking positions on some subcommittees. Junior House members now hold seats on the prestige committees—Appropriations, Rules, and Ways and Means. Newer members now find themselves in important management positions on some legislation. Committee activity is directed more by the desires of its majority caucus than by those of the chair. The sanctions that once meant that junior House members were to be seen and not heard have largely disappeared. Ironically, it is today the junior members who have control of many of the sanctions and rewards for their senior colleagues.

A second theme is that there now exist in the House renewed systems for greater procedural and substantive innovation. The activation of the party caucus organizations means that the ability to raise issues for change and reform of House operations continues. Although there are reactions against the overexercise of caucus activity and the role of caucus leadership as a competitor with other House party leaders, the caucus as an institutionalized organ for the consideration of House reforms is likely to be maintained. In addition, the decentralized structure of the House has improved its capacity for policy innovation and initiation. There are, as a result of subcommittee government, many new points of access for policy ideas in the congressional process, places where the ideas can get a hearing and where information can be gathered.

A final theme that stands out from this period of change is a renewed system of coordination. Much of this involves the transfer of certain activities to the House leadership. In particular, the development of the Steering and Policy Committee, the new range of bill referral authority vested in the Speaker, and the establishment of the new budget process stand out as efforts at centralization designed to bring order in an increasingly complex, decentralized institution. Obviously, not all of the efforts toward centralization and coordination have been successful. The reluctance of the House Democratic leadership to exercise fully the powers available to it and the defeat of the Bolling resolution by the weaker Hansen substitute are indications of the limits House members wish to place on the powers of leadership.

In essence, the House is now faced with the tension that builds from the interaction among these themes. How much power can be given to the leadership without its interfering with the new autonomy that members have achieved? Will some subcommittee chairs give up their piece of the action if it will help the House function more efficiently? With power so dispersed, is there a way to mobilize it to pass legislation and to negotiate effectively with the Senate, the president, interest groups, and agencies in the federal bureaucracy over the final form of legislative policy decisions? Can a strong party caucus exist without its chair's being a political competitor with the Speaker and the majority leader?

A balance between the pull first toward decentralization and then toward centralization in the House now exists, but it is an extremely delicate one that continues to shift. The direction in which it tips, or its institutionalization in its current form, will do much to determine the capacity of the House to play a strong role in national decision making. A move toward a stronger party government and destruction of the committee system would undermine the responsiveness of the House to innovative ideas elicited from a broad range of policy specialists drawn from widely divergent constituent backgrounds. The emergence of a dominant subcommittee government and destruction of the new mechanisms of party leadership probably would cripple the ability of the House to operate as an efficient and coordinated policy-making institution. The emergence of a balance between decentralization and centralization, between innovation and coordination, seems to offer the best hope for a strong House capable of fulfilling its constitutional role as the nation's most representative policy-making entity.

NOTES

1. For a discussion of the House in these general terms, see Samuel P. Huntington, "Congressional Responses to the Twentieth Century," in David Truman, ed., *The Congress and America's Future*, 2d ed. (Englewood Cliffs, N.J.: Prentice-Hall, 1973). For background on the House, see also George B. Galloway, *History of the House of Representatives* (New York: Crowell, 1962); and Neil MacNeil, *Forge of Democracy: The House of Representatives* (New York: McKay, 1963).

2. Charles S. Bullock III, "House Careerists; Changing Patterns of Longevity and Attrition," *American Political Science Review* 66 (1972): 1295–1305. Bullock's operational definition of a House careerist is a member elected to ten or more terms.

3. Huntington, op. cit., p. 9.

4. The ideological groupings in Table 1 are based on conservative coalition support scores published by Congressional Quarterly, Inc. The CQ scores have been adjusted to remove the effect of absences. (This was done by dividing the support score by the sum of the support and opposition scores for each member.) Those with adjusted scores of 0–30 were classified as liberals, 31–70 as moderates, and 71–100 as conservatives.

5. *Congressional Quarterly Almanac, 1974* (Washington, D.C.: Congressional Quarterly, Inc., 1974), p. 855. The almanac will be cited hereafter by the initials *CQA* and the year.

6. On racial composition, see *CQA, 1962*, p. 1047, and *CQA, 1974*, p. 853; on sexual composition, see *CQA, 1974*, p. 853.

7. Herbert Asher, "The Learning of Legislative Norms," *American Political Science Review* 67 (1973): 499–513.

8. On the Democratic Study Group, see Mark F. Ferber, "The Formation of the Democratic Study Group," in Nelson W. Polsby, ed., *Congressional Behavior* (New York: Random House, 1971), pp. 249–67; and Arthur G. Stevens, Jr., Arthur H. Miller, and Thomas E. Mann, "Mobilization of Liberal Strength in the House, 1955–1970: The Democratic Study Group," *American Political Science Review* 68 (1974): 667–81. For a discussion of the reform efforts in the House and the initial role of DSG, see Norman J. Ornstein and David W. Rohde, "Congressional Reform and Po-

litical Parties in the U.S. House of Representatives," in Jeff Fishel
and David Broder, eds., *Parties and Elections in an Anti-Party Age*
(Bloomington: Indiana University Press, 1976).

9. *CQA, 1970*, pp. 117–19.
10. *CQA, 1971*, p. 17.
11. *Congressional Quarterly Weekly Report*, vol. 31, no. 3, pp. 69–72;
no. 4, pp. 136–38.
12. David W. Rohde, "Committee Reform in the House of Representatives and the Subcommittee Bill of Rights," *The Annals* 411
(January 1974): 39–47.
13. *CQA, 1973*, p. 718; *CQA, 1974*, p. 962.
14. See Roger H. Davidson and Walter J. Oleszek, "Adaptation and
Consolidation: Structural Innovation in the U.S. House of Representatives," *Legislative Studies Quarterly* 1 (1976): 37–65.
15. See Lawrence C. Dodd and George C. Shipley, "Patterns of Committee Surveillance in the House of Representatives," paper presented at the APSA annual convention, San Francisco, September
2–5, 1975.
16. See Norman J. Ornstein, "Causes and Consequences of Congressional Change: Subcommittee Reforms in the House of Representatives, 1970–1973," in Ornstein, ed., *Congress in Change* (New
York: Praeger, 1975), pp. 88–114.
17. Rohde, op. cit., pp. 39–47.
18. On Gordon and Richards, see MacNeil, op. cit., pp. 161–70. On
Buckley and Whittington, see James T. Murphy, "The House
Public Works Committee," Ph.D. dissertation, University of
Rochester, 1969.
19. John F. Manley, *The Politics of Finance* (Boston: Little, Brown,
1970), pp. 121–44.
20. *CQA, 1974*, p. 962.
21. *CQA, 1975*, p. 933.
22. See the discussion in Robert L. Peabody, *Leadership in Congress:
Stability, Succession, and Change* (Boston: Little, Brown, 1976),
chap. 2.
23. David R. Mayhew, *Congress: The Electoral Connection* (New
Haven, Conn.: Yale University Press, 1974).
24. On the activity surrounding the oil depletion vote, see *Congressional Quarterly Weekly Report*, vol. 33, no. 9, pp. 419–23. For a
contrasting discussion of earlier action on oil depletion, see Bruce
I. Oppenheimer, *Oil and the Congressional Process: The Limits of
Symbolic Politics* (Lexington, Mass.: Lexington Books, 1974).
25. See the discussion in *Congressional Quarterly Weekly Report*, vol.
34, no. 26, pp. 1631–33.

26. On the Rules Committee in earlier eras, see James A. Robinson, *The House Rules Committee* (Indianapolis: Bobbs-Merrill, 1963). For a more extensive discussion of the new Rules Committee, see Bruce I. Oppenheimer, "The Changing Role of the House Rules Committee," paper presented at the annual meeting of the Southwestern Political Science Convention, Dallas, April 7–10, 1976.

27. These changes, for example, raise questions about the extent to which the postwar House really was an "institutionalized" assembly and the conditions of deinstitutionalization (if that be the case). They also pose for our consideration a question whether different forms of institutionalization exist, with different consequences, and whether the House could develop a new and different structure from the postwar structure that nevertheless would be considered "institutionalized." For the pioneering discussion of the institutionalized House, see Nelson W. Polsby, "Institutionalization in the U.S. House of Representatives," *American Political Science Review* 62 (1968): 144–68.

3. Congressional Dynamics and the Decline of Competitive Congressional Elections

Albert D. Cover and David R. Mayhew

In broad outline the last decade of American politics has been a time of public discontent with political institutions and a consequent search for new modes of public participation. Given the discontent and the search, the record of congressional elections in these years presents something of an anomaly. Down at the constituency level, elections to Congress have become less competitive. Fewer congressmen have been winning their seats by narrow November margins, more by "safe" margins. To be sure, a slow decline in electoral marginality has been visible—on the House side, at least—in time series extending back over the twentieth century.[1] Yet the falloff after the mid-1960s is especially noticeable, enough so to require for the last decade special pondering and special explanations. In this essay we present some evidence on the recent decline in congressional marginality and explore some possible causes and implications of the decline. We give more attention to House than to Senate elections—a choice dictated by the fact that we and others have unearthed more hard evidence on the House. But we marshal some suggestive data on the Senate.

I

The specific phenomenon of interest is that in recent general elections smaller proportions of congressional incumbents have been winning victories in the "marginal" range. No such trend is evident in elections for "open seats" [2]—those 10 to 20 percent of contests each year that offer no incumbents on the November ballot—and in the following data analysis we shall confine our attention to elections with incumbents running. The decline in marginality appears regardless of what definition one chooses for "marginality." Winning with under 55 or under 60 percent of the vote is the customary choice. What makes marginality interesting, of course, is the presumption that congressmen with close victories feel more vulnerable and are more vulnerable to electoral defeat.

The decline in closely contested House and Senate seats is captured in the summary data presented in Tables 1 and 2. Table 1 displays figures on the share of the major party vote won by incumbent House members running in elections between 1956 and 1974. For each election year the table gives the proportion of all incumbent seats in which representatives gathered at least 60 percent of the district vote. (The complement of each listed percentage here is the proportion of incumbent seats in which members won with under 60 percent or lost.) One obvious point emerging from the table is that House incumbents have generally done quite well during this period; if we call a seat safe

Table 1. Decline in Marginality in House Elections, 1956–74

Year	Proportion of Incumbents Winning at Least 60 Percent of the Major Party Vote	N
1956	59.1%	403
1958	63.1	390
1960	58.9	400
1962	63.6	376
1964	58.5	388
1966	67.7	401
1968	72.2	397
1970	77.3	389
1972	77.8	373
1974	66.4	383

SOURCES: Data for 1956–72 elections were taken from David R. Mayhew, "Congressional Elections: The Case of the Vanishing Marginals," *Polity* 6 (1974): 316–17. Data for the 1974 election were taken from the 1974 edition of Richard Scammon's *America Votes* series.

when the incumbent secures at least 60 percent of the vote, then at no point during this period have fewer than half the incumbents won by safe margins.

More important, however, is the changing proportion of safe House seats over time. Before 1966 about three-fifths of the seats were safe, but after the mid-1960s approximately three-fourths of the seats fell into that category. Even in the swing year 1974 about two-thirds of House incumbents won at the 60 percent level—a higher proportion than in any election from 1956 through 1964. The general trend is toward elevation of districts out of the marginal range.[3]

Table 2 presents comparable data on the proportion of safe seats for Senate incumbents. With only a third of the Senate coming up for election at any one time, we must aggregate Senate data over several elections to get enough observations for meaningful comparisons over time. For this reason the table is based on election triplets extending back to 1946.

The Senate pattern is different. The last column of percentages in Table 2 yields no important overall trend toward safeness in Senate elections with incumbents running. Yet regional disaggregation of the figures gives a more precise fix on what has been happening. In the eleven Confederate states, where post–World War II Republican incursions have been especially notable at the Senate level, safe incumbent outcomes have declined from the entire set to about 75 percent. At the same time the proportion of safe northern seats has risen from one-fifth to two-fifths. This decline in Senate marginality in the thirty-nine non-Confederate states has the look of a significant development. Especially noteworthy is the fact that the increase in safe northern

Table 2. Changes in Marginality in Senate Elections, by Region, 1946—74

| Election Triplets | PROPORTION OF INCUMBENTS WINNING AT LEAST 60 PERCENT OF THE MAJOR PARTY VOTE | | | |
	South	North	Total	N
1946–50	100.0%	23.9%	42.6%	61
1952–56	100.0	18.5	35.4	82
1958–62	86.4	24.2	40.5	84
1964–68	72.2	41.9	48.8	80
1970–74	76.9	37.1	44.0	75

SOURCE: A convenient compilation of data on Senate elections is *Guide to U.S. Elections* (Washington, D.C.: Congressional Quarterly, Inc., 1975), pp. 485–509. Senators originally appointed to the Senate are not considered incumbents.

Senate seats coincides quite nicely with the increase in safe House seats; in both cases the mid-1960s emerges as a time of relatively abrupt political change.

Figure 1 gives snapshots of two very recent House elections, showing what elections with eroded marginality have come to look like. For each election year we have sorted seats with incumbents running into classes based on the Democratic percentage of the major party vote. This sorting creates for each year a frequency distribution that makes it readily apparent whether election contests tend to cluster in the competitive region, whether one party wins easily in all contests, or whether each party wins handily in some contests while running quite poorly in others.

The top of Figure 1 presents the frequency distribution based on 1972 House races involving incumbents. Note that all values to the left of the 50 percent mark record Republican victories in incumbent-held districts; almost all of these were victories of Republican incumbents, but six were narrow victories of Republican challengers over Democratic incumbents. Similarly, the values recorded to the right of the 50 percent mark include three narrow victories by Democratic challengers over Republican incumbents. The important message here is that the distribution has a gap in the middle—in roughly the marginal range. If we set aside the most heavily Democratic outcomes—those on the right edge of the figure, in which Democratic incumbents faced no major party opponent in the general election—we see that the 1972 pattern is a bimodal one with a cluster of solid Republican districts on the left, a cluster of solid Democratic districts on the right, and the prominent gap in the competitive middle. This bimodal pattern has become typical; it appears in the years 1966 through 1972, and it will probably appear with regularity in future elections. By contrast, distributions drawn from data on earlier elections are quite different. Earlier distributions are not bimodal but unimodal, with high proportions of incumbent districts clustering in the competitive region.[4] Again, the overall trend is one of declining marginality.

The 1974 election, graphed in the bottom of the figure, offers in one respect an interesting exception to the recent trend.[5] The bimodal pattern is as prominent as in 1972. But the entire distribution has shifted to the right, populating the marginal range with districts that earlier were solidly Republican. What happened in 1974, of course, was that a post-Watergate national swing rendered safe Republican seats marginal. The Democratic share of the national two-party House vote rose a sizable 6 percent between 1972 and 1974, giving the Democrats, at 58.8 percent, their highest vote mark of the twentieth century. Thirty-six Republican incumbents (and four Democrats) lost their seats. The 1974 results make it clear that, bimodal pattern not-

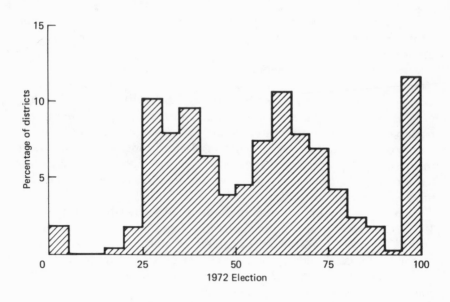

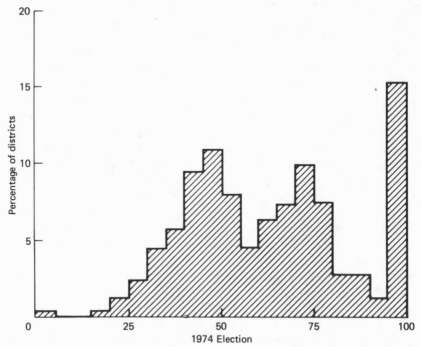

Figure 1. Frequency Distributions of Democratic Percentages of the Two-Party Vote in House Districts with Incumbents Running, 1972 and 1974.

withstanding, a large vote swing can still drive out incumbents and turn safe seats marginal. They also suggest a subtler point, that in a bimodal electoral universe the ratio of seat swing to vote swing is likely to vary with size of vote swing. To be more concrete, in a House election following one like that of 1972, the difference in seat yield between a 4 percent and a 6 percent national swing is likely to be greater for a favored party than the difference between a 1 percent and a 3 percent swing. All of this is to say that it takes a big vote swing to defeat very many incumbents when not many are marginal to begin with. It should be added that the modest shift toward marginality in 1974 (see Table 1) is probably ephemeral. With biennial vote swings smaller in size, the trough in the bimodal distribution is likely to shift back to the middle of the marginal range, yielding what have come to be normal election patterns like the one in the 1972 graph.

II

Why the general reduction in marginality? An inspection of the election careers of individual congressmen supplies a proximate answer. In particular, an examination of critical points in these career patterns shows that the electoral advantage of running as an incumbent has increased in recent years.

Two career points meriting special attention are an incumbent's first and final reelection bids. Running as an incumbent for the first time at the end of his freshman term, a member ought in general to do somewhat better than he did in his first successful election effort. We should expect, therefore, to observe a "sophomore surge" when these first and second elections are compared. The magnitude of this surge is one good measure of the electoral advantage of incumbency.

A second measure can be developed by seeing what happens to the nominee of the incumbent's party immediately after an incumbent voluntarily retires. In general we should not expect the incumbent's successor nominee to do as well as the incumbent did in his final reelection effort. If the successor does not have as much support, then we shall observe a falloff in the party's vote immediately after its incumbent retires. The "retirement slump" constitutes a second measure of how much incumbency is worth.

Table 3 presents sophomore surge and retirement slump data for House elections from 1962 through 1974. Entries in the sophomore surge column were calculated in a fairly straightforward fashion. Consider, for example, the entry for 1962. Forty-six freshmen first elected in 1960 also contested the 1962 election. For each of these members—

Table 3. Sophomore Surge and Retirement Slump for House Members, 1962–74

Years of Sophomore or Successor-Nominee Elections	Mean Sophomore Surge (adjusted)	N	Mean Retirement Slump (adjusted)	N
1962	+2.1%	46	−1.4%	17
1964	+1.6	54	−1.4	25
1966	+3.3	69	−4.7	13
1968	+6.5	54	−7.6	19
1970	+6.7	31	−6.6	36
1972	+7.5	43	−11.0	27
1974	+5.8	57	−6.7	44

SOURCES: Sophomore surge data were taken from Albert D. Cover, "The Advantage of Incumbency in Congressional Elections" (Ph.D. dissertation, Yale University, 1976), p. 21. Retirement slump data for 1962–72 elections taken from David R. Mayhew, "Congressional Elections: The Case of the Vanishing Marginals," *Polity* 6 (1974): 309. The 1974 retirement data came from Cover, p. 19. Data are adjusted to discount interelection swings in the national House vote.

all with major-party opposition both times—we calculated the 1960–62 vote change percentage, using for each year the congressman's percent of the total House vote in his district. The vote change data were then adjusted to take into account the 2.2 percent pro-Republican swing in the national House vote between 1960 and 1962. For each Republican member 2.2 percent was subtracted from his change score; for each Democrat 2.2 percent was added. The 1962 entry, +2.1 percent, is the mean of the 46 adjusted change scores. A similar procedure was used for the entries in the retirement slump column. In the retirement column swing adjustments were applied to changes in a *party's* share of the total vote upon the retirement of its incumbent.

At the outset it should be noted that on balance first-term incumbents do surge and that a party's vote does slump when its incumbent leaves Congress. More interesting, however, are changes in the magnitude of incumbency advantage over time revealed in Table 3. The data in this table do not go back very far, but both the surge and retirement columns indicate that the value of incumbency in House elections amounted to only 1 or 2 percent prior to the mid-1960s. This jibes well with a finding of Robert Erikson, based on somewhat different calculations, that the electoral value of House incumbency was about 2 percent in the years 1952–60.[6] In the mid-1960s, and particularly after 1966, both of the key columns in Table 3 suggest that the value of running as an incumbent representative increased substantially. They differ somewhat in the precise value they ascribe to incumbency, but they both indicate a definite increase at about the same time.

The impact of this increase may be illustrated with a brief example. Between 1972 and 1974 the Republican share of the national House vote fell by 6 percent. For Republican freshmen first elected in 1972 the median vote was −1.3 percent. These freshmen did remarkably well, almost overcoming the pro-Democratic vote shift. In contrast, for seats with Republican retirements in 1974, the median interelection vote change for the party was −15.4 percent. If for some reason the Republican party had been deprived of all its incumbents in 1974, its seat loss surely would have been much greater than it was in fact.

The analysis of critical career points is a bit more difficult for incumbent senators because any given election year has relatively few sophomores or retirees, but aggregating over several elections permits us to explore changes in the value of incumbency for senators. Table 4 summarizes the relevant data for all usable Senate elections regardless of region. In essential respects the arrangement of this table is the same as that of Table 3 on House incumbency. To generate samples large enough for comparisons over time, however, Table 4 goes back to 1940 and aggregates data by decade into election quintuplets. Thus, the 1946–54 row in the table includes entries, under "sophomore surge," for senators who initially won their seats in regular elections in any of the years 1940–48 and who ran again a full term later in any of the years 1946–54. Under "retirement slump," the 1946–54 row includes entries for senators who ran their last races in 1940–48 and gave way to successor nominees a term later in 1946–54. In this Senate table adjustments for national trend are based on six-year interelection swings in the two-party share of the national House vote.

Table 4. Sophomore Surge and Retirement Slump for Senators, 1946–74

Years of Sophomore or Successor-Nominee Elections	Mean Sophomore Surge (adjusted)	N	Mean Retirement Slump (adjusted)	N
1946–54	+0.5%	41	−3.2%	21
1956–64	+1.5	44	−3.2	14
1966–74	+3.9	27	−4.8	28

SOURCE: Data were taken from *Guide to U.S. Elections* (Washington, D.C.: Congressional Quarterly, Inc., 1975), pp. 485–509. Adjustments for national trends are based on six-year interelection swings in the two-party share of the House vote. Senators beginning their Senate service by appointment or by special election are excluded from the sophomore surge data.

These Senate data are scanty but worth comment. Like their counterparts in the House, senators generally do better in their first reelection bids than they did when initially running for office. They tend to
gain less from early incumbency than do House members, but on balance they do pick up some support. Also like their House counterparts, retiring senators usually run more strongly than do their successor nominees. The slim evidence suggests that a senator's party loses
less support upon his retirement than does the party of a retiring representative but that there is still a retirement slump for senators. The
most intriguing House-Senate comparison concerns changes in the
value of incumbency over time. If we examine the three sophomore
surge entries in Table 4, we note that incumbency advantage apparently increased from each time period to the next. The more sizable
increase occurred among senators first elected in 1960–68. Running for
reelection in the 1966–74 period, these senators experienced the increase at about the same time House first-termers were enjoying
theirs. Similarly, we see that the Senate retirement slump value increased modestly in the latest election period, at the same time it was
rising on the House side.[7]

III

What we have, in short, is evidence that the electoral value of
both House and Senate incumbency increased in the 1960s. This increase presumably helped propel many incumbents out of the dangerous marginal category. The evidence presented thus far naturally
raises the question of *why* incumbents are doing better now than they
did only a few years ago. No definitive answer is yet possible, but we
can explore some promising avenues with data collected on House
elections with incumbent candidates.

One plausible explanation offered by Edward Tufte is that House
incumbents have recently benefited more from redistricting than they
had previously.[8] This suggestion gains particular credibility from the
upsurge of redistricting activity that followed from *Baker* v. *Carr*, the
Supreme Court's 1962 decision affirming the federal judiciary's authority to consider apportionment cases. During the 1960s most states
revised district lines at least twice, and some adopted four different
redistricting schemes in efforts to meet increasingly precise judicial
guidelines. The very precision of these guidelines expanded opportunities for congressmen and their allies back home to use redistricting
for political gain, for the guidelines effectively required states to ignore county lines in drawing district boundaries. Unfettered by this

time-honored constraint, states had more freedom in their redistricting arrangements.

Some preliminary evidence suggests that incumbent representatives may indeed have derived political benefit from redistricting during the 1960s. If we examine cases in which an incumbent contests both the last election before district boundaries are redrawn and also the first election after lines are changed, then we can ask whether or not incumbents generally do better after redistricting than they did before it. In making this comparison, we should probably discount national interelection partisan swings to determine what effect redistricting itself has on incumbent vote margins. Of 252 incumbent representatives meeting the relevant criteria in 1962–70, 158 did better than the swing and only 94 fell behind the swing.[9] Although more elaborate controls could reduce this disparity, the preponderance of cases in which incumbents do better after redistricting than they did before suggests that redistricting might have been electorally useful for many.

On the other hand, if redistricting did benefit incumbents, then we should expect the proportion of marginal seats to be lower in sets of redistricted seats than in sets of seats left untouched. In fact, the proportion of marginal seats in the redistricted set did decline in the 1960–74 period, but a decline also occurred in districts that were not redrawn.[10] Furthermore, there is no clear relation between volume of redistricting and the values for incumbency advantage picked up for individual election years in Table 3. For example, there was scarcely any redistricting in either the 1968–70 or the 1972–74 interelection biennium, yet the sophomore surge and retirement slump figures yield high readings for House incumbency advantage in 1970 and 1974. A final point here is that incumbency advantage seems to have risen in the Senate as well as the House even though state lines have, of course, remained inviolable.

While evidence on the contribution of redistricting to the growing advantage of incumbency is weak and inconclusive, stronger evidence is available on the contribution of changes in mass electoral behavior. In particular, we can show that the decline of partisanship in the electorate has benefited incumbents in House elections.

In 1966 Philip Converse wrote of the "serene stability in the distribution of party loyalty" and of the "remarkable individual stability in party identification, even in this period of extravagant vote change."[11] Even then, however, this serene stability was beginning to crumble. Between 1952 and 1964 the distribution of partisan identification did indeed remain remarkably stable, but the next decade witnessed a slow erosion in the proportion of the eligible electorate identifying with either of the major parties. Between 1964 and 1974 Independents increased from 8.2 percent of the electorate to 15.1 percent. If we also consider Independent Democrats and Independent Republicans, the most weakly affiliated partisans, then this augmented pool increased from 23.5 percent of the electorate to 37.5 percent during the same period.[12] Noting that the growth of Independents coincided with the growth of the incumbency advantage, Erikson suggested that "because the recent increase in the number of Independent voters has allowed the incumbent's visibility to tip the balance in an increasing number of voter decisions, the size of the incumbency advantage appears to have grown."[13] The logic is appealing. Evidence developed elsewhere indicates that changes in the distribution of partisanship have in fact benefited incumbents.[14]

The decay of partisanship has had a second, and in some ways more subtle, influence on the advantage of incumbency. Thus far we have been speaking of this decay in terms of the declining proportion of the electorate identifying with the major parties. Even for those continuing to identify with one of these parties, however, party labels may be of less significance than they once were. In particular, partisan identifiers may place less weight on party as a voting cue than they did previously. If so, incumbents may be able to take advantage of this situation. Mayhew, for example, has suggested that "voters dissatisfied with party cues could be reaching for any other cues that are available in deciding how to vote. The incumbency cue is readily at hand."[15]

Of course, an upsurge in defections from partisan identification *may* help incumbents, but it should be said that defections will not necessarily have this effect. Consider, for example, the presumably typical case of a district in which the incumbent carries the party label with which a modal share of voters identifies. A *general* increase in the defection rate will produce a net *loss* of support for the incumbent, since defections favoring the challenger will outnumber defections from the challenger's party. A decline in the importance of partisanship will help incumbents only if defections are "properly" distributed. Survey data allow us to see whether or not defections from party have on balance benefited incumbents and whether the proportions of pro-incumbent and anti-incumbent defections have changed over time.

Using data on party identifiers from the University of Michigan's Survey Research Center, Cover examined defections from party in contested House races involving an incumbent from 1958 through 1974.[16] Defections were divided into two classes, those by respondents identifying with the challenger's party (pro-incumbent defections) and those by respondents identifying with the incumbent's party (anti-incumbent defections). Table 5 presents data on the proportion of all defections favoring the incumbent.

Table 5. Proportions of Voter Defections from Party Identification Favoring Incumbents: House Elections 1958–74

Year	Proportion of Pro-Incumbent Defections	N	Year	Proportion of Pro-Incumbent Defections	N
1958	56.6%	83	1968	66.0%	141
1960	65.0	117	1970	83.6	73
1962	*	–	1972	83.2	113
1964	62.4	125	1974	73.8	126
1966	70.7	92			

* Data not available.

SOURCE: Data on percentage of defections provided by the Inter-University Consortium for Political Research. Only data from contested elections involving an incumbent are included. Percentage defections in 1958, 1960, and 1974 are based on weighted responses.

Throughout this period most defectors have been voters identifying with the challenger's party. This hardly comes as a surprise, since we should generally expect incumbents to draw off more support from the local minority party than challengers draw off from the incumbent's party. Although the number of usable respondents is not large, the trend toward increasingly pro-incumbent defections seems well established. Since 1970 about three-fourths of all defections have come from the challenger's party. The figures capture an important shift in mass electoral behavior.

What lies behind the growing preponderance of pro-incumbent defections? One possibility is that incumbents are inducing defections through a variety of reelection-oriented activities. There is abundant evidence that incumbents have engaged more energetically in such activities since the mid-1960s. For example, the volume of franked mail sent out from congressional offices increased from about 100 million pieces in the early 1960s to about 200 million pieces by the end of the decade; on the House side, district travel allowances were first instituted during the 1964 fiscal year, and by the end of the decade approximately $800,000 was consumed annually in travel reimbursements. The list could be extended to cover other perquisites of office.[17] These data are obviously quite suggestive, but they do not establish that incumbents have been successful in altering mass electoral behavior.

Even if these efforts did pay off, it is not clear exactly what the route to payoff would be. One argument is that the upsurge in incumbent activities should help incumbents by boosting their recognition among constituents. If this is the path through which incumbent activity is translated into votes, then the activity has been a failure. Since 1958 all but two of the Survey Research Center postelection polls have contained some variant of the question "Do you happen to remember the name of the candidates for Congress—that is, for the House of Representatives in Washington—that ran in this district this November?'' Responses to this question permit us to determine which candidates, if any, those surveyed were able to recall. The data are summarized in Table 6. Surprisingly, the share of respondents recalling *neither* incumbent nor challenger has shot up over the last decade—from about half to over three-fifths. The proportions recalling only the incumbent's name have remained stable, and the proportions recalling only the challenger's name have remained negligible. Thus, incumbents have apparently come to inspire *less* rather than *more* name recall than they did in the early 1960s, and the incumbent-challenger gap in name recall has not gotten wider.[18]

Of course, the full impact of incumbent activity may not be mediated through candidate recognition. In an analysis of survey data for 1964–70, John Ferejohn concluded that "voters were apparently using incumbency as a voting cue whether or not they could recall the names of the incumbent candidate in the interview situation."[19] This suggests that recognition does not capture the full advantage of incumbency, and it implies that reelection-oriented activities may have an impact through channels other than the one involving name recall. Alan Abramowitz's recent analysis of Oregon survey data shows that voters can indeed formulate reasonably rich visions of House candidates and act on them without being able to pass the name recall test. Abramowitz argues for a plumbing of candidate "reputations" among voters.[20] In the case of incumbents, it may be that word of their activities reaches many voters by ripple effect, with awareness of name not traveling as far as the ripples but recoverable when needed.

Then there is the possibility that electorally relevant activities of incumbents have changed in nature, inducing contemporary voters to *like* their congressmen more without necessarily knowing them any better. Morris Fiorina offers an underpinning for this case with his argument that congressmen have seized an opportunity supplied by the recent growth of the federal bureaucracy.[21] The modern congressman is more and more an ombudsman, and the beauty of the ombudsman role is that its occupant sends out issue-neutral signals. Cutting red tape can generate pleasure and perhaps support among voters of all political persuasions.

In seeking an explanation for the growing preponderance of pro-incumbent defections, we have considered the possibility that the change in mass electoral behavior has been induced by the activities of incumbents. This explanation is in many ways an appealing one, but we should also note a second plausible possibility. It is conceivable that incumbents are the accidental beneficiaries of behavioral changes they had no part in creating or fostering—most likely a simple

Table 6. Postelection Recall of House Candidates

PERCENTAGE OF RESPONDENTS RECALLING NAMES OF CANDIDATES

	1958	1964	1966	1968	1970	1972	1974
Incumbent Only	18.1	21.7	17.7	18.3	19.8	17.8	18.7
Challenger Only	1.6	1.8	1.2	2.5	0.9	1.2	0.4
Both	26.1	30.3	21.9	31.4	14.9	17.7	15.5
Neither	54.1	46.2	59.3	47.9	64.4	63.3	65.4
Total	99.9	100.0	100.1	100.1	100.0	100.0	100.0
	(N = 1240)	(N = 1117)	(N = 1002)	(N = 1057)	(N = 1096)	(N = 774)	(N = 1778)

SOURCE: Data provided by Inter-University Consortium for Political Research. Respondents have been excluded unless they were in districts with contested races involving an incumbent. The 1958 and 1974 data are weighted.

unraveling of party allegiance among voters and a resultant shift to the incumbency cue in voter decisions. This is a model of noninduced cue substitution—or at least one in which no shift of cues has been induced by changes in the activities of incumbent congressmen. This is, of course, the explanation favored by Walter Burnham.[22] It draws its attractiveness from the abundant evidence of contemporary party erosion, even though we cannot be sure of the specific effects of that erosion.

IV

No doubt we shall have to wait some time to trace out the full consequences of diminishing congressional marginality. Yet some comments seem in order.

A first point is that the shift to safe incumbent seats carries with it an overall change in the sensitivity of the electoral mechanism. The 1974 election notwithstanding, an electoral system with fewer marginals is one in which partisan vote swings yield less in the way of legislative seat swings. As Tufte puts it in his treatment of House elections, the "swing ratio" has declined in recent years.[23] Whether the fall in this ratio should be lamented is unclear. The older American tradition—like the British and the Canadian—was one of electoral exaggeration, with House seat swings magnifying partisan vote swings rather than just reflecting them. This gave great volatility to congressional politics over time, and on occasion it bolstered popular presidents by giving them lopsided House majorities to work with. The argument for high swing ratios is not that they supplied efficient reflection of public opinion at the instant, but that they provided clear political change and empowered party majorities to govern. Lower House swing ratios, reflecting or understating vote swings, bring their own mix of effects—greater stability in partisan seat holdings over time, Congresses less affected by presidential landslides, a clearer separation-of-powers cast to the regime, possibly a displacement of interest onto presidential elections among voters wishing abrupt political change. Membership renewal in the modern Congress becomes more a matter of continuous creation than of big bangs, with the stakes especially high in contests where retirements have supplied "open seats."

Mention of membership stability raises a second and more particular point. We cherish the notion that we have a two-party system at the congressional level, but evidence is building that we may have to abandon that notion. "One-and-a-half party system" may be a more appropriate phrase. The Republicans have now been out of power in both Houses since 1954—a longer drought than any party had had to suffer before that since the 1830s. The chief reason for this losing string is clear enough—a deficiency of Republican identifiers among voters. Yet the rise in incumbency advantage has created an additional burden for the minority party. Most beneficiaries of incumbency advantage are, after all, Democrats. The lowering of swing ratios reduces the probability—both actual and subjective—that a healthy electoral swing will boost the minority into power. Blighted hopes hinder efforts to recruit candidates and marshal electoral resources. The national partisan vote percentage becomes itself in small part an artifact of incumbency advantage; the Democratic share of the House vote dropped to 50.9 percent in 1968, but it might have gone to half or under with a discounting for the fact that more Democrats than Republicans were winning incumbency points. In a highly volatile electoral system a minority party can hope to come to power once in a while; in a more stable system victory may be forever denied.

The division of House Democrats and Republicans into permanent winners and permanent losers seems to be bringing about other structural asymmetries. Voluntary retirement rates have risen higher among Republican members than among Democrats.[24] Dave Martin (R-Neb.), ranking minority member on Rules, retired in 1974 in part because "it is possible that Republicans will never again be in the majority in the House, if you are realistic about it. . . ." [25] Craig Hosmer (R-Calif.), ranking member on Joint Atomic Energy, also stepped down in 1974 with the comment that "as a Republican you don't have many opportunities for promotion in the sense that a ranking member around here doesn't mean very much in relation to what a chairman means. I've been in the minority for twenty years." [26] Most House Democrats can hope to stay around long enough to win at least a subcommittee chairmanship; no Republican can entertain such hopes. In 1975, at the beginning of the 94th Congress, 49 House Democrats (including 28 northerners) had already served ten or more consecutive terms; only three Republicans had stayed that long. In the mid-1970s Republican recruitment efforts were sagging in both House and Senate elections.[27] One gets the sense that in recent years the public and the media have simply given nationwide congressional elections less attention; the last publicized party square-off came in 1970, and then only on the Senate side. It must be said that the homeostatic properties of the American system may yet reassert themselves, incumbency advantage or not; Republicans remain the recourse in a time of Democratic misrule. But in the meantime, the congressional opposition has become lean and has forgotten what it feels like to eat.

But should we be worrying about partisan configurations at all?

Probably less than we used to. A final point here is that incumbency advantage accrues, after all, to individuals rather than to parties, and consequently it can be expected to foster member individualism on Capitol Hill. Congressmen do not know any more than we do about what is causing the rise in incumbency advantage, but, in line with John Kingdon's "congratulation effect," [28] they are powerfully likely to claim, "I did it all myself," and seek out ways to continue doing it all themselves. Hence the electoral patterns probably inspire quests for individual assertion in congressional office. At least on the House side, party voting has reached new lows in recent years.[29] Current institutional reforms have been decentralizing, yielding a House that looks more like the Senate—weak party leadership, nonhierarchical committees, a vast number of subcommittees in which congressmen can do their own thing, an ethic of member equality and member individualism. The revved-up House Democratic caucus has been used less for making policy than for weakening committee chairmen. The House committee declining most in influence in recent years has been Ways and Means—the chief unit for packaging general policy; the committee rising most in influence, although insecurely institutionalized, has been House Administration—the unit dealing in member perquisites, electoral and otherwise. The Congress we shall have to cope with in the foreseeable future is one less of party management than of decentralized individualism—for better or worse a reversion to the original constitutional design.

NOTES

1. See Walter Dean Burnham, "Insulation and Responsiveness in Congressional Elections," *Political Science Quarterly* 90 (1975): 413.
2. See David R. Mayhew, "Congressional Elections: The Case of the Vanishing Marginals," *Polity* 6 (1974):298–302.
3. Note that Table 1 is based on general election data. This leaves open the possibility that the decline of competition in general elections has been counterbalanced by increased competition in primary elections contested by incumbents. This has not happened. See Albert D. Cover, "The Advantage of Incumbency in Congressional Elections" (Ph.D. dissertation, Yale University, 1976), pp. 34–35.
4. For example, see Mayhew, op. cit. For scattered distributions from earlier years, see Donald E. Stokes, "Parties and the Nationalization of Electoral Forces," in William Nisbet Chambers and

Walter Dean Burnham, eds., *The American Party Systems: Stages of Political Development* (New York: Oxford University Press, 1967), p. 200; and Burnham, op. cit., p. 423.

5. On the 1974 election generally, see Burnham, op. cit., pp. 411–35.

6. Robert Erikson, "The Advantage of Incumbency in Congressional Elections," *Polity* 3 (1971): 404.

7. Kostroski has found that in Senate elections over the years 1948–70 the incumbency variable rose in importance as an explainer of electoral outcomes. See Warren L. Kostroski, "Party and Incumbency in Postwar Senate Elections: Trends, Patterns, and Models," *American Political Science Review* 67 (1973): 1222–33.

8. Edward R. Tufte, "The Relationship Between Seats and Votes in Two-Party Systems," *American Political Science Review* 67 (1973):540–54; and Tufte, "Communication," *American Political Science Review* 68 (1974): 211–13.

9. Cover, op. cit., p. 45.

10. Ibid., pp. 36–46. See also John A. Ferejohn, "On the Decline of Competition in Congressional Elections," Social Science Working Paper no. 81, California Institute of Technology, October 1975, pp. 4–8 (also forthcoming in *American Political Science Review*).

11. Philip E. Converse, "The Concept of a Normal Vote," in Angus Campbell, Philip E. Converse, Warren E. Miller, and Donald E. Stokes, eds., *Elections and the Political Order* (New York: Wiley, 1966), p. 12.

12. For 1952–72 data, see Dan D. Nimmo, *Popular Images of Politics: A Taxonomy* (Englewood Cliffs, N.J.: Prentice-Hall, 1974), p. 122. The data are extended through 1974 in Cover, op. cit., p. 47.

13. Robert Erikson, "A Reply to Tidmarch," *Polity* 4 (1972): 529.

14. Cover, op. cit., pp. 103–28.

15. Mayhew, op. cit., p. 313.

16. Cover, op. cit. pp. 51–55.

17. Ibid., pp. 65–102.

18. For a fuller discussion of the recognition data, see Cover, op. cit., pp. 55–64.

19. Ferejohn, op. cit., p. 17.

20. Alan I. Abramowitz, "Name Familiarity, Reputation, and the Incumbency Effect in a Congressional Election," *Western Political Quarterly* 28 (1975): 668–84.

21. Morris P. Fiorina, "The Case of the Vanishing Marginals: The Bureaucracy Did It," Social Science Working Paper no. 100, California Institute of Technology, November 1975.

22. Walter Dean Burnham, "Communication," *American Political Science Review* 68 (1974): 210; Burnham, "Insulation and Responsiveness," pp. 414–15. See also Ferejohn, op. cit., pp. 20–26.

23. Tufte, "Seats and Votes," pp. 549–53.
24. Cover, op. cit., p. 146.
25. Julius Duscha, "Departures: Fun Is Gone," *Washington Post*, September 15, 1974, p. B1.
26. Ibid.
27. See, for example, Alan Ehrenhalt, "Little Evidence of Republican Comeback," *Congressional Quarterly Weekly Report* 34 (February 21, 1976): 351–53.
28. John W. Kingdon, *Candidates for Office: Beliefs and Strategies* (New York: Random House, 1968), p. 31.
29. Julius Turner, *Party and Constituency: Pressures on Congress*, rev. ed. by Edward V. Schneier, Jr. (Baltimore: Johns Hopkins Press, 1970), chap. 2.

II

ORGANIZATIONAL DYNAMICS AND THE CONGRESSIONAL PROCESS

4. *The Conservative Coalition in Congress*

John F. Manley

"Nothing renders Congress less capable of action than the need for it," according to Richard Harris,[1] and numerous students of American political institutions agree. Even when the necessary allowances are made for the hyperbole of catchy phrases, the fact remains that Congress is a ponderous decision-making body, more adept at delaying and diluting legislative proposals than taking clear-cut, decisive action. A policy-making institution composed of 535 diverse individuals is not, in Nelson Polsby's words, "designed to be fast on its 1,070 feet."[2]

If crises are severe enough, such as those of 1933 and 1941, Congress can act swiftly, but in normal times the legislative process takes time. One reason is, of course, structural: Congress is large and complex. But a more fundamental cause is political. In Congress there are lots of conflicting opinions and objectives to be reconciled, and no underlying base of agreement that allows a congressional majority to govern with parliamentary ease. In the absence of an overwhelming consensus on either the need for or the precise form of federal action,

AUTHOR'S NOTE: This essay is part of the author's larger study of the Conservative Coalition being supported by the Brookings Institution. The conclusions expressed are those of the author and do not necessarily represent those of the trustees, the officers, or other staff members of the Brookings Institution.

conflicts over policy are represented in the congressional parties, splitting them into blocs and factions that have to be accommodated before Congress can make any decisions at all. Majorities are built in Congress, not elected to it; hence congressional politics is coalition politics.

To say that congressional politics is coalition politics is not to deny that party affiliation is important in congressional decisions. It is, rather, to emphasize the coalitional nature of the parties and to direct attention toward cross-party coalitions as basic elements of congressional policy making. Party identification may be the best single predictor of congressional voting, as several roll call studies conclude, but it is also true that on many issues party defections determine the results. Moreover, even if party lines hold firm, the reason often lies in the bargains and compromises forced by the influential blocs that constitute the parties. Much of the substance of policy made by Congress hinges on these bargains and compromises; they account for why and how blocs become majority coalitions.

The Conservative Coalition

Since the time of Franklin Roosevelt, one of the most enduring and consequential alliances in Congress has existed between conservative Republicans and conservative Democrats, mostly from the South. At times, the Conservative Coalition has dominated national policy making by passing conservative legislation and/or stalemating liberal bills (80th Congress, 1947–48), and at times it has been so outnumbered that all it could do was raise a faint voice of protest against extending the scope of federal intervention in the nation's life (89th Congress, 1965–66). In general, however, the Coalition has been a potent force behind conservative interests. When the Conservative Coalition joins the issue, it wins far more than it loses.

This essay examines three questions about the Conservative Coalition. First, in what sense is it accurate to say that there is a Conservative Coalition in Congress? Attention to the question is necessitated by the frequent denials inside Congress that such a Coalition exists, and by the possibility that in dealing with roll call votes one is dealing with nothing more than a statistical artifact: simply because southern Democrats and Republicans vote alike in opposition to northern Democrats does not necessarily prove that the Coalition is anything more than a group of like-minded individuals voting the same way. Second, how often has the Coalition appeared and how successful has it been in Congress since 1933? Third, how has the Coalition behaved under the presidency of Richard Nixon, and what can one expect of the Coalition in the years ahead if the Republican party continues to make electoral headway in the South?

The Conservative Coalition: Collusion, Consensus, or Both?

One of the first and most vitriolic debates over the Conservative Coalition occurred toward the end of the 1939 session of the Senate when Senator Claude Pepper of Florida took the floor to denounce those who had undercut Roosevelt's program.[3] It is not clear from the debate precisely whom Pepper meant to include in the "pharisaical alliance," but the Florida liberal's outburst incensed many of his conservative colleagues.

According to Pepper, the 1939 session of Congress showed that a "willful alliance" was bent on withholding "aid and meager succor from the unemployed and the aged of America, in the hope that in their mad misery they might raise their hand against a President and an administration who have tried to restore them to the dignity and the opportunity of American citizens." Pepper, who had reached the Senate with FDR's backing in the 1936 landslide, accused the "designing alliance" of "having prostituted their power to serve the United States Chamber of Commerce, the Manufacturers' Association, and the beneficiaries of special privilege, who hate in their hearts the man who has tried to lighten the burden of toil on the back of labor." The implication was that a group of senators—a "scheming alliance"—had conspired against the working man; but when called upon by Walter George of Georgia to name names, Pepper refused. Senator Josiah Bailey of North Carolina took Pepper's remarks personally and asked if it would be in order to characterize them as "cowardly and mendacious." Bailey closed the colloquy by informing the Senate that he would relay his views to Pepper privately.

Pepper's target was unclear. He did not charge any individual senators with conspiracy, nor did he refer explicitly to southern Democrats and Republicans. He did refer to the opposition to the Fair Labor Standards Act as an example of conservative efforts on behalf of employers, and that act had been fought by Republicans and southern Democrats. But Pepper evidently was content to vary the pejorative adjective before "coalition" and let individual senators speculate on exactly who fit the odious description.

Still, Pepper's remarks came at the time described by the leading historian of the emergence of the Conservative Coalition as the Coalition's "zenith," [4] and it was probably quite clear to his listeners that he was referring to George, Byrd, Glass, Bailey, and their Republican associates. In any event, the debate touched off by Pepper's comments revealed the open rupture in the Democratic party between such all-out New Deal supporters as Pepper and the southern conservatives.

A second discussion of the Conservative Coalition, complete with denials as to its existence, occurred on the Senate floor a few years after the 1939 exchange. Senator Harry Byrd, one of the first and most consistent defectors from FDR's New Deal, took the floor in 1943 to denounce charges made by Pennsylvania Senator Joseph Guffey that northern Republicans and southern Democrats had conspired to deprive members of the armed forces of their voting rights.[5] As quoted by Byrd, Guffey referred to the alliance that passed the voting bill as the "most unpatriotic and unholy alliance that has occurred in the United States Senate since the League of Nations for peace of the world was defeated in 1919." Here was an explicit charge against the southerners and Republicans made by a senator who at the time was chairman of the Democratic Senatorial Campaign Committee.

More interesting than Byrd's categorical denial of the charge is that on this occasion Josiah Bailey expressed what must have been widely held sentiments among southern Democrats as to what it was like to be a Democrat from the South. Expressing his pride in being a southern Democrat, Bailey reminded his colleagues that in the dark days before 1932—"when it [the Democratic party] was not permitted to serve around the altars which our fathers had made holy"—the party had been kept alive in the South. As Bailey noted:

> Down yonder across the Potomac, and the James, and all the way to the Gulf, and beyond the Mississippi, we kept the fires burning upon the altars of our fathers and of our country, and when there was nobody else to vote in the electoral college for the Democratic candidate, southern Democrats were sending 144 votes to the electoral college; and for that we are scornfully referred to as southern Democrats.

For this, Bailey felt, the southern Democrats deserved better than scorn from their northern brethren.

What concerned Bailey was not the unfair distribution of Democratic patronage. Southern Democrats, he observed, "know where the patronage goes in the day of victory, and they know who leads the way to the trough where the pigs feed and the swill is poured out. We know we are not in that number." Not patronage but disparagement upset the southern Democrat: especially obnoxious was the word "unholy." For himself, Bailey was proud not to be part of a holy alliance including Joseph Guffey of Pennsylvania, and he warned that if such attacks continued the Democratic party would be destroyed:

Mr. President, I will be through in a moment. I merely want to say another word, and very solemnly. They can drive us out; yes, they can drive us out. There can be an end of insults, there can be an end of toleration, there can be an end of patience. We can form a southern Democratic party and vote as we please in the electoral college, and we will hold the balance of power in this country.

We can throw the election into the House of Representatives and cast the votes of 16 states.

The presidency of Franklin Roosevelt was, as Bailey's speech makes clear, a mixed blessing to some southern Democrats. FDR's political base included the South, and he normally took pains not to alienate the South, but his national strength weakened the power of the South in the Democratic party at the same time that his domestic policies increasingly violated traditional southern political values. Yet the South had been Democratic so long and the ties binding the southern and northern wings of the party were so strong that it is small wonder that talk of unholy bipartisan alliances with Republicans would upset—indeed infuriate—Democrats like Byrd and Bailey. Interestingly, the Republican half of the alliance has been just as quick to defend their party integrity as the threatened southerners.

"Now I have to say something which all of us know," Paul Douglas of Illinois told the Senate in 1961, "although we seldom speak about it: I refer to the bipartisan, unholy alliance which exists in this body, and also in the House of Representatives, between the conservative Republicans and the conservative Democrats of the South." [6] Douglas got no further before he was interrupted by Minority Leader Everett Dirksen of Illinois: "Mr. President, that is the sheerest nonsense I have ever heard spouted on the floor of the Senate." Dirksen's response touched off some laughter in the Senate, and when it subsided Douglas opined that he "thought that would stir up the alliance. But that statement is true." Dirksen called Douglas's charge an "untruth" and offered to submit to the discipline of the Senate if his choice of words violated Senate rules. "This business of talking about unholy alliances," Dirksen said, "is the sheerest 'stuff.' "

Again laughter came from the Senate, but Douglas persisted. When challenged by John Marshall Butler that the country could use a little more of the benefits of the unholy alliance, Douglas tried to get Butler to admit that such an alliance was real, but Butler refused the bait. Bush of Connecticut—who denied that he was a member of the alliance and said he knew no one who was—wanted to know why it was called unholy. Capehart of Indiana wondered which part of the Coalition, the conservative Republicans or the conservative Democrats, was unholy. Douglas replied that the alliance was unholy because it thwarted the will of the people as registered in presidential elections, and he argued that it was "the chemical combination" that was unholy. "Although individually they may be very fine persons, when they are put together they have a chemical effect which is not good. . . ."

Essentially similar arguments concerning the Coalition were made by a Republican in the House of Representatives the year before Douglas's charge. Reacting to press accounts that House Republicans were refusing to sign a discharge petition on the 1960 civil rights bill as payment for southern votes on the 1959 Landrum-Griffin labor bill, Representative Thomas B. Curtis (Mo.) pointed to the coalitional character of the Democratic party and claimed that the real coalition in Congress consisted of northern and southern Democrats, not southerners and Republicans.[7] In Curtis's view, the Democratic coalition was a coalition for power: control of the House. The unholy alliance among the Democrats therefore explained why the civil rights bill was held up. As he explained it, the fact that Republicans usually join the northern Democrats on civil rights bills refuted the charge that the Conservative Coalition was responsible for the current delay. In the absence of a quid pro quo binding the Republicans and southern Democrats in the same way that northern and southern Democrats were bound by sharing organizational control of the House, the Republican–southern Democratic coalition was fictitious. Curtis's challenge to the Democratic party was to show the same kind of cohesion on civil rights that it showed when electing the Speaker and organizing the congressional committees, a challenge that everyone, including Curtis, knew was impossible.

The Missouri Republican's call for southern and northern Democrats to cooperate on civil rights was answered by Representative Frank Thompson (D-N.J.), a leading member of the liberal House Democratic Study Group.[8] Thompson, citing the "impartial" *Congressional Quarterly* and its studies of Conservative Coalition voting in Congress, argued that the Coalition did indeed exist. "The operation of the coalition is a matter of record," Thompson said, "and has been most successful on legislation such as education, social welfare, public housing, immigration, taxes, labor antitrust, civil rights, public works, and resource development." He thereupon inserted in the *Congressional Record* a brief history of the Coalition from 1937 to 1959 which outlined the ups and downs—mostly ups—of the Coalition.

The basic reason behind the conflicting opinions on the Coalition is that the Coalition is an informal organization which, given its existence in the no man's land between the two major political parties, operates in subtle, hard-to-observe ways. In denying the existence of the Coalition, Dirksen rested his case on the argument that "I have yet to see the time when there has been formalized, on the floor or off the floor, a meeting of Senators on this side of the aisle and a meeting of Senators on that side of the aisle." [9]

At the same time that he made this argument, however, Dirksen also acknowledged that something—agreement on policy—does unite conservatives in Congress:

> The term "alliance" is now used instead of the old, hackneyed phrase "coalition." But whether either one is used, it presupposes some concerted action, and that is derived from the fact that either we see eye to eye with some of our distinguished colleagues on the other side of the aisle, or they see eye to eye with us. However, we can only draw the inference that there is an unholy alliance or that there is a coalition. I have said before, and I shall repeat it, that I reject that kind of inference on every possible kind of occasion.

"Two souls with but a single thought," replied Douglas.

Simple policy agreement may be the single most important element holding the Conservative Coalition together, but the claim that the Coalition is no more than an accidental meeting of minds is excessive. There is substantial evidence of joint planning on the part of Coalition leaders, and Coalition observers have detected a number of cases of overt bipartisan cooperation among conservatives. In the face of this evidence, the fact that no regular formal caucuses of conservatives are held, and the fact that Republicans sometimes vote with northern Democrats against the southern Democrats, are insufficient to support the claim that the Coalition is purely accidental. The Coalition is, in fact, many times a consciously designed force in the legislative process, and this is true for both the committee stage and the floor stage of that process.

Important testimony on the existence and nature of the Conservative Coalition was gathered in an interview (August 19, 1970) with Howard W. ("Judge") Smith, who, until his 1966 primary defeat, was the leading spokesman and strategist for southern Democrats in the House. Judge Smith was first elected to the House in 1931 and, together with Eugene Cox of Georgia, became a leading foe on the House Rules Committee of liberal legislation. When Cox died in 1952, Smith took over as the informal head of the southern Democrats. In the 1950s and 1960s Smith and the Republican leaders Joseph W. Martin and Charles A. Halleck headed the Conservative Coalition in the House. Recalling the early years of the Coalition, Smith observed:

> Joe Martin was a very powerful, very partisan leader. He and Eugene Cox worked together on many issues. Our group—we called it our "group" for want of a better term—was fighting appropriations. We did not meet publicly. The meetings were not formal. Our group met in one

building and the conservative Republicans in another, on different issues. *Then Eugene Cox, Bill Colmer, or I would go over to speak with the Republicans, or the Republican leaders might come to see us. It was very informal.* Conservative southerners and Republicans from the northern and western states. A coalition did exist in legislation. But we met in small groups. There were no joint meetings of conservative Republicans and southern Democrats.

When asked if it is fair to say that a Conservative Coalition existed in the House in the sense that on some issues there was explicit cooperation between southern Democrats and Republicans, Smith replied: "It's fair, sure, but never in a formal way." No formal meetings were necessary because, as Smith said of Halleck's predecessor as minority leader, Joseph W. Martin, "I'd see Joe Martin every half hour on the floor." On one occasion, so close did House conservatives work together, that John Taber (R-N.Y.), a leading conservative on the Appropriations Committee, lent Smith one of his staff men to assist the Judge in finding ways of reducing federal expenditures.

Judge Smith's testimony on the workings of the Coalition is complemented by that of his late partner in Coalition politics, Joe Martin. Martin, who became House Republican leader in 1939 and held that post until defeated by Halleck in 1959, recalls how the Coalition operated:

> In any case when an issue of spending or of new powers for the President came along, I would go to Representative Howard W. Smith of Virginia, for example, and say, "Howard, see if you can't get me a few Democratic votes here." Or I would seek out Representative Eugene Cox of Georgia, and ask, "Gene, why don't you and John Rankin and some of your men get me some votes on this?"
>
> Cox was the real leader of the southerners in the House. He was a good speaker and wielded considerable influence. He and I came to Congress the same year, and we became friends while serving together on the Rules Committee. After I was chosen leader he and I were the principal points of contact between the northern Republicans and the southern Democratic conservatives. A bushy-haired Georgia lawyer, Cox was a typical old-fashioned southern leader, who fought tirelessly for states' rights. His opposition to the New Deal was much more ingrown than mine, and he was ready to fight to any lengths to keep further power out of the hands of Franklin Roosevelt. In these circumstances, therefore, it was unnecessary for me to offer any quid pro quo for conservative southern support. It was simply a matter of finding issues on which we saw alike.[10]

Halleck's turn to be deposed as minority leader came in 1965 when Gerald R. Ford replaced him. Among the reasons for Ford's victory was a widespread feeling among Republicans that they should more actively seek alternatives to Democratic policy proposals, and not simply rest content voting "no." The Halleck-Ford contest was less a contest between ideological opposites than a battle between policy activists and negativists; the former, grouped around Ford, were defined by a diffuse sense that something was wrong with their party rather than by a clear-cut platform for the future. Two years after his ascendancy Ford declared the Republican party's independence from conservative Democrats and announced a new "Southern strategy," as he called it, for House Republicans. As Ford defined it:

> The strategy is to drive Southern Democrats in the House into the arms of the Administration—where they belong—on votes that will hurt them in their home congressional districts.
> *This strategy runs exactly counter to the old pattern of a Southern Democrat-Republican coalition that often prevailed over Administration forces in the House in years past.*
> But I think it is far better to lose a few legislative battles and win the next election. Besides, in following my Southern Strategy we Republicans in the House are staking out positions in which we believe—responsible, constructive positions.
> There will be times when Republicans will win in the 90th Congress. We won't win as many legislative fights as we could if we resorted to the *old coalition tactics* but it's the Big Prize that counts, and that's what we're after.
> The Big Prize is control of at least one House of Congress and control of the White House. We want that prize not because we relish power for the sake of power but because we sincerely believe that our course, our program, is a better way than LBJ's.[11]

Ford's apparent break with conservative Democrats no doubt upset many members of his own party; but the other half of the Coalition was even more disturbed. Omar Burleson (D-Texas), the chairman of the southern Democratic caucus in the House (dubbed "Boll Weevils" by the press), responded to Ford's threat by pointing out that far from driving the southern Democrats anywhere, Ford was likely to have his hands full taking care of the twenty or so Republican liberals and those Republican conservatives who "put the good of this country ahead of party."

The Ford-Burleson exchange exposes the complex relationships among blocs in the House. Burleson, who denied that any surreptitious coalition of conservatives exists in the House, but admitted that conservative Democrats frequently meet to "determine tactics for offering certain amendments," pleaded for the maintenance of what he called "rapport" between his group and the Republicans. By and large Ford stuck to his independent course; but he let the southerners know that although the Republican party would chart its own course on policy, it welcomed whatever Democratic support it could get. Seeing an opportunity to foment dissension within the Conservative Coalition, the House Democratic whip, Hale Boggs, joined the debate by pointing out that, as he learned early in his House career, Republicans are untrustworthy allies who seek to defeat Democrats, not work with them. Two days after the debate a majority of southern Democrats and Republicans banded together against the majority of northern Democrats to defeat rent supplements, a major plank in Lyndon Johnson's Great Society program.

Conservatives in the House and Senate are bonded together primarily by agreement on policy. Sharing a common outlook on policy, they do not need an elaborate organization to hold them together; as Joe Martin said, the major task is finding issues on which they agree and, once this is accomplished, coalescence is to some extent automatic. Under these conditions the task of conservative leaders is twofold: first, shaping issues on which conservatives can act together; second, applying whatever prods are necessary to a united joint effort. For this task an informal organization with some internal lines of communication and with some central direction by recognized leaders is all that is required. And this is precisely what the Conservative Coalition is: an informal, bipartisan bloc of conservatives with leaders who jointly discuss strategy and line up votes.

Coalition Voting in Congress

Congressional conservatives have exerted great influence on public policy through their control of some of the most important committees in Congress. At various times since the New Deal, a bipartisan group of conservatives has largely controlled the decisions of such Senate committees as Armed Services, Finance, Appropriations, and Judiciary. Similarly, conservatives have dominated strategic House committees for long periods of time, including Rules, Ways and Means, Appropriations, Armed Services, Education and Labor, Un-American Activities, and the District of Columbia Committee. In short, powerful committees in both chambers have often been dominated by conservatives, whereas other branches of the government, most notably the presidency, have been in liberal hands.

Conservative strength in committee is matched by conservative strength on the floor, and it is the floor stage of the legislative process that provides the best overview of conservative power. Two questions about Coalition voting will be answered here: (1) how often does the Coalition appear in Congress on roll call votes, and (2) when the Coalition appears, how does it do? [12]

One of the first political scientists to be concerned with Coalition voting was V. O. Key. Key devoted two chapters of his classic *Southern Politics* to southern Democratic strength and voting in Congress. He found that on 275 contested House roll call votes during the years 1933, 1937, 1941, and 1945, a majority of southern Democrats joined a majority of Republicans in opposition to the northern Democrats only 28 times (10.2 percent).[13] In the Senate, Key studied 598 contested votes in the seven odd-numbered years between 1933 and 1945. The Conservative Coalition appeared on only 54 of these votes (9 percent).[14] In addition, rarely did 70 percent or more of the southern Democrats defect to the Republican party. Key reached the conclusion that the "report of the Southern Democratic-Republican congressional coalition has been not a little exaggerated." [15]

A more complete picture of Coalition voting in the House and Senate since 1933 is provided in Figures 1 and 2. In addition, the figures show the won/lost record of the Coalition during these years, a question Key did not go into.[16]

As can be seen from Figure 1, the Coalition in the House did appear on a rather small percentage of contested votes during the years Key studied. Less than 10 percent of the roll calls were Coalition votes during Roosevelt's first three congresses (1933–39), and Coalition voting did not exceed 20 percent until the 78th Congress (1943–44). Since 1943, however, the Coalition has almost always exceeded the 20 percent mark, and in the late 1960s over 30 percent of the votes were Coalition roll calls. From 1946 to 1969 the Conservative Coalition appeared on 544 House roll calls, or about 26 percent of the 2,053 votes. Clearly, the House Coalition has been more salient in the postwar years than it was during the period studied by Key.

Figure 2 shows that, like the House, the Coalition did not appear on more than 20 percent of the contested votes in the Senate until the 1943–44 Congress but that since that time 20 to 30 percent of the roll calls have been Coalition votes.[17] From the Truman years to Nixon, the Coalition appeared on 900, or 23 percent, of the 3,894 contested roll calls in the Senate. Again, the Senate Coalition emerges as a more common voting pattern after World War II than at the time Key examined it.

Figures 1 and 2 also show the ups and downs of the Coalition's success since 1933. Three distinct periods stand out. In both the House and Senate, the 1930s are marked by the relative infrequency of Coalition voting and by its comparatively low batting average when it does appear. Beginning in 1939 in the House, however, and in 1941 in the

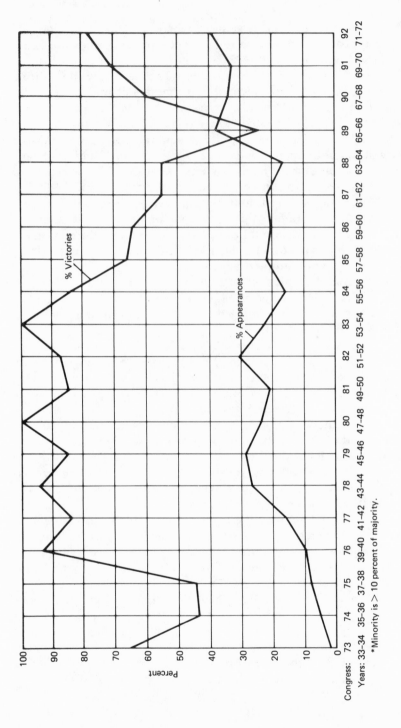

Figure 1. Percentage of All Contested * House Roll Calls on Which the Conservative Coalition Appeared and Won, 73rd–92nd Congress (1933–72)

*Minority is > 10 percent of majority.

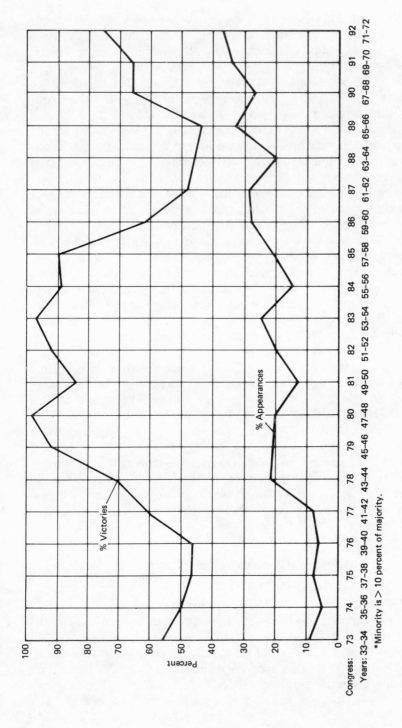

Figure 2. Percentage of All Contested * Senate Roll Calls on Which the Conservative Coalition Appeared and Won, 73rd–92nd Congress (1933–72)

*Minority is > 10 percent of majority.

87

Senate, the Coalition wins a large majority of the votes on which it appears. Throughout the 1940s and well into the 1950s, the Coalition wins 70 percent or more of the votes in both chambers. In the Senate, the Coalition's batting average drops significantly beginning with 1959 (the 1958 Senate elections resulted in a 17-seat Democratic gain), and it never climbs back to its earlier levels. In the House, the Coalition's batting average drops below 70 percent starting in 1957 and stays in the 50 to 60 percent range throughout the 1960s (save for the 89th Congress when it hit an all-time low of 24 percent). The Coalition's win rate in the House for 1957–68 was 55 percent, compared with the 1939–56 average of 91 percent.

Figures 1 and 2 are based on roll call votes and therefore provide only a rough guide to the power of conservatives in the House and Senate. For example, although the Coalition pattern appears on a minority of all contested votes, it regularly includes many of the most consequential issues decided by Congress. These figures do not show how much legislation was watered down or compromised to keep the northern and southern wings of the Democratic party together. These data take into account neither those issues, such as medical care for the aged, that were bottled up for years in committee, nor those issues, such as national health insurance for all Americans, that have yet to see the light of day.

Still, it is significant that the Conservative Coalition, born in the 1930s, has persisted as a relatively common and potent voting alliance for forty years. In both chambers the Coalition was less successful in the late 1950s and in the 1960s than it was earlier, but as the record of the 90th Congress (1967–68) shows, the Coalition was anything but a paper tiger as the 1970s dawned. In that Congress, just prior to Richard Nixon's presidency, the Coalition won 65 percent of Coalition votes in the Senate and 59 percent in the House. With a Republican in the White House, liberals in Congress feared the worst. And, with exceptions, they got it.

The Conservative Coalition and the Nixon Presidency

In 1968 and 1972 Richard Nixon proved that he was a far more acceptable presidential candidate to the South than the nominee of the Democratic party.[18] The so-called "solid South" had been shaking for many years before Nixon's election, but his strength in this traditionally Democratic area far surpassed that of his mentor, Dwight D. Eisenhower. Hubert Humphrey carried only Texas in 1968. Nixon carried five southern states over both Humphrey and George Wallace:

Florida, North Carolina, South Carolina, Tennessee, and Virginia. Wallace won the remaining five states: Alabama, Arkansas, Georgia, Louisiana, and Mississippi. Moreover, in the five states that voted for Wallace, two (Arkansas and Georgia) preferred Nixon to Humphrey. In 1972, with Wallace out of the race and George McGovern as the Democratic candidate, all eleven southern states followed the national trend for Nixon.

Given Nixon's appeal in the South, a resurgence of Conservative Coalition voting in Congress was to be expected, and the Coalition members did not disappoint. Figures 1 and 2 show that during Nixon's first term, in both the House and Senate, the Coalition's appearance reached all-time highs, and Coalition victories approached the high levels of the 1940s and 1950s.[19] In the House in the 92nd Congress (1971–72), the Coalition appeared on 40 percent of the contested votes and won almost eight out of ten. Thirty-seven percent of the contested votes in the Senate during 1971–72 were Coalition roll calls, and 75 percent of them were won by the Coalition. Thus, a fourth period emerges from Figures 1 and 2: Nixon's first term in which the Coalition was a dominant force in both chambers, more dominant than it had been for several years.

On the plus side for the Senate Coalition during Nixon's first term were votes on the Safeguard ABM, closing Job Corps centers, granting governors veto power over legal services programs, military aid to Greece, cutting $292.1 million from OEO, the defeat of the Hatfield-McGovern amendment limiting U.S. troops in Vietnam, modification of the filibuster rule, the Lockheed loan, confirmation of William Rehnquist to the Supreme Court, uniform school desegregation standards for the entire nation, defeat of efforts to strengthen the enforcement powers of the Equal Employment Opportunity Commission, killing the Family Assistance Plan, confirmation of Richard Kleindienst as attorney general, and twenty of twenty-seven amendments dealing with tax reform. In the House, the Coalition won votes on the Safeguard ABM, limiting federal authority in the area of school desegregation, the Cooper-Church amendment barring U.S. troops in Cambodia, authorization of the supersonic transport (SST), strong antibusing legislation, the Lockheed loan, several amendments to end the Vietnam war, diluting a minimum wage bill, and establishing a $250 billion ceiling on federal spending complete with item veto power for the president.

The list of Coalition victories is impressive, but the Coalition does not win all the time. The Coalition lost votes in the Senate on the nomination of Clement Haynsworth and Harrold Carswell to the Supreme Court, the Cooper-Church amendment limiting the use of troops in Cambodia, the SST, expansion of the food stamp program, providing twenty-six additional weeks of unemployment compensation payments to unemployed workers, various amendments to set a timetable for withdrawal of U.S. troops from Vietnam, and a liberal filibuster against strong antibusing legislation passed by the House. In the House the Coalition lost votes dealing with Adam Clayton Powell, voting rights, continuation of the SST, a plan for a comprehensive child development program, prohibition of food stamps to families of striking workers, and a proposal allowing the president to restrict the travel of U.S. citizens to countries with which the United States is in armed conflict. Coalition successes overshadow defeats, but it should be noted that conservative defections and high cohesion among liberals can, and sometimes do, determine the outcome on major issues, even with a Republican in the White House.[20]

Speculations

Enough variations exist in congressional Coalition politics to warn against speculating about future developments, but some factors that may shape the future are fairly clear and deserve special mention. First, the power of the southern Democrats in the House and Senate Democratic caucuses has been declining steadily for several years. Second, House Speaker Carl Albert has increasingly sided with liberals against the conservative Democrats. Third, there is renewed talk, particularly in the House, of a southern Democratic bolt to the Republican party—a realignment of the parties from the top. Should these forces continue in their current direction, radical changes will follow in Congress. An incautious observer might say that we are currently living through a crucial transitional period in American politics, and such a prediction may well prove accurate.

In 1960 seven Republicans were elected to the House of Representatives from the South. Twelve years later there were 34, and the total number of southern Democrats had dropped from 99 to 74. As they decline in numbers, the conservative southern Democrats decline in influence vis-à-vis the northern wing of the party. In addition, the southerners have been losing key leaders and leadership positions (Judge Smith, William Colmer, Carl Vinson, and others are gone from the House). Northern liberals gained ascendancy in the Senate following the 1958 and subsequent elections, and such long-time Senate leaders as Richard Russell no longer skillfully direct the southern cause. As the Republican party gained seats in the South, the ties binding the northern and southern wings of the Democratic party together have been placed under enormous stress. And, further aggravating the southern Democratic decline, House liberals have become increasingly well organized (though still imperfectly organized) through the Democratic Study Group (DSG). There are still enough inconsistencies among northern Democrats, and enough conservative southern Democrats, to prevent absolute liberal control of the Democratic caucus, but the trend is in this direction.

A related development in the House is an important change in the role of the Democratic leadership. In the old days under Sam Rayburn, the leadership served effectively as the balance wheel of the Democratic party. Rayburn, with the support of southern and northern Democrats, played a delicate balancing role in the House. When the DSG was launched in the late 1950s, Rayburn's tacit blessing was essential to the liberals; he held the pivotal position in the House. John McCormack tried to follow the Rayburn script in the 1960s, but strong liberal pressures made his Speakership increasingly difficult. Carl Albert, caught in the same dilemma that faced McCormack, has with increasing frequency responded positively to the demands of the liberal wing of the party. Democratic liberals have not yet toppled senior conservative leaders, but they have forced votes to decide committee chairmanships, they helped pave the way for numerous important reforms in the House, and they have used the caucus for such unusual actions as directing the Democratic members of the Foreign Affairs Committee to report antiwar legislation.

The House Democratic party is not what it used to be; neither is the party leadership. Richard Bolling made headlines in 1967 when he called for McCormack's removal as Speaker. Today Bolling, who lost a 1962 bid for the majority leadership to Albert, is one of the Speaker's closest advisers. Changes such as these are reflective of the basic undercurrents changing, and challenging, the House Democratic party.

If conservative southern Democrats can no longer function effectively within the party, and if they see the party leaders as captives of the DSG, they may seriously consider a formal alliance with the Republicans that would allow the Coalition to organize the House. Under Rayburn, such an idea would have appeared far-fetched; today, the informal leader of the southern Democrats, Representative Joe Waggonner of Louisiana, talks openly about doing it.

Some southern Democrats, like John Connally, have switched parties, but Waggonner has suggested another course: "Don't be too surprised if eventually some efforts are made to take control of the majority in the House through a coalition that wouldn't require change in party registration." [21] Southern conservatives, in other words, could continue to run as Democrats but vote with the Republicans to elect a Republican Speaker and, presumably, organize the committees with Republican majorities. "You wouldn't have left your old Democratic friends back home," Waggonner points out, "you'd have brought them some more influence, instead."

Waggonner's talk may be nothing more than a ploy to scare his liberal colleagues into treating the conservatives with a bit more respect, but if it is more than this it could lead to changes in the House rivaling those of 1910–11, when Joe Cannon lost much of his power. What is interesting about Waggonner's threat is how plausible it seems in the context of growing party competition in the South.

At the moment, Waggonner and other conservative House Democrats are attempting to improve their position in the Democratic caucus. Previous threats to the Democratic party from disaffected elements have not amounted to much. But as the data show, since 1965 southern Democrats and Republicans have been voting together with greater regularity than ever before. When House Republican leaders need votes, they contact Waggonner, and vice versa. Are the internal and external pressures toward party realignment within the House rising? If so, will they lead to a formal cross-party alliance that will allow the Republican party to gain what it has failed to gain electorally, control of the House?

No one, of course, can tell. But the factors pointing in this direction are clear, and may be irreversible. It is not only possible for southern Democrats to become Republicans, many have done it and more will in the future. When William Colmer of Mississippi, chairman of the Rules Committee, retired in 1972, his administrative assistant, Trent Lott, ran for the seat and won it—as a Republican. Realignments of this sort will no doubt continue in the South, and they bode ill for the traditional coalition that is the Democratic party.

Inside the House, the southern Democratic response to their declining influence will be partially decided by the response of the Republican party. When Gerald Ford made his 1967 speech declaring independence from the southern Democrats, he did so for electoral reasons: he wanted Republican control of the House and he felt that the party could no longer afford to write off the South.[22] Ford, like his predecessor, Charles Halleck, has not been choosy about where he searches for votes among the Democrats, and his 1967 speech did not lead to any major changes in the relationship between Republicans and southern Democrats. Given the difficulty of defeating entrenched southern Democrats, Ford decided to work with them on a daily basis and await the openings southern retirements and deaths would bring. In other words, the working relationships between Ford and the southern Democrats have been good enough so that Waggonner's threat might work. What effects the Watergate scandal may have on these questions remains to be seen, but the situation in the House and in the South makes the possibility of a realignment a real one.[23]

The current situation in the House is a paradox, and how this paradox is resolved will profoundly affect future House—and American—politics. As congressional liberals gain power in the Democratic caucus, they run the risk of losing Democratic control of the House. As the southern Democrats have lost power in the Democratic caucus, they have also voted more and more with the Republicans and won more and more of the votes. As a final rebuke to the party that once dominated their region, and that they themselves once dominated, the conservative southern Democrats could in a tight situation tip the balance of power to the Republicans and thereby help bring to fruition some of the hopes of those who desire party realignment in the United States. Liberals inside and outside Congress might be less than happy with the consequences of this action, but at least the parties would be a little less confounding. As for the liberals, they might look back on the old days with a certain degree of nostalgia, unless, of course, the American people take a large unexpected turn to the left. At this writing, a realignment and consolidation of conservative power, though a risky prediction, seems more likely than a massive liberal revival.

NOTES

1. Richard Harris, "If You Love Your Guns," *New Yorker*, April 20, 1968, p. 56.
2. Nelson W. Polsby, *Congress and the Presidency* (Englewood Cliffs, N.J.: Prentice-Hall, 1971), p. 13.
3. *Congressional Record*, August 5, 1939.
4. J. T. Patterson, *Congressional Conservatism and the New Deal* (Lexington, Ky.: University of Kentucky Press, 1967), chap. 9.
5. *Congressional Record*, December 7, 1943.
6. *Congressional Record*, March 14, 1961, pp. 38, 80–86.
7. *Congressional Record*, January 18, 1960, pp. 700–704.
8. *Congressional Record*, January 27, 1960, pp. 1440–44.
9. *Congressional Record*, March 14, 1961, p. 3883.
10. Joseph W. Martin, *My First Fifty Years in Politics* (New York: McGraw-Hill, 1960), pp. 84–85.
11. *Congressional Record*, May 15, 1967, 45408–409; emphasis added.
12. The "Conservative Coalition" appears when a majority of voting southern Democrats and a majority of voting Republicans oppose a majority of voting northern Democrats. "The South" is defined as the eleven former Confederate states.
13. V. O. Key, *Southern Politics* (New York: Random House, Vintage, 1949), p. 374.

14. Ibid., p. 355.
15. Ibid.
16. Following Key, these figures exclude "hurrah" votes on which the minority is less than 10 percent. This has the effect of showing a greater percentage of Coalition roll calls than reported by *Congressional Quarterly* in its yearly studies. *CQ* also includes Kentucky and Oklahoma in its definition of the South. Eliminating nearly unanimous votes gives a more accurate picture of the incidence of Coalition voting than that presented by *CQ*. In 1972, for example, *CQ* shows the Coalition appearing on 25 percent of the roll calls in the House and 28 percent of the Senate votes. My figures show 37 percent of the contested roll calls in the House as Coalition votes and 38 percent for the Senate.
17. Figure 2 is drawn largely from J. Margolis, "The Conservative Coalition in the U.S. Senate," Ph.D. diss., University of Wisconsin, 1973. I am grateful to Professor Margolis for his excellent description of coalition voting in the Senate.
18. In 1960 John Kennedy outpolled Nixon in eight of the eleven southern states—all save Florida, Tennessee, and Virginia.
19. For 1969–72, I have relied on *CQ*'s data for the successes and losses of the Coalition. I removed "hurrah" roll calls from *CQ*'s base to get comparable figures on Coalition appearances. Since *CQ* includes Kentucky and Oklahoma as southern states, these data are not exactly the same as one gets for the 1933–68 part of the graphs, but it is felt that whatever differences there are are of minor significance to the interpretation that follows. For *CQ*'s studies, see *Congressional Quarterly Weekly Report*, January 16, 1970; January 15, 1972; November 18, 1972.
20. Of course, President Nixon's position was not always the same as the Conservative Coalition's. In the 92nd Congress (1971–72), the president stated a position on 46 House Coalition roll calls, agreeing with the Coalition on 40 of them. He agreed with the Senate Coalition 40 out of 43 times that he took a position. See *Congressional Quarterly Weekly Report*, January 15, 1972; November 18, 1972.
21. Quoted in N. C. Miller, "Rep. Joe Waggonner Is a Democrat, but Nixon Finds Him a Loyal Ally," *Wall Street Journal*, April 13, 1973.
22. Personal interview, September 8, 1972.
23. Such a move would no doubt hasten shifts in the opposite direction, such as those of Donald Riegle and Ogden Reid from the Republican party to the Democratic. If all or nearly all of the conservative southern Democrats bolted the party, however, it is doubtful that liberal Republican shifts could fully compensate for

the loss to the Democratic party. At present there are simply not enough Riegles and Reids to make up the difference. Similar forces are at work in the Senate, though less clearly. When, in 1972, it appeared that the Republicans might come close to a Senate majority, there was talk of some conservative Democratic senators (e.g., James Eastland) switching parties, but nothing came of it.

5. The Rules Committee: New Arm of Leadership in a Decentralized House

Bruce I. Oppenheimer

As a political institution goes through a period of change, the functioning of its subunits may also be altered. Some of the institutional changes or reforms may be aimed directly at particular subunits. However, a subunit may change because developments in the larger institution or other subunits cause or offer it new roles to perform in the overall operation of the institution. The purpose of this essay is to explore the changes that have occurred in a particularly important subunit in the House of Representatives, the Rules Committee, resulting both from reforms directed specifically at the committee and from its own need to respond to changes that affected other committees and the House in general. As a result of these changes, the Rules Committee performs different, though no less important, roles in the congressional process today than in years past.

We will look at three major aspects of these altered roles. First, we will see how the committee changed from being a thorn in the side of Democratic House leadership in 1960 to being one of the leadership's strongest allies in the mid 1970s. Second, we will briefly examine how the changes in the committee have resulted in its serving the party

AUTHOR'S NOTE: In addition to those mentioned in the preface of this book, I would like to thank Don Wolfensberger for his extensive comments on an earlier version of this essay.

leadership in two related roles: as new "traffic cop" and as "field commander." And, most important, we will pay detailed attention to the committee's adoption of a new role as "dress rehearsal" for the House in response to needs that have developed from changes in the larger institution.

Reforming the Rules Committee

Less than fifteen years ago the House Committee on Rules was described as a legislative cemetery. The committee and its staunchly conservative chairman, Judge Howard Smith of Virginia, were regularly berated for failing to grant rules to major pieces of liberal legislation. The committee's unique position in the congressional process then and now is one in which nearly every piece of authorizing legislation must receive a rule from the committee before being brought to the House floor for debate. A rule in its simplest form is a resolution that specifies the conditions under which the House may take up a piece of legislation. It will normally include the time available for general debate, how the time will be divided, who will control the time for opposing sides, provisions under which amendments to the legislation may or may not be offered, and a provision allowing for a motion to recommit the legislation to committee to be offered. Although a rule can be much more complex, the important fact is that in failing to hear a request for a rule brought on a piece of legislation by the House committee reporting the legislation or by hearing the request but then denying the rule, the Rules Committee could and still can delay or defeat the legislation.

The Rules Committee under Judge Smith, sometimes through action and other times through inaction, sidetracked federal aid to education, civil rights bills, and other pieces of social welfare legislation. At times, since the committee had no written rules covering its own procedures, Smith would simply refuse to call a meeting or schedule legislation that might receive a favorable vote of the committee despite his own objections. On other occasions the Judge and his southern Democratic colleague on the committee, William Colmer of Mississippi, would join with the four committee Republicans against their six Democratic colleagues to produce a tie vote and thus prevent a rule from being granted.[1] Although there were ways to avoid the Rules Committee or to discharge legislation under its control, such as Calendar Wednesday, discharge petitions, and suspension of the rules, these methods were rarely applied and, when applied, rarely proved successful.

The problems with the Rules Committee reached a head in 1961. With President Kennedy's programs being readied, liberals did not want the Rules Committee to remain an obstacle to their legislation. To make the committee more supportive of liberal programs and responsive to the Democratic House leadership, Speaker Rayburn led a fight to increase the size of the Rules Committee from 12 to 15 members.[2] By a vote of 217 to 212 the House passed the resolution favoring the increase, and two leadership Democrats and one Republican were added to the committee. The change seemingly broke the 6–6 deadlock and provided Rayburn and the Kennedy program with an 8–7 majority.

The enlarged Rules Committee, however, continued to present problems. Although Robert Peabody's study of the committee following the enlargement shows that a majority of its membership perceived the committee as one that should serve the party leadership in its substantive control of legislation, the committee continued to be a legislative stumbling block. As a senior committee member recalls:

> There was never any time when we had the eight that I didn't have a nervous stomach. There was always the opportunity for a pickoff and make an 8–7 win an 8–7 loss. Smith and Colmer together or separately were capable of figuring out who to approach and how, be it in terms of district or personal preference or a trade-off or whatever. They had eight targets sitting there. If they get one, it turns from a majority to a minority.

On given issues, one of the eight might be moved by constituent or independent interests that outweighed the member's desire to serve the party leadership. The most famous case involved the continued fight over federal aid to education.[3] Twice in 1961, following expansion, the committee defeated rule requests on education aid legislation. Moreover, as Table 1 indicates, the trend to deny rules or fail to hear requests continued at substantially the same rate for a number of Congresses following expansion. In the 89th Congress (1965–66), with 295 Democrats in the House, the majority leadership was able to pass the 21-day rule. This provision, similar to one used in the 81st Congress, gave the leadership the ability to bring to the floor bills that were reported to the Rules Committee and after a period of 21 days had not received a rule. During the 89th Congress eight pieces of legislation were discharged from the Rules Committee through use of the 21-day rule. In addition, the threat of the 21-day rule was often enough to cause the Rules Committee to report legislation. Following a loss of 47 Democratic House seats in the 1966 election, the 21-day rule was repealed.

Table 1. Record on Rule Requests, 87th Congress through 94th Congress, 1st Session [4]

	87th	88th	89th	90th	91st	92nd	93rd	94th
Rules granted	*	*	*	*	218	204	255	157
No hearing held †	22	19	26	19	8	12	8	1
Requests denied or deferred	9	7	6	6	5	3	5	2
Total requests not heard, denied, or deferred	31	26	32 ‡	25	13	15	13	3

* Not available.
† Excludes requests withdrawn, use of consent calendar, 21-day rule, suspension, and legislation superseded.
‡ In addition, eight proposals reached the floor through use of the 21-day rule.

Despite this setback, the 1966 election gave the Democratic leadership a major opportunity to improve its control over the committee. Judge Smith at age eighty-three was defeated in a primary contest. This opened up the first opportunity for the leadership to replace one of the committee's conservative Democrats since 1949.[5] William Anderson, a moderate from Tennessee, was selected formally by the Democratic Committee on Committees and informally by the House Democratic leadership to fill the southern vacancy. In addition, the new chairman, William Colmer, was generally viewed as far less politically skilled than his colleague, Judge Smith. Moreover, Speaker John McCormack had a good personal relationship with Colmer. (As majority leader in 1946, McCormack had assured Colmer, who was to be bumped from the Rules Committee when the Republicans took control of the House at the start of the 80th Congress, of reassignment to Rules as soon as a vacancy occurred.) This good relationship is attested to by Rules Committee Democrats, who served during Colmer's chairmanship. They describe Colmer as being far more cooperative with the leadership than Judge Smith had been. One member spoke of Colmer in a particularly sympathetic vein:

> He had set for years and years and years in the shadow of Judge Smith . . . in general philosophical agreement like two peas in a pod. Most people thought he would be an ineffective chairman, that he was basically a lightweight. But he did a good job.
> I know that McCormack tells the story that he didn't ask one thing of Colmer that he didn't get. . . . Colmer felt strongly on the issues. He'd use methods to try and carry his point. . . . I know Carl [Albert] says practically the same thing as McCormack.

Finally, Smith's departure provided an opportunity to weaken the control the chairman had over the Rules Committee. Following Smith's primary defeat, some Democratic House members organized an effort to deprive Colmer of the chairmanship. However, McCormack would not cooperate with the effort. As one member of the Colmer opposition describes it, "McCormack had a vested interest in Colmer. For some reason he wanted to protect him, as well as the concept of seniority, which he believed in." The Colmer opponents were able to extract an agreement that for the first time required the committee to adopt written rules of operation. Among the provisions in the written rules were ones requiring regularly scheduled weekly meetings of the committee and allowing the ranking majority member on the committee to call and preside at meetings in the absence of the chairman. This was a major step in placing control of the Rules Committee in the hands of its Democratic members, who on most occasions would be responsive to the desires of the House Democratic leadership.

Although the impact of this change was small in terms of a decrease from 32 to 25 rule requests not heard, denied, or deferred between the 89th and 90th Congresses (of course, the impact appears larger if one adds in the eight pieces of legislation discharged in the 89th Congress through use of the 21-day rule), it established a trend. In the 91st Congress only 13 rule requests met a similar fate.

Two additional changes in the Rules Committee have cemented the control that majority party leadership has on the Rules Committee. The first took place in 1973 at the start of the 93rd Congress. With the retirement of Colmer, the defeat of William Anderson, and the election of Tip O'Neill as majority leader, three Democratic vacancies opened on the Rules Committee. Speaker Albert formally became a member of the Democratic Committee on Committees for the first time (a reform added the Speaker, majority leader, and Democratic caucus chairman to the Committee on Committees) and had his personal choices selected to fill the Rules vacancies.

Morgan Murphy of Illinois replaced Tip O'Neill, who had become majority leader; Clem McSpadden, a freshman from Speaker Albert's home state of Oklahoma, replaced William Anderson of Tennessee; and Gillis Long of Louisiana replaced the retiring chairman, William Colmer of Mississippi. These three appointments were widely interpreted as showing the new control that Speaker Albert was going to have over the Rules Committee. Although there was little resistance to the Murphy and McSpadden appointments, Albert was under pressure to name Sonny Montgomery of Mississippi to fill the Colmer vacancy. Montgomery, who is similar in ideological temperament to Colmer, was the candidate selected by a caucus of southern conservatives to fill the vacancy. Long, by comparison, is a moderate-liberal and had just returned to Congress following an eight-year absence. (Interestingly, when Long was defeated in his bid for reelection to the House in 1964, a major issue in the campaign was Long's vote in favor of the permanent enlargement of the Rules Committee.) Albert's decision to appoint Long to the vacancy removed the last major foothold of such conservative Democrats from the committee. Although some fairly conservative Democrats remain on Rules, they are individuals who will vote with the leadership when they are needed.

The second change occurred when the 94th Congress organized. The House Democratic caucus, which had already moved the Committee on Committees' responsibilities away from Ways and Means Democrats and to the Steering and Policy Committee, voted to give the Speaker the power to name all Democratic members of the Rules Committee, subject to ratification by the caucus. The resolution, which was introduced by Richard Bolling (D-Mo.), a senior member of the Rules Committee, passed by a vote of 106 to 65. This change formalized a power in the hands of the Speaker that had previously been informal and had been shared by the Speaker and majority leader (as in McCormack's guarantee to Colmer). Moreover, it extended that power so that each incumbent Democratic member of the committee would be formally reappointed at the start of each Congress and would therefore be potentially subject to removal by the Speaker.

Because of the nature of the Democratic Rules members, the Speaker does not have to exercise his leverage. For the most part they have been selected because they are supportive of the leadership in the first place. During the first session of the 94th Congress, Rules Committee Democrats had an average party unity score of 77, or 8 points higher than the average for all House Democrats.[6] Most important, the Speaker no longer has to work with a Rules Committee that has a tenuous 8–7 majority. Only James Delaney (D-N.Y.) and John Young (D-Tex.) vote with a majority of the committee's Republicans with substantial frequency, and both of them are still more likely to vote with their Democratic colleagues. With the committee having 11 Democrats and 5 Republicans (it was expanded to 16 members at the start of the 94th Congress), the Democrats can easily afford the sporadic defection of Delaney and Young. Moreover, the remaining Democrats on this small committee find the vote calculating easy and will rarely vote against the leadership unless an issue affects their constituency deeply—and then only if the final outcome is not affected.

Again, the figures in Table 1 attest to the changes. On only three bills for which rules were requested during the first session of the 94th Congress did the Rules Committee deny, defer, or fail to hear the request. Moreover, most of the bills not granted rules in the 93rd and

94th Congresses have been ones that the Democratic leadership opposed, that involved jurisdictional disputes between committees, or that were sufficiently controversial so that the leadership chose not to bring them to the floor late in the session, thus delaying consideration of other matters.

Many of the changes that Robert Peabody described in 1963 as giving "tenuous control by eight pro-administration" members of the Rules Committee have been extended and solidified. Richard Bolling, the leader of the Speaker's minority on the committee from the late 1950s through 1961 and leader of the "tenuous majority" from 1961 to the early 1970s, leads a comfortable majority in the 94th Congress.[7] He moves the vast majority of controversial rules that are requested; he handles complex parliamentary and political situations that the committee faces; and he speaks for the Democratic leadership. As one Rules Committee staff member put it, "Bolling making a motion tells the leadership position." The difference now is that Bolling and the House Democratic leadership rarely lose in the Rules Committee.

New Roles for the Committee

One might conclude from this brief analysis of changes in the support Rules Committee Democrats give their party leadership that its importance in the congressional process has diminished.[8] After all, power in the House in the past has largely rested with those who could delay or defeat legislation. Now that the Rules Committee acts in that capacity only infrequently, as a traffic cop that prevents legislation from reaching the floor, has it, in fact, become a less significant subunit?

My research on the committee indicates this is not the case. Although it may now receive considerably less public attention, the committee remains vital to the working of the House today. The committee or a group of its members perform in three major role capacities that are significant in the operation of the House. The first is as a new type of legislative "traffic cop"; the second is as a "field commander" operation for the respective party leaderships; and the third is as a "dress rehearsal" for legislation about to go to the House floor. In some ways these roles include many of the functions Peabody described in the perceptions of the Rules members he interviewed in the 87th Congress.[9] In addition, they contain other facets that developed in response to changes in the operation of the House. The first two of these roles will be briefly described, and the dress rehearsal role, the importance of which is highly related to changes in the House, will receive more detailed treatment.

The "New Traffic Cop" and "Field Commander"

Although the Rules Committee now denies rule requests in-frequently, this does not mean that it ceases to be a "traffic cop." The traffic cop role was never limited to stopping legislation from reaching the floor. It also included setting the structure for floor debate in terms of time and the amendment process; ensuring that the legislation met formal and informal technical standards (Did the committee reporting it hold sufficient hearings? Was the legislation in compliance with House rules and procedures?); and taking the heat for House members by keeping some legislation on which they did not want to go on record from reaching the floor.[10] The new traffic cop still performs these functions, but the manner of performance is different. The com-mittee now ensures that legislation the Democratic leadership wants to bring to the floor is not delayed and at times will help expedite legisla-tion delayed elsewhere. It still will delay legislation, but usually this is done to improve its chances of passage or, as discussed earlier, be-cause the leadership wants it delayed. Finally, with the growth of sub-committees in the House, both in number and activity, the Rules Committee is called upon first to protect jurisdictions and second to help settle jurisdictional disputes.

It is important to note that Republican members of the Rules Committee are very critical of the new traffic cop image and feel the committee should again prevent legislation from reaching the floor. As one Republican expressed his discontent:

> It [the committee] should return to more traffic cop functioning and stop bad pieces of legislation. It should be a traffic cop, a cooling-off place, and a filter. The committee should not let every piece of tripe leg-islation go to the floor.

Democrats on the committee agree that the new traffic cop is too le-nient but think they must go along with the wishes of the party lead-ership. However, that leadership is not yet strong enough to allow its Rules members to be a tougher traffic cop with the substantive com-mittees.

The field commander role is closely related to the new traffic cop role, but it is distinct in several ways. First, the role is not one in which every member of the committee, or even every member of the committee majority, participates. Second, although it also involves ex-ecution in the moving and delaying of legislation, it is more elaborate. And, third, while the traffic cop performs functions for the respective party leadership as well as the general House membership, the role of field commander is performed exclusively for the leadership. Thus, for example, the field commander takes the heat for the leadership, while the traffic cop takes it for House members. The role moreover is not an intuitively obvious one. The term "field commander" was first suggested to me and the essence of the role best described by a senior Rules Democrat in the course of responding to a question about the House leadership:

> I don't particularly want to use a military analogy, but it fits. It's sort of like people on the Rules Committee treating themselves as if they were responsible field commanders reporting to the chief in Paris. Intelligence comes from us to the leadership. Our responsibility is to inform, advise, and execute. We're in charge of the field operation and sometimes you have to act on your own best judgment. You can't always confer. Sometimes you need reserves like Biemiller calling up Madden. At times you make leadership decisions for leadership. Even in a military operation it works the same way.[11]

An example will help to illustrate the field commander role. During the 94th Congress Jack Brooks (D-Tex.) introduced a resolution to allow for the broadcasting of floor sessions of the House. Brooks, as chairman of the Joint Committee on Congressional Operations, which had recommended that floor activity be broadcast (and televised), and as chairman of the House Commission on Information and Facilities, which would oversee the proposed broadcasting operation, appeared before the Rules Committee to request that it report the legislation. (In this instance Rules had original jurisdiction over the issue and thus had to report the legislation and a rule providing for its consideration on the floor.) Several of the field commanders spotted some difficulties with Brooks's proposal, especially since plans for control of the operation were vague and left too much discretion to the Commission on Information and Facilities. Two of them took the matter to the Speaker:

> ———and I had a long talk with the Speaker. He wanted to compromise and try it on radio first. ———and I thought that was a mistake and no way to go. There hasn't been enough study yet. Jack Brooks has too much to do already to give it sufficient attention. We really need to look at it carefully and how it affects the House and its rules. We prevailed upon the Speaker. . . . We were the ones who went to the leadership on it.

Thus, they informed and advised Speaker Albert about problems of which he was not fully aware. When the committee met again on the broadcasting resolution, a motion was introduced to create an ad hoc subcommittee of Rules to hold hearings and to investigate the matter further. As the following report from a Rules member indicates, the committee wound up taking the heat for the leadership.[12]

> Take the broadcasting subcommittee. The Speaker doesn't want broadcasting of sessions now. Yet Jack Brooks, who's been pushing the resolution, he came up to me to press for us to act the other day. Jack told me the Speaker wants it and told him that yesterday. I told Jack that he didn't really know. And Jack has served over twenty years here, and he doesn't understand in this case.

With some differences, some Republicans on the committee also serve in field commander capacities. Two of them, Jimmy Quillen (R-Tenn.) and John Anderson (R-Ill.), are formally members of the House Republican leadership. With Republican control of the White House, they operate as field commanders for both the president and the leadership.

Not every member of the committee serves in the field commander capacity. Some are rarely relied upon by party leadership to act in this capacity, and some do not see it as a role they want to play. The most important distinction, at least among the Democratic members, between the field commanders and non-field commanders is that the former have internalized and understand the need for the committee to be an extension of the leadership and want to develop its capacities to assist the leadership, whereas the latter tend only to varying degrees to accept that as being the case.

Dress Rehearsal Role

It is no accident that Capitol Hill participants and observers alike often refer to the Rules Committee as the "best show in town." Aside from the entertaining cast of House members who hold seats on the committee, the committee provides the spectator with the opportunity to see committee members question their House colleagues, people with whom they work on a day-to-day basis, about the content of legislation produced in their respective committees. This is done in the confines of a small hearing room with a large chandelier overhead, while members and witnesses, like actors, enter from and exit to anterooms on the left and right. The audience consists almost entirely of committee staff and press, with a few members of the public allowed to squeeze in for each performance.[13]

And yet it is not really a show per se. It is more like a dress rehearsal, a tryout, or a preview. The audience is small. The show is often interrupted by the noise of bells, the need to vote, or the committee members' desire for lunch. And the committee members are at the same time members of the cast and members of the audience scrutinizing the performance of witnesses. One almost has the feeling of watching the rehearsal of a play within a play. The few who regularly observe these activities feel that they provide a good indication of what will happen when and if the particular piece of legislation arrives for its opening on the House floor.[14]

Perhaps the analogy is overdrawn and in any case imperfect, but after nearly a year of observing Rules Committee sessions and speaking with the committee's members, staff, and spectators, I became convinced that the committee hearings do really function as a dress rehearsal or critic's preview and as such perform a vital role in the congressional process. Whatever the imperfections are in the analogy, the similarities with a dress rehearsal provide valuable insights for analysis of the committee's behavior.

First, if one goes to a Rules session at which a committee or subcommittee chairman is presenting the case for granting a rule and his minority counterpart is opposing a rule, one is usually able to hear the same statements that will be repeated when these individuals debate the bill on the House floor. Sometimes there are changes in the floor speeches, but these are usually made to account for some problem in the original statement presented at Rules. As one Rules Democrat member describes the committee:

> . . . on controversial and major legislation, it serves as a trial run. Like Eddie Hebert and the others. Hebert would come before the committee with a fifteen-minute text which he'd read. And others do the same. Some don't, you know. But the text Hebert would read to the Rules Committee would be the same one as he'd use on the floor. It's a way to prepare and to learn the various arguments.

Another Democrat commented that he did not know "if it was meant to be that way or if it used to be, but that's what happens. Members make almost the identical speeches on the floor as they do in the committee."

The floor managers are not the only ones who try their statements out at the Rules session. Often members who wish to offer an amendment on the floor will testify at Rules to publicize the amendment. If they are not cut off by the chairman or a member of the committee asking, "Is there any question as to the germaneness of your amendment? Won't you be able to offer under the requested rule?" they can test their arguments. For example, when the Tax Reduction Act of 1975 was before Rules on February 26, a major debate hinged on making two non-germane amendments in order. Both dealt with changing the depletion allowances on oil and gas. The preceding day the House Democratic caucus had voted to instruct Rules Committee Democrats to make the amendments in order. The first of the amendments, by William Green (D-Pa.), would have repealed the allowance for oil and gas retroactively to January 1, 1975. It had received wide publicity. The second amendment, by Charles Wilson (D-Tex.), would amend the Green amendment to maintain certain levels of depletion for independent oil and gas producers provided the money was plowed back into further exploration. The Wilson amendment was complex and was given little chance of passage. Wilson, however, went before Rules to discuss his amendment. He brought with him an elaborate set of charts and graphs and went through his entire presentation (during which he kept the attention of every member of the committee, which is no mean feat in itself). The next day Wilson appeared before a couple of hundred members on the House floor. He used the same charts, the same delivery, and in large part the same speech. Wilson's amendment was defeated 197 to 216, but the margin was far closer than anyone would have supposed twenty-four hours earlier.

Second, the Rules Committee members act as critics as well as performers. They provide feedback on the dress rehearsal. If the individual presenting the bill before the committee receives few questions or challenges, he can expect smooth sailing on the floor. This, however, is rarely the case. More often the interchange that occurs at Rules provides the floor manager with information as to where challenges will develop and how strong they will be. One Rules member calls it an "early warning system," and another calls it a "preview movie." But in essence it is no different from a theater critic's review of a play in Boston before it goes to New York. It provides a good indicator of strengths and weaknesses; the main difference is that the director learns that the first act needs a rewrite, whereas the floor manager learns that he might have to accept an amendment to Title 1.

The Rules Committee membership is representative enough of the House as a whole so that provisions that do not sit well there are almost certain to face a floor challenge. If a floor manager comes before Rules and finds that all the Republicans, including John Anderson, the lone moderate, are strongly opposed to the legislation and, further, that John Young, James Delaney, and B. F. (Bernie) Sisk, the more conservative Democrats, are willing to support the rule but have strong reservations, he knows he is going to have serious trouble. As one committee Democrat put it: "When legislation comes to the committee for a rule, you know where the complaints are coming from because the members of the Rules Committee are so diverse in their outlooks." Another Rules member chose to discuss this point in the context of problems with substantive committees:

> There's a problem with being a good legislator on other committees. The legislation only gets tested in the environment of the committee from where it comes. The members of the reporting committee feel they have the right to get it to the floor because it got out of their committee. We're getting more and more isolated proposals because of the disintegrating consideration in committee and subcommittee. Rules is the integrating force. Until it gets to Rules, it's like someone who hasn't gone out of the house into the neighborhood. Rules is the neighborhood. It may not be ready for the world yet, that is, the House.

At times during the period in which I observed the Rules Committee, representatives of reporting committees would appear claiming that an overwhelming majority of the members of the reporting committee support the bill. Then they discover that a problem gets raised in Rules that was not even considered in their committee. When exposed to the outside critic for the first time, small oversights or weaknesses suddenly become glaring flaws.

A third facet of this dress rehearsal role, and one that is closely related to the first two, is that the Rules members are sought out by the other House members and report to them on the status of particular pieces of legislation. This was certainly evident in the case of the Wilson amendment. The word went out that Wilson had a well-developed case to present. Similarly, in late May 1975, when the House leadership wanted to bring H.R. 6860, the Ways and Means Committee's energy bill, to the floor right before the Memorial Day recess, the word went out from the Rules hearing that the bill had opposition from different segments of House membership. This happens not only on major legislation such as tax and energy bills but also on less controversial matters. Rules members frequently mentioned that they regularly received inquiries about legislation from other House members. As one Democratic member described his relationship to other House members since going on Rules, compared with his earlier assignments:

> I get a lot of questions from other members. They want to know what's scheduled, when it's going to be on the floor, or something about its provisions. They think we know what's scheduled. Many times they give us more credit than we deserve.

A Republican member put it more simply: "People expect you to know a little bit about everything." Moreover, the Rules members do not handle all the inquiries. Many calls come to their offices from other member's offices. Again, however, the expectation is that the Rules member knows whether or not a rule will be granted, specifics about the legislation, its chances on the House floor, and probable amendments to be offered.[15]

This reporting system by the dress rehearsal critics on Rules again encourages House members to use Rules to publicize their amendments. One Republican member of the Rules Committee claims that he tells his colleagues to use the committee for this purpose:

> I have recommended to my fellow colleagues who want to offer amendments, "Come before the Rules Committee and make your plea there. Use any excuse you want to." Wilson did it on the tax bill. He got himself worked up for the floor. I've suggested this to Bud Brown, Bill Archer, and John Rousselot.
>
> I think the minority should do more than it does. I suggested to——and——[Rules minority members] that we meet with the minority on the substantive committees. We should sit down and explain what we can do to help them . . . how we can bring out things not discussed in the committee hearings.

This strategy is not without its disadvantages, as one Democratic Rules member observed in discussing an attempt by Charles Wiggins (R-Calif.) to bring attention to an amendment in the nature of a substitute that he intended to offer to the 1975 extension of the Voting Rights Act.

> I like the idea of a dress rehearsal. From the point of view of the committee chairman or subcommittee chairman, that's exactly what it is. If they get asked questions at the Rules Committee, they're likely to get the same questions on the floor. It sets guidelines for the floor. Take Wiggins's amendment the other week. Judiciary did not really know about it until he brought it to the Rules Committee. It was deceptive and sounded very reasonable at first. If they had just sprung it on the floor, it might have passed.

Following that Rules session, House members were bombarded with information attacking and defending the Wiggins substitute. The Rules Committee session backfired on Wiggins. It allowed Judiciary Democrats to prepare for Wiggins before going to the floor.

There are other features of Rules proceedings that have similarities to a dress rehearsal. Although they are of less significance than the features mentioned above, they add a certain richness to the metaphor.

Just like actors performing for the critics, many House members who come before Rules are visibly nervous. At times their voices quiver, their hands shake, and they perspire profusely. Yet these are individuals who are accustomed to speaking in public and who appear relaxed when going before other committees. Most Rules members are aware of this "stage fright" and think it usually indicates the witnesses are poorly prepared, are unfamiliar with the legislation they are managing, or know they have a weak bill. One Rules Democrat, when asked why he thought witnesses tended to be nervous, was reluctant to comment at first; then, after a long pause, he replied:

> I'd hate to think that the committee did anything that made the witnesses nervous. There's no reason that a witness who knows his bill should be . . . [pauses, then laughs]. Of course, you know what I mean by that. Those who come to the committee unprepared or with a weak position on a bill are the ones who get nervous.

Another Rules member recalled his discussion with a nervous witness after the committee session:

> You know, like poor old ———. He just gets so nervous now. I went up to him after the Amtrak bill and said, "———, you're here with your colleagues. There's no need to be nervous." And he responded to me, "You know I'm going to be nervous. I'm always afraid someone there will ask me a question that I can't answer. And I just don't want to look bad in front of my colleagues."

Several of the committee members thought that witnesses were nervous because of lack of preparation but also felt that it was because many of them were coming before Rules for the first time, especially given the number of new subcommittee chairmen who are now expected to make presentations to Rules. One Rules Republican was particularly strong in making this case.

> As a member gains in seniority, he becomes a subcommittee chairman or a full committee chairman. And when he first gains the position, he's unsure of himself. But the more he comes to Rules, the less nervous he gets. It's like baseball. You have rookies who are uncertain of themselves in tight situations and old pros who've been through it before. . . . Mahon is an old pro but not a good example because he only comes for waivers. Staggers is not really an old pro . . . [pauses]. Manny Celler, Bob Poage, Eddie Hebert, Wayne Aspinall, people who had been around for years and years. Now we have a new breed.

The staff assistant to a new subcommittee chairman was surprised at his member's first appearance before Rules as the manager of a bill. He commented that although his subcommittee chairman did not appear nervous during his presentation, the presentation was disorganized and generally below par. Later, in discussing the performance with this fourteen-year House veteran, the staffer reported, "——— said he was very nervous. He claimed it was like his maiden voyage."

One other reason mentioned as contributing to the nervousness of witnesses before the Rules Committee is that they have a combined sense of "fear and respect" for the committee. It comes from the knowledge that, despite the fact that few rule requests are now denied, the potential exists for losing the bill there or for the committee to find some source of objection that will become damaging when the legislation reaches the floor. Moreover, there is a realization that members' performances before the Rules Committee can affect their reputations in the House.

Whether one thinks these are sufficient explanations for the nervousness of witnesses or not, the Rules performance, like the dress rehearsal, is a good indicator of what is to come. One committee member, while admitting that the correlation is not perfect—"Some days you can remember names and some days none come to you; it's the same thing"—still put forth the general relationship: "Those who do badly before the committee do badly on the floor."

One final similarity to the dress rehearsal is worth noting. Witnesses and committees, like actors and playwrights, develop reputations that affect how the critics evaluate their performances. Thus, a witness may find that his early reputation as being nervous and uncertain will be a handicap in future appearances before Rules. On the other hand, a witness can make a good impression. A Rules Republican, speaking about one witness's successful performance, noted:

> Mike can come back with another bill and probably won't have any trouble. Everyone there was impressed with him. He had a command of his subject. . . . And just the opposite can happen. I don't know whether it's subconsciously or consciously, but somehow you have confidence with some members and not with others.

Usually reputations take a longer time to establish than just one appearance. But knowing that particular witnesses are going to appear at a Rules session makes some committee members cringe. One committee chairman, in particular, usually brings a response like this: "He doesn't know anything about his bills, and he never answers any of the questions we ask. He just comes in and says, 'this is for the good of the American people,' and expects us to grant a rule."

More important is the fact that committees have differing reputations. Rules members from both parties complain about the Banking and Currency Committee and the Education and Labor Committee for bringing forth legislation that really requires writing on the floor, for failure to settle major disputes, and for being poorly prepared. Of course, much of this may result from the subject matter with which these committees must deal. But when they appear before Rules, it is anticipated that they will have tough sledding. Not surprisingly, that condition carries over to the floor proceedings.

Committee reputations can be altered especially when there is a turnover in chairmen. The change in the Ways and Means chairmanship from Wilbur Mills to Al Ullman (not to mention the other changes on that committee) offers an excellent example of how committee reputations change. Mills had relatively high success with the Rules Committee and on the House floor. Ullman, however, had substantial difficulty with both during 1975. By an 8–8 vote, the Rules Committee barely defeated a motion that would have allowed for consideration on the floor of "any amendment pertaining to oil depletion" to the Tax Reduction Act of 1975. If adopted, this rule could have delayed floor passage of the bill considerably. As mentioned earlier, when Ullman presented H.R. 6860, the Energy Conservation and Conversion Act, he ran into major problems in Rules, and the granting of the rule was delayed. Finally, in November 1975 Ullman ran into trouble with his rule request for the Tax Reform Act of 1975. Another tie vote (7–7) prevented it from being reported with an open rule.

Although Rules members note a variety of reasons for the difficulties Ways and Means is having, Ullman's skill and knowledge are usually among the factors cited. One Rules Republican claimed:

> The biggest difference you can see is with Ways and Means with Ullman as chairman instead of Mills. Why, there were 120 some amendments to the energy bill. I'd wager 100 to 1 Wilbur would never let a bill like that get out.

In the next breath, however, this Republican demonstrated that his comments were not just partisan. He noted the fine job Tom Foley (D-Wash.) had done in handling a controversial agriculture bill: "There was opposition to it on substantive grounds and the veto was sustained, but that wasn't Foley's fault. He was a craftsman."

Dress Rehearsal: An Overview

Some observers might argue about the importance of the Rules Committee's dress rehearsal role to the effective functioning of the House of Representatives. In addition, some may believe that this role has always been performed to a certain degree by the Rules Committee. But in a legislative institution like the House that in recent years has become more decentralized and specialized in its decision-making processes, has dispersed its work load to over 140 subcommittees, and has increasingly given junior members important responsibilities in its workings, the ability of one committee to serve in a dress rehearsal capacity takes on new significance in the effective working of that institution.

We have seen how the dress rehearsal gives the proponents and opponents a chance to test their presentations on a committee that is broadly representative of the entire body. This not only provides them with important feedback and makes them aware of problems they will face on the floor, but also supplies an important opportunity to publicize their positions and to set the boundaries for debate by the entire body. In this sense the dress rehearsal serves each of these decentralized, highly specialized committee environments.

But more important, by serving as critics at the dress rehearsal, the Rules members serve the House. It is impossible for House members to keep track of the legislation forthcoming from all the committees and subcommittees of which they are not members. They need someone whose judgment they can trust, who is not intimately involved in the writing of the legislation, just like the theatergoer needs a good critic to sort through the many available entertainment offerings. From the Rules critic the House members can learn whether the committee producing the legislation has done its job well. What strengths and weaknesses exist? Has consensus been built? Is it likely to pass? Have his interests been protected? When is it scheduled for the floor?

Although there is ample room for discussion as to how well the Rules members are performing in this capacity, it is hard to deny the importance of this role. As House members, or members of any large legislative institution, become more specialized, their need to rely on such critics increases and correspondingly the role becomes a more valuable one. The critic is relied on for information, opinion, and protection by the audience. And just like the theater critic, the information and opinion provided by the Rules member can affect the success or failure of various productions.

Conclusion

As we have seen in this essay, the roles the Rules Committee plays in the House have been altered both by reforms directed at the committee and by those directed at the House in general. By gaining full control over the recruitment of Democratic members to the committee and by filling vacancies carefully, the Speaker has turned the committee into an arm of the leadership. It can now be relied on to be a traffic cop that serves the leadership instead of one that serves the chairman of the committee.

Throughout the 1960s, with only narrow leadership majorities on Rules, the role of the Speaker's supporters on the committee was limited to guarding against an upset in the flow of legislation. Now, with an ample leadership majority, the Speaker's strongest supporters on the committee are free to pursue new activities as field commanders for the leadership. Reforms that brought about greater decentralization in the House have given new attention and importance to the committee's dress rehearsal role. The need of House members for critics to comment on the wide variety of legislation before it comes to the floor from isolated subcommittees and the need of bill managers to publicize their cases and to have a trial run before going to the floor are growing ones.

The mix of roles played by the Rules Committee and its members may continue to change. Within a few years there will be a substantial turnover in the committee's Democratic membership. An active Speaker could use the opportunity to turn the committee into his cabinet and thereby achieve better control over the flow and quality of legislation and over subcommittee government. At the least, the Speaker could allow the Rules Committee to be a tougher traffic cop than it has been during the 94th Congress and keep the House floor clear of poorly written legislation.

It is unlikely, however, that any of the committee's current roles will soon be dropped. Even if the Republican party takes control of the House, it is likely that its members would want the committee to continue its dress rehearsal role and that its leadership would find it convenient to maintain field commanders on the Rules Committee. True, the traffic cop role might return to its earlier form. But in a decentralized House, party leadership, be it Republican or Democratic, liberal or conservative, will not allow one of its vital arms of influence to wither.

NOTES

1. For an analysis of Rules Committee operations in this period, see Richard Bolling, *House Out of Order* (New York: Dutton, 1966), chap. 10; Milton C. Cummings, Jr., and Robert L. Peabody, "The Decision to Enlarge the Committee on Rules: An Analysis of the 1961 Vote," and Robert L. Peabody, "The Enlarged Rules Com-

mittee," both in R. L. Peabody and N. W. Polsby, eds., *New Perspectives on the House of Representatives*, 1st ed. (Chicago: Rand McNally, 1963), pp. 167–94 and 129–64, respectively; and James A. Robinson, *The House Rules Committee* (Indianapolis: Bobbs-Merrill, 1963).

2. See Cummings and Peabody, op. cit.
3. On the fight over federal aid to education, see especially Frank J. Munger and Richard F. Fenno, Jr., *National Politics and Federal Aid to Education* (Syracuse, N.Y.: Syracuse University Press, 1962); James L. Sundquist, *Politics and Policy* (Washington, D.C.: Brookings Institution, 1968), chap. 5; Eugene Eidenberg and Roy Morey, *An Act of Congress: The Legislative Process and the Making of Education Policy* (New York: Norton, 1969).
4. The data in this table come from several sources. For the 87th through the 90th Congress I used data reported by Douglas M. Fox and Charles P. Clapp, "The House Rules Committee and the Programs of the Kennedy and Johnson Administrations," *Midwest Journal of Political Science* (November 1970): 667–72; and "The House Rules Committee's Agenda-Setting Function, 1961–1968," *Journal of Politics* (May 1970): 440–44. Data on the 91st and 92nd Congresses come from statistical reports compiled by the committee's staff. I compiled the data on the 93rd Congress from the final calendar of the committee. For the 94th Congress, first session, an unofficial count was made by a member of the committee's staff.
5. In 1949 William Colmer was reappointed to the Rules Committee after having been bumped in 1947 when the Republicans became the majority party.
6. These figures are based on scores published in *Congressional Quarterly Almanac*, 94th Congress, first session. The party unity score is based on all roll call votes during that session on which a majority of Democrats was opposed by a majority of Republicans. The party unity score derives from the percentage of the time on those roll calls that a member votes with the majority of his party.
7. Peabody, op. cit.
8. Despite the changes, Rules remains what Fenno has described as a committee that gives its members influence within the House. See Richard F. Fenno, Jr., *Congressmen in Committees* (Boston: Little, Brown, 1973).
9. Peabody, op. cit., p. 147. I would like to thank Bob Peabody for the access he gave me to interview material he gathered for this earlier study.
10. Ibid., pp. 133–45.

11. Biemiller refers to Andrew Biemiller of the AFL-CIO, and Madden to Ray Madden, chairman of the Rules Committee in the 93rd and 94th Congresses.

12. During the 2nd session of the 94th Congress, following a report by its ad hoc subcommittee, the Rules Committee decided not to report a broadcasting resolution. The Democratic leadership in this case formally opposed the legislation.

13. Until mid-1975 the committee members and witnesses all sat at one large table. With the addition of a sixteenth member, it was necessary to go to the standard design of semicircular elevated hearing desks, at which the members sit, with the witness facing them at a small separate table. This design in the long run may reduce the informality of the proceedings. See Richard L. Lyons, "Rules Panel Room Has a New Look," *Washington Post*, August 3, 1975, p. A:5.

14. It is important and interesting to note that in the course of studying the Ways and Means Committee, John F. Manley uncovered the same dress rehearsal notion when Ways and Means bills went before Rules. Manley discusses it as a "test run." See his *The Politics of Finance* (Boston: Little, Brown, 1970), p. 238.

15. Peabody, op. cit., p. 142, discusses this as information and cue giving. The dress rehearsal role surely includes the information and cue-giving function, but it is more extensive. Dress rehearsal acts to integrate these functions in a broader pattern of operation.

6. Committee Reform and the Revenue Process

Catherine E. Rudder

The Old Ways and Means Committee and Its Transformation

The 94th Congress will be recorded as a "reform Congress," one that altered rules, procedures, and, consequently, power relationships in the House.[1] A major target of House reform was the Ways and Means Committee and its former chairman, Wilbur Mills (D-Ark.), who had often been cited as the single most powerful person in the House. Constitutionally empowered to originate tax legislation, the House delegated that duty to the Committee on Ways and Means, whose jurisdictional vortex has drawn into itself numerous matters of national concern: trade, social security, unemployment compensation, national health insurance, and public assistance. Mills could prevent congressional action in these areas. For example, with the support of his committee, which he assiduously maintained, it was Mills who set the terms for medicare, the 1968 tax surcharge, the 1969 tax reform act, and revenue sharing in 1972.[2] Mills was an expert substantively in Ways and Means legislation and politically in maintaining his preeminent position in his committee and in the Congress.[3]

Under Mills, the Ways and Means Committee was structured to

facilitate committee autonomy and independence from the House and, at the same time, to press upon the House committee decisions without alterations from the floor. The committee was small relative to other House committees; it had 25 members with a constant 3-to-2 party ratio. Those recruited to the committee were "reasonable" and "responsible" lawmakers who, upon first joining the committee, experienced an apprenticeship period of learning the subject matter and practicing deference to more senior members. There was a spirit of group identification and fraternity that led members to practice norms of reciprocity and restrained partisanship and to defend committee decisions outside the committee.

Decision making was highly centralized around Chairman Mills. Having abolished subcommittees a short time after he became chairman in 1958, Mills became the keystone of the committee arch, the central conduit for interest group and member demands. His technique in dealing with his committee was to discuss thoroughly an issue, in meetings closed to the public and the press, and to devise a compromise that could create consensus in the committee and that could pass on the floor of the House. Mills's power stemmed from his ability to forge consensus, his sense of timing, his eventual willingness to change his own position, his reputation of being the knowledgeable tax expert in Congress, his past performance in the committee, House, and conference, and, of course, his position as chairman of a committee whose substantive importance and political autonomy were considerable.

It was claimed by Ways and Means members that the complexity of the committee's subject matter and its national significance required insulation from short-term electoral forces and particularistic district concerns. The committee needed to be free to forge bills that could take into account various philosophies and interests. This delicate balance could not withstand floor amendments, any one of which could undo the compromise or could cost the Treasury millions of dollars. Thus, the freedom of movement was bestowed upon the committee because it did what the House wanted it to do: produce tax bills that were widely acceptable to House members. Political scientists John Manley and Richard Fenno both maintain that these bills were widely accepted because members of the House approved of the committee's decisions rather than because individual members lacked the expertise, time, energy, procedural ability, organization, or willingness to risk reprisals.[4]

Several procedural reforms established in the 93rd Congress set the stage for frontal challenges to Ways and Means in the 94th Congress. First, the caucus mandated that all committee mark-ups thenceforth would be held in public unless a majority of committee members with a quorum present publicly agreed in a roll call vote to close the meeting. Only those hearings covering matters such as national security issues or personnel concerns could be closed to the public. This change was directed especially at Ways and Means. As a spokesman for Common Cause commented after the vote, "We're going to try very hard to keep Ways and Means open. They're perhaps the worst offender, except possibly for Armed Services." [5]

A second change in 1973 was the establishment of a secret ballot vote to approve each nomination for committee chairman made by the newly formed Democratic Steering and Policy Committee. This change, in conjunction with a 1971 change that allowed committee chairmen to be approved individually rather than as a group, would give the caucus an opportunity to remove committee chairmen whose performance the majority of Democrats considered unacceptable.

The third relevant change was an alteration of the procedure by which major legislation would go to the floor under a closed rule. In the past Ways and Means bills had been granted a rule from the Rules Committee which prevented amendments on the floor of the House. This procedure meant that House members had been given the opportunity to vote only on an entire Ways and Means bill as an all-or-nothing proposition. In 1973 the caucus altered this procedure. Under the caucus change, 50 Democrats can propose to the caucus an amendment to the bill under question. If a majority of the caucus approves, then the Democratic members of the Rules Committee are instructed to report a rule to allow that specific amendment to be voted upon by the entire House. Although this modification of the use of the closed rule was apparently "aimed at the Ways and Means Committee and its chairman, Wilbur D. Mills," Mills was not present during the vote on the change and "made no apparent attempt to fight" this resolution.

Despite these changes, the caucus was unwilling to alter drastically the power relationships in Ways and Means at this time, and in fact was thrown in the unlikely role of protecting the committee from attempted encroachments into its jurisdiction. Although the Bolling Committee reported to the caucus in March 1974 a plan for committee reorganization including significant jurisdictional changes for Ways and Means and other committees, the Democratic caucus decided to send the Bolling plan to a study committee chaired by Julia Butler Hansen (D-Wash.), which in turn reported out a much less radical plan. After six days of floor debate, a modified Hansen plan was passed on October 8, much to the relief of the Ways and Means Committee.

However, although Ways and Means was permitted to retain most of its old jurisdiction, the committee was dealt an important blow: the

Hansen plan required that all committees with twenty or more members must have at least four subcommittees. This reform was aimed specifically at Ways and Means, for Mills had abolished subcommittees after he assumed the chairmanship and had refused to set up subcommittees despite an increasingly heavy work load that the committee could handle less and less well.

The Hansen plan provided for an early organization of the House in December. The Democratic caucus of the 94th Congress met from December 2 to December 5, 1974, immediately after Chairman Mills had been widely publicized for engaging in erratic personal behavior involving a striptease dancer. After a year of frequent absences from the committee by Mills, of Mills's defiance of the caucus, and of little legislative productivity in the areas of tax revision and health insurance, the caucus, which now included 75 new freshmen Democrats to provide the margin of votes, was now prepared to dismantle the power of Chairman Mills and the Committee on Ways and Means. First, the caucus stripped the power of the Democratic members of Ways and Means to make the Democratic committee appointments, a duty they had been performing since 1911 when the committee-on-committees function was originally given to the Democratic members of Ways and Means in a reform movement at that time.

Not only did the Ways and Means Committee lose the assignment function, but the committee was enlarged, not by three members, as the Rules Committee had been in an effort to liberalize it in 1961, but by almost 50 percent, from 25 members to 37 members.[6] Moreover, the previously permanent party ratio of 3 to 2 was altered to reflect the overwhelmingly Democratic Congress of 2 to 1. The large influx of new participants and the increase in the size of the committee was bound to affect the way the committee operated, but the method of recruitment to the Ways and Means Committee also changed, and this in turn affected what kind of person was likely to be a member of the committee. The composition of the committee was also affected by the fact that the freshman caucus had exacted a promise from the Steering and Policy Committee that at least two freshmen would be appointed to the Ways and Means Committee.

Strengthening the requirements of the Hansen resolution, the caucus required that five, rather than four, subcommittees be established. The caucus also dealt with the method that should be used in assigning members to subcommittees. Ways and Means members immediately formed subcommittees and selected assignments before the expiration of the 93rd Congress in order that they could claim two seats before the new members could claim any. They established six committees, five required by the caucus and an oversight committee, as set forth in the Hansen reforms.

Besides the establishment of subcommittees, an additional task had been added to the committee. The Budget and Impoundment Control Act of 1974 had created a House Budget Committee, five members of which were to be members of the Ways and Means Committee. Since representation on the Budget Committee was considered tantamount to chairing a subcommittee, those members who served on the Budget Committee could not also chair a subcommittee. This rule spread responsibility within the Ways and Means even further.

In the midst of the caucus-mandated changes, Chairman Mills was hospitalized on December 3, 1974, and later that month formally resigned as chairman of the committee. Mills was not well; the caucus was obviously in a "reform mood"; and Mills would have had to face nomination by the Steering and Policy Committee and secret ballot election by the restive caucus. Mills was replaced as chairman by Al Ullman of Oregon, the next most senior Democrat on the committee.

Reform: Purposes and Consequences

Although procedural reform of Congress and of the Ways and Means Committee has been advocated for a variety of reasons, at least three closely related but conceptually distinct purposes of reform can be identified. One purpose has been to democratize procedures and to remove the negative "veto points" in Congress. Given the *modus operandi* of the Ways and Means Committee under Chairman Mills, with closed mark-ups and closed rules, Ways and Means was a key target for those who wanted Congress to be run by more democratic procedures.

The argument in favor of democratizing procedures is that democratic institutions ought to employ rules and procedures that are fair, allow people to express their concerns, operate on the basis of majority rule, and permit public scrutiny—in other words, democratic rules of procedure without reference to any particular interest or ideology. The problem with this view is that, as Ralph Huitt is fond of pointing out, rules and procedures are not neutral: rules structure conflict to the advantage of some and the disadvantage of others, although it is not always possible to predict who or what interests are going to be advantaged.[7] Moreover, it turns out that simple democratic concepts such as majority rule are not nearly as simple nor necessarily as democratic as they at first may seem.[8] There is a need for some control mechanisms to aggregate interests and to provide for responsible governing.

A second purpose of procedural reform is to alter *who* makes the decisions. It seems that those who are most eager for certain kinds of reform are those who stand, or at least think that they stand, to benefit from the changes. For example, freshmen and non-committee members who have been excluded from the decision process in the past may wish to become participants. However, in adding participants, no one may be better off in the long run if, as a result, coherent legislation cannot be produced.

A third purpose of procedural reform is to alter legislative outcomes. Many people complained about the Ways and Means Committee, for example, because of the particular bills it was producing and those, such as national health insurance, that it was not producing. But to attempt to control legislative outcomes by the indirect route of altering structures and procedures is a highly risky business. For instance, an expanded committee with presumably more "liberal," more "responsive" members might not concomitantly produce more "liberal" and more "responsive" legislation. Nor will open meetings necessarily ensure any particular legislative outcome, despite the expectation of some that more liberal legislation would result. The legislative consequences of reform may be quite different from anything that is anticipated by the reformers. In general, reforms often produce outcomes that are neither intended nor necessarily consistent with their original purposes.

Thus, the primary purposes of procedural reform of Congress have been to democratize its operations, to change who is making the decisions, and to modify the substance of legislation. In accomplishing one of these purposes, by necessity another one may be affected. For example, democratizing decision making entails changing who is making the decisions. However, accomplishing one purpose may interfere with one of the other purposes or may make one of them not worth accomplishing. For instance, the power of the chairman may be sufficiently diluted to make the second purpose of reform—changing personnel—meaningless. If the chairman has little power, who cares who is chairman? Reform, in short, is not the simple matter that it may at first appear.

The reformed Ways and Means Committee provides an intriguing arena in which to consider the results of procedural reform. Even though some of the effects of the changes in the committee may be temporary and some may not have yet emerged, it is worth examining Ways and Means in light of how well the changes may have accomplished the three purposes of procedural reform identified here and in light of what other impact the reforms may have had which were probably not anticipated.

In addition to secondary sources, the author used two sources of primary data in examining the impact of the reform. First, the author was a participant observer of the meetings of the Ways and Means Committee and its subcommittees on trade and social security from April to August 1975. As a staff assistant of Representative Abner Mikva (D-Ill.), a new member of the committee, she was specifically assigned to cover the Committee on Ways and Means. This assignment provided contextual knowledge of and firsthand experience with the committee and two of its subcommittees. The second main source of original data derives from personal interviews that the author conducted with twenty-seven members of the committee in July 1975. A fair representation of old and new members, Republicans and Democrats, southerners and nonsoutherners, and conservatives and liberals were included among those interviewed.[9] The length of the interviews ranged from thirteen to forty-five minutes each, and a common core of questions was asked each member.

Democratizing the Committee

Most of the changes in the Ways and Means Committee have had the effect of democratizing procedures. The committee operates more openly, more democratically than in the past, and members of the committee and of the House are better able to influence its legislative product. But this accomplishment has been achieved at the expense of the ability of the committee to operate efficiently and to enforce its legislative will in the House. Moreover, there are some unexpected changes. The beneficiaries of at least one of the democratizing reforms, for example, are the organized interest groups.

The Enlargement of the Committee and the Establishment of Subcommittees

Forming six subcommittees whose chairmen can hire their own staff has been a means, as one member expressed it, of "spreading the cookies around." The changes have given more House members an opportunity to participate in committee deliberations and to take leadership roles in the committee. On nontax legislation the establishment of subcommittees has actually allowed the committee to act more quickly, to work on more than one subject at a time, and to hold hearings on and report out legislation that they might not otherwise have had time to complete or to consider in detail.

At the same time, however, the demands on members' time have been considerable. It is not uncommon for meetings of the entire committee and its subcommittees to consume an entire day from 8:00 A.M. to 8:00 P.M. Moreover, the enlarged committee operates slowly and inefficiently, especially on tax matters for which there is no subcommittee. Thus, all 37 members were involved in 1975 in the most time-consuming efforts of the committee: tax reduction, energy taxes, and tax revision. Both old and new members complained that the enlarged committee was "unwieldy" and "bulky." As one veteran Democrat observed in an interview, "The difference in trying to get a consensus of 35 members as opposed to 25 is tremendous, and it's more than the numbers would indicate."

Despite these difficulties, the expansion of the committee has lessened the ability of a small group in the committee to block legislation. For instance, it was noted by one prominent member of the committee that in a "big committee it is harder for one clique to be dominant. . . . On a small committee little factions or cliques develop. You used to have to cater to the Republicans and southern Democrats. That happened on taxes last year. We never got anywhere."

Open Hearings and Mark-ups

Open hearings and mark-ups have also democratized the committee. In 1973, 30 percent of the meetings of the Ways and Means Committee remained closed to the public. By 1975 the public and press were excluded from only 2 percent of Ways and Means hearings and mark-ups. The ability of the chairman to form majorities in secret session with no roll call votes was correspondingly diminished, although committee Democrats have frequently caucused in secret.

Despite the apparent ideological neutrality of the rule to operate in the open, in practice this rule has worked more to the benefit of some people and groups than others. Specifically, it is interest group activity which has apparently been most profoundly affected by the open mark-ups, according to the Ways and Means members who were interviewed. Although no specific question on interest groups was asked in the interviews, 12 members volunteered comments on the effect of open mark-ups on the activities of lobbyists.

One veteran Democrat, for example, observed, "The open meeting is not as fruitful as I thought it would be. . . . The public's not there, but the interests are. . . . Open meetings put special interests into the process and gave them an active input." Several members mentioned the presence of lobbyists in the committee room during mark-up sessions. Said one, "A member now goes out to the audience and comes back with a question or amendment [prepared by a lobbyist]."

The open meetings have affected the committee "adversely," according to another veteran, who said:

> . . . and remember, I'm a liberal Democrat. Under the old system we made effective trade-offs and had effective discussion which produced effective legislation. Now there is reason for more suspicion than there was before. During the energy [tax bill] mark-up, members went down and sat in the audience and talked with a very specific interest and wrote an amendment, came back up and offered it. The media should be there but not the special interests. Those are the people who are out there day after day.

The member continued, "With the open meetings a member has to play to his special interest"—especially, he said, if the member is not from a safe district.

Apparently one technique that lobbyists employ is to call an important constituent in a member's district as a proposal is being considered in committee and have that constituent call the member immediately in the committee room during the meeting to express a position on the issue at hand. A Republican reported, "People are on the phone before adjournment."

The "public" interest groups are also increasingly active and are becoming more respected by members. Common Cause and Ralph Nader's tax group monitor all Ways and Means meetings and have worked with and even organized sympathetic members on tax proposals. They have also provided members with detailed information on tax "loopholes" and how they work. Another group, Taxation with Representation, publishes analyses of the voting patterns in committee and reports on mark-ups in Ways and Means. Still, the activities of these kinds of groups are insufficient to counter the "private" interest groups. One member, for example, felt that there are "no true representatives of the public. There are neglected areas. Common Cause and Nader have their own particular areas to represent." To the extent that these groups do constitute an appropriate counter to other interest groups, they themselves admit that they are "outgunned." [10]

One set of beneficiaries of the open meetings has been the personal staffs of the representatives who had been excluded from executive sessions. At least 12 members now have staff assigned to cover Ways and Means meetings.[11] This change provides congressmen with information and assistance that was not previously available to them. Several representatives have even combined their resources and hired a tax expert to assist the lawmakers in their Ways and Means work.

It seems that open meetings have been a mixed blessing for the Ways and Means Committee. Members' votes are now public and publicized. The press can cover the committee directly rather than through "sources." The aides from Treasury and the committee staff less exclusively control the information that members receive. However, the change in interest group activity provides an unexpected twist to open hearings and mark-ups. Opening meetings to the public has meant opening meetings to everyone, including lobbyists, who, it has been claimed, take an even greater part in writing Ways and Means legislation than they did in the past. As one member commented, "Now if a deal is struck, they'd [the member] better support whatever measure they've promised. If they renege on agreements, the other party is going to know it." Thus, the open meetings have made members more accountable to whoever cares to pay attention. What originally looked like a neutral procedural reform has thus far had an effect that is hardly neutral.

Closed Rule Reform

Like the open meeting reform, the alterations in the use of closed rules has contributed to democratizing the committee and the House: more people directly influence Ways and Means legislation. This reform has broken Ways and Means's exclusive control of the taxation decision process in the House. As a consequence, the making of tax law has been fundamentally altered. Instead of a tightly controlled committee whose decisions are enforced in the House, the decision process has been opened to the Democratic caucus and to the entire House membership. At the same time, the ability of any person or group to produce and pass a coherent piece of taxation legislation whose content is satisfactory to a majority of the House may have been severely hampered.

In the past it had been argued that a closed rule was necessary for Ways and Means legislation because of its complexity and because of the delicate compromise constructed in committee which could be destroyed by modifying amendments on the floor. At the same time, closed rules gave the Ways and Means Committee a considerable amount of power to determine the shape of the tax law and gave members who disagreed with sections of Ways and Means bills little recourse other than voting against the entire bill. Until the closed rule reform, for example, opponents of the oil depletion allowance had had no chance to remove that preference from the tax code since its original enactment in 1926. Since the majority of Ways and Means members supported the allowance, it was retained, although it was modified by the committee in 1969.

Interestingly, it has been dissident committee members rather than noncommittee Democrats who have made use of the 1973 procedural change. In 1974 Charles Vanik (D-Ohio) and William Green (D-Pa.) each proposed an amendment to a tax revision bill. The caucus instructed the Rules Committee to permit a floor vote on these two amendments, one to change the foreign tax credit for businesses to a foreign tax deduction and the other to eliminate the oil depletion allowance. Both of these amendments were devised to reduce the tax preferences of businesses even though Ways and Means had not recommended this course of action.

This defiance of Wilbur Mills and the majority of the Ways and Means Committee was met with defiance. Mills refused to bring the bill before the Rules Committee with the excuse that he had been given contradictory instructions: for a closed rule by Ways and Means and for a modified closed rule which allowed the two amendments from the caucus. The bill died. The closed rule reform had ended in deadlock.

In 1975, however, there was again a challenge, this time on the 1975 Tax Reduction Act, and the outcome was quite different. Again Ways and Means refused to remove the oil depletion allowance. Chairman Ullman supported this position with the suggestion that the matter be taken up in a subsequent bill, but Green and Sam Gibbons (D-Fla.), along with five new members of the Ways and Means Committee, gathered the required 50 signatures and petitioned for a caucus vote. That amendment and another which would retain the allowance for independent oil producers were permitted. Green and his allies won the removal of the allowance on the floor of the House. (The special provision for independent producers, however, was added to the bill in conference at the insistence of Senator Long.)

Having lost that battle, Ullman began to realize his subservient position vis-à-vis the caucus. In short, the Ways and Means Committee had been and would probably continue to be overruled on certain matters, given the current predilections of the Democratic caucus. As a consequence of this realization and of his political situation in the committee, a situation which often required 19 Democratic votes to form a majority in the face of unified Republican opposition, Ullman began to help the dissidents short-circuit the caucus procedure to add amendments to Ways and Means bills. On the tax revision and extension bill, in order to form a majority, Ullman agreed to request a modified closed rule that would permit six strengthening amendments to the bill. Hence, Ullman gained the Democratic votes needed to report out the bill, and the dissidents were spared the choice of no tax reform or of appealing to the caucus.

Thus, the use of the new procedure to modify closed rules on Ways and Means bills was first tried in 1974 and first succeeded in

1975. It worked to the benefit of disgruntled Ways and Means Democrats and those who desired to strengthen Ways and Means legislation by reducing tax advantages for certain business operations.

In contrast to the new "appeal" procedure, the gradual use of modified-open and open rules is less demonstrably salutary. There is general agreement that the energy tax bill, reported under an ironically entitled "orderly open rule," was completely gutted on the floor of the House with over 200 amendments proposed, not all of which were actually considered on the floor. Many people have argued that it was the open rule which prevented the House from producing a coherent and tough bill. And it is probably that experience which led the Ways and Means Committee later on in the year to shy away from requesting open rules on, for example, H.R. 10210, the unemployment compensation system revision.

It can be argued that the House's performance on the energy bill was less an indication that Ways and Means bills should not be reported out on an open rule than it was that the House and the country are not politically ready for a strong energy policy. The open rule simply allowed the House to work its will, or nonwill, as the case may be.

In any case, the reform of the closed rule has lessened the ability of Ways and Means to determine taxation policy univocally. For the first time the House has been given an opportunity to vote on specific provisions in taxation legislation. The long-run effect of the new procedure for allowing amendments on tax bills will be determined by the composition of the Democratic majority and the Congress.

An open rule provided individual House members more say in the intricacies of Ways and Means legislation and reduced the committee's exclusive claim on tax bills in the House. At the same time, the open rule permitted a significant weakening of the energy tax bill to the extent that some people have dubbed it a "nonpolicy." Complained one veteran Democrat, "Now we have 435 independent Democrats and Republicans. . . . The modified rules have destroyed the opportunity for strong leadership and will potentially destroy the institution." There are already suggestions to "reform the reform." For example, one proreform observer of the energy debacle observed, "The 'orderly open rule' proved to be a near disaster. . . . It seems obvious that a more restrictive rule is needed."

The Loss of the Democratic Committee Assignment Duty

If open rules have lessened the ability of the Ways and Means Committee to enforce its will on the floor of the House, the loss of the Democratic committee-on-committees duty has exacerbated that difficulty. How important the committee assignment duty was in securing floor support for Ways and Means bills is a matter of some dispute among committee members. That this duty was important to the Democratic members is underscored by John Manley: "Thus the Ways and Means Democrats . . . see this [committee assignments] as one of the most important things they do." [12]

Most veteran Democrats see the loss as inconsequential, as affecting primarily the committee's prestige, and feel that the assignment power was never employed to exact support for Ways and Means bills. In their view the threat of using the committee assignment process as a means of reprisal against opponents of Ways and Means bills was slight, for members receive their committee assignments before they vote on Ways and Means legislation, and Ways and Means had no power to take away an assignment from an opponent. Said one veteran Democrat, "I never saw it used to gain support for a bill." Said another, "That [committee-on-committees function] amounted to nothing. It only happened once every two years." A third felt that the loss of the function affected the committee "not a bit. Once they get on a committee, they forget how they got on it." With this loss, he continued, "we lost prestige, not power."

It might be argued that prestige was perceived as power by those representatives who did not have it. Perhaps the old Ways and Means Democrats in fact did *not* consciously use their assignment duty to enforce support, but other Democrats may have *perceived* that assignment power as a threat. Another explanation is that the loss of this function was sufficiently embarrassing and perhaps demeaning that senior members prefer to discount its value.

New members, on the other hand, tended to emphasize the importance of the loss. One new Ways and Means Democrat, for example, felt that the loss of the assignment duty has had a "tremendous" effect on the committee's operation. "It constitutes a substantial diminution in power for the committee. It is exactly where Ways and Means people had their power." A senior Republican concurred:

> From the standpoint of pure politics the most important change on the operation of the committee is that the Democrats lost their committee-on-committees power, the power to appoint House members to committees in the House. This power provided them with an element of respect and gave House members second thoughts about crossing them on the floor or not going along.

One likely result of the loss of the assignment duty is that as the committee becomes less prestigious and powerful, different people will be attracted to the committee. As both Fenno and Manley have pointed out, the major goal of Democrats on the old committee was one of internal influence in the House. Presumably, as the committee is less able to meet that goal, members will readjust their goals, and the committee will begin to attract members with different personal objectives. Perhaps the predominant goal for "safe seat" Democrats will begin to shift to the predominant Republican goal of making good public policy, while Democrats from less sure electoral districts will probably have to focus their primary attention on the goal of reelection.[13]

Changing the Decision Makers

Of course, democratizing the decision process automatically alters who makes and influences the decisions. Expansion of the committee, for example, has increased the number of people who are involved in committee decisions. The closed rule reform has increased the influence of liberal dissidents on the committee, and it has in part taken the decision process out of the hands of the Ways and Means Committee. Subcommittees have provided new positions of leadership for some committee members.

One personnel change that has not yet been discussed is the change of chairmen from Wilbur Mills to Al Ullman. This change has received as much attention in the press as any of the committee reforms, and yet this change is probably not as important as any of the other changes (that is, except to Mills and Ullman personally).

Over the years in Congress, Ullman had apparently moderated his liberalism considerably to the point that in the last few years his voting pattern (on the basis of conservative coalition scores) has become similar to that of Mills. Mills and Ullman have shared another similarity as chairmen. The composition of the Ways and Means Committee is such that there is no automatic majority coalition. Winning coalitions more often have had to be developed. Both Mills and Ullman have frequently found themselves in the enviable position of being the crucial swing vote on the committee. The two chairmen also have largely had the same tax staff accessible to them. The staff of the Joint Committee on Internal Revenue Taxation, with Lawrence Woodworth as its chief of staff, has continued to serve the Ways and Means Committee on matters of taxation.

There are differences between the two chairmen—in their personal styles, for instance—but the drastic changes in the committee, the demands which the committee faces from the caucus, the different legislation confronting the committee in 1975, and the lessened power of the chairman make it impossible to compare the two chairmen.

Their situations are entirely different, and style is circumscribed by opportunity. One member of the committee, for example, commented, "The changes in the Ways and Means Committee and the House changes are tied together. The chairman must react differently from the way he reacted in the past. He's not protected by seniority. This causes a tremendous change in the way the committee operates."

To the extent that the changes have undercut Ullman's ability to lead the committee, Ullman has tried to overcome this difficulty by making use of the Democratic caucus on the committee. He tries to forge agreement in closed meetings among the Democrats. He employed this method with the energy bill by setting up task forces composed of Democrats and with the tax revision bill in which the final compromise was hammered out in a secret caucus meeting. Inevitably, this method of operation arouses the ire of Republicans whose response is to vote en masse against Ullman in committee. This method also breaks up the conservative coalition of Republicans and southern Democrats on the committee. A senior Republican complained, "The Republicans feel cut out and therefore resist supporting the chairman. . . . The committee is polarized. It's partisan. The Republicans are responding to being cut out of the process." Said another, "The Republicans have to act together. . . . It's the only way we have to make our position felt." Ullman, in turn, has publicly mentioned that he resents the consistent and staunch Republican opposition that he has confronted in the committee.

Another consequence of the chairmanship change is that Chairman Ullman is challenged in the committee, on the floor, and in conference to a much greater extent than Mills ever was. The fact that Ullman is successfully challenged reduces his own power and the power of the committee to determine tax law. One Republican member explained, "There's a group on the Democratic side testing the chairman all the time. It's sort of the middle-level, middle-management group who were on the committee under Mills—Gibbons, you've probably noticed him the most, but also [Joseph] Karth [D-Minn.], [James] Corman [D-Calif.], and Green." Said a senior Democrat, "There's a different atmosphere. Members feel freer to challenge Ullman."

Ways and Means's success in getting its bills passed on the floor unamended has declined since Wilbur Mills's departure, if for no other reason than that individual members now have a *means* by which they can challenge Ullman and his committee's decisions. When Mills finally brought a bill to the floor, he was sure of its passage and was protected from amendments by bringing his bills out under a closed rule. When he went to the floor, he could count on his own committee to support him, and the non-committee members "assumed he knew what he was talking about, and they would go along," explained one veteran committee member. "But the new members have changed the whole complex of the House."

If Ullman has confronted opposition on the floor of the House, he has also experienced considerable difficulty in dealing with the Senate Finance Committee and its chairman, Russell Long (D-La.), in conference. Two senior Democrats who have participated in many conferences over the years both noted this phenomenon. The fact that Ullman can command less authority in the committee and the full House than Mills could has reduced Ways and Means's bargaining position in the conference. "Ullman doesn't have the votes in his pocket the way Wilbur did, but even Mills wouldn't have them anymore." Not only can the Ways and Means Committee no longer offer a solid front in conference, Ullman is less experienced than Mills in dealing with Long, who has made a point of humiliating Ullman in conference.[14]

The power of the chairman of Ways and Means apparently has been decimated. The opportunities for forceful leadership are much fewer. More committee and House members are getting a say in Ways and Means legislation at the expense of the chairman and the committee as a whole. In turn, the House is itself apparently experiencing a weakened ability to deal with the Senate in conference.

Changing the Substance of Legislation

Assessing the degree to which the substance of Ways and Means legislation has been altered as a result of the procedural reforms is probably the most difficult and most interesting aspect of the changes in the committee. It is probable that the change in chairmen, given the other changes, has not particularly altered the legislative product of Ways and Means, with the exception that the House is in a weakened position in House-Senate conference. Nor have open meetings apparently had much effect other than giving interest group lobbyists more direct opportunity to influence legislation. One member, for example, commented, "It [open meetings] has had no effect. That surprised me. . . . I miscalculated. . . . Members are as willing to support special interests in public as they are in private."

The reform of the closed rule, however, has definitely put its mark on the taxation legislation produced by the House. The caucus procedure of forcing floor votes on specific amendments, for example, has meant that the tax reduction act and the tax extension and revision bill are somewhat more liberal than they would have been without the new procedure. That is, tax preferences for businesses were reduced by the House to some extent from those in the bills that Ways and Means reported out of committee. More generally, the decision process is no longer exclusively a committee process but has been extended to the Democratic caucus and to the entire House.

There is another change in the committee which has had an impact on legislative outcomes, although the impact is less noticeable than one might have expected. That change is the enlargement of the committee, or, more exactly, the change in the composition of the committee. The committee is considerably different from that of previous years. For instance, for the first time in this century there is a black, Charles Rangel (D-N.Y.), on the committee. Also for the first time, a woman, Martha Keys (D-Kans.), was selected to serve on the committee.

Prerequisites for membership on the committee in the past included considerable prior service in the House and a moderate style. But the average length of prior service for Democrats has dropped from 8.0 years in the 92nd Congress to 4.5 years in the 94th. Four freshmen Democrats, two of whom had served in the House previously, received unprecedented appointments to the committee. Moreover, the new members, including the freshmen, are more outspoken and more integral to the committee than new members had been in the past.

The composition of the new committee has thus changed in that the new members are more diverse, less legislatively experienced, and much more likely to participate in the committee. The committee members are also on the average somewhat—but only somewhat—more liberal in their voting patterns on the floor of the House (with conservative coalition scores as a criterion for comparison). Committee Democrats and Republicans vote more often with their party than committee members voted in the past. Thus, the committee, because of its additional Democratic members, is more likely to reflect the position of House Democrats, but the Democratic side is only slightly more liberal than in the past.

Despite the increased number of liberals on the committee, there is not a dependable liberal majority. A useful comparison of the old and new committees is provided by the proposal to end the oil depletion allowance, which had given the oil industry a lucrative tax reduction. This proposal was considered by the old committee in 1974 and again by the new committee in 1975. In both years the proposal lost, but on the second vote oil opponents almost doubled their strength. In 1974 the proposal lost 6 (25 percent) to 19 (75 percent); in 1975 the proposal gained ground in a vote of 14 (40 percent) to 22 (60 percent). Thus, the increased proportion of liberals on the committee has not always been sufficient to constitute a majority even in the new committee.

One reason for the unstable support of "liberal issues," as conceived by the members, is the need for new members, especially those who for the first time hail from unsafe districts, to respond to interest group and district demands. If a representative is dependent upon the United Auto Workers for support, he will tend to vote with them even though their position on automobile efficiency taxes, for instance, may not be the "liberal" one. Or if a number of multinational corporations have their home offices in a representative's district, it is difficult to vote to eliminate an important tax advantage, such as the Domestic International Sales Corporations (DISC), even though DISCs may constitute a substantial tax "loophole" in the eyes of tax reformers. With regard to the substance of the legislation that the committee has produced, one liberal veteran member expressed it this way: "The expansion of the committee has not had as much impact as reformers thought it would. The committee is only slightly more liberal."

A comparison of the two tax reduction acts written by the committee in 1975 is instructive on this point. In February 1975 the Ways and Means Committee reported out a tax rebate bill of $2.3 billion. Although the committee persistently rejected two "liberal" attempts to remove the oil depletion allowance, the tax bill did include "liberal" provisions that redistributed the tax burden away from low-income persons. The taxes sustained by low-income persons had increased more than those of any other income group over the last twenty years, but the effect of the 1975 tax cut as designed by the new Ways and Means Committee was proportionately greater for those with low incomes. In short, the new committee reversed the regressive twenty-year trend.

In the fall of 1975 the Ways and Means Committee considered the extension of the Tax Reduction Act and a revision of the tax code, popularly referred to as "tax reform." At first the committee voted to reduce tax expenditures or "loopholes" which favored large businesses (considered a "liberal" position by committee members), but three days before reporting out the bill, the committee reversed itself. The $2.6 billion in additional revenues which had been tentatively proposed was trimmed to $752 million. Chairman Ullman was faced with solid Republican opposition (12 votes) because the Republicans refused to support the bill without spending ceilings, as requested by the Republican president. Since the committee had rejected such ceilings, Ullman was faced with the fact that without any Republican votes a mere seven Democrats could block the passage of the bill. In order to be able to report a bill out of committee at all, the chairman had to work to weaken the bill to pick up support from wavering Democrats. In some cases lobbyists actually provided the weakening language. Members, especially new ones who are not impervious to district demands, responded to lobbying from those industries hailing from their districts.

From these two tax bills some patterns do emerge. The committee is probably more liberal in fiscal policy than the old committee was. Further, the redistribution of the tax burden created by the Tax Reduction Act suggests that the committee is willing to support a more progressive income tax system.

Where observers are probably thrown off, however, is in the tax revision bill in which the committee retrenched from a tax reform position. The votes simply were not there, and the reason probably inheres in the composition of the new members of the committee. The majority of the new members are liberal in fiscal policy in that they support a fairer distribution of the tax burden. But many of the new members are not from safe districts; thus they are not guaranteed reelection and must listen and respond to interest group demands.

Hence, the committee reform which included a new kind of member was double-edged: new members were selected with an eye to removing the Ways and Means Committee from its past insulation from the Democratic caucus, the Congress, and national forces, but this receptiveness is by definition not selective. The committee is as little able now to reduce tax expenditures or "plug loopholes" as the old committee was, but some substantive changes have resulted from the enlargement of the committee.

Conclusion

The Committee on Ways and Means has been successfully reformed from three perspectives. Internally, the committee operates in the open. The committee's procedures have been democratized: subcommittees have been established, with the important exception that taxation remains a full committee matter, and some staff have been distributed among subcommittee chairmen. Meetings are held in the open, with the result that there is more direct participation in the deliberations of the committee by whoever cares or is able to participate. The effective power of the chairman, and, especially with the expansion of the committee, of the individual members of the committee, has been reduced.

Second, the reforms have successfully altered *who* is making the decisions. With the committee's expansion, closed rule reform, the establishment of subcommittees, and change in the chairmen, different people and more people are involved in making decisions that previously had been controlled by the chairman. The closed rule appeal procedure has given liberal Democrats in the committee more leverage within the committee. The new members have also made their mark on the committee. From their arrival they have actively participated in committee deliberations. In some respects they are somewhat more liberal than the older members, and the new Democrats are especially more likely to support party positions. Finally, they are less legislatively experienced and less electorally entrenched than some of the older members.

Third, the reforms have affected the substance of the legislation that is produced. The new procedures and the new participants (both committee and non-committee members) have enabled the House to pass legislation that might not otherwise have been passed, for example, the removal of the oil depletion allowance. However, the addition of the new committee members and the altered party ratio which increased the percentage of Democrats on the committee have not consistently translated into more liberal legislation emanating from the committee.

Probably the most important impact on the substance of legislation has derived from the changes in the closed rule. Those changes have meant that the Ways and Means Committee and, in particular, its chairman have lost control of the decision process.[15] Increasingly, the substance of legislation is determined in the caucus and on the floor. Given the current composition of the caucus, liberal positions have benefited from the closed rule appeal procedure. In effect, the new procedure has provided an appeal process for dissatisfied Ways and Means Democrats (or any other Democrat, for that matter) and thus has paved an avenue of greater accountability of the Ways and Means Committee to the Democratic caucus, as the new (1973) caucus procedure to select committee chairmen by secret ballot has forced more accountability of committee chairmen to the caucus.

In sum, the consequences of the reforms have been to democratize procedures, to alter who the decision makers are, and to change the substance of legislation, particularly in the caucus and on the floor. But there have been other consequences as well, consequences that, if not surprising, were probably not explicitly anticipated. There are, for example, a different kind of interest group activity and influence, more partisanship in the committee, more closed meetings among Democratic committee members, more dissension within the committee, fewer opportunities for leadership, and less House influence in conference with the Senate.

The fact that new committee members hail disproportionately from unsafe seats has had its secondary effects on the committee as well. While the inclusion of these new members has led to more diversity and more responsiveness to public or popular opinion, it has also lessened the ability of Ways and Means members to make taxation decisions from a national point of view. If individual members' first goal is reelection, those from "unsafe" districts must cast their votes with reference to how those votes will affect their reelection prospects. Thus, the process has been altered such that members are more accountable to whomever of their constituents pay attention, in particular, interest groups.

One might argue that congressional reform, if anything, has been too successful, especially that democratization has been too complete. Ways and Means, for example, has been stripped of its power to make binding decisions. In the reformed committee no decision is final but is subject to change in the caucus and on the floor of the House. What this means, beyond the obvious point that more people are able to participate in Ways and Means decisions, is that a compromised legislative package cannot be developed in the committee with any assurance that that package will be passed intact on the floor.

Democratization of the Congress has coincided with a national realization that resources are finite, that legislative solutions cannot be found in the relatively painless route of distributive policies. The new "politics of scarce resources" requires redistributive and regulative policies. An example of this kind of politics is found in the energy tax bill. The Ways and Means Committee "bit the bullet," as some members like to express it, and reported out a tough piece of legislation that included a 23-cents-per-gallon gasoline tax for most consumers, along with incentives to save gasoline. When the bill went to the floor, the incentives were retained, while every stringent section of the bill, including all of the gasoline tax, was either eliminated altogether or weakened substantially. Many Ways and Means members voted against their own bill, as it was considered title by title on the floor. Even though the energy tax bill might have failed had it been voted upon as an entire package, in general, logrolled bills that call for sacrifice or for redistribution will have a better chance of passing without being gutted if coalitions can be built and maintained around an indivisible legislative package.

Finally, democratization places emphasis on only one side of the concept of "representative democracy," and that side is one that emphasizes the need for governmental responsiveness. However, there is another aspect of representation that has been slighted by the zeal to break down unaccountable structures of power. That aspect is the obligation to govern and to govern responsibly.

In order for Congress to function, to produce coherent, responsible legislation, structures of power are needed. In the case of taxation legislation, for instance, some group, presumably Ways and Means, has to have the ability to aggregate interests and to maintain the coalition that it develops.

The problem with the old structures of power, it was claimed, was that they were often anonymous, unaccountable, unresponsible, and unresponsive. Democratization has addressed the problem of responsiveness but has lessened the ability of Congress to govern responsibly. Thus, structures of power will have to be built in the Congress again. Both the obligation to govern responsibly and the politics of scarce resources require it.

There are already deliberate efforts in this direction: the new budgetary process, the active Democratic caucus, and the two adjuncts to the majority party leadership, the Rules Committee and the Steering and Policy Committee. As these new structures develop, they will need to be accountable and responsible, if they are to be improvements over the dismantled structures. What needs to be dealt with in a conceptually coherent way is the perennial question: To *whom* should these structures be accountable? to themselves? to the congressional parties? to the entire House membership? to the national parties? or to home districts which, after all, send people to Congress in the first place?

NOTES

1. I would like to acknowledge the assistance of a number of people without whose help this research could not have been undertaken. First, the American Political Science Association through its Congressional Fellowship Program provided me with firsthand experience in Congress. Representative Abner Mikva graciously assisted me in gaining the interviews with the members, and he, along with his staff, shared their congressional "home" with me during my stay on the House side. Genie Irmoyan, Jacques DePuy, and Zoe Gratzias deserve special mention. I would not have been able to accept the Congressional Fellowship without the support of the University of Georgia. Joyce Murdoch provided helpful editorial assistance. Finally, the extensive and thoughtful comments of Terry Sullivan shaped my thinking fundamentally.

2. John F. Manley, *The Politics of Finance: The House Committee on Ways and Means* (Boston: Little, Brown, 1970); Gary Orfield, *Congressional Power: Congress and Public Policy* (Washington, D.C.: Brookings Institution, 1975); Lawrence C. Pierce, *The Politics of Fiscal Policy Formation* (Pacific Palisades, Calif.: Goodyear, 1971), pp. 135–78.

3. The following account of the Committee on Ways and Means prior to 1975 is heavily indebted to Manley, op. cit.

4. Manley, op. cit.; Richard Fenno, *Congressmen in Committees* (Boston: Little, Brown, 1973), p. 18.

5. Factual information and background on the reforms that affected the House Committee on Ways and Means and on its subsequent behavior have been drawn from the *Congressional Quarterly Almanac, 1973, Congressional Quarterly Almanac, 1974*, various issues of *Congressional Quarterly Weekly Report*, and contemporaneous news reports, unless otherwise noted.

6. On the expansion of the Rules Committee, see James A. Robinson, *The House Rules Committee* (Indianapolis, Ind.: Bobbs-Merrill, 1963).

7. See, for example, Ralph K. Huitt and Robert L. Peabody, "Foreword," in Fenno, op. cit., p. vi.

8. See, for example, Duncan Black, *The Theory of Committees and Elections* (Cambridge At the University Press, 1968).

9. Members interviewed include Al Ullman (Oreg.), James A. Burke (Mass.), Dan Rostenkowski (Ill.), Phil M. Landrum (Ga.), Charles A. Vanik (Ohio), Omar Burleson (Tex.), James C. Corman (Calif.), William J. Green (Pa.), Sam M. Gibbons (Fla.), and Joseph E. Karth (Minn.)—veteran Democrats; Herman T. Schneebeli (Pa.), Barber Conable (N.Y.), John J. Duncan (Tenn.), Donald B. Clancy (Ohio), Bill Archer (Tex.)—veteran Republicans; Richard F. Vanderveen (Mich.), Henry Helstoski (N.J.), William Cotter (Conn.), Fortney H. Stark (Calif.), James R. Jones (Okla.), Andy Jacobs, Jr. (Ind.), and Abner J. Mikva (Ill.)—new Democrats; Philip M. Crane (Ill.), Bill Frenzel (Minn.), James G. Martin (N.C.), L. A. "Skip" Bafalis (Fla.), and William M. Ketchum (Calif.)—new Republicans.

10. Thomas J. Reese, *Tax Notes*, June 30, 1975, p. 9.

11. Thomas J. Reese, *Tax Notes*, May 19, 1975, p. 21.

12. Manley, op. cit., pp. 77–78.

13. Fenno, op. cit., pp. 1–14.

14. Aaron Latham, "Behind Closed Doors: How Russell Long Won the Battle of the Tax Bill," *New York*, May 5, 1975, pp. 61–68. A veteran of Ways and Means conferences commented that Latham's article is uncannily accurate.

15. See Terry Sullivan, "Voter's Paradox and Logrolling as an Initial Framework for Committee Behavior on Appropriations and Ways and Means," *Public Choice* 25 (Spring 1976).

7. Congress in Organizational Perspective

Joseph Cooper

The purpose of this essay is to apply organization theory to the study of Congress. There are a number of ways in which this objective could be pursued. The approach I shall follow will be to sketch out a general framework in terms of which congressional operations and behavior can be conceptualized and relationships among important variables identified. Of necessity, given the mélange of organization theories and theorists, the results of such an approach will be highly influenced by the types or strains of organization theory emphasized.[1] It is appropriate, therefore, to specify at the outset the basic guidelines that will be relied upon in making choices. First, organizations will be broadly conceptualized as rational, goal-oriented entities, as planned social units that are created and structured to perform certain functions or tasks. Second, concepts will be drawn eclectically from a variety of sources, the test being their ability to contribute in a coherent fashion to the construction of a comprehensive framework.[2] Third, emphasis will be placed on distinguishing Congress as a non-bureaucratic organization rather than on developing its similarities to other types of organizations.

The framework that will be presented consists of four basic categories: (1) the context of performance, (2) the basis of performance, (3) structure and process, and (4) adaptation. In each case the analysis will first present some general propositions drawn from organization theory and then apply them with specific reference to Congress.[3]

Context of Performance

General Propositions

1. Society may be seen to be composed of various networks or subsystems of social units that arise to satisfy basic societal needs. These networks or subsystems vary in their degree of differentiation and integration. They may be seen to be differentiated to the extent that they specialize in the performance of specific functions. They may be seen to be integrated to the degree that relationships among units are normatively specified or controlled rather than determined by exchange or market considerations. Organizations exist as elements of such networks or subsystems. They thus operate within broad functional environments or contexts.

2. Shared expectations concerning an organization's relationship to other units in its functional environment define or constitute an organizational role. The nature of such roles varies in relation to three prime components of the functional environments in which organizations operate: cultural values, structural ties, and the character of the work. Cultural values relate to the value patterns that are dominant in a discrete functional environment. Structural ties relate to the forms of linkage between an organization and its environment. The character of the work relates to the nature of the desired product, the type of raw materials required, and the state of knowledge concerning the conversion of raw materials into outputs.

3. Roles express broad and abstract conceptions of the nature of the functional relation between an organization and its environment. They must be actualized or realized in the form of discrete products or outputs. The output or mix of outputs an organization produces is thus constrained and shaped by its role. Nonetheless, organizations have leeway in determining what output or mix of outputs best fulfills their roles. Such leeway permits and leads to the conflict over output goals that is endemic to all organizations.

4. To produce outputs, organizations need inputs from their environments. Over time the ability to secure inputs rests on environmental satisfaction with organizational outputs. Nonetheless, the terms of exchange vary substantially in different functional contexts in relation to the values, linkages, and work that characterize the environment. Different types of organizations thus vary in the quantity

and quality of the inputs they require and in their ability to secure inputs on the basis of their outputs.

5. Organizations have domains as well as roles. Domain pertains to an organization's actual relationship to its environment—to the scope of its activities and its degree of autonomy. Organizations that are successful in fulfilling their roles, in satisfying environmental expectations regarding their functional contributions, maintain their roles and domains. Organizations that are unsuccessful suffer diminutions of role and domain. In competitive environments losses of role and domain tend to occur in a balanced or symmetrical fashion. In integrated environments losses of domain tend to exceed and precede losses of role.

Applications to Congress

The functional environment in which Congress operates is the political system. The political system may be seen as a particular network or subsystem of units that is differentiated to satisfy the goal attainment and integrative needs of national societies. It serves, in short, to provide national societies with the capacity to define and attain collective goals and to manage and control social conflict.

Political systems constitute highly structured or integrated environments for the units that operate within them. Thus, many important aspects of the relationships among units are normatively predetermined and specially protected through legally defined spheres of jurisdiction. The roles of units nonetheless vary among and within political systems in relation to the character and impact of the prime components that define their environments. In the case of Congress, its role is a resultant of the values, linkages, and work that characterize or define the American political system.

The value component of Congress's environment is defined by two broad sets of values: democratic values and separation-of-powers values. Both have a critical impact on Congress's role.

As a key unit in a democratic political system, Congress must contribute to satisfying the needs of such a system. The hallmark of democratic political systems is that they seek to provide both for governmental capacity to maintain social harmony and realize collective purposes and for societal consent, that they seek to balance government's ability to act and society's ability to control such action by basing governmental action on citizen preferences and judgments. Democratic systems thus require structures and processes that foster the articulation of citizen demands, that provide such demands with access to official decision-making units, and that ensure some meaningful degree of responsiveness on the part of these units. Furthermore, since demands inevitably conflict, the structures and processes of democratic systems must also foster the accommodation and aggregation of demands without setting the levels of agreement required so high as to vitiate the capacity for action. Finally, since officials at all levels must be accorded discretion if collective goals are to be defined and implemented, the structures and processes of democratic systems must satisfy one last prerequisite. They must provide for accountability, for holding officials responsible for their decisions and actions.

In all democratic systems the legislature furnishes one of the key sets of structures and processes required to satisfy these needs. The American political system, however, is not simply a democratic political system but one that is organized in terms of a separation-of-powers principle. Congress's role as the national legislature in this system is accordingly greater and the system more dependent on it as a mechanism for balancing consent and action than is the case in parliamentary systems. On the one hand, the separation-of-powers principle vests legislative power in the legislative branch. This, to be sure, does not mean that all policy discretion must be exercised by Congress. But it does mean that within the limits of the Constitution the basic or determining features of collective goals are to be decided by Congress, acting on the basis of its own volition. On the other hand, the separation-of-powers principle also charges the legislature with serving as a prime guardian of executive performance. Once again, this does not mean that Congress should acknowledge no limits, that it should regard itself as directly and immediately responsible for supervising the administrative process. But it does mean that the system places a substantial degree of reliance on Congress to ensure that the law is executed in a responsible, efficient, and nonarbitrary manner.

The structural linkages that tie Congress to its environment are, of course, shaped by the value component of that environment. Nonetheless, by structuring the channels and modes of interaction, these linkages critically impact Congress's relationship to its environment and thus define an important aspect or feature of its role. The two primary segments of Congress's environment overlap but should still be distinguished. One primary segment is the electorate. Congress is linked to this portion of its environment both formally, through a legally defined electoral or constituency system, and informally, through a variety of organized mediators, including parties, pressure groups, presidents, and bureaucrats. The other prime segment of Congress's environment is the executive establishment itself. Congress is linked to this portion of its environment both formally, through legally defined responsibilities and relationships, and informally, through various patterns of interaction that arise and proliferate on the basis of the formal linkage.

The character of Congress's work is shaped by the value and structural components of its environment. Here too, however, the abstract and value-laden nature of Congress's work has an impact of its own and defines an important dimension of Congress's role. Congress's work consists of decisions and actions that specify basic or determining aspects of collective goals and enforce executive accountability. The raw materials out of which it must fashion its outputs are demands that issue from the electoral process and decisions or actions that are taken in the administrative process. The state of its knowledge or expertise depends on the degree of understanding of means-ends relationships in broad policy and performance areas.

Congress's work thus involves both quantitative and qualitative dimensions. Quantitatively, Congress must produce a sufficient number of decisions and actions to satisfy its responsibilities as the unit in the system that is charged with deciding the basic or determining features of public policy and serving as a prime agent of executive accountability. Qualitatively, its decisions and actions must satisfy the canons of both rationality and representativeness. They must be rational in the sense of serving as effective means of remedying the problems or dissatisfactions they are designed to overcome. At the same time, they must be representative. They must be made in a manner that satisfies the system's democratic decision-making needs.

Moreover, to perform its work, Congress must rely on a variety of forms of action or decision. In controlling the content of government policy, both the norms of the system and the realities of power require that it act primarily through law. However, Congress cannot acquit its policy responsibilities under the Constitution unless it also directs or influences policy through other forms of legislative action: investigations, control of funding levels, subjection of executive plans or decisions to legislative veto, instructions in hearings or reports, and so on. Similarly, in reviewing and correcting the character of executive performance, it must act not only through law but also through other forms of legislative action.

Congress's domain is defined by its actual outputs, by its actual product mix. Congress possesses considerable leeway in defining this mix, in choosing the aspects of policy and performance that merit its attention and in deciding whether to act through law or through other forms of legislative control or influence. Nonetheless, constraints also exist. Congress must meet the political system's need for action as well as consent. Over time, inability to respond effectively to pressing national problems leads to net losses in the scope of Congress's policy control and in its ability to make its own decisions. Losses in domain are, however, not matched by adjustments in role expectations, since the values and symbols of the political order buttress traditional conceptions even when performance is poor. What occurs, then, in eras in which Congress encounters continuing difficulties in fulfilling its role is a widening gap between Congress's designated role and its actual domain.

Basis of Performance

General Propositions

1. To produce outputs that will fulfill their roles and maintain their domains, organizations must satisfy three basic internal needs: division of labor, integration, and motivation. The need to divide labor derives from the need for effectiveness and efficiency in the productive process, from the need to bring intelligence to bear and to conserve the time and energy of members. The need for integration derives from the need to combine and relate what division of labor separates. For a variety of reasons, cooperation in organizations is problematic, not guaranteed. It is therefore necessary not only to organize intelligence and effort but also to coordinate them and control conflict. Finally, organizations must meet the human needs of the individuals who compose them. They must motivate such persons to fulfill both the common and diverse aspects of their responsibilities as organization members.

2. Division of labor has a variety of dimensions: the degree of complexity or specialization, the degree of vertical and horizontal structural elaboration, and the degree of formalism or dependence on rules to control discretion. These dimensions, however, can vary greatly in their proportions relative to one another in different types of organizations.

3. Various modes of providing for integration and motivation exist, and in each case organizations rely on some combination of them.

4. Modes of integration may be classified in terms of the source or basis of integration. One primary source derives from the internal power resources of an organization. Two basic forms of power exist: authority and influence.[4] Authority is normative in character. It pertains to the ability to secure compliance by asserting rights to control the decisions and actions of others on the basis of obligations that are involved in organizational membership and derive from general or diffuse commitments to organizational values and purposes. The role structures of an organization thus define and distribute authority. Influence rests on direct and specific inducements of various kinds. It pertains to the ability to secure compliance through the control and

distribution of a variety of specific rewards and penalties that organizations involve or generate. The role structures of an organization thus distribute influence as well as authority. Nor is the distribution of these two forms of power random. Authority and influence rather are distributed in an ordered and related fashion, since the authority conferred on a role involves claims for the control of particular rewards and penalties that pertain to the exercise of such authority. In addition, personal skills or qualities can serve as sources of authority and influence. Expertise or competence as well as office can provide a basis for authority. Skill in applying rewards and penalties or attractive personal qualities can augment influence. Nonetheless, imbalances typically exist between the authority persons possess in leadership roles and their ability to secure compliance, their actual power.

Two other modes of integration exist. Integration can be based on the adjustment or reconciliation of differences as well as power. Indeed, the more limited the power resources of an organization, the more it must rely on adjustment or reconciliation. This mode, in turn, involves two basic types of adjustment: adjustment through rational persuasion on the basis of shared values and goals and adjustment through bargaining and the exchange of advantage. Finally, integration can be based on technological mechanisms or processes in cases in which agreement on output goals is high and cause-and-effect knowledge regarding the conversion of raw materials into outputs is sophisticated.

5. Modes of inducement may be classified in terms of the source or basis of inducement. Normative inducements pertain to the moral or ideal satisfactions involved in participating in the achievement of shared values and purposes. They thus derive both from general or diffuse commitments to organizational roles and from specific commitments to particular output or policy goals. Material and psychological inducements pertain to the gratification or denial of personally oriented needs. Material inducements are tangible and derive from specific sources or means of reward or punishment, e.g., pay or physical coercion. Psychological inducements are intangible and can result from specific facets of a role, e.g., the prestige or influence conferred, or from specific or diffuse features of the group life of the organization, e.g., friendship, social approval, or feelings of importance and solidarity.[5]

6. The values, linkages, and work that define an organization's environment constrain its ability to satisfy its division of labor, integration, and motivational needs. Organizational capability in these regards thus varies among different types of organizations and even among similar types of organizations in relation to the character and impact of the prime components of their environments.

Applications to Congress

The values, linkages, and work that define Congress's functional environment serve to impose several broad and continuing constraints on its ability to satisfy its internal needs.

In contrast to bureaucratic organizations, Congress has a low tolerance for hierarchy, for highly differential distributions of authority in its formal or official role structure. Congress must be operated in a manner that is consonant with basic aspects of democratic values both to satisfy systemic needs and to legitimize its product. Congress accordingly cannot be run like an army or even a business corporation. Members formally must have equal standing and decision making must be collegial, even if such collegiality in turn must be limited by the majority principle. Top roles in the formal structure thus cannot be authorized to command or control the full range of decisions or actions accorded to other roles. Nor, given the value-laden nature of decisions, can expertise compensate for structural deficiencies in authority. Rather, the prime type of authority that can be distributed is parliamentary authority, authority to arrange and order the consideration of business.

This does not mean that Congress possesses no internal power resources. Even forms of parliamentary authority involve control over rewards and penalties that are of consequence to members. Moreover, parliamentary authority can be differentially distributed in ways that concentrate control over the rewards and penalties that the formal structure generates. In short, if Congress cannot tolerate highly differential distributions of organizational authority in any general sense, power in the form of influence can be concentrated. Such distributions, however, run counter to individualist and egalitarian aspects of democratic values and are difficult to legitimize and sustain. As was demonstrated by the 1910 revolt against czar rule and again recently by the reforms aimed at the power of committee chairmen, the sources of power-authority imbalances in Congress, in contrast to bureaucracies, derive not from deficiencies in influence but rather from deficiencies in the ability of concepts of authority to legitimize concentrations of influence.

Another basic constraint concerns Congress's lack of control over the productive factors it requires to perform its work, as compared with most bureaucratic organizations. Because of the character of environmental values and linkages, Congress has minimal control over the quantity or quality of its members. Similarly, because of the character of its linkages and work, Congress has highly restricted alternatives with regard to raw materials. It must fashion effective and representative solutions to pressing national problems out of conflicting demands that issue from the electoral process, no matter how coherent or malleable such patterns of demand are, or else risk losses of domain.

A third basic constraint concerns Congress's fragile sources of inducement, as compared with most bureaucratic organizations. Because of the character of environmental values and linkages, it can neither dismiss members for poor performance nor distribute pay on the basis of performance or role. Indeed, even with regard to perquisites, such as office staff or allowances, the need to treat members as equals imposes severe limitations on differential distributions. Equally important, Congress's linkages to the electoral system and the executive and the character of its outputs or work foster dual loyalties among its members. Both the electoral insecurities and the policy desires of members can undermine their loyalty to Congress and facilitate losses of domain.

A final constraint concerns technological capability, that is, the ability to apply regularized techniques or methods to transform raw materials into outputs. The state of technology with reference to a particular type of work depends on the character and applicability of cause-and-effect knowledge regarding the production of the desired output. In Congress technological capability is necessarily limited, since the most critical aspects of its work are interlaced with value decisions. This does not mean that Congress cannot routinize or even mechanize some aspects of its work or that it cannot use cause-and-effect knowledge to varying degrees in different areas to identify the likely consequences of alternative courses of action. The point is simply that, compared to an oil refinery, a steel factory, or even a hospital, its capability to routinize or standardize the work involved in transforming raw materials into outputs is quite low.

These broad assumptions and continuing constraints define the contours of Congress's operational capabilities.

Congressional capability for division of labor is highly limited in a number of regards. Its potential for organizational complexity is restricted by limited technological capability and lack of control over the quantity and quality of members. Indeed, even though Congress can compensate to some degree by adding staff, its small and fixed size imposes harsh limits on the number of staff it can effectively supervise and control. Similarly, Congress's capability for vertical structural elaboration is constrained by its low tolerance for hierarchy and its lack of control over personnel resources. In both these regards, however, the limitations are more severe in the Senate than in the House. In contrast, both the House and the Senate equal and perhaps exceed most bureaucratic organizations in their capability for detailed specification of decision-making procedures and arrangements. This is true because parliamentary authority and collegial decision making are highly amenable to formalization in procedural terms.

Congress's capability for integration is also constrained in significant ways. Unlike most bureaucratic organizations, Congress cannot rely on hierarchy and/or technology to coordinate effort and control conflict over output goals. It rather must rely on a particular form of power—that is, influence—and on the adjustment or reconciliation of differences. Leadership skill is thus an important feature of integration in Congress at all times, since personal skills contribute to influence and are also involved in adjustment, whether achieved through persuasion or bargaining. As for differences between the House and the Senate, sources of leadership influence are greater in the House and potentially more expandable, since the forms of parliamentary authority are more extensive. In contrast, the Senate possesses advantages in achieving integration through adjustment, given its smaller size and the broader expanse of individual constituencies.

Finally, Congress's capability for motivation is constrained in basic and distinctive ways. Given its lack of control over the conditions of membership and its inability to manipulate material rewards, it is more dependent on normative and psychological inducements than most bureaucratic organizations. In the former regard, it is particularly dependent on actual performance, on satisfying the specific policy goals of members, since diffuse commitment to Congress's role in the system can be undermined by the dual loyalties of members. In the latter regard, it is particularly dependent on the specific and diffuse inducements that proceed from the group life of the organization both as a means of bolstering organizational loyalty and as a means of compensating for the frustrations that service in Congress involves for the ordinary member. In both these regards, however, the Senate possesses greater overall capability for motivation than the House, owing to its smaller size and longer tenure.

Structure and Process

General Propositions

1. In order to satisfy their needs for division of labor, integration, and motivation, all organizations give rise to instrumental or task structures. Role relationships in this structure are oriented to the production of outputs for the environment and thus are patterned by norms that are specific, nonaffective, performance-directed, and universalistic in character.

2. The nature of the instrumental structure in any particular organization is shaped by the constraints on organizational capability imposed by its functional environment. Certain aspects of instrumental structure therefore tend to be constant, since they are tied to aspects of

value, linkage, or work that are stable and continuing. Others, however, are subject to change, since they are tied to aspects of value, linkage, or work that are unstable and even fluctuating.

3. All organizations give rise to social structures as well as instrumental structures. The social structure arises out of the instrumental or task structure and overlaps and interpenetrates it. This structure consists of sets of relationships that link members as persons, not as holders of organizational roles. The types of norms that pattern relationships are thus the obverse of those that govern the instrumental structure. That is, they are affective, diffuse, quality-oriented, and particularistic in character. The social structure organizes and embodies the group life of the organization. It therefore shapes and distributes the specific and diffuse psychological inducements that the group life generates. In addition, the social structure can displace the instrumental structure and assume tasks or functions in the productive process.

4. Leadership styles in organizations vary in relation to differences in the nature of their instrumental and social structures. In addition, these structures shape the basic character of organizational processes and the broad contours of individual behavior.

Applications to Congress

The broad and continuing constraints that govern Congress's organizational capability define the parameters of its instrumental structure.

In the context of highly limited capability for organizational complexity and vertical structural elaboration, division of labor is provided for through extensive formalization of the work and through reliance on committees.[6] The work is organized into three basic stages and is controlled at all stages through detailed rules that define the procedures to be followed. Committees, subcommittees, and committee staffs, whose operations constitute the first stage and whose influence is also substantial at the agenda and floor stages, serve as the main instruments of organizational complexity. Specialization is thus provided for through horizontal structural elaboration and through emphasis on subject matter divisions of the work. Formalization at all stages is, however, more extensive in the House than in the Senate. So too is the degree of specialization on the part of members, elaboration of committee units, and dependence on them.

Congress must also satisfy its integrative needs in a distinctive manner. In bureaucratic organizations the formal structure and the instrumental structure are largely the same, since the same structure of roles that provides for division of labor also serves as the primary source of integration. Such operation, however, rests on highly differential distributions of authority in the formal structure and often on sophisticated technology as well. Congress, in contrast, cannot rely on either hierarchy or technology as primary modes of integration. As a consequence, virtually since its inception it has elaborated and been dependent on a second structure of roles to enhance its integrative capability—the party structure.[7]

In Congress party roles and units duplicate and interact with the structure of roles and units defined by the rules. In so doing, this complementary structure fosters the successful operation of the two modes of integration on which Congress must rely.

Party ties reflect the broadest alignments of groups and interests that emerge in the electoral process, and partisan policy orientations accordingly provide the strongest bases for uniting members across constituency lines. Party thus facilitates integration through adjustment by providing the largest and most stable building blocs with which to construct majority coalitions in important areas of policy. Indeed, the stronger the potential for party cohesion, the more this mode can be confined simply to the party structure.

Equally important, party provides a critical foundation for augmenting Congress's internal power resources, for concentrating rewards and penalties in the hands of congressional leaders. On the one hand, party values and norms offer a counterweight to highly individualistic and egalitarian views of what democratic values require. In so doing, they provide an alternative basis for distributing authority and can legitimize the concentration of inducements in leadership roles in both the formal and party structures. Thus, the stronger the equation between party and majority rule, the more the needs of representative democracy can be interpreted so as to limit the atomistic implications of democratic values and to justify concentrations of power in the form of influence. On the other hand, the party structure itself serves as a source of enhancing power in the form of influence. The party structure involves a variety of units for controlling the distribution of positions in the formal structure and the behavior of partisans in their member and committee roles. The strength and viability of these mechanisms vary over time. But to some degree at all times they place rewards and penalties generated by the formal and party structures in the hands of party leaders. Moreover, when party cohesion is high and belief in party government strong, these mechanisms can produce such high concentrations of influence in the hands of party leaders as to provide a basis for centralized rule. The potential for such rule is, however, greater in the House than the Senate, owing to its more elaborate and complex formal structure.

The constraints that Congress's functional environment impose on its ability to satisfy its motivational needs have primarily a negative impact on its instrumental structure. They deny it elasticities in the generation and distribution of material and psychological inducements that larger and more hierarchical organizations in competitive environments possess to a high degree. However, in compensation, many of these constraints promote a strong and highly functional social structure. Thus, the restricted size and collegial nature of the instrumental structure nurture a vibrant and intense group life. Moreover, the friendships, feelings of importance, and forms of approval this group life produces serve as essential means of sustaining morale and loyalty in the face of the drudgeries, policy disappointments, and personal frustrations of congressional life. Important differences nonetheless exist between the House and the Senate. Group life is more intense in the Senate and so, too, is the ability of its instrumental structure to satisfy the desire of members for influence and prestige.[8]

Yet, within these parameters, the precise shapes of the instrumental and social structures have varied over time in relation to changes in aspects of the values, linkages, and work that define Congress's environment. Both the complexity of the committee system in terms of units and staff and the degree of formalization at all stages of the legislative process have increased substantially over time in response to a variety of difficulties caused by increases in size and work load. Similarly, the character of the party structure and its impact on integration have varied over time. Most of the party offices and units present today evolved during the course of the nineteenth century in response to changes in size, work load, and concepts of representative government. As for impact, the effectiveness of party as an integrating force has varied in relation to electoral patterns. When electoral conditions produce coherent and conflicting party alignments, party cohesion tends to be high and attachment to party values strong. In such periods party roles and units become more operative and controlling, the power of party leaders expands, and Congress's internal capacity for integration increases substantially. In most periods, however, party values and cohesion have not been strong enough to provide a basis for strict party rule.

The strength and importance of the social structure have also varied over time. Increases in work load and tenure have increased the intensity of group life in Congress. At the same time, increases in size and tenure have increased the importance of the specific and diffuse psychological rewards generated by such group life. Aside from these general trends, some elements of fluctuation can also be noted. In periods in which party is strong enough to provide an effective basis for integration, policy rewards lessen the need for psychological re-

wards. In contrast, in periods in which party is weak and important
policy outcomes are restricted, the psychological rewards generated by
the social structure assume more importance, as do the psychological
rewards generated by organizational roles, e.g., personal prestige and
influence. Moreover, when integrative difficulties exist, there is a tendency for the social structure to displace the instrumental structure.
This is particularly true in the Senate. In periods of party weakness or
disunity, cliques based on friendship and mutual regard can assume
exceedingly important roles in integration if party leaders are not extremely skillful in husbanding and applying their sources of influence.

Both the House and the Senate have thus been quite different
bodies in different eras of their history, quite apart from the broad
trend toward increasing complexity and formalization.[9] Leadership
styles vary in relation to the strength of party roles and units. In strong
party eras leaders tend to punish disloyal behavior, to work through
established units, and to be impersonal in their relations with members. In contrast, as party declines in strength, leaders become more
permissive, ad hoc, and personal in their approach to majority construction. Similarly, the relative emphasis on influence vis-à-vis adjustment as modes of integration varies. In strong party eras influence
is primary, supplemented by adjustment. In contrast, as party strength
declines, the balance shifts and quickly reverses. Finally, the broad
contours of individual behavior vary. In strong party eras general and
prevailing norms sanction and encourage party loyalty, collective action and interests, party conflict, and broad policy orientations. In
contrast, as party declines in strength these norms alter and increasingly sanction and encourage individual independence, bargaining
and reciprocity, restrained partisanship, and constituency orientations
and service.

Adaptation

General Propositions

1. Strain may be conceived as weaknesses or discrepancies in an
organization's productive capacity relative to its role in its environment. Strain is thus a contingent, not an absolute, condition or phenomenon. However, since the internal capabilities of all organizations
are constrained by their environments, strain is an endemic feature of
organizational life.

2. Two basic types of strain may be identified. Demand strain
pertains to the pressure that environmental expectations exert on productive capacity, to gaps between environmental expectations and or-

ganizational outputs that derive from the stringency of environmental demands. Structural strain pertains to the pressure that conflicts among internal needs and limited organizational capabilities exert on productive capacity, to gaps between environmental expectations and organizational outputs that derive from the difficulties of simultaneously satisfying division of labor, integration, and motivational needs.

3. Organizational strain varies in intensity over time. In general, it intensifies as a result of broad societal forces or trends that alter the character and/or impact of the prime components of an organization's functional environment. However, in the case of structural strain the effect may be indirect, rather than direct, and may derive from the intensification of demand strain. In addition, structural strain can intensify as a result of declines in leadership skill or effectiveness.

4. Stress may be conceived as a particular form of strain, as a condition in which strain becomes so intense that it threatens the patterns of accommodation that an organization has established between its domain and its role. Demand stress thus exists when the requirements of role fulfillment are increased so substantially as to create severe discrepancies between existing levels of performance and role expectations. Similarly, structural stress exists when limits on productive capacity increase so substantially that the ability of organizational outputs to meet environmental expectations is seriously impaired.

5. Organizations adapt to stress by expanding productive capacity and/or by altering their domains in ways that reduce the degree of discrepancy between performance and role fulfillment. Expansion in productive capacity hinges on fuller exploitation of organizational capabilities. The basic approaches that can be employed in doing so are shifts in leadership, shifts in structure and work force, and shifts in motivational bases and strategies. Alterations in domain can involve changes in the scope of activity, in products or outputs, and/or in autonomy relative to other units. Success in relieving stress hinges on enhancing environmental satisfaction with organizational performance by altering the character of ouputs and/or by inducing changes in role conceptions.

6. Organizations typically prefer to adapt to stress by expanding productive capacity. However, constraints on internal capabilities limit the range of such action. Changes in domain occur when attempts to expand productive capacity provide inadequate or highly inefficient responses to stress and serve to compensate for deficiencies in the effectiveness of internally oriented forms of adaptation. In integrated environments, however, the relief of stress through domain change is far more difficult to achieve than in competitive environments, since the roles of units are closely regulated and strongly main-

tained by fundamental systemic values. The net result of domain change can thus easily be to increase tension between performance and role expectations rather than to relieve it. Any substantial amount of adaptation through domain change therefore generally requires basic alterations in systemic values and occurs as a consequence of the corrosive effects of gaps in performance on such values.

Applications to Congress

Congressional vulnerability to organizational strain, to gaps in productive capacity relative to role, is substantial.

Demand strain can easily intensify, given the broad and multifaceted nature of Congress's role. Within the limits of the Constitution, Congress is charged with making the basic or determining decisions on governmental policy and with serving as a prime guardian of executive performance. Nor do the broad substantive requirements of Congress's role exhaust its dimensions. Congress not only must determine where collective action is needed and define and control the content of such action, but must also perform these functions through collegial decision making and majority rule. It must, as emphasized earlier, provide for both consent and action. This is no easy task. Indeed, when party cohesion is not strong, the concentrations of influence necessary to bolster integrative capacity threaten majority rule and in so doing create severe disharmonies between Congress's ability to act on behalf of society and its ability to base such action on consent.

Structural strain is also readily subject to intensification. Key aspects of division of labor, integration, and motivational needs inherently conflict, and in the case of Congress these conflicts are exacerbated by the constraints that limit its organizational capabilities. Thus, for example, growth in the number of committee units heightens integrative difficulties, and this is especially true in periods in which party is weak and leadership influence is decentralized. Conversely, increases in the activity and control of party units and leaders involve decreased freedom of action for specialized committees and subcommittees. As for motivation, specialization increases the drudgery of committee work and narrows personal influence; concentrations of influence in party leaders are difficult to legitimize and strip ordinary members of dignity and importance. In sum, then, though Congress could not have survived since 1789 if it did not possess some leeway in balancing or accommodating its internal needs, the amount of leeway it possesses is relatively restricted. As a consequence, internal strains that impair productive capacity can easily intensify when changes occur that heighten some significant aspect of organizational need and/or reduce capabilities in some important regard.

In the twentieth century a number of broad societal trends have combined to intensify the strains endemic to congressional operation and transform them into forms of stress, into conditions of strain so intense that they have shattered the balance between domain and role established by Congress in the nineteenth century.[10] Demand strain has been transformed into demand stress by the huge expansion in the scope of national responsibilities and federal activities since 1901 and especially since 1932. Such expansion has multiplied the qualitative and quantitative burdens of congressional work. It has necessitated far more attention to oversight while simultaneously expanding the range and complexity of formal legislation. It has aggravated the difficulty of balancing the system's need for action and consent both by increasing demands for governmental action and by increasing the number and variety of interests to be accommodated. Similarly, structural strain has been transformed into structural stress. In part, this has occurred because demand stress has increased the dimensions of internal needs and thus has intensified conflicts among them. In large part, however, it has occurred as a consequence of societal trends that have eroded the strength of American parties. Since 1910, attachment to party norms and levels of party cohesion within the Congress have declined substantially.[11] This decline, in turn, has intensified structural strain both directly, through the impairment of integrative capacity, and indirectly, through the deleterious impact of impaired integrative capacity on the satisfaction of other needs.

Congress has sought to adapt to the stress that the conditions of modern government have generated by expanding its productive capacity. Both the House and the Senate have reorganized their committee systems, increased the number and autonomy of subcommittees, and augmented their staff resources. In addition, Congress has tried to protect the integrative capacity it has retained by seeking in various ways to limit the opportunities for minority obstruction that the dispersion of organizational influence since 1910 has created, e.g., enlargement of the Rules Committee, caucus election of chairmen, and so on. Moreover, Congress has substantially increased the salaries and perquisites of members. Nonetheless, the steps taken to aid productive capacity have provided only transitory and limited forms of relief for the stress to which Congress has been subject in this century. As a consequence, Congress has been under steady and intense pressure to redefine its domain, and the amount of domain change that has resulted has in fact been extensive. Such change has involved alterations in product or output goals and in the degree of dependence on executive officers. In the former regard, large and at times even awesome delegations of discretionary authority have been made to presidents and lesser executive officials both in traditional and new areas of policy. Moreover, in some important areas of policy Congress has not even been able to protect its traditional prerogatives from simple aggrandizement by the president. In the latter regard, congressional dependence on executive officials for detailed information, advice, and proposals has substantially increased. So, too, has dependence on the president for program planning and coordination and political muscle, for supplying Congress with the elements of integrative capacity it so sorely lacks.

Such extensive changes in domain have led to important changes in conceptions of Congress's role. The president is now expected to assume an open and leading role in directing the lawmaking process, in defining the main items on Congress's agenda, and in controlling results. Similarly, Congress now expects to vest the president and lesser executive officers with large amounts of discretion and to rely to an increasing extent on forms of action other than legislation to fulfill its policy and performance responsibilities. Conceptions of Congress's role thus have shifted and place far more emphasis on its functions as critic, modifier, and overseer than was true in the nineteenth or even the early twentieth century.

Ironically enough, however, these changes have also failed to stabilize Congress's position in the political system. In part, this is true because the broad societal trends that have intensified strain have persisted and stress has therefore not abated but rather has been continually renewed. In large part, however, Congress's inability to create a new equilibrium between what it actually does and what it is expected to do derives from the strength and impact of the traditional democratic values that define and support its role. Though these values allow some flexibility in reformulating aspects of Congress's relationship to the president and bureaucracy, they cannot cede its substantive and representative primacy. Yet, in fact, many of the changes in domain that have occurred have involved substantial incursions on such primacy. As a result, domain change has to a large degree not relieved the tension between domain and role that stress in the twentieth century has created, but rather has maintained and even increased it. It is not surprising, then, that Congress has been in a continual state of crisis since the 1930s or that it typically enjoys low levels of public support or approval.

All this is not to say that Congress has become a cipher in the American political system or that it will soon become one. Nonetheless, there is little reason to believe that in the decades to come congressional scope and autonomy will not continue to erode, unless modern sources of stress relax and/or the adequacy of congressional performance materially increases. Nor can we expect high levels of tension between actual performance and role expectations to continue indefinitely without having a decisive impact on the character of the American political system. If such tension persists, it will in the long run be relieved by loss of faith in representative government and basic transformations in the nature of our political institutions.

NOTES

1. For a cogent review of the major variants of organization theory, see J. E. Haas and T. E. Drabek, *Complex Organizations: A Sociological Perspective* (New York: Macmillan, 1973), pp. 23–95.

2. Authors whose works have significantly influenced the construction of the framework are Talcott Parsons, George C. Homans, James D. Thompson, Charles B. Perrow, Amitai Etzioni, Peter M. Blau, Herbert A. Simon, James G. March, Fred E. Katz, Joan Woodward, David Easton, James Q. Wilson, and Richard F. Fenno.

3. Aspects of the framework are spelled out in greater detail in Joseph Cooper, "Strengthening the Congress: An Organizational Analysis," *Harvard Journal on Legislation* 12 (1975): 307–68; and Joseph Cooper and David W. Brady, "Organization Theory and Congressional Structure," paper presented at the annual meeting of the American Political Science Association, September 1973. For other works applying organization theory to Congress, see Lewis A. Froman, "Organization Theory and the Explanation of Important Characteristics of Congress," *American Political Science Review* 62 (1968): 518–27; and Roger H. Davidson and Walter J. Oleszek, "Adaptation and Consolidation: Structural Innovation in the U.S. House of Representatives," *Legislative Studies Quarterly* 1 (1976): 37–65.

4. For the purposes of this paper, power may be conceived in general terms as the ability to direct or control the behavior of others. Brief surveys of major approaches to the concepts of power, authority, and influence may be found in *International Encyclopedia of the Social Sciences* (New York: Macmillan, 1968).

5. For insightful discussion of the various types of inducements and their significance, see Talcott Parsons, *Politics and Social Structure* (New York: Free Press, 1969); Amitai Etzioni, *A Comparative Analysis of Complex Organizations* (New York: Free Press, 1961); and James Q. Wilson, *Political Organizations* (New York: Basic Books, 1973).

6. Lewis A. Froman, *The Congressional Process: Strategies, Rules and Procedures* (Boston: Little, Brown, 1967).
7. Richard F. Fenno, "The Internal Distribution of Influence," in D. B. Truman, ed., *The Congress and America's Future* (Englewood Cliffs, N.J.: Prentice-Hall, 1965); and Robert L. Peabody, *Leadership in Congress: Stability, Succession and Change* (Boston: Little, Brown, 1976).
8. Nelson W. Polsby, *Congress and the Presidency*, 3rd ed. (Englewood Cliffs, N.J.: Prentice-Hall, 1976).
9. Joseph Cooper, "The Origins of the Standing Committees and the Development of the Modern House," *Rice University Studies* 56 (1970): 1–167; and David W. Brady, *Congressional Voting in a Partisan Era* (Lawrence: University of Kansas Press, 1973). In addition, see Randall B. Ripley, *Power in the Senate* (New York: St. Martin's, 1969), and *Congress: Process and Policy* (New York: Norton, 1975).
10. Samuel P. Huntington, "Congressional Responses to the Twentieth Century," in Truman, op. cit.; and Davidson and Oleszek, op. cit.
11. Brady, op. cit.; and Julius Turner, *Party and Constituency: Pressures on Congress*, rev. ed. by Edward V. Scheier (Baltimore: Johns Hopkins Press, 1970).

III

CONGRESS,
THE EXECUTIVE,
AND PUBLIC POLICY

8. The New Congressional Budget Process: The Hows and Whys of House-Senate Differences

John W. Ellwood and James A. Thurber

In 1974 Congress initiated the most wide-ranging budget reform since the passage of the Budget and Accounting Act of 1921. The nature and implementation of this new congressional budget process raise a number of interesting issues that should be of concern to students of the Congress.[1] There is an intrinsic interest in the process itself. How does it work? What are the new institutions created by the reform? What are the new requirements imposed on traditional units of Congress and the executive branch? There are also basic questions related to enactment of the reform. Why was it enacted? Where did the support for the new budget process come from?

Beyond this intrinsic interest, however, a study of the implementation of the new budget process can shed light on some fascinating questions. How does the new budget process seem to be working? Will the new process lead to changes in congressional behavior and ultimately in congressional spending policy?

The new budget process affects just about every existing unit of Congress. The procedures call for modification of the behavior patterns of appropriations committees, revenue committees, and author-

AUTHORS' NOTE: The views expressed in this paper are those of the authors and should not be attributed to the Congressional Budget Office nor to the Temporary Select Committee to Study the Senate Committee System.

izing committees, as well as party leadership. This development will necessarily cause modifications of the power relationships among the preexisting institutions as they in turn modify their behavior to take account of the new process and institutions. Therefore, the new budget process also presents the student of Congress with a case study that will be useful in determining (1) what changes in power relationships take place among existing units of the House and the Senate, (2) how existing units of Congress modify their behavior to take account of new units and the requirements of a new process, and (3) how a new committee seeks to build its own power base within a preexisting legislative body.

The new process is also of special interest to students of House and Senate committees. The budget committee is unique among major committees of the House because twelve of its twenty-five membership slots must be filled by congressmen from specific committees or leadership positions and because it alone among major House committees has a rotating membership. In the House the behavior pattern associated with the new budget process during the first year and a half of its existence was so different from that of the Senate, as well as from usual House patterns, as to warrant serious attention.

Because the new process has been under way for only a year and a half, the data base upon which each of these questions is to be judged is extremely thin. However, the pattern of behavior of each of the new institutions created or affected by the process has been so consistent as to give us some courage.

This chapter is divided into five sections: a description of reasons for the enactment of the new process, a review of how the new process works, a history of the first year and a half of the implementation of the process, an examination of the differences between how the new process has worked in the House and in the Senate, and a tentative explanation of these differences.

Reasons for Enactment

The Budget and Impoundment Control Act of 1974 took only two years to work its way through the legislative process. This is a remarkably short period for such a sweeping and complex piece of legislation. Its final passage was accomplished by the overwhelming majorities of 75 to 0 in the Senate and 401 to 6 in the House. This quick and overwhelming passage reflected the power of the forces and factors that had coalesced behind such a reform in the early 1970s.

Traditionally, the history of budgeting in Congress was that of war between the parts and the whole.[2] Each year, Congress would take the president's total budget, chop it up into many small pieces, and parcel it out among many committees and subcommittees. Each committee or subcommittee would work on its own piece with little regard for the impact the changes might have on the total. Indeed, few within Congress were even aware of the emerging totals.

Evidence of the prereform approach to congressional budget making was found in the scattered jurisdictions for various spending programs. While the executive branch experienced a series of reforms designed to concentrate policy- and budget-making authority in a central office—formerly the Bureau of the Budget and now the Office of Management and Budget—the congressional budgetary process became merely the sum of a series of isolated, competing, and unrelated actions. Even the many appropriations subcommittees could claim annual authority over only 44 percent of all federal expenditures.[3] Large entitlements, such as social security expenditures, were controlled by the tax-writing committees. Authorizing committees also gained control over large sums by granting agencies the authority to contract in advance of appropriations or to borrow from the public. This process was found wanting by different groups for the following reasons.

Fear of Rise in Spending and Deficits

Conservatives, joined by increasing numbers of moderates and liberals, were alarmed by the rapid growth of federal spending and the ever-increasing number and size of deficits. Since 1956, federal outlays had increased more than 500 percent, rising from $70.5 billion in fiscal year 1956 to $394.2 billion for the current fiscal year. Even in constant dollars, federal spending had more than doubled. At the same time, the federal government had run a deficit in sixteen out of the twenty years. The total federal debt, while declining as a percentage of the gross national product, had increased by about $350 billion.

Large segments of the public and Congress became increasingly upset. These groups advocated and supported the new process so that spending could be limited. They frequently referred to the fact that federal spending was "out of control," by which they meant that there was no way to limit or decrease it.

Lack of Control in the Appropriations Process

Budget control, of course, can have another meaning besides the ability to limit or decrease spending. One can speak of the congressional budget process being out of control in the sense that Congress finds itself without the mechanisms to work its budgetary will through the appropriations process, regardless of whether that will is in the direction of decreased or increased federal expenditures.

Used in this sense, the lack of congressional control was evidenced by the increasing percentage of expenditures that could not be altered without changing the basic authorizing statute, by the fact that less than half of the budget was subject to annual appropriations, and by the inability of Congress to meet its own budgetary deadlines.

Before the reform, about 75 percent of the budget was considered "relatively uncontrollable under existing law," [4] and, because of backdoor spending measures, only about 44 percent of the budget in fiscal 1974 could be directly controlled by the appropriations committees on an annual basis. The rise in permanent budget authority (resulting in most part from the various forms of backdoor spending) led to a diminished relationship between congressional budgetary decisions in any given year and the actual outlays of that year.

This inability to control large amounts of federal spending was exacerbated by the timing of budgetary decisions. Appropriations bills were rarely completed by the beginning of the fiscal year, causing many federal agencies to operate on continuing resolutions. Before the new process, not one appropriation bill since 1968 was enacted before the beginning of the fiscal year. In fact, the Labor-HEW appropriations bill for fiscal 1973 was never completed. Supporters of reform in this area sought to impose deadlines and jurisdictional limitations that would increase the power of the appropriations committees and at the same time force them to meet deadlines as to when bills would be reported out.

Need to Control Priorities

Since World War II, Congress, except in a few instances, has been able to avoid making difficult priority choices. The rapid growth of the economy has allowed it to resolve conflicts between competing interests by giving most parties larger amounts, if not larger percentages, of the federal budget. This is not to say that the old congressional budgetary process was not able to change priorities. In fact, over the last twenty years, the percentages of the budget allotted to defense and to aid to individuals have roughly reversed. However, the reduction in defense spending (as a percentage of the budget) was accomplished without reducing the amount of money being spent on national security.

As political and economic factors eliminated the "fiscal dividend" that had been promised for the 1970s, it became clear that hard either/or choices would have to be made between programs. These would be choices that could not be resolved by increasing the size of the pie. Those who saw this future felt that congressional budgetary reform was needed in order to unify the disaggregated budgetary process and to create a mechanism for making the hard priority choices.

Need to Control Fiscal Policy

Because the traditional budgetary process involved a series of isolated, unrelated decisions, Congress had no mechanism through which it could set fiscal policy—that is, the proper level of economic stimulus or restraint that should be exercised through the federal budget.

Some members, mostly conservatives, felt that if congressmen and senators were forced to vote on the deficit or surplus, the tendency toward larger and larger deficits would be reversed. To this extent, they saw the vote not as a way to exercise fiscal policy but as a means to limit spending. Other members, however, saw a need for a vote on the overall deficit or surplus so that Congress would have the capability to challenge the executive branch's dominance of the setting of fiscal policy.

Need to Reassert Institutional Authority—Information

Congress's lack of budgetary information was widely perceived. Since the Office of Management and Budget—part of the executive office of the president—was the only federal budget body, Congress was frequently forced to rely on the president for the information needed to review and oversee the president's budget. Naturally, presidents of both political parties tended to forward information favorable to their policy choices and priorities.

It became a frequently mentioned axiom among members that Congress would never be able to assert its proper budgetary role unless it could begin to right the imbalance of information and expertise that existed in favor of the executive branch. Many supporters of reform felt that the creation of new institutions that specialized in budgetary matters would bring this about.

Need to Reassert Institutional Authority—Impoundment

Fresh from his landslide reelection in 1972, President Nixon decided to launch a public relations campaign to reduce the growth of federal spending and to assert his own budgetary priorities by branding Congress as "fiscally irresponsible." Being only partially successful in reducing spending through his recommendations and the use of the veto, Nixon attempted to increase his power by expanding his use of impoundment—the refusal to spend funds provided by Congress.

Nixon's use of impoundment began early in his administration but intensified in November 1972 with the impoundment of $9 billion in clean-water funds and in December of that year with the termination of many agricultural programs. In January 1973 the fiscal 1974 budget was presented; it contained an eight-page table listing program reductions the president planned to make. Only 6 of 109 items were listed as requiring congressional approval; other changes were to be made by presidential fiat. An examination one year later showed that the president had been able to achieve most of his stated reductions.[5]

This unprecedented use of impoundment was a constitutional as well as a political challenge to Congress. By challenging Congress's institutional integrity, Nixon created a coalition supporting budget reform made up of those who wanted to reassert legislative authority over budget making and those who simply opposed his economic policies. This coalition not only advocated budget reform to help check the power of the presidency and to help reassert Congress's constitutional power of the purse, but also supported reform to refute Nixon's claim that Congress was fiscally irresponsible.

The stage for congressional budget reform was set when different groups in Congress felt it was in their best interest to change the status quo. Along issue lines, conservatives sought a new institutional system that would force the membership to limit the growth of federal spending and balance the budget. Members of the appropriations committees sought a new system that would increase the percentage of the budget that would be under their control. Members, in general, sought a new system that would reinstitute the power of the Congress over spending. Long-term academic advocates of congressional budget reform, through their allies on the Hill, sought a system that would give Congress a means to make priority decisions and set fiscal policy. Finally, Democrats, reacting to the Nixon administration's economic policies and the increasing use of impoundment to frustrate congressional will, supported the reform. It gave them a means to reassert their policies; furthermore, failure to do so would have been politically damaging.

This broad-based coalition of support meant that:

1.   Both conservatives who wanted to cut spending and liberal Democrats who wanted to increase spending and change priorities saw the reform as a means to achieve their ends.

2. Both members of the appropriations and revenue committees, who wanted to limit backdoor and uncontrollable spending, and liberal Democrats, who tended to be on the very legislative committees that would be most hurt through such control, supported the reform.

3. The reform was supported by members who saw the elimination of backdoor and uncontrollable spending as a first step toward allowing greater short-term congressional control over the budget, and by members who felt that the only way to achieve congressional budget control was some form of forward planning and/or advanced budgeting.

Thus, given the conflicting expectations that led to passage of budget reform, one could expect the long-term acceptance of the new budget process to be very difficult.

Congressional Response: Characteristics of the Budget and Impoundment Control Act

The congressional response to these internal and external pressures for reform was the Budget and Impoundment Control Act of 1974 (P.L. 93-344), which was signed into law on July 19, 1974. The reform movement started in earnest in 1972 with the creation of the Joint Study Committee on Budget, which was charged with examining the budgetary process for the purpose of improving decision-making procedures. Most of the work on the final legislation was done in late 1973 and early 1974.

The budget reform that emerged was an overlay to the old budgetary process; the existing structure of Congress was not altered. The reform created new House and Senate budget committees, the Congressional Budget Office (a full-time professional staff for analytical studies), a complex set of budgetary procedures, a timetable for budgetary actions, a change in the fiscal year, requirements for standardized budget terminology and information for the president's budget, and provisions for controlling presidential impoundments.

Committees

The new House and Senate budget committees have many similarities and some significant differences. Each must report at least two concurrent resolutions on the budget each year, analyze the impact of existing and proposed programs on budgetary outlays, and oversee the operations of the Congressional Budget Office. Thus, in terms of statutory authority, the two committees are basically the same.

The differences between the committees are in terms of the nature and tenure of their membership. The 16 members of the Senate Budget Committee (SBC) are selected in the same manner as are members of other Senate committees—by the Democratic and Republican conferences. Membership is not restricted in any way, and tenure on the committee is not limited. The Senate rule that a member can serve on only two major committees has been waived until the start of the 95th Congress.

The House Budget Committee (HBC) has 25 members. Under the present division of the House, 17 are Democrats and 8 are Republicans. Twelve out of the 25 membership positions on the committee are restricted in that 5 members have to be drawn from the House Appropriations Committee (3 Democrats and 2 Republicans), an additional 5 members from the Ways and Means Committee (with the same party split), and 2 members from the respective party leaderships.[6]

The tenure of the members of the House Budget Committee is also restricted in that no member may serve for more than four years out of any ten-year period. At present, all 8 Republicans are in the second year of their four-year terms. However, on the Democratic side, in order to maintain some continuity of committee membership, 9 out of 17 Democratic members are serving the last year of a two-year term. Thus, in the future, the four-year terms of the Democratic members will be staggered.

Committee Staff

The staff of the House Budget Committee consists of approximately 40 professionals and 25 support personnel. Because of the rotating nature of committee membership, an early decision was made by the committee's first chairman, Al Ullman, and its first staff director, Walter Kravitz, to hire a staff with a great deal of programmatic expertise. As a consequence, the staff of the House Budget Committee initially had a relatively small amount of Hill experience. In addition, the lack of subcommittee staff and the small size of the partisan core staff has meant that committee members have had to rely on the core staff for support.[7]

The Senate Budget Committee has a larger staff than its House counterpart. In all, its staff consists of approximately 55 professionals and 30 support personnel. However, under the Senate arrangement, each member of the committee is allowed to hire two staff persons—

one professional and one support. Thus, the core staff consists of approximately 34 professionals and 15 support personnel.

As compared to their counterparts on the HBC, the staff of the SBC has had less programmatic and budgetary but more political experience. They also tend to be younger. In this, they follow the traditional House/Senate staffing patterns.[8]

Analytic Support

In addition to the quality of their staffs, the performance of the budget committees will depend, in part, on their support from the third element of the new budgetary triad, the Congressional Budget Office (CBO). The CBO is the major analytical and informational component of the budget reform. Its first director, Dr. Alice M. Rivlin, has been appointed to a four-year term by the Speaker of the House and the president pro tem of the Senate, upon the recommendations of the two budget committees. The CBO has been given broad, analytic responsibilities. These fall into three general categories: (1) monitoring the economy and estimating its impact on the budget, (2) improving the flow and quality of budgetary information, and (3) analyzing the costs and effects of alternative budgetary choices.

New Process Timetable

The new congressional budgetary process sets October 1 as the beginning of the fiscal year. On November 10 the president must submit a current services budget, and on the fifteenth day after Congress meets he must submit his budget.[9] Congress must adopt at least two concurrent resolutions: one on or before May 15 (before revenue and expenditures bills have been passed) and the other by September 15 (after action has been taken on all appropriations bills). (See Table 1.)

It is possible to break this timetable down into four general stages:

STAGE 1. Information gathering, analysis, preparation, and submission of congressional budget by Congressional Budget Office and budget committees (November 10 to April 15)
STAGE 2. Debate on and adoption of congressional budget by both Houses; establishment of national spending priorities (April 15 to May 15)
STAGE 3. Enactment of spending bills (May 15 to early September)
STAGE 4. Reassessment of spending, revenue, and debt requirements

Table 1. Congressional Budget Timetable

Deadline	Action to Be Completed
November 10	Current services budget received
January 18 *	President's budget received
March 15	Advice and data from all congressional committees to budget committees
April 1	CBO reports to budget committees
April 15	Budget committees report out first budget resolution
May 15	Congressional committees report new authorizing legislation
May 15	Congress completes action on first budget resolution
Labor Day +7 †	Congress completes action on all spending bills
September 15	Congress completes action on second budget resolution
September 25	Congress completes action on reconciliation bill
October 1	Fiscal year begins

* Or fifteen days after Congress convenes.
† Seven days after Labor Day.
SOURCE: U.S. Congress, Senate, Committee on the Budget, *Congressional Budget Reform*, 93d Cong., 2nd sess., March 4, 1975, p. 70.

in second budget resolution; enactment of reconciliation bill (September 15 to September 25)

The objectives of this elaborate timetable consist of the following:

1. *To set targets and ceilings.*   The aggregate totals of the first concurrent resolution will establish expenditures and revenue targets in the spring. During the summer the budget committees, with the analytic support of CBO, will use their influence to see to it that the traditional appropriations, authorization, and revenue processes stay within these targets. In the fall a second concurrent resolution will set a ceiling for expenditures and a floor under revenues. This second resolution must be reconciled with the reality of the summer's congressional budgetary activity. Once this reconciliation process has been completed—and it must be completed before Congress is allowed to

adjourn—any bill that exceeds the expenditure ceilings or revenue floor will be subject to a point of order when brought up for consideration.

2. *To allow for priority choices.* The first and second concurrent resolutions will also contain first targets and then ceilings for each of the functional categories of the budget. As such they will provide a mechanism for Congress to choose between different types of activities in an either/or format.

3. *To allow for the setting of fiscal policy.* Through each concurrent resolution, Congress will vote on a proper level of budget authority outlays, revenues, and the resulting deficit or surplus. Thus, the resolutions will give Congress a mechanism for setting what it feels is the proper degree of fiscal stimulus or restraint.

4. *To limit the growth of uncontrollable and/or backdoor spending.* Although all current programs are exempted (grandfathered) and future changes in several programs—such as social security—are exempted, the budget reform does have provisions that prohibit the creation of future or the expansion of many present forms of backdoor spending.

5. *To limit presidential impoundment power.* The new process classifies impoundments into two categories—deferrals and rescissions—and establishes procedures to control them. The president can defer the spending of appropriated funds until the end of the fiscal year *unless* either house, by a majority vote, passes an impoundment resolution. Deferrals are supposed to be made on the grounds that the funds need not be spent to achieve congressional intent. If, however, the president desires to change congressional intent by not spending appropriated funds, he must submit a rescission bill that must achieve majorities in *both* houses within forty-five days. The comptroller general is given the authority to go to court if he feels that the president is deferring funds that should be rescinded and/or if the president does not spend funds that have been supported by a rejection of a rescission bill.

6. *To assure that all regular budget bills are passed before the start of the fiscal year to which they apply.* By beginning the consideration of the budget in November with the release of the president's current services budget, and by shifting the start of the fiscal year from July 1 to October 1, Congress will have almost eleven months in which to work on the budget before the new fiscal year. These changes, combined with a series of deadlines, could decrease the need for continuing resolutions.

Implementation of the Reform

Passage of the Resolutions

Because of the breadth of the coalition that supported the passage of the Budget and Impoundment Control Act of 1974, different supporters expected different outcomes from its success.[10] However, there is one necessary condition that has to be achieved for any of the expectations to be fulfilled: Congress has to pass a minimum of two concurrent resolutions on the budget each year.

One should not belittle the difficulty in achieving this minimal requirement. The very passage of these resolutions requires that Congress do that which it is least successful at accomplishing— aggregating interests and making the tough trade-offs between competing programs. The last time Congress attempted a unified budget process—as part of the Legislative Reform Act of 1946—the two houses could not agree on the same set of priorities, and the reform failed.[11]

So far, the prime achievement of the new budget process is that Congress has been able to pass concurrent resolutions. It has set targets through two first concurrent resolutions, it has been fairly successful in staying within those targets, and it has set ceilings for expenditures and floors for revenues by passing two second concurrent resolutions.

The first two resolutions ever attempted under the new process barely passed. Significantly, the crisis occurred in the House. First, on April 8, 1975, at the close of its mark-up of the first concurrent resolution, the House Budget Committee failed by an 11–13 vote to adopt its own resolution. The committee was only able to report out a resolution when Republican representatives Barber Conable (R-N.Y.) and Elford Cederberg (R-Mich.) switched their votes in order to let the process have a chance to go through its trial year.[12]

The first vote in committee set the pattern that was to make the passage of budget resolutions in the House one of the most interesting battles in Congress. Republican voting was characterized by extreme partisanship, with none of the committee's Republican members (with the exception of Conable and Cederberg) supporting the resolution. The Democratic side saw negative votes being cast by liberals, such as Representative Elizabeth Holtzman (N.Y.), who felt that the budget resolution did not contain enough stimulus to get the nation out of its economic recession, and by conservatives, such as representatives Omar Burleson (D-Tex.), Butler Derrick (D-S.C.), and Phil Landrum (D-Ga.), who felt that the deficit was just too large.[13]

A similar close vote occurred on the final House passage of the resolution. The May 1 vote for final passage carried by only four votes:

200 to 196. According to Chairman Brock Adams (D-Wash.) and Staff Director Walter Kravitz, it was impossible to create a plurality coalition for any given set of budget totals.[14] It became clear that if the process was to stay alive through its first year, it would be from support of the process rather than the content of the resolutions.

This same pattern was repeated during House floor action on the second concurrent resolution. On November 12, the House amended the committee's resolution by increasing budget authority by $7.5 billion and outlays by $1.0 billion. This so-called O'Neill amendment had to be passed if the resolution was to get the needed liberal support for final passage. It passed by a vote of 213 to 203. The 10-vote margin is deceiving because, when the clock ran out, the amendment had failed by a vote of 207 to 208. Normal procedure calls for the Speaker—or, in this case, the chairman of the Committee of the Whole—to ask members if they want to change their vote. This process usually takes a minute or so. In this case, Chairman Richard Bolling continued to ask members if they wanted to change their votes until the leadership had enough time to work the floor to get the required number of members to switch in order to ensure passage.[15] Once again, in a very crucial vote, the resolution was supported because of loyalty to the new process (in this case, leadership loyalty) rather than agreement with its content.

The final instance of this pattern occurred on December 12 with the vote on the acceptance of the conference report on the second concurrent resolution. The 2-vote margin of victory in the 189–187 vote is somewhat misleading in that the roll call was taken on a Friday, when many of the supporters of the resolution were out of town or otherwise unable to vote. In any case, this close vote reinforced the perception by the members and staff of the House Budget Committee that it would be extremely difficult to pass first and second concurrent resolutions during the second year of the new budget process.

Actually, this was not the case. On April 29, 1976, the House easily passed a first concurrent resolution on the budget for fiscal year 1977. Gains in support of the resolution were achieved among major party groups with significant improvements in support from liberal Democrats and Republicans and from moderate southern Democrats. Thus, there appears to be some evidence that the new process is becoming institutionalized in the House. However, the degree of partisan voting—both in the budget committee and on the floor—is still very high in the House. The data in Table 2 clearly demonstrate the extremely high degree of party cohesion among House Republicans.[16]

But not only are House Republicans more cohesive than their Senate counterparts, they also are more cohesive than House Republicans have traditionally been over time. Julius Turner and Edward

Table 2. Party Cohesion Scores for Floor Roll Calls in Which Parties Were in Opposition and for Budget Committee Votes to Report Out Concurrent Resolution

	94TH CONGRESS, 1ST SESSION		94TH CONGRESS, 2ND SESSION		94TH CONGRESS, 1ST AND 2ND SESSIONS, COMMITTEE VOTES	
	House	*Senate*	*House*	*Senate*	*House*	*Senate*
Republicans	81.4	13.9	73.5	14.5	83.3	33.3
Democrats	52.3	77.3	54.1	50.5	59.6	100.0
	(N=9)	(N=4)	(N=7)	(N=3)	(N=6)	(N=3)

NOTE: The number of votes used to compute each average cohesion score is shown in parentheses at the bottom of each column.

Schneier present cohesion data that indicate that in fourteen selected congressional sessions from 1921 through 1967, House Republicans' cohesion averaged 67.2.[17] This is quite low compared with the average cohesion scores of 81.4, 73.5, and 83.3 amassed by House Republicans in their voting on budget resolutions.

The difference between the voting patterns in the Senate and in the House is to be found in these differing cohesion patterns. In the House, supporters of the budget resolutions are faced with almost solid Republican opposition. Thus, to obtain passage, they need overwhelming Democratic support. Yet almost a fifth of House Democrats voted against the resolutions either because they were insufficiently stimulative or because they called for too large a deficit.

In the Senate, on the other hand, both resolutions have received a plurality of Republican votes. In addition, the resolutions in the Senate have received the same (if not higher) levels of Democratic support as they have in the House. This has led to a pattern of bipartisan support for the resolutions in the Senate.

Conflicts among Committees

As previously explained, in order to build a broad coalition supporting passage of the reform, the new budget process was laid on top of the old procedure. The aim was to convince as many members as possible that the new process would lead to a maximum number of winners and a minimum number of losers. Thus, the appropriations, revenue, and legislative committees all were led to believe that the new process would be beneficial to their interests.

However, with the establishment of a new committee in each house, conflicts were bound to arise between the new budget committees and the preexisting committees. This is because, at the beginning of their existence, the new budget committees lacked power. During the first year and a half of the new process, both budget committees attempted to increase their power. The fact that they sought to build their power in differing ways tells us much about the differing nature of the two committees.

The Senate Budget Committee has gone out of its way to challenge the appropriations, authorizing, and revenue committees of the Senate. A number of instances stand out. First, early in its existence, the Senate Budget Committee demanded—and got from the Democratic caucus—the right to have joint jurisdiction with the Senate Appropriations Committee over rescissions and deferrals (the means for dealing with impoundments under the Budget and Impoundment Control Act). The comparative advantage to the Senate Budget Committee in this action was quite small. Yet Chairman Muskie and his fellow committee members acted because they wanted, early in the development of the new budget process, to assert the authority of their committee. No similar action has yet been taken by the House Budget Committee.

Second, Senator Muskie and his colleagues, unlike the members of the House Budget Committee, actively sought to enforce the targets of the first concurrent resolution by opposing legislation on the floor of the Senate. In contrast, Chairman Adams tried to enforce his targets through persuasion before legislation actually got to the House floor. It is true that differing procedures in the House and the Senate tend to dictate these strategies. But it is also true that, by successfully challenging the legislation of other committees on the Senate floor, the Senate Budget Committee expanded its own power in the Senate.

These two approaches are reflected in other areas: the two committees' differing attitudes toward authorizing committees, toward revenue committees, and toward the proper format of the "scorekeeping" reports that determine when a particular target will be, or is being, broken.

On several occasions the Senate Budget Committee has gone out of its way to assert its authority on budgetary matters. During the summer of 1975 the committee successfully challenged two conference reports on the Senate floor. Their argument was that, although the cost of the original Senate bill that went into the conference was within the targets of the first concurrent resolution for fiscal 1976, the compromise conference report that came out clearly exceeded those targets. The most notable of these cases took place on August 1, when the Senate sent the Military Construction Authorization Bill back to conference by a 48–42 vote. Similar action was taken in early September on the School Lunch Authorization Bill.

Two important facts should be kept in mind. First, the Senate Budget Committee was successful in this effort only because four Republican members (two-thirds of the Republican members of the committee), who under normal circumstances would vote in favor of higher defense spending, chose in this case to support the new budget process and their committee's actions. This presents a clear example in which committee members see an advantage to themselves in supporting the position of their committee and the process it represents. Such a case has yet to occur in the House.

Second, and of equal import, was the frequently overlooked fact that the two bills that the Senate Budget Committee chose to challenge in the summer of 1975 were both authorization bills. One would normally expect the budget committees to enforce the targets of the first concurrent resolution primarily on appropriations bills. Yet it is the position of Senators Muskie and Bellmon that the new budget committees and the new process cannot gain control over the budget unless and until authorizations are brought under congressional control. Thus, although it was very difficult to show exactly how a slightly higher military construction authorization level would lead to the breaking of the expenditure targets during the 1976 fiscal year over which the first concurrent resolution had control, Senators Muskie and Bellmon specifically chose this as the battle ground where they wanted to make their stand.

The actions of the members of the House Budget Committee have been in the exact opposite direction; extreme deference has been shown to the authorizing committees of the House. The best example of this approach occurred during the conference on the fiscal year 1976 second concurrent resolution. The Senate conferees wanted to place ceilings on expenditures for the three-month transition period that would result as the federal government switched the beginning of its fiscal year from July 1 to October 1. In doing so, the Senate conferees wanted to prevent the House Public Works Committee from authorizing a large sum of budget authority for the federal highway program during this "transition quarter." Although a programmatic issue—the proper method of forward-funding the highway program—was also involved, a clear distinction developed within the conference over whether the new budget process gave the budget committees the power to enforce their will over the authorizing committees. The following exchange between Representative Jim Wright (D-Tex.) and Senator Frank Moss (D-Utah) clearly focuses the issue:

WRIGHT: The Senate position presumes a change in existing law. If that comes about through the appropriate committees and actions of the House and Senate, fine. But we take the position that the Budget Com-

mittee has not got any business putting those committees and the House
and Senate in a straight jacket saying you have to change that law and
resolve it according to the Senate [Public Works] committee's decision.
Now, we think that would prejudice the rights of our House committee. . . .

Moss: Well, that is what I object to. I reject entirely what you have to say. I
think our process that we went through already on 76, if that is preju-
dicing a committee, we did the same thing. When we came to military
[authorizations] the conference report came back, both Houses agreed to
it, we in the Senate rejected it. . . .

WRIGHT: Why in the hell set a ceiling that you know is going to breach what
they have in committee?

Moss: If they breach it we will have to do the same thing. Send it back. . . .

WRIGHT: If the budget committee assumes that right, Ted, do you understand
what is involved? It is not a matter of what will be expected? It is man-
dating them to change a law that they have apparently liked because it
has been on the books all these years, 20 years.

Moss: It may be that the budget act is going to mandate a great many things.
We hope it is, because we hope finally to get control of the budget
ceilings here and have a target and mandate back to all of those authorizing committees as well as the Appropriations Committee certain ceilings they have to observe. That is the whole purpose of the law.[18]

This insistence on the part of the House conferees to "keep the
faith" with their authorizing committees is repeated throughout the
conference. It is also frequently stated by members of the House
Budget Committee in their own committee deliberations.[19]

There are advantages and disadvantages to each committee's
power-building strategy. As we will show, the House Budget Committee's reliance on a behind-the-scenes persuasion strategy is in
many ways mandated by the unique nature of its membership. The
strategy follows partly from the nature of the House. It also follows
from the fact that the House Budget Committee, because of its mandated and rotating membership, will have to continually seek allies
among the major power units of the House.

The Senate Budget Committee's confrontation strategy is based on
an attempt to increase its power vis-à-vis that of other Senate committees. But such a bold strategy, while allowing for the possibility of
great success, can also lead to great failure. In its early confrontations
with the appropriations and authorizing committees, the Senate
Budget Committee appeared to be at least a marginal, if not an outright, winner. In July of 1976, however, it chose to challenge Senator
Russell Long (D-La.) and the Senate Finance Committee over the con-
tents of the Tax Reform Act of that year. In this conflict, the budget
committee came out at least a marginal loser.

The central question in the conflict was whether the tax bill should be modified to comply with the revenue assumptions made in the fiscal year 1977 first concurrent resolution. That resolution had called for a revenue target of $362.5 billion. However, in a report accompanying the resolution, the budget committees stated that they assumed that the $362.5 billion target would be met through a $2 billion increase resulting from tax reform. The tax bill that was reported out of the Senate Finance Committee not only failed to raise the $2 billion, but actually called for additional revenue losses through additional tax expenditures.[20] Thus, the two committees came into conflict over whether the budget resolutions could mandate not only the amount of revenue to be raised but also, to some extent, the manner of raising that revenue.

The technical arguments between Senators Muskie and Long are too arcane for this discussion. However, the important point is that the Senate upheld Senator Long's position when Senators Muskie and Bellmon attempted to modify the tax bill to make it comply with the Senate Budget Committee's assumptions.[21] The SBC lost this confrontation because, unlike in its previous confrontations with authorizing committees, it failed to gain the support of its Republican members and it faced the overwhelming opposition of other committee chairmen, who appeared to see this as a test case of the budget committee's power to mandate action to other committees.[22]

The contrasting House and Senate strategies were also reflected in differing views of how best to "keep score," i.e., to determine whether the action of the House or the Senate had broken or would break the targets of the first concurrent resolution.

The Senate Budget Committee, seeking to act as a positive restraint on expenditures, emphasized the degree to which the Senate would exceed the targets *if all* the bills floating around the Senate were to be passed. The House Budget Committee, seeking not to offend the Democratic majority that had passed the budget resolution, chose to stress the amount between what had already been passed and what the targets would allow. Thus, while the Senate Budget Committee focused on the probability of exceeding the targets, the House Budget Committee told the Democrats of the House that they had additional funds to appropriate before the targets would be broken.

In addition, the Senate Budget Committee wanted to emphasize the influence of authorization bills on spending levels. Therefore, the Senate Budget Committee wanted to include proposed authorizations in the scorekeeping reports. The House Budget Committee chose to keep score largely on the basis of appropriations bills. Again, we have an example of the House Budget Committee wanting to "keep faith" with their authorizing committees.

Differences between the Budget Committees

In most ways the two budget committees are alike. Their jurisdictions and legislative requirements are identical. Each committee's function is to report out at least two concurrent resolutions on the budget each year. In addition, each committee monitors the actions of its house to determine whether first the targets and then the ceilings and floors of the resolutions are about to be breached. Finally, each committee is equally involved in the provisions of the budget process that relate to the controlling of new "backdoor spending" and the regulation of impoundments.

Yet, given these similarities, what strikes the observer is the degree to which the two budget committees have gone about their business in differing ways. This, in turn, has meant that the Senate and the House have approached the new budget process in very different ways. Examples can be found in the areas of degree of partisanship, power-building strategy, and decision-making process.

Partisanship

Within the Senate Budget Committee and on the Senate floor, budget resolutions have received bipartisan support, whereas voting on the resolutions in the House Budget Committee and on the House floor has been extremely partisan. This is particularly true for House Republicans, whose party cohesion scores are at record levels when voting on concurrent resolutions.

Power-Building Strategy

The Senate Budget Committee has sought to exercise its will through confrontations on the floor of the Senate. Chairman Muskie and ranking minority member Bellmon have followed an aggressive strategy of opposing legislation on the floor of the Senate that they feel is not included within the targets, ceilings, and floors of the resolutions.

On the other hand, Chairman Adams of the House Budget Committee has avoided floor confrontations. Rather, he has sought to meet with committee chairmen informally when he and the House Budget Committee felt that a particular piece of legislation was not included in a resolution. This cautious strategy is a reflection of the desire on the part of House Budget Committee members to avoid dictating actions to other House committees. Most often this caution is expressed in a desire not to "break faith" with the other committees—particularly the authorizing committees—of the House.

The Decision-Making Process in Committee

The two budget committees have followed very different decision-making processes in putting together their concurrent resolutions. *First*, it is important to remember that, in an effort to avoid jurisdictional conflict between the budget and appropriations committees, the new budget process called for the targets and ceilings of the concurrent resolutions to be applied to sixteen functional categories of the budget.[23] Thus, while the appropriations committees set budget authority for approximately 1,250 appropriations accounts, the budget resolutions were to operate at a much higher level of aggregation.

But in order to determine whether a given bill will exceed a target, it is necessary for the budget committees to have some idea of the specific make-up of what is included in each functional category. This creates a quandary: the budget committees, in order to avoid jurisdictional conflict with the appropriations committees, must operate at a high level of aggregation, but that high level of aggregation makes it almost impossible for them to monitor legislation to determine whether the targets are about to be broken.

The House Budget Committee has chosen to put together budget resolutions at a very low level of aggregation—with a few exceptions at the appropriations account level. On the other hand, the Senate Budget Committee has operated at a much higher level of aggregation. During mark-ups, members of the Senate Budget Committee frequently suggest spending levels for an entire function without supplying information as to how much each program within that function will receive. This leads to the *second* major difference in the decision-making process of the two committees: the use of chairman's mark by the House Budget Committee.

So far, Chairman Adams has presented a suggested budget resolution—called a chairman's mark—as a starting point for committee debate at each mark-up. His chairman's mark is very specific. It consists of the president's budget level for each function and any changes recommended by Adams. Because Adams's changes are mostly at the appropriations account level, it is possible to create an appropriations account–level budget from the chairman's mark. Amendments to the chairman's mark within the House Budget Committee are also made at the appropriations account level. Thus, the budget resolutions that are reported out of the House Budget Committee can easily be broken down to a very low level of aggregation. Chairman Muskie has yet to provide a chairman's mark for the Senate Budget Committee's deliberations. Rather, as each function is taken up, senators move to adopt a given spending level for the entire function.

Third, the decision-making processes of the two committees differ in that the House Budget Committee continues to use the president's budget as the baseline from which alternatives are measured, whereas the Senate Budget Committee has used the current services budget (what this year's budget would be like next year if there were no policy changes) as its baseline.

Based on these procedural differences, one should expect the House Budget Committee—with its almost account-level decision-making process—to be in constant conflict with the House Appropriations Committee. But it has been the Senate Budget Committee that has had a series of conflicts with the Senate Appropriations Committee. Why is this so?

Why the Process Differs in the House and in the Senate

One possible explanation for the much higher degree of partisan voting on budget resolutions in the House Budget Committee and on the House floor is that House Republicans are more partisan on all issues than their Senate counterparts. However, voting data do not support this notion. The CQ party unity index, which measures the degree to which members vote with their party, is 65.5 for House Republicans for the second session of the 93rd Congress—only slightly higher than the 61.5 registered by Senate Republicans.

The party unity data indicate that the Republicans on the House Budget Committee are slightly more partisan (73.4) than Republican House members as a whole, but this fact does not explain the extremely high degree of Republican partisan voting on budget resolutions on the floor of the House. Moreover, the data also indicate that the Republican members of the House Budget Committee are not significantly more partisan in their general voting behavior than their SBC counterparts, whose index is 71.5. Yet Republicans on the Senate Budget Committee, unlike their HBC counterparts, have evidenced a bipartisan voting record on budget resolution roll calls as indicated by their low cohesion index scores (see Table 2).

Rather, it would appear that the major distinctions between the new budget processes of the House and the Senate flow from the relative differences in power, within their respective bodies, of the House and Senate budget committees. It is our belief that the power of the two budget committees differs in quantity and kind because of the restrictions on membership and tenure that apply to the House but not the Senate Budget Committee.

The stature of members within Congress is largely determined by the power they gain through their committee assignments. Because of the tenure limitation, it is impossible for representatives to build a career around service on the House Budget Committee. Since representatives have only one major committee assignment, members of the House Budget Committee, when faced with a conflict, will give their time, effort, and loyalty to the duties and viewpoints associated with their major committee assignment. Thus, when there is a clash between the interests of the House Budget Committee and those of their main committee, HBC members will side with the position of their major committee.

In contrast to this pattern, senators on the Senate Budget Committee can identify their membership on that committee with their power and stature in the Senate. As indicated by the data in Table 3, the Senate Budget Committee has attracted a much more junior group of members than has its House counterpart. Of particular interest is the fact that HBC Republicans on the average have three times as much seniority as their counterparts on the Senate Budget Committee.

It appears that the Senate Budget Committee is populated with junior members who can build their career in the Senate around their budget committee membership. This alternative is not open to members of the House committee. This career opportunity also means that SBC members realize that their power in the Senate will be associated with the rise in stature and power of the committee. Therefore, it is in the interest of SBC members to see to it that the budget resolutions reported out by the committee are successfully passed on the Senate floor. This motivation of self-interest goes a long way toward explaining the bipartisan nature of Senate Budget Committee proceedings.

Table 3. Mean Seniority of the Membership of the House and Senate Budget Committees

	SBC	HBC
Republicans	5.0 years	14.6 years
Democrats	11.0	14.8
Total	8.8	14.8

For example, during the mark-up of the fiscal year 1976 first concurrent resolution, Chairman Muskie and other liberal Democrats on the committee ended up on the losing side in 14 out of 26 votes held during the mark-up. In these votes, Muskie and other liberals tried unsuccessfully to reduce expenditures for defense and to increase expenditures for stimulative programs to fight the ongoing recession. But having lost their fight in the committee, all these liberals supported the resolution on the floor of the Senate. Moreover, Chairman Muskie opposed amendments on the Senate floor that would have had the same effect as those which he proposed, and which were defeated, in the committee.

The same pattern emerges among the Republicans. In the debate over whether to recommit the Military Construction Authorization Bill to conference, the Senate Budget Committee's position was supported by Senator Bellmon and three of the other five Republicans on the committee. In the past these senators had established strong promilitary positions, but in this case they supported their committee and voted against higher defense authorizations.[24]

This self-interest motivation does not exist for the members of the House Budget Committee. Republicans, not having the votes to determine the nature of the resolution in committee, have no stake in supporting the resolution when it comes to the floor. Thus, House Budget Committee membership has no effect on the roll call behavior of its members.

This situation is magnified by the mandated membership provisions that apply to the House Budget Committee. Because 12 out of the 26 positions are mandated (5 from Appropriations, 5 from Ways and Means, and 2 from the respective party leaderships) and because (owing to tenure limitations) little committee loyalty exists, members of the House Budget Committee tend to view their function as representative of the interests and viewpoints of their respective major committees.

There is also evidence that the Appropriations and Ways and Means committees have assigned some of their most senior and powerful members to the budget committee to guarantee that the interests of the traditional money committees are taken into account during the House Budget Committee's deliberations. Thus, while the total HBC membership averages 14.8 years of House seniority, the five Appropriations Committee members average 16.8 years and the five Ways and Means members 20.8 years of House seniority.[25]

All of the above leads to the hypothesis that the House Budget Committee, compared with its Senate counterpart, is in a relatively weak position within its house. This weakness has had a major impact

on the partisanship, decision-making process, styles, and strategies
followed by Chairman Adams and the other members of the committee.

As to Partisanship

Since House Budget Committee members tend to represent the
viewpoints of their major committee or their party's leadership, it is
not surprising, in a time when the presidency and the Congress are
controlled by different parties, that Republican members express the
administration's view while Democratic members—particularly in the
case of the chairman's mark—express the Democratic leadership's
view. This would naturally lead to extreme partisan voting—particularly over such a fundamental issue as a budget.[26]

As to the Decision-Making Process

It is its very weakness that allows the House Budget Committee to
operate almost at the same decision-making level as used by the Appropriations Committee. The Senate Appropriations Committee can
see the Senate Budget Committee as a potential threat to its power
over the budget. But even if it operates at the account level, the House
Budget Committee does not pose a threat to the House Appropriations
Committee. The House Appropriations Committee knows that it has
five of its senior members on the budget committee to see to it that the
interests of the Appropriations Committee are taken into account.
Also, the mandated turnover of budget committee membership will
mean that just as budget committee members build the expertise to
gain stature with their colleagues, they will be forced to leave the
House Budget Committee.

As to Style and Strategies

The aggressiveness of the Senate Budget Committee and the caution of the House Budget Committee are a direct result of their power
positions. The House Budget Committee, because of its unique status,
must seek alliances with the major power centers in the House in
order to pass its resolutions. Thus, unlike the Senate Budget Committee, the House Budget Committee must avoid confrontations with
other committees of the House.

During its first year and a half of existence, the Democratic majority of the House Budget Committee has turned to its party's leadership for support. Consequently, a consistent pattern has developed. The chairman's mark is made public. It elicits criticism. Then the leadership—acting in consort with Chairman Adams—introduces its amendment. In the case of the first two resolutions, the amendment was introduced on the floor of the House, but for the fiscal year 1977 first concurrent resolution, it was introduced during the committee's mark-up, just before a final vote was taken to report the resolution to the House. In all cases the leadership amendment was introduced by Majority Leader O'Neill, holder of the Democratic leadership position on the House Budget Committee.

The object of each amendment has been to guarantee a minimal winning coalition for the resolution. In each case Chairman Adams and the leadership, fearing that there might not be enough votes to pass the resolution, have sweetened the pot by moving to increase expenditures in the human resources area to the degree necessary to attract extra liberal votes without alienating already existing moderate support. Under this process the budget resolutions, as they come out of the House Budget Committee, can be seen as trial balloons that are followed in each case by an O'Neill perfecting amendment. The O'Neill perfecting amendments have been necessary because, given the almost unanimous opposition of House Republicans, it has been necessary for the leadership and the Democratic majority of the House Budget Committee to develop a coalition among House Democrats that would represent a plurality of the total House.

Conclusion

Because the Democratic leadership and the majority of the House Budget Committee have been forced to build their minimum winning coalitions almost totally within the Democratic ranks of the House, the budget resolutions in the House can truly be said to represent a majority party budget. This, in turn, implies that the relative weakness of the House Budget Committee is also its greatest strength; for by forcing the committee to seek allies among the major Democratic groups in the House, the budget committee's lack of power ends up by producing a clear choice between the parties.

Two major aims of the new budget process were to give Congress the tools to set fiscal policy and to make priority choices among competing types of programs. The new budget process in the House has clearly established very real differences between the political parties on each of these choices.[27] To that extent, the budget process in the House has been unique in American congressional behavior in that it has followed the "responsible party model." If this continues to be true, the pattern of voting associated with the passage of budget resolutions in the House will come to resemble that found with votes on budgets in European parliaments.

Although this might be seen as a great step forward in terms of clearly defining the issues that separate the parties in the House, a question remains: Can the American legislative party produce the necessary party cohesion consistently to achieve the passage of these resolutions? Based on past experience, the answer will probably be no. But the very fact that the question can be raised means that the new budget process in the House is bringing about greater change than in the Senate, where voting, committee support, and alliances continue to follow the traditional patterns.

NOTES

1. The new congressional budget process was created with the passage of the Budget and Impoundment Control Act of 1974 (P.L. 93-344).
2. This phrase is attributable to Allen Schick of the Congressional Research Service. See also Richard F. Fenno, Jr., *The Power of the Purse* (Boston: Little, Brown, 1966), for an excellent discussion of the traditional budgetary procedures in the House. See also Aaron Wildavsky, *The Politics of the Budgetary Process*, 2nd ed. (Boston: Little, Brown, 1974).
3. U.S. Congress, Senate, Committee on the Budget, *Congressional Budget Reform*, 93rd Cong., 2nd sess., March 4, 1975, p. 3.
4. For a discussion of uncontrollables, see *The Budget of the United States Government, Fiscal Year 1977* (Washington, D.C.: Government Printing Office, 1977), pp. 6–10.
5. See Dennis M. Sherman, "Impoundment Reporting by the Office of Management and Budget: A Preliminary Analysis," *Congressional Research Service*, January 7, 1974, printed in *Congressional Record*, daily edition, January 29, 1974, p. S.66.
6. At present, Representative Barber Conable (R-N.Y.) holds two of these positions in that he is both on the Ways and Means Committee and chairman of the Republican Policy Committee. Thus, in effect, only 11 positions on the House Budget Committee are mandated at this time.
7. Interview with Walter Kravitz, November 28, 1975.
8. See Harrison W. Fox and Susan Hammond, "The Growth of Con-

gressional Staffs," in Harvey C. Mansfield, Sr., ed., *Congress against the President* (New York: Praeger, 1975), pp. 112–24.

9. The Current Services Budget is defined by Section 605(a) of the Congressional Budget and Impoundment Control Act as "the estimated outlays and proposed budget authority which would be included in the Budget . . . for the ensuing fiscal year if all programs and activities were carried on during such ensuing fiscal year at the same level as the fiscal year in progress and without policy changes in such programs and activities."

10. For a fuller discussion on this point, see John W. Ellwood and James A. Thurber, "The New Congressional Budget Process: Its Causes, Consequences, and Possible Success," paper delivered at the Symposium on Legislative Reform and Public Policy, University of Nebraska, Lincoln, March 11–12, 1976.

11. For a description of the reasons for the failure of the 1946 attempt at reforming the congressional budget process, see ibid., appendix A.

12. "Budget Committees Move toward Firm Figures," *Congressional Quarterly Weekly*, April 12, 1975, pp. 735–36.

13. For a statement of Representative Holtzman's position, see U.S. House of Representatives, Report No. 94-145, *First Concurrent Resolution on the Budget—Fiscal Year 1976: Report of the Committee on the Budget, House of Representatives, to Accompany H. Con. Res. 218* (Washington, D.C.: Government Printing Office, 1975), pp. 111–12. For Representative Derrick's views, see ibid., pp. 115–19. For the views of Representatives Burleson and Landrum, see ibid., pp. 107–10.

14. Interview with Walter Kravitz, November 28, 1975.

15. Eyewitness account.

16. The Rice Index of Cohesion is used. According to Anderson, Watts, and Wilcox: "For the purposes of the index, Rice defined cohesion as the extent to which the distribution of votes on a legislative roll call deviates from the distribution that would be expected if all influences operated in a random fashion. The argument states that, if one hundred votes were cast in a purely random manner, they would distribute themselves equally on both sides of the issue, i.e., fifty 'yeas' to fifty 'nays.' This instance is defined as the case of minimum cohesion and is assigned the index value of 0. The opposite extreme occurs when all members vote on the same side of an issue—that is considered complete cohesion and is assigned the index value of 100. The index is thus established as having a range from 0 to 100.

"Intermediate values in this range are determined by the degree to which the percentage 'yea' vote deviates from 50.0 in either direction, toward 0.0 or toward 100.0. For example, when 75 percent vote 'yea' on an issue, there is a 25/50 or 50 percent departure from 0 cohesion toward complete cohesion, the index is 50.0." [Lee F. Anderson, Meredith W. Watts, Jr., and Allen R. Wilcox, *Legislative Roll-Call Analysis* (Evanston, Ill.: Northwestern University Press, 1966), pp. 32–33.]

17. Julius Turner, *Party and Constituency: Pressures on Congress*, rev. ed. by Edward V. Schneier (Baltimore: Johns Hopkins University Press, 1970), p. 20.

18. U.S. Senate, Committee on the Budget, *Transcript of the Conference on the Second Concurrent Resolution for Fiscal Year 1976*, pp. 317–18.

19. During the mark-up sessions of the first concurrent resolution for fiscal year 1977, Representatives Robert Leggett (D-Calif.) and Robert Giaimo (D-Conn.) made frequent reference to the fact that the members of the House Budget Committee should be wary of cutting back on all the March 15 requests from the authorizing committees. Leggett made specific reference to the difficulty encountered in passing budget resolutions on the floor of the House and the resulting need to avoid offending members of the authorizing committees. (Eyewitness account.)

20. Tax expenditures can be defined as "losses of tax revenue attributable to provisions of the federal tax laws which allow a special exclusion, exemption, or deduction from gross income or which provide credit, preferential rate of tax, or a deferral of tax liability." General Accounting Office, "Initial Proposed Definitions to Be Published under Section 202(a)(1) of the Congressional Budget Act of 1974" (Washington, D.C.: General Accounting Office, October 17, 1975), p. 27. "Loopholes" are tax expenditures that one does not like.

21. The crucial test came on two procedural votes to table motions relating to whether individual income tax reductions would be extended through 1977. The Senate Finance Committee position carried by votes of 53 to 39 and 49 to 42.

Of the 18 standing committee chairmen, 11 voted to support the Finance Committee's position. Only Senators Bellmon and Beall among the Senate Budget Committee's Republicans supported the budget committee's position. Finally, whereas a plurality of Senate Republicans had supported each of the concurrent resolutions, Republicans voted against the Senate Budget Committee's position in both cases by margins of 26 to 9. See "Senate Rejects House Tax Shelter Curbs," *Congressional Quarterly Weekly*, June 26, 1976, pp. 1639–41, 1679, and 1688.

22. Ibid.

23. The General Accounting Office defines the budget's functional categories as "a means of presenting budget authority, outlay, and tax expenditure data in terms of the principal purposes which federal programs are intended to serve. Each account is generally placed in a single function. . . . The best represents its major purpose, regardless of the agency administering the program. The Congressional Budget and Impoundment Control Act of 1974 requires Congress to estimate outlays, budget authority, and tax expenditures for each function." [General Accounting Office, op. cit., p. 17]

   At present the federal budget is divided into sixteen functions (plus interest): (1) National Defense, (2) International Affairs, (3) General Science, Space, and Technology, (4) Natural Resources, Environment, and Energy, (5) Agriculture, (6) Commerce and Transportation, (7) Community and Regional Development, (8) Education, Training, Employment, and Social Services, (9) Health, (10) Income Security, (11) Veterans' Benefits and Services, (12) Law Enforcement and Justice, (13) General Government, (14) Revenue Sharing and General Purpose Fiscal Assistance, (15) Allowances, (16) Undistributed Offsetting Receipts, and Interest.

24. For example, on the "1976 National Security Voting Index" (put together by the promilitary American Security Council), the four senators (Beall, Bellmon, Dole, and Domenici) averaged 87.0. This compares favorably (from a promilitary point of view) with the Senate Republican average of 75.6 and the Senate-wide average of 52.8.

25. There is also some indication that the Appropriations and Ways and Means committees have sent some of their most conservative members to fill the mandated slots on the House Budget Committee. Cathy Rudder has shown that House Budget Committee members from Ways and Means average 24.8 percentage points above the Ways and Means Committee average (for all members) on the Congressional Quarterly Conservative Coalition Index. See Catherine E. Rudder, "The Reform of the Committee on Ways and Means: Procedural and Substantive Impact, 1975," paper delivered at the annual meeting of the Southwestern Political Science Association, Dallas, Texas, April 9, 1976, p. 12A, table 9.

26. Julius Turner and Edward Schneier, among others, present data to indicate that party cohesion is at its highest in European parliaments in roll call voting on budget questions. See Turner, op. cit., p. 22.

27. This essay has concentrated on process aspects of the new con-

gressional budget procedures. However, there is also a good deal
of evidence to indicate that the new budget process has changed
the policy output of the Congress. We go into considerable detail
on this point in our Nebraska paper. See Ellwood and Thurber,
op. cit.

It is worth noting here, however, that the budgets proposed
by the president and set out by Congress in its First Concurrent
Resolution for Fiscal Year 1977 are quite different both in terms
of the degree of fiscal stimulus and the priorities choices reflected
by the distribution of funds among types of programs. The following table is illustrative:

**Comparison of President's Budget with First Concurrent Resolu-
tion for Fiscal Year 1977 (in billions of dollars)**

	President's Budget (March 25)	First Concurrent Resolution	Difference in Dollars	Difference in Percentage Increase
Outlays	$395.8	$413.3	+$17.5	+4.4%
Budget authority	431.2	454.2	+23.0	+5.3
Revenues	351.3	362.5	+11.2	+3.2
Deficit	44.6	50.8	+6.2	+13.9

9. Congress and the Intelligence Community

John T. Elliff

Over the three decades from World War II until the 1970s, no major field of national policy making was more immune from congressional involvement than intelligence. The foreign intelligence community—composed of the Central Intelligence Agency, the Defense Intelligence Agency, the National Security Agency, the intelligence arms of the military services, and the State Department—was nominally overseen by small subcommittees of the Senate and House Armed Services and Appropriations committees. The principal domestic intelligence agency—the Federal Bureau of Investigation—regularly reported only to a House Appropriations subcommittee. Professional staff assistance was minimal, and the subcommittee chairmen developed close personal relationships with the agency heads. The attitude of the members was expressed by one senator assigned to oversee the CIA who declared in 1956 that "it is not a question of reluctance on the part of CIA officials to speak to us. Instead it is a question of our reluctance, if you will, to seek information and knowledge on subjects which I personally, as a Member of Congress and as a citizen, would rather not have." [1]

This attitude has changed in the aftermath of Watergate and the Vietnam war. Both the Senate and the House of Representatives have begun, in different ways and with varying degrees of success, to assume more significant roles in the making of intelligence policy and the oversight of intelligence operations. Each house created a temporary select committee in 1975 to investigate intelligence activities, although the two committees adopted contrasting approaches to their common assignment. In 1976 the officially published report of the Senate Select Committee and the suppressed, but leaked, report of the House Select Committee called for additional legislative action; and the Senate established a permanent Select Committee on Intelligence. The role of Congress in this area is still evolving and is unlikely to stabilize for some time to come.

The purpose of this essay is to describe how Congress has attempted to assert its influence over intelligence activities in recent years. This process of change in executive-legislative relations has several dimensions, including (1) the specific resources, skills, and strategies available to the participants, (2) the larger political environment of events, public attitudes, and elite opinions, (3) the constitutional arrangements prescribing the way each branch is expected to perform its institutional responsibilities, and (4) the consequences for public policy outcomes. Each of these aspects of the relationship between Congress and the executive branch suggests a basic question about congressional efforts to affect intelligence policy and oversee the intelligence community:

•Which of its resources has Congress chosen to use, with what degree of skill and according to what strategies?
•How has the congressional effort been linked to developments in the political environment?
•Are changes taking place in the constitutional framework governing the respective roles of Congress and the executive?
•What have been and are likely to be the results for public policy in the intelligence field?

The Legacy of Congressional Passivity

The place to begin looking for answers to these questions is the period from World War II onward, when Congress devoted few resources to intelligence policy. It had the power to write authorizing legislation assigning intelligence functions to specific agencies, setting their objectives, and imposing legal standards. But such legislation was inadequate or nonexistent. The CIA had a general statutory charter, enacted as part of the National Security Act of 1947.[2] However, there was no legislation authorizing the National Security Agency, defense intelligence, or the domestic intelligence functions of the FBI. These latter operations were based on executive orders, sometimes secret and often couched in vague language placing few meaningful limits on intelligence activities.

For example, when the FBI's internal security role was established in the late 1930s, the executive intentionally kept the decision away from Congress. FBI Director J. Edgar Hoover advised that it was "undesirable to seek any special legislation which would draw attention to" the program. He urged "the utmost degree of secrecy in order to avoid criticism or objections which might be raised to such an expansion by either ill-informed persons or individuals with some ulterior motive." [3] However, even after the FBI's intelligence assignment was made public shortly before World War II, Congress deferred to the executive's initiative. Presidents Roosevelt, Truman, Eisenhower, and Kennedy issued directives authorizing the FBI to investigate "subversive activities," without defining the term themselves or seeking legislation to limit such investigations.

The CIA's legislative charter demonstrated that Congress could be equally vague in its authorization of intelligence activities. The National Security Act of 1947 allowed the CIA not only to evaluate intelligence information, but also "to perform such other functions and duties related to intelligence affecting national security as the National Security Council may from time to time direct." Thereafter, secret National Security Council directives cited this clause as the basis for CIA covert action abroad, although there is little evidence that Congress intended to grant such authority beyond clandestine intelligence gathering. [4]

Another legislative resource, the appropriations process, was used to protect rather than to limit or regulate intelligence activities. The congressional oversight subcommittees learned of CIA covert action operations by 1949 and regularly approved the agency's appropriations. However, neither the purposes nor the amounts of the CIA appropriations were disclosed to the Congress as a whole, since they were buried within the budgets of other agencies. Similarly, J. Edgar Hoover provided "off the record" briefings to the House Appropriations subcommittee on the FBI's domestic counterintelligence programs for disrupting and discrediting Communist and Communist-influenced groups and the Ku Klux Klan, and the members did not question their propriety. Thus, Congress did not formally confront the issue of covert action by the intelligence community, at home or abroad, despite knowledge of such operations by the members assigned to review intelligence appropriations.

The executive branch consistently succeeded in forestalling congressional investigations of intelligence activities. In fact, the modern doctrine of executive privilege was elaborated under the Truman and Eisenhower administrations as a rationale for withholding from congressional investigators FBI files on alleged "security risks" and information about the handling of allegedly disloyal government employees. The executive resisted such investigations not only in the interest of protecting the rights of innocent persons or the confidentiality of executive deliberations, but also on the ground that disclosure to Congress might reveal intelligence sources and thereby hamper the ability to obtain information.[5]

It was unnecessary to invoke executive privilege to deflect different kinds of congressional investigations in the 1960s. When a Senate Judiciary subcommittee began looking into wiretapping and other surveillance techniques in 1966, Justice Department and FBI officials informally persuaded the subcommittee chairman, Senator Edward V. Long, not to seek information on "matters of a national security nature" and to bypass the Bureau altogether. The FBI thus kept secret its mail opening, surreptitious entry, and electronic surveillance practices, although the risk posed by the Long subcommittee apparently contributed to Director Hoover's decision to curtail sharply the use of such techniques. Congress also failed to conduct an investigation following disclosure in 1967 of secret CIA subsidies for the overseas programs of the National Students Association and numerous other American labor, educational, and cultural organizations. President Johnson appointed a committee composed of Undersecretary of State Nicholas Katzenbach, HEW Secretary John Gardner, and CIA Director Richard Helms to study the matter and, according to Katzenbach, to head off a full-scale congressional inquiry. It recommended terminating covert financial support to "any of the nation's educational or private voluntary organizations," and President Johnson adopted this policy, although it had no firm legal status as an executive order or act of Congress.

The general view of Congress toward oversight of the intelligence community was reflected in the defeats (by 2-to-1 margins) of Senate resolutions in 1956 and again in 1966 to create a standing committee on intelligence. This proposal was initially made by a Commission on Organization of the Executive Branch, headed by former President Herbert Hoover, which warned of "the possibility of the growth of license and abuses of power" without closer outside review. However, the Senate votes were expressions of confidence in those of its senior members already assigned to oversee the CIA. Many senators also accepted the notion that intelligence activities were the exclusive constitutional prerogative of the chief executive and his subordinates. The chairman of the Appropriations Committee, Senator Carl Hayden, asserted that legislative interference "would tend to impinge upon the constitutional authority and responsibility of the President in the conduct of foreign affairs." And Senator Richard Russell, the Armed Services Committee chairman and titular head of the Senate "establishment," declared forthrightly, "If there is one agency of Government in which we must take some matters on faith without a constant examination of its methods and sources, I believe that agency is the Central Intelligence Agency." [6]

On the domestic intelligence side, Congress deferred less to the presidency or the importance of secrecy than to FBI Director Hoover. Representative John McCormack, later to be Speaker of the House, expressed the prevailing view during the 1947 debate over tenure for the CIA director: "The best we can do is as in the case of J. Edgar Hoover . . . a man who impresses himself so much upon his fellowmen that permanency accrues by reason of the character of service that he renders." Former Secretary of State Dean Rusk once summarized the sources of Hoover's extraordinary independence as "a combination of professional performance on the job, some element of fear, very astute relations with the Congress, and very effective public relations." [7] Among the FBI's techniques for dealing with Congress was the compilation of data from its files and from public sources on every congressman for use in "selling" hostile legislators on "liking the FBI."

In short, Congress declined to use any of its resources to participate in intelligence policy making. It did not provide statutory guidance on crucial policy issues, with the result that there were no standards by which even the poorly staffed and fragmented subcommittees engaged in oversight could evaluate administrative performance. Nor did it insist upon receiving information about intelligence operations, either through the appropriations process or by investigation. Such activities as CIA clandestine intervention overseas and FBI wiretapping without judicial warrant nonetheless became widely known in the 1960s, and Congress allowed the executive branch exclusive control over them.

The Assertion of Congressional Powers

Recent congressional interest in the intelligence community has not been solely the result of a desire to strengthen the institutional position of Congress vis-à-vis the president and the bureaucracy. This objective has been reinforced by more specific changes in public and elite attitudes, including disenchantment with American intervention abroad in the wake of the Vietnam war, concern for protecting individual rights of privacy against governmental surveillance, and fear of the demonstrated ability of presidents (and sometimes agency heads) to use intelligence resources against their political "enemies."

Charges that U.S. intelligence agencies had been misused by the White House played a central part in the disclosures leading to President Nixon's resignation in 1974. The second article of impeachment adopted by the House Judiciary Committee cited as abuses of presidential power certain FBI wiretaps and other investigations authorized by the president, the concealment of wiretap records, establishment of a special White House intelligence unit that unlawfully used CIA resources and burglarized a psychiatrist's office in search of information about the former Defense Department official who leaked to the press the "Pentagon Papers" on Vietnam policy, the attempt to have the CIA curtail the FBI's investigation of the Watergate break-in, and the use of intelligence resources against the president's partisan opponents. Congress moved slowly but decisively, in tandem with the Watergate special prosecutor, to bring to account the high officials responsible for these actions.

The question remained, however, whether removal of the president and other officials and criminal prosecutions for some of the offenses were enough to remedy the abuses linked to intelligence operations. Former Watergate Special Prosecutor Archibald Cox attributed much of the problem to "a neurotic passion for spying as a means of ensuring loyalty and coping with supposed threats to domestic security." [8] The prime example was the so-called Huston Plan developed (but partly rescinded) in 1970 for the use of illegal surveillance techniques against Americans.[9] President Nixon and his defenders were not the only ones to suggest that similar misconduct had occurred under previous administrations. Allegations that the FBI had committed numerous burglaries before 1966, that journalists were wiretapped under the Kennedy administration, and that President Johnson had ordered an FBI check on vice-presidential candidate Spiro Agnew's phone records during the 1968 campaign surfaced as a byproduct of the Watergate investigations. Following President Nixon's resignation, Attorney General William Saxbe issued a report on a fifteen-year FBI program, labeled COINTELPRO, carried out until 1971 to disrupt domestic groups and discredit Americans with tactics he described as "abhorrent in a free society." [10] Shortly thereafter, major newspapers published charges that the CIA had engaged in "massive" surveillance of Americans in violation of its charter and that the FBI had spied on political activities at the 1964 Democratic National Convention for the Johnson White House. Watergate had unleashed a torrent of revelations about questionable domestic intelligence activities going far beyond abuses tied to the Nixon administration.

On the other hand, U.S. foreign intelligence activities abroad were not involved with Watergate. Instead, it was the reaction against the Vietnam war that produced growing concern about secret foreign intervention, including covert political and paramilitary intelligence operations. Beginning with the War Powers Act of 1973, Congress sought to regulate the president's authority to commit United States resources unilaterally overseas. The disclosure in 1974 of CIA covert action in Chile, apparently contradicting previous official denials, led to significant congressional debate over such operations.

Thus, intelligence policy came to be viewed as a crucial test for Congress. With the prestige of the presidency at a low ebb, could the Congress act decisively? One course was to proceed directly with consideration of legislation restructuring and redirecting the intelligence community. Bills were introduced to make the FBI and the Justice Department independent from White House interference and to forbid CIA covert actions "for the purpose of undermining or destabilizing the government of any foreign country." [11] Congress was not, however, ready to exercise its lawmaking power in this area. The legacy of decades of inaction was widespread lack of confidence by the members in their ability to make decisions on complex matters which they knew little about and which, despite the apparent abuses, still carried the imposing label of "national security."

The alternative, then, was to obtain adequate information and develop the necessary expertise as rapidly as possible, so that intelligence reforms would not turn out to be misguided or politically embarrassing. For example, both the House and the Senate defeated measures banning CIA covert action in the fall of 1974, but several opponents stressed only that the legislation was premature in the absence of sufficient knowledge about covert operations and full consideration of the matter in committee. Reform opinion in the Senate was divided between members who wanted a total prohibition and those who sought more effective legislative oversight to insure against unnecessary foreign intervention. Hence, with the aim of providing Congress with the data needed to resolve the issue, the Hughes-Ryan Amendment was added to the Foreign Assistance Act of 1974. It required that the appropriate committees, including the Senate Foreign Relations Committee and the House Foreign Affairs Committee as well as the more sympathetic Armed Services committees, be advised in a "timely fashion" of the nature and scope of any CIA operations conducted for purposes other than obtaining intelligence information. The measure also required the president to make a finding "that each such operation is important to the national security." Thus, Congress took the first tentative step toward regulating foreign intelligence activities, although its proponents saw it as a temporary arrangement pending development of more permanent standards and procedures.

On the domestic side the House Judiciary Committee, in the midst of its impeachment investigation, requested the General Accounting Office to investigate FBI domestic intelligence operations. The GAO, headed by the comptroller general, is an independent arm of Congress created in 1921 to investigate the use of public funds. Under the Legislative Reorganization Act of 1970, the GAO received wider authority to "review and analyze the results of Government programs" and to assist congressional committees "in developing a statement of legislative objectives and goals and methods for assessing and reporting actual program performance in relation to such legislative objectives and goals." Although the Judiciary Committee asked the GAO to "focus on policies, procedures and criteria" for current domestic intelligence investigations, rather than on specific allegations of past misconduct, and despite the attorney general's refusal to allow the GAO direct access to FBI investigative files, such an outside inquiry was unprecedented for the intelligence community and the traditionally autonomous FBI.[12]

Moreover, the question of past intelligence abuses could not be put aside. Neither the Hughes-Ryan Amendment on CIA covert action nor the GAO investigation of the FBI, designed as they were to help the standing committees evaluate present intelligence activities, addressed this problem. The various existing committees also lacked the resources and the specific mandate to conduct a full-scale investigation. On the other hand, President Ford acted promptly to appoint a commission chaired by Vice-President Nelson Rockefeller to examine charges of improper domestic CIA activities; and Attorney General Edward H. Levi's first significant action upon taking office in 1975 was to report numerous instances of past political abuse of the FBI to the House Judiciary Committee. The executive branch sought to regain the initiative by admitting past errors (which could not be attributed to the Ford administration) and promising to keep intelligence operations under tighter control.

Congressional Investigations and Their Aftermath

In the political environment of 1975, these assurances did not deter Congress. Appointment of the Rockefeller Commission had the contrary effect of confirming the existence of serious problems and placing Congress in the embarrassing position of appearing less concerned about them than the new president. The Senate responded immediately by setting up a temporary select committee to investigate intelligence activities headed by Senator Frank Church (D-Idaho), a member of the Foreign Relations Committee who had criticized CIA covert actions.

The House followed suit, and Lucien Nedzi (D-Mich.), who already headed the House Armed Services subcommittee assigned to oversee the CIA, became the House select committee's first chairman. However, the House committee's work was delayed for several months by internal controversy. It was disclosed that Nedzi had been secretly briefed the year before on questionable CIA domestic operations, and one committee member, Michael Harrington (D-N.Y.), was alleged to have leaked classified information about CIA covert action in Chile. The committee was finally reconstituted under a new chairman, Otis Pike (D-N.Y.), and without either Nedzi or Harrington as members.

It is impossible to summarize all the work of the two select committees in a few pages, but several aspects deserve special attention. The first is the sharp disparity in their strategies. The House committee, born in turmoil, lacking the resources of its Senate counterpart, and controlled by members eager to dramatize publicly any weaknesses in the intelligence community, adopted a strategy of confrontation with the executive. Its chief accomplishment was to uncover and expose cases in which the intelligence community failed to supply advance warning of major international developments, such as the 1973 Mideast war.[13] However, when the committee unilaterally released secret data that the executive branch had refused to declassify, it lost the support of the full House of Representatives in its demands for additional secret materials and its attempt to issue a final report containing classified information. The leak of this report to the press and its publication after the House had voted against its public release raised doubts about the ability of congressmen to exercise oversight duties in conformity with their mandate.

By contrast, the Senate select committee attempted to show that Congress could uncover misconduct and evaluate intelligence performance without risking improper disclosure of secret information. It sought the cooperation of the executive, held most of its hearings in closed session, concentrated its substantial resources on intensive staff investigations of particular abuses and studies of basic policy issues, and produced sweeping recommendations for new oversight procedures and legislation to govern the intelligence community. The Senate committee also took on the unforeseen task of investigating alleged assassination plots involving foreign leaders—a difficult assignment willingly passed on to it by the president—and prepared a unanimous report that the Senate, after debating the issue in rare secret session, allowed the committee to publish over White House objections.[14]

In spite of their divergent strategies, both select committees reached similar conclusions on central policy issues. Neither proposed a flat prohibition against CIA covert action. Instead, they recommended that such operations be conducted only when "required to protect the national security of the United States" (House committee) or "to deal with grave threats to American security" (Senate committee). And both stated that the intelligence oversight committee(s) of Congress should have some form of prior notice. The two committees also agreed that FBI security investigations should not go beyond the bounds of the criminal statutes, although the Senate committee allowed for "preventive intelligence investigations" of terrorist activity and hostile foreign intelligence activity.

One of the Senate committee's unique contributions to the institutional strength of the Congress involved its access to classified or otherwise confidential materials. In the past the executive had occasionally supplied such materials to sympathetic committees but had resisted more critical inquiries by invoking the constitutional doctrine of executive privilege. The Supreme Court ruled in *United States* v. *Nixon* that the "generalized interest in confidentiality" of "presidential communications" had to "yield to the demonstrated, specific need for evidence in a pending criminal trial." But the Court also declared that this executive interest was "fundamental to the operation of government and inextricably rooted in the separation of powers under the Constitution." Thus, it remained uncertain how the Court would deal with executive privilege issues not raised by the Nixon case, including "a claim of need to protect military, diplomatic or sensitive national security secrets" and "the balance . . . between the confidentiality interest and congressional demands for information."[15]

Therefore, in view of the delays of litigation and the risk of an adverse judicial decision, the Senate committee adopted a political rather than a legal strategy to get the material it needed for its investigation. Often proceeding step by step and carefully framing detailed requests based on facts already established in witness testimony or previous executive responses, the committee tried to avoid the charge that it was engaged in a "fishing expedition." When responses were tardy or materials delivered with major deletions, the senators did not move to open confrontation but held lengthy meetings with high executive officials to insist upon their specific requirements. The committee did not waver in its adherence to the constitutional principle that Congress had the right to whatever information it needed; however, it was willing to tailor access procedures to the particular concerns of the executive. Sometimes this meant examining documents in the first instance at the agencies to determine their relevance, restricting access to the senators themselves and specifically designated staff, or assuring the executive an opportunity to review committee reports before publication and state the case for secrecy.

The executive branch, for its part, did not abandon its constitutional right to claim executive privilege and occasionally asserted the doctrine as the reason for withholding certain materials. Nevertheless, there were no classes of documents that the committee did not obtain, although it agreed that in general the names of agents and their methods of conducting certain intelligence activities should remain in executive custody. The committee's access to types of materials rarely, if ever, provided to Congress was not so much a victory for the absolute principle of the congressional right to information as it was a triumph for the process of accommodation and the constitutional concept of "comity" between the branches. Whether this success will be a precedent for future oversight in a different political environment depends on the ability of the Senate committee's immediate successors to institutionalize the executive-legislative relationships developed in the course of its investigation.[16]

The Senate acted promptly in 1976 on the recommendation for a permanent intelligence oversight committee having the power not only to investigate but also to review intelligence appropriations and consider authorizing legislation. With exclusive jurisdiction over the CIA and joint authority with the Armed Services and Judiciary committees over defense intelligence and FBI intelligence, respectively, the new Select Committee on Intelligence was mandated to draft statutory charters for each component of the intelligence community. Several senators expressed the hope that the House of Representatives would do likewise and ultimately agree to a single joint committee.

The executive branch did not wait for Congress to finish its investigations before instituting intelligence reforms. President Ford issued an executive order revising the structure for intelligence decision making and limiting domestic CIA activities along the lines recommended by the Rockefeller Commission.[17] Attorney General Levi also issued "guidelines" for FBI domestic security investigations after consultation with congressional committees (although not with their full or final agreement). At least one presidential initiative failed because the administration did not go as far as some senators wanted. The Senate's failure to act in 1976 on a Ford-Levi bill to require judicial warrants for FBI intelligence wiretapping showed how difficult it was to enact new legislation on complex intelligence issues.

While the White House was controlled by the Republicans, the Democratic Congress was better at saying no than at legislating policy standards or operating procedures. In an unprecedented exercise of its power of the purse over intelligence operations, Congress amended the Defense Appropriations bill to terminate American covert intervention in Angola. The chairman of the Senate Foreign Relations Subcommittee on Africa, Senator Dick Clark (D-Iowa), led the opposition after being briefed under the procedures of the Hughes-Ryan Amendment. The inevitable public disclosure of a secret operation served, in this instance, the will of the Congress; and in the short run the Angola controversy was a warning that the executive should proceed with caution. Similarly, enactment in 1976 of a law setting a ten-year term for the FBI director warned the president that, while his formal power to replace an FBI director is unlimited, Congress expects him to give "good reasons" if he does so. Whether or not to replace FBI Director Clarence Kelley, who he had criticized in his campaign, was one of President Jimmy Carter's first decisions.

Conclusion

Recent experience demonstrates that Congress has the resources that, if used skillfully in the pursuit of an effective stategy, can win for it a share in control of the intelligence community. However, the intensity and direction of congressional interest depend on the movement of larger political forces. The national consensus supporting cold war foreign policy from the Truman to the Johnson administrations offered little incentive for congressmen to question the foreign intelligence activities carried out to implement a policy of containing Communist expansion wherever it was threatened throughout the world. Similarly, public hysteria about Communist "subversion" in the 1940s and 1950s, followed by comparable hostility in the 1960s toward the Ku Klux Klan, black militants, and antiwar protesters, frequently encouraged congressmen to seek more rather than less surveillance of domestic political activities. There is no guarantee that public and elite opinions will not move once again in favor of international intervention, or that events at home will not inspire new antagonisms against groups on the extremes of our political life. Even the apprehension about presidential misuse of intelligence resources may dissipate under a popular chief executive belonging to the same party that controls the Congress.

Nevertheless, it appears doubtful that the atmosphere of congressional passivity and acquiescence will soon return. Whatever may be the ultimate resolution of such issues as the procedures for oversight or the enactment of new legislative charters for the intelligence agencies, there has been a profound constitutional change in the relationship between Congress and the executive. Intelligence is no longer viewed as the exclusive domain of the executive branch. The staunchest supporters of a strong U.S. intelligence community, represented on the Senate select committee by Senators John Tower (R-Tex.) and Barry Goldwater (R-Ariz.), did not question the need for expanded legislative involvement in intelligence policy and practices. Although neither side has retreated on the question of executive privilege, progress in supplying adequate information to Congress has been made through joint efforts to achieve "comity" between the branches.

As for the impact on policy, the immediate consequence has not been to dismantle the intelligence community or even to eliminate such controversial policies as CIA covert action or FBI intelligence investigations. Instead, subject to stringent limits and controls, both functions would be legitimated if Congress carried out the recommendations of the Senate select committee. Of greater concern to the intelligence community and in Congress as well is the danger that individual congressmen could effectively sabotage intelligence policies—even policies supported by congressional majorities—by leaking information about actions that can only be successfully taken in secret. Therefore, the Senate committee saw the challenge to Congress as one of finding a "realistic" and "credible" system of accountability that could "substitute for the public scrutiny through congressional debate and press attention that normally attends government decisions." It is easy to envision circumstances in which the desires of Congress itself could be frustrated by the exposure resulting from open discussion of intelligence operations.

NOTES

1. Statement of Senator Leverett Saltonstall (R-Mass.), cited in Harry Howe Ransom, *The Intelligence Establishment* (Cambridge, Mass.: Harvard University Press, 1970), p. 169.
2. The Central Intelligence Agency Act of 1949 exempted the CIA from Civil Service regulations and laws requiring publication of agency functions.
3. U.S., Congress, Senate, *Intelligence Activities and the Rights of Americans*, Book II, Final Report of the Select Committee to Study Governmental Operations with Respect to Intelligence Activities, 1976, p. 28.
4. U.S., Congress, Senate, "Congressional Authorization for the Central Intelligence Agency to Conduct Covert Action," Appen-

dix I, *Foreign and Military Intelligence,* Book I, Final Report of the Select Committee to Study Governmental Operations with Respect to Intelligence Activities, 1976, pp. 475–509.

5. Raoul Berger, *Executive Privilege: A Constitutional Myth* (Cambridge, Mass.: Harvard University Press, 1974), pp. 5–6, 211–13, 224–28, 234–36, 294–97, 375–76.

6. Ransom, op. cit., pp. 161, 166–67.

7. U.S., Congress, Senate, "The Development of FBI Domestic Intelligence Investigations," *Supplementary Detailed Staff Reports on Intelligence Activities and the Rights of Americans,* Book III, Final Report of the Select Committee to Study Governmental Operations with Respect to Intelligence Activities, 1976, pp. 460, 469–70. (Cited hereafter as Book III.)

8. Archibald Cox, "Reflections upon Watergate," the Louis D. Brandeis Memorial Lecture, Brandeis University, April 24, 1974.

9. U.S., Congress, Senate, "National Security, Civil Liberties, and the Collection of Intelligence: A Report on the Huston Plan," Book III, pp. 921–86.

10. U.S., Congress, Senate, "COINTELPRO: The FBI's Covert Action Programs Against American Citizens," Book III, pp. 1–77.

11. The latter proposal, introduced by Representative Elizabeth Holtzman (D-N.Y.), was defeated, 291–108, by the House of Representatives on September 30, 1974. A similar measure, proposed by Senator James Abourezk (D-S.Dak.). was defeated by the Senate in October 1974.

12. *FBI Domestic Intelligence Operations—Their Purpose and Scope: Issues that Need to Be Resolved,* Report to the House Committee on the Judiciary by the Comptroller General of the United States, February 24, 1976.

13. U.S., Congress, House, *U.S. Intelligence Agencies and Activities: The Performance of the Intelligence Community,* Hearings before the Select Committee on Intelligence, 1975.

14. U.S., Congress, Senate, *Alleged Assassination Plots Involving Foreign Leaders,* An Interim Report of the Select Committee to Study Governmental Operations with Respect to Intelligence Activities, 1975.

15. *United States* v. *Nixon,* 418 U.S. 683 (1974).

16. U.S., Congress, Senate, "Introduction," *Foreign and Military Intelligence,* Book I, Final Report of the Select Committee to Study Governmental Operations with Respect to Intelligence Activities, 1976, pp. 7–8, 11–14.

17. Executive Order 11905, February 18, 1976; *Report to the President by the Commission on CIA Activities within the United States,* June 6, 1975.

10. *Congressional Oversight: Structures and Incentives*

Morris S. Ogul

Legislative oversight of the bureaucracy involves some of the most complex forms of behavior that Congress undertakes.[1] Oversight—defined as behavior of legislators, individually or collectively, formally or informally, that affects bureaucratic behavior in policy implementation—is less understood than almost any other aspect of congressional behavior. This lack of understanding results in large part from a reliance by political analysts on the "conventional wisdom" about legislative oversight, a wisdom that blinds us to the reality of oversight activity.

Legislative Oversight: The Conventional Wisdom

Like Pavlov's dog, Congress responds to cries for more and better legislative oversight of the bureaucracy by practicing its own form of salivation: Congress provides itself with more staff, increases budgets for committees, buttresses its information collection facilities, and issues itself more detailed instructions to do a better job. With equal predictability, these measures fail to close or even significantly narrow any perceived oversight gap in either its quantitative or qualitative dimensions. And so the pursuit of effective oversight goes on. If the plot seems circular or the theme repetitive, that is because it is. The influence of the conventional wisdom is pervasive.

The conventional wisdom of Congress is to vote more authority, add some staff, increase committee budgets, and add to information resources. The conventional wisdom at work can be illustrated by watching Congress prescribe itself invigorating potions through grants of additional authority to oversee.

Legislative Authority

The formal history of legislative oversight, though not of course the performance of the function, is frequently said to begin with Section 136 of the Legislative Reorganization Act of 1946 (P.L. 79–601):

> To assist the Congress in appraising the administration of the laws and in developing such amendments or related legislation as it may deem necessary, each standing committee of the Senate and the House of Representatives shall exercise continuous watchfulness of the execution by the administrative agencies concerned of any laws, the subject matter of which is within the jurisdiction of such committee; and, for that purpose, shall study all pertinent reports and data submitted to the Congress by the agencies in the executive branch of the Government.

Congress amended this provision in the Legislative Reorganization Act of 1970. In 1974 the House of Representatives modified the House rules concerning oversight, establishing general and special oversight responsibilities for committees and subcommittees.

This repeated tinkering with legislative authority suggests continual congressional concern with oversight and dissatisfaction with the performance of the function. The most interesting question about this evolution is: Do additions to legislative authority to oversee affect legislative behavior? Although research on oversight is too scanty to support firm conclusions, the evidence points toward a modest impact of authority on behavior. Almost all of some forty congressmen interviewed during the middle 1960s believed that the Legislative Reorganization Act of 1946 created a full and direct obligation to oversee. In addition, they saw that obligation as appropriate for the Congress. In brief, congressmen believe that systematic oversight *ought* to be conducted.

Why then the continuing gap between expectations and behavior? One possible explanation is that congressmen do not really believe in oversight; they only say that they do. Interviewing suggests that such is not the case. A second reason for the gap between expectations and behavior might lie in the nature of the expectations. The plain but seldom acknowledged fact is that systematic, all-inclusive oversight is simply impossible to perform. No amount of congressional dedication and energy, no conceivable increase in the size of committee staffs, and no boost in committee budgets will enable Congress to oversee policy implementation in a comprehensive and systematic manner. The job is too large for the members and staff to master. A third explanation is that, in particular situations where a congressman could realistically do something about oversight, such as when he holds a key status on a committee or subcommittee, factors other than a general desire to oversee govern his behavior. Among these are his multiple priorities as well as his policy preferences.

Committee Staffing

A second recommendation almost guaranteed to emerge from congressional self-examinations is to increase the size of committee staffs. Former congressman Roman Pucinski provided a typical statement in defense of this position:

> I am suggesting a substantial increase in committee staffs of professional people because it is becoming abundantly clear that within the framework of our present facilities, more and more the legislative branch of our Government must rely on the executive branch as the basis for information on which to judge legislation.[2]

Legislative reforms tend to reflect this feeling. The Legislative Reorganization Act of 1946 stipulated four professional and six clerical staff persons for each committee except for Appropriations. The Legislative Reorganization Act of 1970 called for six professional and six clerical staff persons. H. Res. 988, effective in January 1975, set staff size at eighteen professional staff members and twelve clerical persons except for two House committees, Appropriations and Budget.

The actual size of committee staffs is usually much larger. The growth of committee staffs is shown below in data for the House of Representatives collected for the Bolling Committee.[3]

	PROFESSIONAL	CLERICAL	INVESTIGATIVE	TOTAL
1946	47	102	33	182
1960	84	143	190	417
1970	126	149	372	647
1971	147	170	431	748

The figures are clear but their consequences are not. There is no hard evidence to suggest any strong correlation between the size of committee staffs and the quantity or quality of legislative oversight of the bureaucracy. Congressmen themselves seldom correlate staff size and effectiveness. Samuel C. Patterson found similarly in interviewing staff persons that ". . . professional staff people themselves did not feel that, in the main, their own staff operations were too small." [4] A discussion of the rise of congressional committee spending and of the increase in information resources yields the same pattern. In each case, the figures go up but the basic deficiencies in the performance of legislative oversight remain. The conventional wisdom about legislative oversight does not seem to resolve the dilemma of how to get more and better oversight.

The Judiciary Committee and Civil Rights

The deficiencies of conventional wisdom concerning oversight become even more apparent when we look at committee behavior. The civil rights oversight activities of the House Judiciary Committee, especially subcommittee #5, for the period 1965–67 provide a good example.

The House Judiciary Committee suffered no lack of authority to oversee in the area of civil rights. The committee staff was substantial. In interviews, a preponderance of committee members and staff persons attested to the adequacy of committee staffing. The following comments are representative:

> The staff is adequate for our activities.

> If other staff members were added, they would be drawn toward the current activities of the committee.

> More staff is not crucial because if we had more staff and they developed more materials, they would still have to come to us to act.

> There is plenty of staff to handle the problems in the civil rights area.[5]

Conventional wisdom would suggest that a committee with full authority, appropriate staffing, and an adequate budget would be an extensive and systematic overseer. Yet analysis reveals a strikingly different picture, one in which almost no formal civil rights oversight was being performed. The major exception might be the school guidelines hearings in 1966. An examination of these hearings is instructive.

In 1964, the Congress had passed the Civil Rights Act, Title VI of which permitted the Office of Education to cut off federal funds from programs that discriminated on the basis of race. Section 602 required that

> Each Federal department and agency which is empowered to extend Federal financial assistance to any program or activity, by way of grant, loan, or contract other than a contract of insurance or guarantee, is authorized and directed to effectuate the provisions of section 601 with respect to such program or activity by issuing rules, regulations, or orders of general applicability which shall be consistent with achievement with the objectives of the statute authorizing the financial assistance in connection with which the action is taken. No such rule, regulation, or order shall become effective unless and until approved by the President. . . .

The Office of Education, to implement this provision, drew up guidelines in Spring 1965 and again in March 1966. Objections from many southern school districts, relayed through their congressmen, were intense.

The clamor for the repeal or modification of Title VI heightened the demand for congressional oversight activity. The House Rules Committee in late September and early October 1966 held hearings on H. Res. 826 calling for the establishment of a select committee to investigate school guidelines and policies of the Commissioner of Education in school desegregation. Faced with a possible loss of jurisdiction, Chairman Emanuel Celler (D-N.Y.) of the Judiciary Committee, not previously enamored with the idea of civil rights oversight, now promised the Rules Committee a full and fair investigation.

Despite Celler's assurances, the Rules Committee voted to create the select committee provided for in H. Res. 826. Chairman Celler then promised to create a special judiciary subcommittee on civil rights if the Rules Committee, in exchange, would not implement the resolution. Chairman Celler fathered the Subcommittee on Civil Rights in November 1966. Hearings followed quickly in December. These happenings, bizarre in the context of previous committee behavior, were rather simply explained by committee members: "We were sort of pushed into it. We were forced into it. We might have lost our jurisdiction if we didn't." The dual threat of a loss of jurisdiction and of the creation of a select committee not likely to be favorable to desegregation had moved the Judiciary Committee when internal pressures could not.

No report emerged from these hearings because, as Chairman Byron Rogers succinctly put it, "None is needed." In the 90th Congress (1967) this special subcommittee was reconstituted as the

School Guidelines Subcommittee. In reality, its jurisdiction was civil rights. Reconstitution occurred because as part of the "Treaty of September of 1966," Chairman Celler had promised Chairman Howard Smith of the Rules Committee that southerners could call witnesses. The lengthy interrogation of Education Commissioner Harold Howe in December had prevented this.

No hearings were held by this special subcommittee in 1967. Chairman Rogers, with a notable lack of enthusiasm, asserted: "We will probably hold some hearings in this session. If we go into anything, it will probably be school guidelines." One staff member commented later: "The chairman is not particularly enthusiastic about having more hearings."

With the immediate pressure lessened and attention shifting elsewhere, the school guidelines subcommittee faded away. The Judiciary Committee had made motions toward oversight but only in the face of intense, immediate, and sustained external pressure. In this one clear example of a formal oversight effort, the intent was to defuse external pressures rather than to probe and assess administrative conduct.

Formal versus Informal Oversight

A sparse record of formal oversight from a committee that is highly active in a policy area suggests the possibility that informal oversight may be the prevailing practice. Interview evidence indicates that most members prefer informal methods of oversight where possible. Formal methods are seen as an indication of the breakdown of informal efforts. Only a distinct minority prefer formal methods of oversight as a first tactic.

Chairman Celler saw his informal relations with those in charge of civil rights activity in the Justice Department as excellent. Operationally, this meant that Celler agreed with much of what the Justice Department was doing and *that he was regularly and fully consulted by the department on civil rights matters.* Those members of the Judiciary Committee who advocated more formal oversight had to persuade a strong and reluctant chairman that their views were correct. Their inability to do so is evidenced in what might be called the Kastenmeier caper.

Representative Robert Kastenmeier (D-Wisc.), a member of the full committee and of subcommittee #5, was a vocal advocate of a special constitutional rights subcommittee to deal with questions of civil liberties and constitutional guarantees. He was concerned especially with the implementation of the Voting Rights Act of 1965. He asked Chairman Celler in September 1965 to create a special voting rights subcommittee. Kastenmeier and a few other members wanted a formal mechanism in the Congress for overseeing the implementation of the civil rights bills passed since 1957.

After complicated negotiations, a special ad hoc committee on civil rights which was to report to subcommittee #5 emerged in October 1965. The ad hoc subcommittee was to assess the desirability of establishing an oversight subcommittee. According to one committee member, "We were not encouraged to hold hearings." Informal conferences were held over six days with federal officials and with spokesmen for interested groups. Others submitted written statements for the record.

According to one staff member, no verbatim records were kept. Most of the testimony centered around Title VI of the 1964 Civil Rights Act, which provided for the withholding of federal funds under specified circumstances. Kastenmeier asserted that "Throughout the conferences, it was the opinion of all parties that an oversight committee be established within the Judiciary Committee." [6] The ad hoc committee presented its report to subcommittee #5 in February 1966 and then disbanded. The report was not published as a committee print; instead, Kastenmeier inserted it in the *Congressional Record* on September 21, 1966, during the debate on H. Res. 826, the proposal for a select oversight subcommittee.

The ad hoc committee made four recommendations:

> *First:* That a subcommittee, existing or special, within the House Judiciary Committee be authorized and directed to attend to matters involving voting and civil rights on a continuing basis.
> *Second:* That such subcommittee be authorized to travel within the continental limits of the United States for the purpose of conducting appropriate on-site hearings and/or investigations.
> *Third:* That adequate funds for professional staff and for other purposes be obtained for such subcommittee.
> *Fourth:* That authority to require the attendance of such witnesses and the production of such books or papers or other documents or vouchers by subpoena or otherwise be obtained for such subcommittee.[7]

Chairman Celler did not implement the recommendations unilaterally. He had reportedly taken similar actions in the past but now referred the matter to the full committee, where it lay dormant. One staff member, attempting to explain the absence of a positive committee reaction, stressed the pressures of other business. Many observers were convinced that this explanation provided less than the whole story.

Why did this effort seem to fail despite the support of members who shared the chairman's views on civil rights questions? The answer can be found in some judgments about political efficacy. Chairman Celler, supported by enough members to kill the proposal, had apparently reached two conclusions. First, the net impact of formal oversight would probably be pressure for less enforcement rather than for more effective enforcement. Second, sufficient oversight was being carried on through informal means.

Latent Oversight

Those who accuse Congress of not doing much oversight may be seeing only part of the picture. A committee, while devoting its efforts to legislation and other activities, may be conducting some oversight latently. The presence of latent oversight—that accomplished in fact while another legislative activity is ostensibly being performed—can be ascertained by looking at civil rights activities in the Judiciary Committee. Subcommittee #5, in the course of hearings on proposed legislation, latently gave some attention to oversight. The product of their efforts was less than systematic but more than minuscule.

Most subcommittee members and staff persons supported this latent presence:

> We achieve much oversight as we consider legislation. Hearings for legislation are the major instrument for performance of the oversight function on this subcommittee.

But others on the committee saw the formal distinction between legislation and oversight as an accurate reflection of behavior:

> Our big question is legislation. This is what we spend our time on. We are not primarily an oversight committee.

> The Congress hears too little of the widespread activities undertaken under these statutes. Most pertinent data on civil rights are presented in hearings on the current year's proposals.

How much oversight goes on in legislative hearings can only be determined by an examination of the record. A careful reading uncovered enough examples of oversight to merit attention, but only enough to slightly modify the earlier generalization about the committee's oversight activities. An analysis of committee oversight, formal and informal, manifest and latent, provides a more useful and complete picture of oversight than the formal record of investigations alone yields.

Why So Little Oversight?

How did the committee members explain the absence of systematic oversight? Most asserted that the committee was simply too busy legislating to do much overseeing. Some data do build a prima facie case. In the 89th Congress (1965–66) the Judiciary Committee was given responsibility for 35.8 percent of all measures introduced in the House of Representatives.[8] Included were such items as constitutional amendments on presidential inability, voting rights bills, measures proposing assistance for law enforcement agencies, bail reform proposals, and assorted civil rights bills. Subcommittee #5 held hearings on 371 bills, including the proposed voting rights act for which there were thirteen sessions of hearings, four days of subcommittee deliberation, and eleven days of full committee deliberation.[9] On the proposed civil rights bill of 1966, the subcommittee held ten days of hearings, deliberated on the bill for six days, and sent the bill to the full committee, which devoted nine sessions to it.[10]

The record confirms that the Judiciary Committee was in fact extraordinarily busy and productive on civil rights and other questions. The usual excuse offered by members of many committees—we are too busy legislating—did have some validity here. But even on this committee an element of rationalization loomed large. The committee did not oversee very much, partly because of the press of its schedule but mainly because its leadership, firmly in control of events, wanted to limit the scope of oversight efforts.

During this period, Chairman Celler was the dominant force on this committee, and he wanted little oversight effort. Why? The reasons were to be found in the interaction between personal, policy, and partisan factors—surely one of the most potent packages conceivable.

PERSONAL POWER. Chairman Celler had great respect for Justice Department officials with responsibilities for civil rights matters. They, in turn, consulted him with all the deference due to a powerful patriarch of the House of Representatives who had the added virtue of being the dominant voice on his committee. Consultation here was more than ritualistic. Instead, Celler's views seemed to be given great weight. Celler then lacked the incentives to oversee that rudeness, slights, and lack of attention sometimes provide.

POLICY PREFERENCES. If oversight efforts more frequently flow from policy disagreements than from policy consensus, then little oversight was to be expected here. Celler and Justice Department officials seemed in basic agreement about what needed to be done and about how to proceed. Moreover, Celler genuinely feared that formal oversight efforts in civil rights might expand the scope of conflict and thus upset existing policy patterns. Because the issues were so volatile, Celler felt that oversight efforts would provide room for segregationists and others whose views Celler did not share to jeopardize constructive policy implementation in the Justice Department.

PARTISANSHIP. One member of the committee stated the issue succinctly:

> We are of the same political party as the president and, of course, we do not want to do anything to embarrass him unless there is something absolutely wrong with a program.

Thus, another incentive for oversight was removed.

The story seems to have two morals. First, the general obligation to oversee falls before the specific realities of personal power, policy preferences, and partisan attachment. Second, motivations and incentives do a better job than structures in explaining the conduct of oversight or the absence thereof.

An Afterthought

In February 1971 Chairman Celler assigned jurisdiction for civil rights oversight to subcommittee #4. What accounted for a type of action that had been rejected previously? The answer was to be found in new circumstances. The flood of civil rights legislation beginning in 1957 had ended. A Republican administration was perceived by Celler as eroding established civil rights legislation. Celler's personal influence in the Justice Department had diminished.

In 1973, with a new committee chairman, Peter Rodino (D-N.J.), this new pattern persisted. When the Judiciary Committee ended its long-standing practice of having numbered subcommittees, one of the new units created was the Subcommittee on Civil Rights and Constitutional Rights.

Incentives and Oversight

The experience of the Judiciary Committee suggests two conclusions. First, the conventional wisdom concerning oversight provides an inadequate basis for analysis and reform. Second, granted a base of adequate resources, a situation that describes most committees and subcommittees in the Congress, the motivations of members are more central to oversight efforts than are structural factors. Increasing budgets, adding staff members, and gaining new authority may indeed help Congress to oversee more effectively in specific situations, but these acts cannot address the core problems because they ignore a central factor—member motivation and incentives to act. A focus on member motivation and incentives, however fruitful, leads analysts rapidly into barely explored territory. A brief glance at two topics begins to sort out this incredibly complex problem.

The Multiple Priorities of Members

Each member of Congress is faced with a variety of obligations that are legitimate, important, and demanding of time and energy. In principle, he should be working hard at all of them. In fact, since he does not weigh them equally, he is unlikely to give them equal attention. Because the weights assigned change with status and circumstance, the interests of each congressman in oversight will wax and wane despite his belief in the importance of performing oversight. When action is perceived to contribute directly and substantially to political survival, it is likely to move toward the top of any member's priority list.[11] Extra incentives to oversee come from problems of direct concern to one's constituents or from issues that promise political visibility or organizational support. Conversely, problems not seen as closely related to political survival are more difficult to crowd onto the member's schedule. In the choice phrase of one member: "Our schedules are full, but flexible."

In making their choices about what to do, members of Congress will do those things considered important to them at the time. In these calculations, oversight frequently falls into the neglected category. The price of multiple priorities is selective neglect.

Oversight becomes more difficult if most members assign a low priority to a committee's work. The House Post Office and Civil Service (POCS) Committee provided a spectacular example. Examining the POCS committee from 1965 to 1967 from the perspective of conventional wisdom yields an opaque picture. In the years 1965–66 the committee had a staff ranging from 32 to 42 members, and its expenditures in 1965 alone were $147,418.24. Despite this, the overall operations of the committee were in such low repute that the House Select Committee on Committees (the Bolling Committee) in 1973 seriously considered abolishing it altogether. Examining the record of the POCS committee through the lenses of member motivation can considerably clarify one's understanding of its oversight failures.

The low status of the POCS committee in the House of Representatives guaranteed that few would want to serve on it. In 1965–66 most members of the committee did not want to be there. Two members spoke for their peers:

> I didn't really choose the committee. It was assigned to me.

> I was assigned to this committee. I will get off of it as fast as I can.

Members of the committee left it in droves as soon as seniority permitted. Low initial attractiveness and high turnover meant relatively uninformed and largely indifferent members.

Almost all POCS committee members were assigned to more than one standing committee, and some 80 percent of these members listed the POCS committee as their second priority. The consequences were predictable. Those who remained on the committee seldom did so because of an intense interest in its subject matter. More particularistic reasons governed their behavior. On low-status committees, such as this one, subcommittee chairmanships tend to come rather quickly. Some enjoyed their perquisites of power and stayed to maintain them. Others stayed to guard specific interests in their district. Some found the slow pace of the committee appealing. Some were linked to committee-oriented interest groups vital to their reelection. Motivation here for comprehensive or systematic oversight was modest. The close ties of many of the "stayers" to interest groups, primarily postal employee organizations, and associations of mail users, provided strong incentives to attend primarily to two aspects of committee jurisdiction: employee wages and benefits, and the mail rates of user groups.

Policy Preferences

The relationship between policy preferences and the motivation to oversee is intimate. Interviews across several committees revealed that congressmen are seldom eager to monitor those executive activities of which they approve. A member who is indifferent to a program seldom presses for oversight. Disagreement on policy provides an important incentive to oversee. Almost all members feel a general obligation to oversee; the behavioral consequences are slight. When that responsibility merges with policy disagreement, oversight is much more likely.

The ties between policy preferences and oversight were spectacularly clear in the Judiciary Committee case study. This committee was an able group; many of its members were vitally interested in civil rights policy making and administration. Because Chairman Celler approved of what the Justice Department was doing, the Judiciary Committee did very little formal overseeing in the period studied. The absence of oversight could be explained by a rather simple formula: when policy preferences and the general obligation to oversee lead in differing directions, policy preferences normally prevail as a guide to conduct.

Structures, Resources, and Incentives

Why do so many congressmen approach oversight from a structural-resource perspective when the limitations of doing so are clear? The evidence suggests several answers: (1) Congressmen have found that structural and resource changes can have some impact on what they do. (2) Structures and resources are tangible. Something can be done about them. Congress can readily require oversight subcommittees or vote more money for investigations. (3) Motivations are difficult to ascertain and may be politically dangerous to uncover. They are linked in exceedingly complex ways to behavior. They are frequently hard to do a great deal about. (4) Congressmen tend to avoid painful topics especially when the costs of doing anything about them are high and the benefits uncertain. (5) Like all of us, congressmen may not always assess their situation very astutely.

Why do analysts prefer structural-resource approaches and solutions? The answer is that they used to, but most do not any longer. As one reads the research of Bibby, Fenno, Mayhew, Ogul, Scher, and Vinyard, among other political scientists, one can posit a consensus on the central relevance of motivations and incentives.[12] Translating this relatively recent awareness into analytically fruitful projects is the next major step if research on legislative oversight is to take any great leap forward. However, the danger of creating new strawmen to replace old ones is ever present. A focus on incentives should not distract us from the importance of relating individual impact to personal *and* situational factors.[13] Not all members are equal in their abilities, nor are they equally well placed to successfully pursue their interests. Even an intense desire to oversee depends for its fruition on more than the individual member's wants. Individual members conduct very little oversight themselves. Oversight efforts are centered in the committees and subcommittees. Where one is placed in the committee system is a vital element in translating desire into performance. *A focus on the intersections between incentives and structures is imperative.*[14]

Congressmen do what they do and slight what they slight for reasons that seem persuasive to them. The bases for choice are many. Balancing reasonable requests for time and action is central. Most congressmen feel that they can justify much of what they do in terms that their constituents would find quite acceptable. Most staff members do what their employers, the members of Congress, want them to do. The incentives for conducting more intensive and extensive oversight are great in the abstract and modest in many concrete situations. Any analysis of legislative oversight has to be grounded in this reality.

In the face of imperfect performance, congressmen still believe in doing a good job at oversight. Concurrently, many members seem comfortable while not doing much to narrow the gap between expectations about oversight and the actual performance of it. Many members of Congress are insufficiently dissatisfied with their oversight behavior to feel a strong enough stimulus to alter existing patterns.

How comprehensively Congress could do oversight and how systematic its efforts might be are questions that defy absolute answers. In relative terms, Congress can do more and better oversight. The primary question concerning legislative oversight of bureaucracy is not what Congress can do but what the members, individually and collectively, want to do and how badly they want to do it. Put another way, ask not only what oversight Congress can or should perform, *but also what oversight congressmen want to perform.*

NOTES

1. For related comments on oversight, see Joint Committee on the Organization of Congress, *Organization of Congress,* Hearings pursuant to S. Con. Res. 2, June 1965, pt. 4, 594; John Culver, *Committee Organization in the House,* Hearings under the authority of H. Res. 132, June 1973, vol. 2, p. 17; Theodore Lowi, "Congressional Reform: A New Time, Place, and Manner," in Theodore J. Lowi and Randall B. Ripley, eds., *Legislative Politics U.S.A.* (Boston: Little, Brown, 1973), p. 371; and Roger Davidson, David Kovenock, and Michael O'Leary, *Congress in Crisis: Politics and Congressional Reform* (Belmont, Calif.: Wadsworth, 1966), p. 174.
2. *Organization of Congress,* August 1965, pt. 9, p. 1333.
3. H. Rept. 93-916, pt. 2, p. 356.
4. "Staffing House Committees," working paper prepared for the House Select Committee on Committees, in "Committee Organization in the House," panel discussions, June 1973, vol. 2, p. 675.
5. All unattributed quotations are from interviews conducted by the author. Anonymity to the interviewees is assured.

6. U.S., Congress, House, *Congressional Record*, 89th Cong., 2nd sess., September 21, 1966, pp. 22547–548 (daily edition).
7. Ibid., p. 22547.
8. Committee on the Judiciary, *Legislative Calendar, Eighty-Ninth Congress*, p. 9.
9. Ibid., p. 18.
10. Ibid., p. 19.
11. The best discussion of this problem is David R. Mayhew, *Congress, the Electoral Connection* (New Haven, Conn.: Yale University Press, 1974).
12. Richard F. Fenno, Jr., *Congressmen in Committees* (Boston: Little, Brown, 1973); Davidson, Kovenock, and O'Leary, op. cit., p. 174; David Mayhew, op. cit., pp. 110–40; John F. Bibby, "Committee Characteristics and Legislative Oversight of Administration," *Midwest Journal of Political Science* 10 (February 1966): 78–98; Fenno, op. cit.; Morris S. Ogul, *Congress Oversees the Bureaucracy* (Pittsburgh: University of Pittsburgh Press, 1976); Seymour Scher, "Conditions for Legislative Control," *Journal of Politics* 25 (August 1963): 526–51; Dale Vinyard, "Congressional Checking on Executive Agencies," *Business and Government Review* 11 (September-October 1970): 14–18; Vinyard, "Congressional Committees on Small Business," *Midwest Journal of Political Science* 10 (August 1966): 364–77; Vinyard, "The Congressional Committees on Small Business: Pattern of Legislative Committee–Executive Agency Relations," *Western Political Quarterly* 21 (September 1968): 391–99.
13. This point is made especially well by Fred Greenstein, *Personality and Politics* (Chicago: Markham, 1969).
14. Chapter 7 of Ogul, op. cit., offers additional analysis leading to this conclusion.

11. *Congress and the President: Enemies or Partners?*

James L. Sundquist

Capacity in government depends, in the United States as elsewhere, on leadership. But even the ablest leaders—and the haphazard nomination and election processes of a democracy do not ensure selection of the ablest—cannot transcend the limits of the institutional structures in which they labor. In the United States, that has a special meaning. The institutional structure bequeathed to twentieth-century America by the eighteenth century is more complex than that of any other democratic country in the world. The United States stands alone in the degree to which governmental powers are shared among competing institutions—nation and states, Congress and the president, Senate and House of Representatives, all checked in turn by an independent Supreme Court.

The problem of governing, since the beginning, has been to assemble those dispersed powers in a working combination sufficiently harmonious to permit decisions to be made. Some of the divisions of power have been bridged in the course of past crises. A civil war and the ordeal of a great depression buried the doctrine of states' rights and established national supremacy in matters on which the nation elects to act. And with the depression and the New Deal revolution, the Supreme Court ceased trying to conform both the president and Congress to—as Mr. Justice Holmes put it—Mr. Herbert Spencer's

Social Statics. But one great division of power remains unabridged. That is the division of national governmental authority between the president, the Senate, and the House—three competing institutions that have the power to checkmate one another on most matters if they choose to press their authority to its limits.

That division has, if anything, become more crucial because of a phenomenon peculiar to the past two decades. From 1954 to 1976 the electorate did most of the time what before that date it did only on rare occasions—sending to Washington a president of one party and a Congress dominated by the other. For fourteen of those twenty-two years, the executive and the legislature confronted one another across not only an institutional but also a partisan political gulf, each branch compelled by the dynamics of party competition not to cooperate with the other but rather to attempt to use its power in such a way as to discredit the other. On any major issue, if a Republican president sent a bill to a Democratic Congress, the Democrats had to find reason to belittle and reject it—or else they were publicly pronouncing their political adversary to be a wise and able leader and his party's policy to be the right one. Conversely, if Congress initiated a bill, or a modification of the president's bill, he was under the same compulsion to find reason to denounce and veto it.

The public tends to dismiss the denunciation and counter-denunciation that flow from divided government as so much "playing politics," and much of it is. Often, after both sides have made their statements for the media, compromises are worked out. Nevertheless, President Ford's over half a hundred vetoes, reflect the different conceptions the two major parties have of the national interest. That, of course, is the reason for the party system, and something would indeed be lost if the parties failed to disagree or compromised too soon. To give the electoral processes vitality the parties must find ways not to conceal their fundamental differences in outlook and approach but to sharpen them as they apply them to concrete legislative issues. That this results so often in immobilization of the policy-making process is the consequence of the party system's operation within a structure of checks and balances.

The Cult of the Strong Presidency

For the first two-thirds of this century those who pondered the problem of how to unite the fragmented powers of government came to widespread agreement on what seemed a clear and feasible solution—the strong presidency. If the party is the web that unites the executive and legislative branches—when it controls them both—the leader of the party is the president. He carries the party's mandate in the presidential campaign. His program becomes the party's program, his appointees the party's spokesmen, his record the party's record. Members of Congress accept his leadership; senior members refer to past presidents they have served *"under,"* not *"with."* If the government is unified, it is through presidential energy, presidential skill, presidential force. A succession of strong leaders—Theodore Roosevelt, Woodrow Wilson, Franklin Roosevelt—dramatized the great potential of the presidential office.

The creaky machinery of the American government could be made to work after all, it seemed clear, if the president were strong enough. So half a century of agitation and effort went into building up his office. The president, a man, became the presidency, an institution. The Executive Office of the President was formed, made up of staff assistants who would extend the president's reach and his authority. In a whole series of legislative acts, he was assigned specific responsibilities of leadership. The Budget and Accounting Act of 1921 required him to devise annually a comprehensive program for the whole of the government, embodying a fiscal policy—which, before that time, a president did not have to do and usually did not. With the consent of Congress, he became the single spokesman on legislative policy for the whole of the executive branch; no agency could speak to Congress without his clearance. By the Employment Act of 1946, he was compelled to have an economic policy for maximum employment, production, and purchasing power. Before that date a president did not have to take responsibility for maintaining prosperity and economic growth, and before Franklin Roosevelt most did not. And, of course, he was still expected to fulfill his traditional roles of chief diplomat, chief global strategist, and—since World War II—leader of the free world.

Here was the answer. If parliamentary countries had a cabinet in which the powers of government were united, the United States had a presidency that served a comparable purpose. The president became the acknowledged leader of the legislative branch, as well as director and general manager of the executive. Congress waited for the State of the Union Message, the Budget Message, and the Economic Report of the President to set the agenda for its session. Then it waited for the administration bills. Presidents transmitted them with an increasing flow of special messages. It was on the administration program that media attention focused. An enterprising journal, *Congressional Quarterly*, devised an index to measure individual congressmen by the degree to which they supported the presidential program.

After Vietnam and Watergate, it is hardly necessary to dwell upon the dangers of the strong presidency that half a century of aggrandizement has produced. Those episodes tell us that a president could, after all, be recreant. Decisions could be made by the president alone, or by him in consultation with a small group of his own selection, confined, if he chose, to subordinates whom he could dominate. The president, in other words, could withdraw into a tight little circle from which critical or independent spirits could be excluded. He could defy popular and congressional opinion, if he chose. He did not even have to tell anyone what he was doing.

Most presidents don't act that way, of course. Lyndon Johnson and especially Richard Nixon are now seen as aberrations. Gerald Ford is the norm—open, outgoing, responsive. So people have stopped worrying. After all, Johnson was forced to retire and Nixon to resign, which proves, we are accustomed to saying and hearing, that the American system *did* work. Yet the experience of ten years of headstrong and unsuccessful presidential leadership compels an earnest reexamination of the faith that the strong presidency is a safe and reliable solution to our constitutional dilemmas.

In any institution, if power reposes in a single person, what happens when that person turns out to be rash or impulsive or erratic or touched with megalomania or bent on corrupting the purposes of the institution to serve his own? These traits may be uncommon, but they are hardly unknown. Hence most human institutions hedge the personal power of any individual executive by making him or her responsible to a plural body—a board of directors, a governing council, a board of trustees, or something comparable. In a parliamentary government, that plural body is the legislature itself, which selects and removes the chief executive. Among American governments, plural bodies are commonly in charge at the local level, where city councils and school boards select, control, and dismiss managers and superintendents.

The problem with the presidency, in essence, is how to pluralize the exercise of its power. Congress cannot serve as the necessary restraint upon the power of the president because it has no right to participate in the decision-making process, no right to be consulted. Presidents have even denied its right to be informed and have succeeded in defying its demand for information. The effective restraining force must therefore come from within the executive branch itself. Yet here a determined president can usually take command. He can dismiss or reassign officers in the departments and executive agencies who oppose him; the Supreme Court has affirmed that power. Richard Nixon found a way to rid himself of Archibald Cox, though he lost an attorney general and a deputy attorney general in the process. It may take a little time, but the White House can always learn who in the bureaucracy is loyal and organize around the others, and it can fill any key positions in the departments with its own henchmen. If necessary, it can take foreign policy out of the State Department, or any other policy out of any other department, and place it directly in the White House, and it can organize its own task forces—"plumbers," perhaps—to do jobs it prefers not to entrust to the permanent civil service.

Even the powers of Congress to take corrective action *after* the fact have their limits, for they often cannot be used directly to alter the behavior that may be deemed offensive. Congress may pass a new law, if the existing law is in fact unclear—provided each house can muster two-thirds of its members to override a veto. The War Powers Resolution, enacted over a veto, is an example of such a clarifying law. Yet if the existing law is satisfactory but simply maladministered, changing it is obviously no recourse.

Congress may cut appropriations for an agency it feels has abused its power, and this can work in instances where the abuse arises from an excess of governmental activity. The legislators could have dealt with Vietnam that way at any time with a simple clause in an appropriations bill—again assuming it could override a veto or outmaneuver the president in a legislative deadlock. But if the problem is the misuse of funds that Congress wants to see spent, but properly, cutting the budget only injures the program. In case of an outright violation of the law, its members can sometimes go to court, like any other citizen, and obtain an order to the president or a subordinate. Finally, there is the ultimate remedy of impeachment and removal of the chief executive. But in practice that depends on catching him in a clearly illegal act, and even then the process is so extreme and divisive as to be beyond consideration in any but the most extraordinary circumstances.

So the corrective action often has to take an indirect form. Congress has to hold as a hostage things the president is asking for— laws, appropriations, confirmations—and use them for purposes of bargaining.

But bargaining—or blackmail—on a broad scale is almost insuperably difficult to organize in a Congress of dispersed power, and it often cannot be carried out without damage to agencies and programs that have public and congressional support. To hold up all the president's appointments would mean judicial vacancies unfilled, cabinet posts empty, major agencies without direction. Also, the programs the president wants are usually programs that large segments of the public want. It would be easy for the president and his party to drum up public sentiment against Congress for impairing the normal and useful function of government and injuring innocent third parties in its vendetta against the chief executive. Within Congress, the committee or the house aggrieved by a presidential act may have to depend for retribution upon another committee or the other house, whose reaction may be, "Don't ask us to carry your fight against the president; we sympathize with you, but we're not going to let our program be your hostage."

Moreover, a branch made up of 535 equals has a hard time bargaining with a branch whose authority is concentrated in one executive. No one can commit Congress. No one can even speak for it. The elected leadership cannot be sure of its support. And the president can use his own bargaining devices to divide and conquer the diffused and plural legislature.

These are the dilemmas that have faced Congress since it set out a few years ago, with much public support, to bring to bay what it had finally concluded was an overgrown, overbearing, overweening presidency.

The Resurgence of Congress

Even before the full scope of the Watergate scandal had been uncovered, Congress had been aroused to an extraordinary mood of determination and resolution: the balance between the executive and legislative branches had to be restored. The turning point came at the opening of the 93rd Congress in January 1973 as the result of a whole series of conflicts with President Nixon that had reached a climax in the preceding autumn.

The most important of these was a conflict over spending, in which the Republican president defeated and humiliated the Democratic Congress. In the middle of the 1972 election campaign and just before Congress was scheduled to adjourn, the president challenged it with a demand that expenditures in that fiscal year be cut from the $256 billion already authorized by the lawmakers to $250 billion in order to stem inflation. If Congress could not make the cuts, he demanded that it give him a blanket authority to do so. The House of Representatives listened to pleas from its leaders that to give the president that kind of power would be, in the words of Speaker Carl Albert, to "knowingly and willingly abdicate not only our powers—but our responsibilities." But then it acquiesced to the president's request. The Senate, however, heeded the pleas of its Democratic leaders and refused to go along. It agreed with the president's request but proposed a formula for making the $6 billion cut that restricted the president's discretion. That alternative the House members of a House-

228 • CONGRESS AND THE PRESIDENT

Senate conference committee rejected as unworkable, and Congress adjourned in deadlock.

The Senate had succeeded in preserving the prerogatives of Congress but only at the cost of publicly demonstrating the impotence of the whole legislative branch. Here were both houses agreeing that the president was right, that aggregate spending authorizations of Congress did add up to unsound policy. But having acknowledged its cumulative mistakes, Congress then proved incapable of pulling itself together to rectify them. Accepting the president's leadership, it could not even organize itself to follow. The president won a public relations victory to exploit in the campaign, Congress suffered another loss in public esteem, and the country presumably suffered more inflation.

Confident that public opinion was behind him, the president then proceeded to rub another congressional sore by impounding still more money that Congress had appropriated. In January the administration reported that a total of $8.7 billion was being held in reserve.[1] And he was defying the Congress in other ways as well. Without consulting Congress, which by then was dominated by peace sentiment, he had stepped up the Vietnam war by renewing the bombing of North Vietnam and blockading Haiphong harbor. He was claiming for his administration an unlimited right to withhold from Congress any information on any subject, solely at his own discretion, under the doctrine of executive privilege. And he was proceeding to put into effect indirectly a reorganization of the executive branch that Congress had rejected; when they refused to consolidate seven domestic departments into four, he appointed four supra-cabinet officers in the White House to exercise, insofar as possible, the powers the four new department heads would have held.

Congress convened in January 1973 in a fighting mood. In the ensuing months, it mustered a rare unity of purpose and firmness of will in its confrontation with the president, and it was aided immeasurably by the collapse of the Nixon presidency as Watergate unraveled— an unraveling to which the congressional investigative power had made its own important contribution. A president in a desperate struggle just to retain his office—and a losing struggle, as it turned out—is in no position to ward off the demands of a resurgent Congress, and so the legislative branch did succeed in reviving those of its lost powers that had been most at issue. The president canceled the supra-cabinet appointments that had offended Congress (and had outraged the subordinated departments as well). Over the president's veto, Congress enacted the War Powers Resolution, which requires the president to report to Congress within forty-eight hours any commitment of American military forces and obtain the legislature's approval within sixty days. It passed the Congressional Budget and Impoundment Control Act to restore congressional authority over fiscal policy and spending decisions. It extended the confirmation power to the top officials of the Office of Management and Budget. It experimented with various "legislative veto" devices to give it a chance to review certain types of executive actions before they were taken. Meanwhile, in the case of the Nixon tapes, the Supreme Court had overruled unanimously the president's claim of unlimited executive privilege, although it did not define exactly what the limits are.

By the time the 93rd Congress adjourned at the end of 1974, then, each of the specific causes of the anger and unrest that had marked its opening had been removed. The Nixonian aggressions against the legislature had been repulsed, the offending president himself had been actually driven from office, and Congress had set up barriers through legislation that would prevent new "usurpations." Not only had the pre-Nixon status quo been restored, but also the pre-Johnson and in some respects even the pre-Franklin Roosevelt and pre-Theodore Roosevelt relations between the branches. In fact, in some matters Congress was on firmer ground than any it had ever occupied before. Yet a caveat has to be entered: if a determined president chooses to interpret even the new laws in his own way, Congress is essentially back where it started. While the intent and spirit of these laws is clear, so have been earlier laws and the Constitution itself, and all are encompassed equally within the general limitations, discussed above, on what Congress can do whenever it feels the president has overstepped his powers.

Viewed in the perspective of history, the changes in the executive-legislative power balance wrought by a single Congress—the 93rd—are truly momentous. Ever since the era of congressional government at the close of the Civil War (when Congress succeeded in writing reconstruction policy in defiance of President Andrew Johnson), the flow of power had been all one-way, in the direction of the president. In just two years, the trend of a hundred years was dramatically reversed. An extraordinary abuse of presidential power triggered a counteraction equally extraordinary, and the ponderous processes of institutional change were expedited.

This leads to a critical question about the flow of power back to Congress. If the legislative branch has succeeded in restoring its "constitutional prerogatives," how well is it equipped to exercise them? The resurgence of Congress compels a fresh look at what have been seen over the years as the endemic weaknesses of Congress. These may be summarized under four headings: parochialism, irresponsibility, sluggishness, and amateurism.

Parochialism

Individual senators and representatives depend for survival not on pleasing the nation as a whole but on satisfying the limited constituencies from which they are elected. So being national-minded can be a positive hazard to a legislative career. The politically safe course for almost any newcomer to Congress is to attend assiduously to his or her duties as a delegate—interceding with the executive branch on cases involving constituents, promoting local projects, speaking and acting for the particular interests of the state or district—while leaving the statesmanship to others. Even if the member later assumes responsibility for leadership on broader questions, he had better never forget who sent him to Washington and who keeps him there.

This has its merits, up to a point. The parochialism of Congress ensures that local and narrow interests can get a hearing, that they are not ridden over arbitrarily, which is not necessarily the case in the executive branch. Yet whatever the merits of the local or regional claim, it must be pressed. Representatives of Texas must see the national interest in terms of oil, those of South Dakota in terms of cattle, and those of Detroit in terms of automobiles. Foreign policy seen through the eyes of a constituency may predispose a representative toward the Greek, the Israeli, or the Irish view of particular problems. The budget appears as a "pork barrel" to be distributed among districts as well as a fiscal program for the country. What weapons the military forces should get are liable to be judged by what factories are located in a state or district. And so it goes across the whole range of policy. Political incentives propel the member—especially the House member who represents more specialized constituencies—from the broad to the narrow perspective. To avoid invidious reference to the living, one may reach into history for a case and come back with, perhaps, the story told by Henry Stimson about the chairman of the House Naval Affairs Committee of sixty years or so ago. Asked one day whether the navy yard in his district was too small to accommodate the latest battleships, the chairman replied, "That is true, and that is the reason I have always been in favor of small ships." [2]

Defenders of Congress argue that the national interest is, in the last analysis, the sum of the local interests. This argument, however, rests on a mythical conception of how a legislature with the work load of the American Congress operates. Decisions—except for the greatest ones—cannot really be made by the collectivity of both houses. Issues have to be parceled out instead for piecemeal action by committees and subcommittees, and these are unlikely to be fully representative. Committee assignments are determined by what the members want to do. Farm state members want to deal with agriculture while city people do not, so the agricultural committees are rural and proagriculture in their composition. The military affairs committees are dominated by partisans of the military, urban affairs committees by members from the cities, interior committees by proreclamation westerners, and so on. By custom, the judiciary committees are made up exclusively of lawyers. Within each committee, there is further specialization of committees and of individual members. The decisions of the specialists have to be accepted by their colleagues most of the time without more than a cursory examination; a fresh and exhaustive review of every question by every member is obviously impossible. And through logrolling, the advocates of various local interests form coalitions of mutual support.

Specialization is properly advanced as one of the strengths of the houses of Congress, and they could not function without it. Yet if specialization is to prevail, then by definition the effective power of decision is delegated mainly to individuals and small groups who reflect the views of relatively narrow geographic segments of the population; if the sum of those views turns out in some cases to be the equivalent of the national interest, that has to be coincidental.

The presidency, in contrast, has a nationwide and governmentwide perspective. Responsible only to the largest of constituencies, the president can, if need be, sacrifice a local interest to the general welfare. Moreover, the hierarchical structure of the executive branch facilitates the weighing and balancing of local and narrow interests. If separate departments speak for the cities and the countryside, for the producer and the consumer, for employers and for labor, the White House and the Executive Office of the President command a broad view of the entire government and can discern from the clash of separate interests, in a judicious and deliberate fashion, where the national interest—defined by some as the "greatest good of the greatest number" concept—lies.

Irresponsibility

How does the electorate exercise control over a plural body chosen from half a thousand separate constituencies? It is not even possible, sometimes, to fix responsibility within Congress for what the body does or does not do. If a popular measure dies in committee, who killed it? Republicans may blame Democrats and Democrats Republicans, members may blame the chairman and the chairman the members, liberals and conservatives may blame the others' tactics, and so on. The individual member tells his constituents, "I did the best I could; it was the fault of all those other fellows." And from all indications, this tactic works. Even as opinion polls show public confidence in Congress as a whole to be extraordinarily low—13 percent gave it a favorable rating in one recent test—the voters tend to approve their own representatives and return them to office. And anyway, if a voter is unhappy with Congress and seeks to alter it, he can cast his ballot against, at most, only 2 of 535 members in any one election.

The members of Congress can hide not only behind one another but behind the president as well. If they intervene in a casual or piecemeal way in economic matters or in the complex world of U.S.-Soviet or U.S.-European relations, it is still the president who must bear most often the electoral responsibility for the consequences of their acts. The continuing management of the economy and of diplomacy are the president's responsibility. He is the one held accountable by the electorate for results, and normally a plea that Congress interfered is not an acceptable excuse. After all, the president was sent to Washington to lead and manage Congress, too. So if the public, or any substantial segment of it, is aroused by events in Cyprus, say, or inside the Soviet Union or anywhere else, and a majority in Congress feels a surge of emotion to strike a blow, it can usually be done with relative impunity. The members reap the political reward and go on to the next item on their agenda, while the administration is left to pick up the pieces of its wrecked policy and reorder its relations around the globe.

When a president exercises power, on the other hand, responsibility is clear. Further, he must take personal responsibility for the way the whole executive branch exercises its discretion. He cannot escape by putting the blame on his colleagues, as can a congressman; the plaque on Harry Truman's desk announced, "The buck stops here." And popular control—eventually, at the end of the president's term—is real: everybody can vote for president. If not for or against the incumbent, at least for or against the candidate of the incumbent party, whom the president will be supporting.

Sluggishness

It takes time for a legislature to blend and reconcile disparate views. But it takes more time in the American Congress than in other national legislative bodies because of certain peculiarities of Congress—its division into two houses that must concur on all legislative matters, the further fragmentation of power within each house among numerous committees and subcommittees, the Senate rule requiring an extraordinary majority for the closure of the debate, and the virtual absence of party discipline. In each of these respects, the

United States Congress occupies a position among national parliaments that is either unique or extreme.

The result is that any piece of legislation must surmount an obstacle course of unparalleled difficulty. At each point along that course, the action may be delayed, if not killed—in the House by the subcommittee, the full committee, the Rules Committee (or even by the chairmen of one of these, through the device of not scheduling it for action), or on the floor; in the Senate by the subcommittee, the committee (or, again, by a chairman), or on the floor by a majority or by a minority large enough to forestall cloture of debate (41 members, or as many fewer as there are absentees at the time of the vote); or in a House-Senate conference committee. As a result, few things happen quickly. Policies eventually adopted are often approved too late; a fiscal policy designed to counter one economic trend may not win approval until that trend has disappeared and the opposite trend set in, at which time it may be exactly the wrong policy. And in the process of overcoming the countless legislative hurdles, policies may be compromised to the point of ineffectiveness.

The inherent slowness of Congress gives the president infinite advantages as policy leader. Only the president, indeed, can be trusted with power where quickness of decision and action is imperative. This has been recognized not only in time of war but also to a degree in peacetime when the government must be able to respond quickly to events beyond its control. In foreign relations, therefore, the president has often been granted broad latitude to commit the nation, and the War Powers Resolution appears to acknowledge a continuing if limited authority even for the use of military force. The president has been granted discretionary powers in such domestic matters as price and wage controls. There is strong reason to make his economic powers permanent in a manner corresponding to his war powers —covering rates of taxation and expenditure as well as direct controls—on the ground that only the president can act quickly enough to counter sudden inflationary or recessionary trends in the economy. Presidents can procrastinate, too, but unlike Congress they are not compelled to by any institutional structure. When their minds are made up, they can act within the limits of their statutory power.

Amateurism

An executive branch decision is presumably derived from expert judgments. The president is himself an amateur, and so may his cabinet members be, but they have in their employ experts on every subject of accepted governmental concern—often the leading experts in the country. From their accumulated experience in the administration of government programs, these experts can advise on the workability of proposed new policies. They can assess the side effects and predict the consequences. They may be overridden by the politically responsible amateurs for whom they work, but at any rate their judgment is normally sought and considered sympathetically.

When Congress elects to compete with the president in policy initiation, quite the opposite may be the case. Members of Congress do not have equal access to the executive branch expertise, and they may not trust it, especially when the two branches are under differing partisan control. Moreover, in those circumstances, as suggested earlier, they are under some compulsion to reject in whole or in part the executive branch's leadership. So they need experts of their own. This can be salutary. The executive branch has no monopoly on either wisdom or data, and it is good for experts in the bureaucracy to be checked and challenged by experts on the outside.

However, the solid expertise Congress needs for overruling the executive branch and substituting its own judgment is not easily or reliably assembled. The legislative branch does contain research and information-gathering organizations that match their executive branch competitors in quality of staff—the General Accounting Office, the Congressional Research Service of the Library of Congress, the new Office of Technology Assessment, and the even newer Congressional Budget Office. But the older of these organizations, at least, have not been intimate participants when the members of Congress were actually making legislative policy. They have been a step removed from the policy process, as nonpartisans in a climate of partisanship and as bodies independent of the legislative committees and subcommittees and their individual members; the heads of the General Accounting Office and the Library of Congress are presidential appointees. How the expertise of these agencies is used depends heavily on the circle of staff advisers who are at the core of the policy-making process. These are the committee and subcommittee staffs and the personal staffs of senators and representatives, who are chosen and appointed by the members of Congress themselves and who reflect the partisan orientation, and are sensitized to the political needs, of their sponsors.

Again, there are committee and subcommittee staffs that compare well with executive branch agencies in specialized knowledge and general competence. Yet even when the backup resources of the GAO, the CRS, the OTA, and the CBO are taken into account, they can rarely match their rivals in depth, despite enormous expansion in recent years. The range of responsibility of each committee is too broad, and the attention given most subjects too intermittent, to permit the engagement of specialists on each. Hence committee and even subcom-

mittee staffs have tended to be composed of generalists, often knowledgeable about many things but usually truly expert only in legislative
manipulation and in knowing where in the executive branch to turn
for reliable data and the best advice. When in a period of intense and
partisan interbranch competition executive branch sources dry up for
them, the shortage of qualified specialists on Capitol Hill becomes
more glaring and acute.

As Congress has tried during the Nixon-Ford years to remedy its
shortages, the weaknesses of its personnel system have been exposed.
Neither house has a merit system or central facilities for recruitment or
a tenured career service. The fragmentation of the hiring process ensures that at best the structure of staff assistance will be spotty. Since
each chairman has the responsibility for assembling his own staff, the
competence of the staff available to cope with a given legislative issue
depends on the chairman's conception of how much genuine expertise
he needs. Sometimes he may not see the need for any at all; he may be
content to rely for information and argument on the interest groups
supporting his position—always a dubious source. Or a chairman may
feel a need for expert assistance but have no acquaintance with the
universe of talent in that particular area and no ready means of tap-
ping it, in which case he falls back on amateurs. Moreover, the need is
apt to develop quickly, and established experts are difficult to obtain
on short notice for jobs that offer no security of tenure. So the recruitment field may be limited to persons not yet established in careers; in
other words, the young and inexperienced.

Finally, an element of expertise almost invariably lacking on Capitol Hill, even in experienced and permanent staff, is the comprehen-
sion of administrative necessities that can only come from responsibility for program operation. Even when the congressional majority
and the president are political allies, the separation of administrative
from legislative responsibility reduces the degree of attention given in
the legislative process to questions of administrative feasibility—an
aspect both of the administrative amateurism of Congress and of its
lack of responsibility and accountability for administrative results.

Congressional Reform and Its Limits

As Congress in 1973 surveyed its loss of standing vis-à-vis the
president, it was not unaware of its endemic weaknesses. "The fault
lies . . . in ourselves," Mike Mansfield has said.[3] So even as Congress
looked outward and resolved to do battle with the president, it looked
inward to its own organization and procedures. Since then, in internal

reform as in relations with the executive, it has made more dramatic progress than at any time in more than half a century.

The new reforms—particularly the new budget process, a dramatic modification of the seniority system, and an assertion of greater power by the House majority caucus—may well prove lasting. But the reform impulse has now run up against a stubborn fact of congressional life, which has dampened the urge for further change. For the typical member of Congress, reform inevitably means a sacrifice of individual freedom and individual power. Each of the weaknesses enumerated above—parochialism, irresponsibility, sluggishness, and amateurism—results from, or is accentuated by, decentralization of power within the institution. It is the individual decision maker who is parochial and amateur; it is the multiplicity of veto points that makes for delay and indecision; it is the scattering of authority that hides its exercise and permits each member to escape a clear responsibility. To remedy these defects would require the individual decision makers in the committees and subcommittees to be effectively subordinated to some form of central authority in each house—an authority that could make timely decisions on behalf of the membership, from a national viewpoint, with expert assistance, and with clear responsibility. Congress, in other words, would have to become something of a hierarchy, like the executive branch, with a power of decision somewhere. Yet individual members cherish their independence and their shares of dispersed power. Beyond that, it is obviously impossible to go far in centralizing power in Congress without changing the fundamental character of that institution and losing the very real values that come from its pluralism and diversity.

The dilemma becomes clearer when one attempts to design the specific nature of the centralizing mechanisms that might be employed. Powers that might be recovered from the committees, subcommittees, and individual members could be centered in the leadership of the majority party, in an authoritative central policy committee, in the majority party caucus, or in some combination of these. The alternatives are more than theoretical; each has at one time or another been tried, and a review of these experiments is revealing.

The apogee of leadership power came during a period of about twenty years with its midpoint at the beginning of this century. That was a time of tightly organized and well-disciplined party "machines" at state and local levels, held together by patronage, and the politicians who made their way to Congress were accustomed to follow leaders—or obey bosses, as the progressive enemies of machine politics preferred to phrase it. In the Senate, the majority leadership was collective, an oligarchy of like-thinking Republican stalwarts whose leading figure was Nelson Aldrich of Rhode Island. But in the House, the power of the Speaker was all but absolute. That was the time of the fabled Republican "czars" of the House—Speaker Thomas B. Reed of Maine and, after him, Joseph G. Cannon of Illinois. The Speaker held sway by virtue of his power to control all committee assignments; his championship of the House Rules Committee, which cleared all measures for floor debate; and his right of recognition, which controlled access to the floor.

During the reigns of czars Reed and Cannon, Congress was unquestionably powerful. President Theodore Roosevelt's legislative program was at the mercy of Speaker Cannon and Senator Aldrich and his fellow oligarchs. They told him what their houses would or would not accept, and they spoke with authority; they could deliver or withhold majorities. No problem of sluggishness here, but the other weaknesses remained and by the concentration of authority were even magnified. In the House in particular, Uncle Joe Cannon became parochialism and irresponsibility writ large. As the nation grew and urbanized and Cannon failed to grow and broaden with it, Cannonism became a national issue. But Cannon's power over the majority of the controlling party in the House sustained him in office, and only his Illinois constituents could defeat him at the polls. So progressives had to aim their attack at the institution of the Speakership, and in 1910 a coalition of Democrats and progressive Republicans seized the opportunity to strip that office of its most important powers. The Speaker's control of committee assignments was wrested from him, and as a safeguard against a return of Cannonism, both parties guaranteed their committee members continuous tenure, with rank determined automatically by seniority. In the Senate, too, seniority came to be the protector of individual rights.

Since that period, the antiboss, antimachine ethic of the progressive movement that toppled Cannon has become even more deeply ingrained in the American politician and in the electorate, and any return to czarism in either house has been unthinkable. Even the strongest leaders of our own era—the two Texans of the Eisenhower period, Senate Majority Leader Lyndon Johnson and Speaker Sam Rayburn—therefore fell far short of being bosses in the old sense. They could not direct the committees; quite the contrary, on every issue they were at the mercy of the committees and their chairmen, in whom the power of decision actually resided. Neither Johnson nor Rayburn had at his command any sanctions to compel the making of the decisions they desired, or even to get decisions made at all. They could not depose or penalize recalcitrant committee chairmen or reconstitute committee membership. They had no significant rewards to offer beyond the original assignment to committees, and they lacked full control even over that. All they could do, really, was to use their personal prestige, extraordinarily high in Rayburn's case, and their ability to wheedle, cajole, and persuade, which was legendary in Johnson's.

The use of an authoritative policy committee as a central repository of power had its heyday too, even earlier than the Cannon-Aldrich period. If there was a time that can be called the golden age of congressional supremacy—when the legislature laid down the policies that governed the nation, in defiance of the president, if necessary—it was during the Reconstruction Era. The instrumentality was the Joint Committee of Fifteen on Reconstruction, which came closer than any other group in the history of Congress to performing the legislative functions of a British cabinet. (President Andrew Johnson compared it, instead, to the Directory of the French Revolution.) It rejected the Lincoln-Johnson program of reconstruction and wrote its own Radical Republican alternative, which was enacted over a series of Johnson vetoes. And to put the program into effect against executive resistance, the radical-dominated Congress went so far as to take from the president the power to remove cabinet officers—a type of derogation that in a later case the Supreme Court held unconstitutional—and in the end impeached him.

But the circumstances of the time were exceptional. Rarely has Congress been so ideologically cohesive, so dominated by a single faction of a single party. The two-thirds majorities necessary to override presidential vetoes could be mustered almost automatically. But that could happen only in a Congress whose natural minority had disappeared from its halls, when the Confederate states seceded. Once those states were readmitted, Congress lost its homogeneity, and its partisan majorities were no longer large enough to crush a president.

The use of the majority party caucus as the centralizing instrument had an even briefer, though distinguished, life, amounting to a single Congress, that of 1913–14. The central measures of Woodrow Wilson's New Freedom, notably tariff reform and creation of the Federal Reserve System, were enacted through the caucus mechanism. Democratic members of the regular Senate and House committees having jurisdiction over those subjects developed the bills with the leadership or collaboration of the Wilson administration—and the exclusion of Republican participants. The measures were then submitted for approval to a "binding" Democratic caucus, one that pledged the members (unless they were formally excused for any of several specific reasons) to vote for the bills on the floor. After the caucus votes, the standing bipartisan committees went through the motions of considering the bills, but the results were ordained. Majority party unity had been attained, a clear party policy had been adopted, and the minority was easily overridden.

The use of the Democratic caucus as a regular mechanism for making policy ceased after only a brief experiment in a single Congress, despite the success of that trial. It might have survived the opposition attacks on King Caucus if the party had retained its unity on basic policy. But it did not. It fell apart on issues of preparedness; the House majority leader was among those who split with President Wilson, and from that point on the use of the caucus to establish binding policy was out of the question. The institution has never been revived.

In its post-1972 reform mood, the House of Representatives (and to a minor degree the Senate) has moved gingerly in the direction of all three centralizing models. The House Democratic majority has been holding caucuses more frequently than at any time in recent decades. And although the caucus has not attempted to bind individual members concerning votes on the floor, it has taken some other revolutionary steps. For one thing, it has brought an end to the rigid seniority system that had prevailed for sixty years. In 1975 it finally exercised on three occasions its option to depose committee chairmen who were out of step with the party rank and file, or too old to be effective, or both.

The House majority caucus also transferred the task of filling the party's vacancies on standing committees from the Democratic members of the Ways and Means Committee, where it had resided since the overthrow of Cannon, to the caucus's own steering and policy committee. This is a body at once more representative and more directly subject to caucus and leadership control. The Speaker is its chairman and appoints 9 of its 24 members, but Speaker Carl Albert—never a seeker after personal power in the Reed-Cannon or even the Rayburn tradition—has tried to develop the committee as a collective leadership structure. At the beginning of 1975, the committee attempted to act as a policy coordinator in the field of energy, where jurisdiction was divided among several standing committees—but without conspicuous success. A corresponding special committee of Senate Democrats on energy likewise had little impact. Both efforts were abandoned, and the experiment was not extended to other areas.

In one crucial field of overlapping jurisdictions, however—that of budget and fiscal policy—Congress in 1974 established a permanent coordinating mechanism. It created in each house a new bipartisan standing committee on the budget, with the Congressional Budget Office as an analytical resource to serve both. These committees have begun presenting annually to Congress a comprehensive fiscal plan governing revenues, expenditures, and deficit or surplus, which upon adoption sets limits on all subsequent fiscal actions. To the surprise of many who predicted that the combined power of the old standing committees would be concentrated on scuttling their new rival, the system survived its trial year of 1975 and then the 1976 cycle. Congress can now claim to have brought under orderly policy control the piecemeal appropriations process that so embarrassed it in its 1972 feud with Richard Nixon.

Except in this one field of fiscal policy, there remains no regular institutional structure in either house to deal effectively with matters that cut across the jurisdictions of two or more committees. With its power dispersed, Congress remains organized to deal with narrow problems but not with broad ones. Its structure still impels it to think parochially. It can skirmish for limited objectives but it cannot think strategically. It can, for instance, devise policies affecting energy but not a *national energy policy*. It can enact measures affecting the nation's growth but not a *national growth policy*—even though in 1970 it committed itself by statute to do so. It cannot have a comprehensive economic policy (apart from fiscal policy) or a policy on intergovernmental relations. It has no machinery for the coordination of foreign policy with military policy. The breadth of each of these policy areas, like the budget area, calls for a body of some kind with jurisdiction cutting across those of existing committees. The leadership in neither house has shown a disposition to improvise with temporary special committees for coordination purposes, and it is clear that a multiplicity of permanent committees dealing with broad, cross-cutting policy questions would create a jungle of conflicting jurisdictions that could only make the present situation worse. Congress still has no way of setting an agenda, or priorities, for its own activities, no way of ensuring consistency and completeness in its consideration of the country's problems. For the good and largely inescapable reasons set out above, it does not appear likely that a much greater degree of centralization of responsibility for these purposes can be attained—in the leadership, in the new committees, or in the caucuses.

In short, if presidential government has its perils, a pendulum swing to some ideal of congressional government is not the safeguard. That goal is unattainable within the American constitutional framework and tradition.

The Prospects for Collaboration

So the president and Congress are compelled to live together in a marriage arranged by matchmakers of a long-gone era, a marriage that, however loveless, is without the possibility of divorce. So how can the partners live together in a reasonable degree of harmony, attaining enough unity of purpose to make the government functional?

The indispensable requisite for fruitful collaboration is that the president and the congressional majority be of the same party. When the two branches are in the hands of partisan adversaries, the president will not consult freely and share with congressional leaders his crucial decisions, which is essential to preventing the abuse of power. Nor, in those circumstances, will Congress accept the presidential leadership that is needed to compensate for the diffusion of its own internal structure. Partisan consistency is the first requirement for interbranch collaboration, though it has not always proved to be enough.

Now that the voters have chosen, however, to put their trust in a president and congressional majority of the same party, a development of great significance, suggests that for the next few years, at least, the chances of a durable peace between the branches will be better than at any time in this century. That development is the realignment of the parties in Congress, which reflects the changes that have been taking place in the country—the final working out, that is, of the realignment of the 1930s, when the issues of the Great Depression and the New Deal gave the United States its present party system. Since then, as new generations of voters have come along, those who were not committed by inheritance found themselves attracted to the Democratic party if they were liberals in the New Deal sense and drawn to the Republican party if they were conservatives. In this process, both parties have become more homogeneous. By now, all the northern states have realigned generally on the national pattern. So have the metropolitan areas of the South, and the realignment is progressing in the rural areas.[4]

With some time lag, these changes have affected the party composition of the Senate and the House. On the Republican side, the once deeply divided party has coalesced into a far more homogeneous group. On the Democratic side, the old anti-New Deal "bourbon" wing that thwarted and frustrated Democratic presidents from Franklin Roosevelt to John Kennedy has been dwindling rapidly. The conservative stalwarts who once made up one-third to almost half of the Democratic strength in both houses, and by virtue of seniority held an even larger proportion of actual power, are now reduced to not much more than half a dozen in the Senate and thirty to forty in the house. Moreover, since the Democratic caucus no longer is forced by the seniority system to bestow automatic chairmanships upon them, a Democratic president and his congressional leaders will be able to ignore or override them.

The country has become so accustomed to seeing the president and the Congress at each other's throats that this seems almost a permanent and normal condition of American government. Some may even think it beneficial because it suggests that any future Watergates will be exposed more quickly and surely. But more important consideration in forming a government is to make possible affirmative, positive action. So the quiet revolution going on within the party system, which provides a new basis for presidential-congressional collaboration, is one of hope and promise. The prospects for interbranch cooperation when the president and the congressional majority are of the same party are brighter than at any time in the memory of anyone now living, and they will become even brighter in the future as party realignment completes its course. Responsible party government under the president as party leader will be possible—not just in times of extraordinary majorities but on a continuing basis. One has to go back to the nineteenth century for a time when that could be said about either party.

There are still things that can keep this promise from being realized, of course, even if the president and the congressional majorities are of the same party. Much depends on the skill of the individual who happens to be president; many in the past have failed as party leaders. The central mechanism for developing solidarity and capacity to act within the congressional majority still must be attended to. And it remains to be seen whether the vastly expanded congressional facilities for policy analysis, such as the new congressional budget machinery, will be a bridge between the branches, facilitating collaboration, or a barrier. Set up by a congressional majority bent upon equipping itself for confrontation with a president of the other party, will these mechanisms display an institutional bias toward confrontation, even when the White House falls into friendly hands?

These are not minor considerations. But there is at least solid reason to believe that the prospect for an effective, lasting partnership between the president and Congress has never been better than it will be during the era that the inauguration of President Carter has ushered in. The long season of hostility and stalemate between the branches should have passed. The American government should begin to work again. And some, at least, of the recent appalling loss of confidence by the people in their governmental institutions should be recouped.

NOTES

1. Louis Fisher observes that this figure rested on a narrow definition of impoundment that excluded another $9 billion in impounded funds. *Presidential Spending Power* (Princeton, N.J.: Princeton University Press, 1975), p. 172.

2. Stimson testimony in *National Budget System*, Hearing before the House Select Committee on the Budget, 66:1 (Washington, D.C.: Government Printing Office, 1919), p. 641.
3. Address to the Senate Democratic Conference, January 4, 1973, reprinted in *Congressional Record*, vol. 119, p. 324.
4. This realignment process is described in James L. Sundquist, *Dynamics of the Party System: Alignment and Realignment of Political Parties in the United States* (Washington, D.C.: Brookings Institution, 1973), especially chaps. 11 and 12.

IV

CONGRESS AND THE FUTURE

12. *Will Reform Change Congress?*

Charles O. Jones

The moment is at hand. Reform is absolutely mandatory. The House of Representatives must regain its authority. A Democrat eloquently states the case:

> This is not a personal fight, so far as I am concerned. . . . This is a fight against the system. We think it is a bad system. . . . It does not make any difference to me that it is sanctified by time. There never has been any progress in this world except to overthrow precedents and take new positions. There never will be. . . . We had to make up our mind months ago to try to work the particular revolution that we are working here today, because, not to mince words, it is a revolution. . . . We are fighting to rehabilitate the House of Representatives and to restore it to its ancient place of honor and prestige in our system of government.[1]

Mary Russell reconstructed the story for the *Washington Post*.

> The revolt that rocked the House last week, leaving two committee chairmen deposed and the seniority system crippled, was full of charges of conspiracies, pettiness and passion, selfishness and opportunism.
> By last week's end it was clear that a major shift in power had taken place. Committee chairmen, who, as autonomous barons, secure in their seniority, had often ignored the leadership and undermined programs

that a majority of the Democrats wanted, were served notice that their heads might roll for such action.[2]

So seniority as a virtually inviolable rule was drastically modified by a series of actions dating back to 1971. A "revolution"? "The word . . . has been freely used—in both joyous and fearful tones—in the wake of the stunning events in the House Democratic steering committee and caucus." [3]

I have, in fact, drawn these quotes from two different reform eras. The eloquent Democrat cited first was Champ Clark (D-Mo.) and the occasion was the famous 1910 House debate on a resolution introduced by George Norris (R-Nebr.), which said, among other things: "The Speaker shall not be eligible to membership on said committee" (i.e., the Committee on Rules). I favor the juxtaposition of these reform efforts for this essay because I want to speak here about reform and change, about short-term reordering and long-term effects, or, if you will, about removing the Speaker from the Rules Committee and the rise of "autonomous barons."

My central question is: Will reform change Congress? And the short answer is: Of course it will. Wright Patman, Wilbur Mills, W. R. "Bob" Poage, and F. Edward Hebert were powerful committee chairmen in the 93rd Congress and were not in the 94th Congress. And the caucus was being used by the House Democrats to a greater extent in the 94th Congress than at any time since 1910–16. But what are the long-term implications of these reforms? What happens now? What is the effect on how Congress does its job? And, indeed, what is the job of Congress? Has it changed? Will these reforms help Congress and the nation solve their critical leadership problems? These are some of the questions I wish to treat in this essay. To do so in orderly fashion, I have organized my remarks to discuss the job of Congress, the nature of congressional leadership, why we got reform, and how these reforms might lead to a more effective Congress.

What Congress Does (and What It Can Never Do)

The United States Congress remains the most powerful legislative body in the world because we continue to assign it a major, if not the primary, function in the American democratic system. It is peculiarly well structured to fulfill certain necessary prerequisites if democracy is to be realized. First, its election system fosters representation—the awareness of a need to be responsive and accountable. Second, the unique committee system acknowledges the plurality of interests and public problems and facilitates orderly access to decision making for some legitimate groups. Third, the elaborate set of rules, precedents, and unwritten agreements provides for variable forms of debate and deliberation in the two chambers. And finally, the party system plays an essential organizational role in relationship to these three primary activities of representation, providing access, and deliberation. Properly exercised, this organizational function should lead to effective lawmaking—the principal task of a legislature. The other activities are of little moment if conclusions are not reached about what problems deserve legislative attention, how these problems should be analyzed, what should be done about them, and how the resulting laws should be administered. My view is that the parties, through their leadership, must see to it that these conclusions are reached. If they do not, the job won't get done. Therein lies my indictment of Congress, on the one hand, and my agenda for change, on the other.[4]

Part of the genius of our legislative system is that these functions are variably performed by the two chambers. The House is the principal place of access—the epitome of direct representation—a truly public institution. It is naturally pulled toward specialized and segmented views of public problems. It is a collectivity constantly fighting the battle to institutionalize itself. The centrifugal forces are strong, and therefore the House faces the difficult task of designing means by which "it can be maintained as an on-going institution." [5] Seniority has been such a mechanism; its destruction (if, in fact, it has been destroyed) does not rid us of the problem it was designed to solve.

The Senate is perhaps the most distinctive legislative body in the world. After many years of trying to characterize it, I have finally come to define it as an institution of "functional self-indulgence"—a sort of adult "Summerhill." Its structure is based on a remarkably human proposition: that social gain will be realized by permitting, indeed supporting, self-promotion among the membership.[6] Such an institution is, by definition, self-checking. Strict adherence to written rules is not necessary. Nor may one expect frequent reform, or that reform, when it comes, will be any more than a confirmation of change already in effect. Thus, I will have little to say about the Senate here. Though an important modification was made in Rule 22, the Senate was less an object of reform in 1975 than the House (as we would expect, if my description is at all accurate).

I am quick to emphasize the positive benefits of this peculiar Senate institution. In particular, permissive egocentrism can result in highly imaginative policy searches, "random innovation," [7] and a potential for intellectual debate in the public interest.[8] *These are significant contributions to the public weal* and they should not be lightly dismissed, interrupted, or quashed.

Another approach to understanding what Congress does is to inquire into what it cannot do. What I have described above does not lend itself well to the initiation and development of large-scale, integrated, and comprehensive policies. Congress is not now and never has been well designed to create its own agenda and then act on it in a coordinated way to produce a unified domestic and/or foreign policy program. It is particularly well structured to react to many publics (including other governmental institutions) and, in reacting, to criticize, refine, promote alternative proposals, bargain, and compromise. Reforms directed away from these strengths are unlikely to improve Congress or, in fact, to be taken very seriously for very long.

Leadership in Congress

In describing the Speakership before the reforms of 1910–11, George Rothwell Brown argued that its great power was essential to the constitutional balance. "No more paradoxical action has ever been committed by the American people than in the destruction of the power of the Speakership in the name of popular liberty." [9] According to Brown:

> Organized leadership in the House prevented disintegration of opinion, and tended to check actions springing from imperfect comprehension, passion, selfishness, and personal idiosyncracies. . . . The organization of the House, under the rigid system of party government, was such that no chairman of a committee . . . could risk the inevitable conflict with the vast power of the Speakership which would have been precipitated by insubordination. Hence the power of the appointment of committees came to carry with it the power of the inner organization, headed by the Speaker and his trusted lieutenants, to determine the whole of a legislative program. . . .[10]

With the destruction of these powers as a result of the excesses of Speaker Joseph G. Cannon, party leadership in the House came to depend on the personal resources of incumbent Speakers. Sam Rayburn was particularly adroit at "sleight-of-hand" leadership—now you see it, now you don't. Other Speakers, with the exception perhaps of Nicholas Longworth, were less resourceful in accommodating themselves to the post-Cannon balkanization of authority. Until very recently, of course, one might have made the case that those anxious for power would do better chairing one of the major committees, e.g., Ways and Means, leaving the Speakership to those comfortable with the trappings, but not the substance, of power. The virtual acceptance of the right of succession in the Democratic party—whip to floor leader to Speaker—would seem to support this conclusion as party "accommodators" moved into leadership positions.

If my description of the Senate and its functions comes close to the mark, then we may not expect strong leadership to emerge very often. How can one senator lead another? Those who have been acknowledged as successful leaders in the Senate—in particular Nelson W. Aldrich (R-R.I.) and Lyndon B. Johnson (D-Tex.)—had to develop very special techniques that essentially capitalized on the individualism so characteristic of the chamber. That is, they individualized their approach—tailoring their appeals to each senator's interests.[11] Their compelling styles cannot be expected to surface very often in the Senate.

All of this suggests that the Mike Mansfield and Carl Albert style of leading by following is the rule, not the exception, in the twentieth-century Congress. *An analysis of their leadership turns out to be an essay on the idiosyncratic manner in which each chamber has organized to do its job.* For the fact is that neither the House nor the Senate has until recently favored strong party leadership. If they do now, and it is too early to say for sure, then clearly we may expect that *reform will change Congress.* Whether we will return to the days when "organized leadership . . . prevented disintegration of opinion" is uncertain, but strong party leadership can come only by sacrificing strong committee leadership, and that means major change. One would expect any such development to be fully realized only when the present leadership stands aside, however, since they were selected to suit other purposes.

Why Did We Get Reform?

Congress is an institution that reforms itself, and therefore special conditions must obtain before the membership will be moved to upset familiar ways of doing business. In the past, majority support for reform has followed periods of leadership excesses (as with Speaker Cannon in 1910–11 and House Rules Chairman Howard W. Smith in 1961–63) or conditions leading to widespread congressional awareness of incapacities (as with the growth of presidential authority during the 1930s and 1940s and Nixon's use of this authority—before the Watergate revelations—in a manner highly threatening to Congress).

The 1974–75 reforms did not appear to follow from either of these conditions. President Nixon was aggressive no more—he had been brought to the brink of impeachment before resigning. President Ford promised close cooperation with Congress from the time of his taking the oath of office. So why should a Democratic Congress feel moved to enact reforms? I believe that an answer to this question is of fundamental importance in assessing whether and how these many reforms will change Congress.

Given that Congress is a self-correcting institution, the roots of reform are to be found in how the members look at themselves and their perceptions of how others look at them. In this respect, events in 1974 were nearly as important for Congress as for the presidency. For however poor the image of the White House, the congressional image among the public was consistently worse. The Harris Poll over the past decade shows a rather steady decline in the public ratings of Congress—from a high of 64 percent positive ratings in 1965 (when a Congress with large Democratic majorities was essentially ratifying the Johnson Great Society programs) to a low of 21 percent in January 1974 (when President Nixon's popularity, too, had dipped to a new low).[12] At least superficially, it would appear that the public ratings of Congress are associated with those of the president, though always a bit lower. This finding lends little support, therefore, to the theory that the public turns to Congress as an alternative when the president fails. Rather, the public would appear to group the two—disillusionment with one leads to disillusionment with the other.

As has been stressed, however, Congress is more than an institution; it is also a group of individually elected public officials who respond both to constituency demands of themselves as representatives and to national demands of the institution as a policy-making body. This dual role helps to explain the puzzle that Richard F. Fenno, Jr., identified—i.e., why is it that "we love our congressmen so much more than our Congress"? Fenno's response was, in part, that we don't often connect the two—we don't seek to understand the complex relationship between what congressmen are and what Congress is.

> "Who Runs Congress," asks the title of the Nader report, "The President, Big Business, or You?" . . . it is none of these. It is the members who run Congress. And we pretty much get the kind of Congress they want. We shall get a different kind of Congress when we elect different kinds of congressmen or when we start applying different standards of judgment to old congressmen.[13]

These conditions were met in 1974. In particular, those of us who bothered to vote "elected different kinds of congressmen." Further, we gave old congressmen reason to think that new standards were being applied to them. Let's consider the second phenomenon first. The low rating given all politicians as a result of Watergate clearly affected the members of Congress as well as the president and his staff. This is demonstrated in public opinion polls, editorials, and the 1974 campaign itself. Thus, Watergate came to erode that supportive relationship between the members and their constituencies—or at least to disorient the membership in the 1974 campaign. Alienation and cynicism, which have been increasing among the voting public in recent years anyway, were certain to grow even more, with voter apathy and low turnout the results. Therefore, members could no longer so conveniently disassociate institutional unpopularity from how their publics viewed them personally.

Though I do not have direct evidence on the point, it seems that other factors, too, played an important role in creating a congressional mood receptive to reform. On the positive side, congressional self-images were raised by television coverage of the impeachment proceedings before the House Committee on the Judiciary. Members had a view of the heights to which they might aspire. On the negative side, the Nixon pardon ended the honeymoon period for President Ford but, in all probability, also adversely affected Congress as the question of trust in politics was once more dramatically raised. Then, of course, the Wilbur Mills Tidal Basin incident violated the improved self-image developing among members of Congress, while lending support to the low esteem for politicians evidenced in public opinion polls. Finally, the delay and eventual modification of the House Bolling Committee recommendations cast doubts on congressional capacity for self-improvement.

Here, then, were a number of conditions supportive of change. But reform probably would not have been realized if all incumbents had been returned. If nothing else, the members would have been reassured that Watergate failed to have the influence on their own political careers they had earlier imagined. Many Republican incumbents were defeated, however, and a huge class of freshmen stormed into Washington.

Fenno says that a different kind of Congress follows when we elect different kinds of congressmen. Well, we did just that in 1974. First, consider the number of new faces—the largest freshman class since 1949, constituting 26 percent of the House Democratic party and 12 percent of the House Republican party. Second, they represented the first large infusion of the "1960s awareness" into the House. Our election system seldom responds quickly to new social movements—indeed, a certain amount of lag was intentionally built into the system. Table 1 displays one dimension of this resistance. During the turmoil of the late 1960s, incumbents were returned to office at record-

Table 1. The Return of Incumbents, U.S. House of Representatives, 1956–74

Year	Incumbents Seeking Reelection	Those Losing in the Primary	Those Losing in the General Election	Those Returned	As a Percentage of Those Seeking Reelection	As a Percentage of the Total House
1956	411	6	16	389	94.6	89.4
1958	394	3	37	354	89.8	81.4
1960	403	5	26	372	92.3	85.5
1962	393	11	14	368	93.6	84.6
1964	397	8	44	345	86.9	79.3
1966	407	5	40	362	89.0	83.2
1968	404	3	5	396	98.0	91.0
1970	398	8	12	378	95.0	86.9
1972	381	7	13	361	94.8	83.0
1974	391	8	40	343	87.7	78.9

SOURCE: Calculated from data in *Congressional Quarterly Weekly Report*, various issues.

breaking rates. An incredible 98 percent of those seeking reelection were returned at the height of the antiwar protest in 1968—representing 91 percent of the full House. Only with the effect of reapportionment in 1972 was there a large freshman class, and most of these freshmen (73 percent) were elected in districts with no incumbent or where the incumbent was not seeking reelection. As noted in Table 1, nearly 95 percent of incumbents seeking a return to the House were reelected. In 1974, however, only 87.7 percent of those seeking reelection were returned—representing 78.9 percent of the House (the lowest return for the full House in the period measured).

Further evidence of the arrival of the last decade comes when one looks at the ages and educational experience of these new members. The average age of the Democrats is forty-one. I was shocked to discover that forty-seven of them (63 percent) were born after I was. Many of these members were obviously in college in the 1960s—thus able to experience firsthand the revolt against institutions, traditions, hierarchy, old values, and experience. Over one-half of the freshmen Democrats received undergraduate, graduate, or law degrees in the 1960s or later; one-third received degrees in 1965 or after. Yes, the healthy disrespect for "whatever was"—for those procedures "sanctified by time"—has arrived in Washington. I call it "the greening of Congress" and propose that it will have a continuing effect on the institution.

There is ample evidence that these many new candidates campaigned on a reform theme in 1974. But fervor for change must be combined with an opportunity to act. In the past one could expect a cooling of campaign ardor during the two months between election and swearing in. In 1974, however, all this anxiety was brought to town three weeks after the election. Never before in history could congressional candidates move so directly from campaign promise to political performance. The December caucus instituted as a part of the Bolling Committee reforms permitted the 75 freshmen Democrats and their 216 concerned colleagues to devote undivided attention to critical organizational matters. Further, the drama was to be played out before the watchful eyes of the media and their publics—grown demanding and expectant from campaign images, the Ervin and Judiciary Committee probes, and the escalating sanctimoniousness of the Watergate era.

Other developments also accommodated the transition from campaign rhetoric to political reality in the new Congress. The 1971 and 1973 changes in the procedures for selecting committee chairmen provided means for violating the seniority principle. The unusually large number of former congressmen in the freshmen class (including such reform-minded Democrats as Abner Mikva of Illinois, Andrew Jacobs of Indiana, James Scheuer and Richard Ottinger of New York, and Robert Duncan of Oregon) provided a leadership capability normally lacking in the freshman class. And the combination of weak top party leadership and a new, liberal caucus chairman, Philip Burton, (D-Calif.), gave freshmen Democrats unprecedented influence in organizational politics.[14]

What hath all this wrought? Certainly the distribution of power in the House has been adjusted. *But we know much more about who has lost than about who has won.* On paper it would seem that the Speaker and the party apparatus have gained authority at the expense of the committee chairmen. What does that say, however, unless the Speaker is willing to take charge, and has the support to do so? For a time it seemed that the caucus would dominate. Whether that pattern can continue for very long is the subject of the concluding comments.

Will Reform Change Congress?

I want to return now to my comments on what Congress can do and the importance of party leadership in realizing those responsibilities. For it is within those contexts that we must analyze the current reforms. Are these changes likely to increase congressional capabilities for doing the job? Will they result in responsible and accountable party leadership? If so, then change will have occurred in a direction I personally favor; if not, then another opportunity for strengthening Congress will have passed, though we may in fact get change.

The central point to emphasize is that we cannot yet be certain of the effects of the "revolutionary" reforms on congressional performance. It is simply too soon to tell whether the procedural, organizational, and personnel changes have increased responsiveness, promoted access and deliberation, and facilitated reaching conclusions in lawmaking. Established access and deliberative procedures have been disrupted. The committee system has been dealt a heavy blow. Whether its authority will now be assumed by party leaders, the caucus, or a growing congressional bureaucracy remains to be seen. One can make a persuasive case that the short-run effect is to enhance the president's authority. To paraphrase Job, "Oh, that mine adversary had reformed." [15] Weakening the committee system without strengthening the policy-making role of the party surely makes Congress more vulnerable to presidential direction and manipulation, not less.

Consider the possible outcomes in the flow of authority. First, as noted, a less autonomous committee system may actually enhance presidential power. The committees have been the great strength of Congress since the reforms of 1910–11. They have often successfully challenged or thwarted presidential programs. Reduction of this capability may give the president an advantage. Indeed, if a Democrat wins in 1976, it is not unrealistic to expect that presidential power will steadily grow once more—not necessarily because the president wants it but *because Congress gives it to him or because issues demand that someone act decisively.*

Second, perhaps the next Speaker will seek to exert the full measure of authority granted to him in recent months and years. If so, we might witness the emergence of a much stronger policy role for congressional parties. His chairmanship of a revitalized Steering Committee, his power to appoint members of the Committee on Rules, his new authority in assigning bills to committees, and so on, are all potential sources of power in managing a stronger programmatic orientation of the majority party. Speaker Albert is unlikely to test the limits of this authority—a fact greatly facilitating the expansion. His retirement may change all of that.

Third, it is conceivable that the open, unled, and unpredictable caucus may emerge as an important force in congressional decision making. Such an outcome would probably mean the further demise of Congress as a viable policy-making institution. However attractive it may be to pure democrats, the undisciplined caucus has little to recommend it as a means for effective lawmaking in a complex modern society. Such a development may in fact be the condition leading to the first alternative—increased presidential authority.

Fourth, a new balance of authority between party and committee might emerge. It is hard to imagine any further blows being struck at the committee system. Rather one might expect a period of adjustment to the many changes in the past five years—a little breath-catching by the old body. Nor is it likely that future party leaders will be as unassertive as those presently in office. Surely any candidate with the support of the "new politics" in the House may be expected to use his authority. One should not be misled by reformist rhetoric into believing that what has happened in the House is something other than an old-fashioned power struggle. The winners will use their power for purposes they support—if, in fact, they can agree on a set of goals. Therefore, the final result might be a sort of balance between "party battalions and committee suzerainty" in which the old politics holds on to some committees and the new politics captures other committees and some party leadership posts.

Finally, if one takes an interstitial look at reforms in the past five years, a case can be made for greater decentralization even than has existed with the strong committee system. The Subcommittee Bill of Rights, dispersal of staffing, requirements for establishing subcommittees, caucus approval of Appropriations subcommittee chairmen—all potentially could lead to a diffusion of authority so extensive as to cancel any centralizing effects of increased authority for the Speaker.[16] Any such decentralization, combined with the ever-growing congressional bureaucracy, could affect the traditional representational and deliberative functions of Congress. Few would deny the need for greater expertise in Congress; many rightly fear the growth of a legislative technocracy, however.

What in fact happens in the future depends at least on the following factors:

1. Who wins the White House in 1976.
2. Who returns to Congress.
3. Who leads the 95th Congress.[17]
4. How the congressional agenda changes over time.

Richard Bolling, no stranger to the topic or the politics of congressional reform, was reported to have observed: "It's easy to punish or remove but awfully hard to be creative legislators." [18] That is the perspective emphasized here. The real question is: Will reform change Congress for the better? An answer to that question demands identification of what one thinks makes a good Congress. I sought to clarify my own preferences while discussing what Congress can and cannot do in the political system. Acknowledging the potential for effective change in recent reforms, I withhold judgment as to the ultimate effect, while continuing to emphasize the urgency of strengthening Congress. For however satisfied we may be in having forced the resignation of President Nixon, the more positive test of this democracy is whether we can make Congress an effective working partner in solving the complex problems of a highly technological society. I personally will not permit myself to be other than optimistic for the simple reason that if the legislature fails, democracy fails, and accepting that as a possible outcome contributes to its realization.

NOTES

1. *Congressional Record,* March 19, 1910, p. 3430.
2. *Washington Post,* January 19, 1975.
3. *Washington Post,* January 20, 1975.
4. See my earlier essay for *Time* Magazine, "Somebody Must Be Trusted: An Essay on Leadership of the U.S. Congress," reprinted in Norman J. Ornstein, ed., *Congress in Change* (New York: Praeger, 1975), pp. 265–76.
5. Richard F. Fenno, Jr., "The Internal Distribution of Influence: The House," in David B. Truman, ed., *The Congress and America's Future* (Englewood Cliffs, N.J.: Prentice-Hall, 1965), p. 52.
6. Speaker Thomas Reed enjoyed tweaking the Senate's institutional ego. Once visiting the chamber, he noted, "There doesn't seem to be a quorum in the divine presence today." And in an unpublished manuscript he fictionalized a situation in which the president had come to be elected by the Senate. At the first election, the chief justice announced the result: "Seventy-six Senators [the total number of senators] had each received one vote. For a moment a stillness as of death settled upon the multitude. Never until that moment had the people realized that, like the Deacon's One Hoss Shay, the Senate of the United States was one level mass of wisdom and virtue, perfect in all its parts, and radiant from North to South with that light of intelligence which never shone on sea or shore." Quoted in Samuel W. McCall, *Thomas B. Reed* (Boston: Houghton Mifflin, 1914), p. 252.
7. I borrow this term from Alice Rivlin, *Systematic Thinking for Social Action* (Washington, D.C.: Brookings Institution, 1971), pp. 87 ff.
8. For a brilliant analysis of the Senate's functions, see Nelson W.

Polsby, "Strengthening Congress in Nanal Policymaking," *Yale Review* (Summer 1970): 481–97.

9. George Rothwell Brown, *The Leadership of Congress* (Indianapolis: Bobbs-Merrill, 1922), p. 13.

10. Ibid., pp. 16–17.

11. The Johnson "treatment" has been frequently described. (See particular Ralph K. Huitt, "Democratic Party Leadership in the Senate," *American Political Science Review* 55 [June 1961]:331–44.) Does not the Aldrich "treatment" sound similar?

"He is using his chloroform bottle," once remarked Senator Hansbrough of North Dakota, when Aldrich was moving from one Senator to another. "When Aldrich wants to put something over, either to pass or defeat a bill, he goes about with what I call his chloroform bottle. It is invisible, but I am confident that he carries it in his pocket all the time. He sits down beside a Senator and the first thing that Senator knows he has been chloroformed, and is completely under the Aldrich influence." [Arthur W. Dunn, *From Harrison to Harding*, vol 2 (New York: Putnam, 1922), p. 64.]

12. See "Congressional Unpopularity: Five Views from the Inside," *Congressional Quarterly Weekly Report*, March 9, 1974, pp. 600–603.

13. See Richard F. Fenno, Jr., "If, as Ralph Nader Says, Congress Is 'the Broken Branch,' How Come We Love Our Congressman So Much?" reprinted in Ornstein, op. cit., p. 287.

14. Herbert B. Asher records that changes have been occurring in the status of freshmen since even before 1974. See "The Changing Status of the Freshman Representative," in Ornstein, op. cit., pp. 216–39.

15. I must acknowledge that I learned of Job's observation, "Oh, that mine adversary had written a book," from Speaker Cannon's foreword to L. White Busbey's book on his political career. Joe Cannon was doubting the wisdom of a book by him—or even a written speech. "I never wrote a speech and held it in respect long enough to deliver it." See Busbey, *Uncle Joe Cannon* (New York: Holt, 1927), p. iii.

16. For a review of these reforms, see Norman J. Ornstein, "Causes and Consequences of Congressional Change: Subcommittee Reforms in the House of Representatives, 1970–73," in Ornstein, ed., op cit., pp. 88–114.

17. The 1976 election results put a Democrat in the White House and returned nearly all of the 1974 Democratic freshmen. Thomas P.

(Tip) O'Neill, Jr., was elected Speaker; James C. Wright, Jr., won the majority leadership post, and John Brademas was appointed the majority whip. Early indications suggest a period of consolidation as majority than further reform.

18. *Washington Star-News*, January 21, 1975.

13. *Strengthening a Congressional Strength*

Richard F. Fenno, Jr.

During recent years Congress has expended a great deal of effort on internal reform. Yet it is still an awkward time to talk about the subject. It is too late to describe the reforms; we all know what they are. But it is too early to evaluate them; none of us knows how they will work. The new budget system is only one case in point. As reform architect Richard Bolling has said, "There's change, but I don't know what it means." If prediction seems premature at this point, so too does the suggestion of still more internal reform. We shall have to know what we have got before we can know what more we want.

Besides, Congress deserves some applause for its efforts, along with a little breathing room. There has been a perceptible strengthening of congressional self-confidence—partly as a result of its proven ability to reform itself. Timidity and lack of will have been central themes of journalistic commentary in recent years.[1] But it would be unfair to make them central themes now. Congressional self-confidence is a national asset and should be nurtured as such. Today's question is whether or not Congress can convert the self-confidence it gained in an extraordinary, temporary set of circumstances into a self-confidence more routine, more permanent, more institutionalized. For the moment, that is an open question; and we shall not help Congress today by rushing to a verdict in the matter.

262 • STRENGTHENING A CONGRESSIONAL STRENGTH

Congress will stabilize its self-confidence to the degree that its reforms build upon its inherent strengths as a national political institution. So it will not take us too far away from the subject of self-confidence if we use the present lull to explore the relationship of internal reform to basic institutional strength. The strength I wish to focus on is the unique representational character of Congress.

The Supreme Court, of course, makes no claim to be a representative institution. On the other hand, the president, every president, does—notably when he claims to be "president of all the people." But that is just how we should treat his statement—as a claim, as an attempt to win political support, not as a statement of fact. Congress, not the president, best represents the diversity of views that exists in this country. Congress, not the president, is most closely in touch with the people who live beyond the nation's capital. Our recent experience—with two presidents who lost their constituencies and a third who cannot find one—helps remind us that Congress remains our most representative institution. And we can view several of the recent reforms as efforts to strengthen its representative strength.

If members of Congress are to have an equal opportunity to represent the views of their constituents, they ought to have a more or less equal share in the making of decisions inside Congress. One steady stream of internal reform has focused on giving an increasing number of members a piece of the action, by eliminating gross inequalities in internal influence. The informal idea that junior senators and representatives should serve a legislative apprenticeship has suffered a gradual demise. The Johnson Rule of 1953, guaranteeing all freshmen Senate Democrats a major committee assignment, was the first of a string of similar guarantees in both parties and both chambers. Limitations on the number of committee and subcommittee chairmanships one person could hold have provided more people with leadership positions. The weakening of committee chairmen has allowed influence to flow to the more numerous subcommittees. The strengthening of the House Democratic caucus has increased the scope of influence of each one of its members. The new budget system has produced a wider dispersion of influence by adding a new set of participants to budgetary decision making within each chamber. And so forth. Altogether, influence is more broadly distributed inside Congress than it was twenty, ten, five—or even two—years ago.

Constituents cannot know whether their views are being represented unless they can know what their representatives are doing. Such, in part, is the logic behind a second stream of internal reform— the opening up of congressional proceedings to public view. The abolition of unrecorded teller votes in the House in 1970 established more public voting on the floor. The subsequent opening of executive committee hearings was followed by the opening of committee mark-up sessions and, now, of many conference committees. House Republicans have just opened their party conference; and House Democratic caucus votes are a matter of public record. Few stages of the legislative process remain hidden from the scrutiny of interested outsiders. Television coverage of the House Judiciary Committee's impeachment inquiry could be regarded as the high point of the move toward openness. More people saw Congress at work than ever before. (And part of what they saw—or should have seen—was the representative character of that body.) Proposals for televising House and Senate floor proceedings are being talked about, as the next logical extension of the stream of antisecrecy, "sunshine" reforms. Increased equality of representation and increased visibility of representation both work to strengthen the representative strengths of the Congress.

Although the two streams of reform may enhance the representative possibilities of Congress, we should also acknowledge that they will probably slow down the productivity of Congress. The greater the fragmentation of influence, the harder it is to develop or assert internal leadership. And the more open the internal operation, the easier it is for external groups to interpose their wishes at all stages of the process. That is, the weaker the leadership and the more the external demands, the slower will go the lawmaking. If what we want from Congress is action, neither type of reform can be viewed as a blessing.

On the other hand, it might be helpful if we simply acknowledged that Congress is, and always will be—for better or worse—our slow institution. Surely the president is, and always will be, faster at decision making. Maybe the Supreme Court, too, can act more quickly. But an institution that is representative and slow has its own merits. It can work out and reflect a consensus view in the country, in circumstances where that consensus takes a considerable length of time to jell. Surely that is one of the lessons of the impeachment inquiry; and the pundits who criticized the Judiciary Committee for its lack of speed missed the whole point of the slow but sure consensus building that was going on—in the country and in the country's committee.[2]

Consensus-type decisions, furthermore, are likely to be regarded as fair decisions. And what we shall be needing from our national institutions now—more than speed—are decisions that are felt to be fair. As we try to convert a society based on assumptions of plenty to a society based on assumptions of scarcity, the government will have to call on the citizenry to sacrifice. People are willing to sacrifice; but they will be totally unwilling to sacrifice until they believe the government's allocative decisions are fair. An institution that is both representative and slow, and effective at consensus building, may be our best candidate for "the fair institution."

Whatever their impact on decision making, both streams of reform place additional burdens on our senators and representatives. For them, there is no such thing as a free reform. All reforms carry costs—in this case an increased obligation of Congress's members to educate the people they represent. As influence gets dispersed internally, more members will have a stake in the success of the institution. The greater a member's influence and his stake, the more of his legislative activity he will need to explain and the more willing he should be to accept some responsibility for the performance of his legislature. More members should be willing to resist the temptation—which seizes them when they talk to their constituents—to see Congress as "them" instead of "we," and to run for Congress by running against Congress. Similarly, the more a legislator's activity goes on public display, the more willing he should be to explain to his constituents what he is doing individually and what Congress is doing collectively. It will be a fraud that can only lead to greater public disillusionment, however, if members fail to explain that all the sunshine reforms in the world cannot (and should not) put the totality of legislative politics on public display.

Members of Congress have prescribed for themselves, it seems, added responsibilities of explanation and education. If they accept the responsibility, the representative character of Congress will be strengthened. But there is nothing self-executing about these prescriptions. So Congress-watchers on the outside should help the members to face up to the consequences of their reforms. A problem is, however, that Congress is an institution in which performance is collective and accountability is individual. A large part of the Congress-watcher's task is to encourage individual members to take some responsibility for the collective performance. And that is not easy. The case of the 75 freshman Democrats gives evidence, however, that it can be done. Their reform-centered campaigns and their spearhead support of reform in the early days of the 94th Congress indicate that they associate their individual career success with the performance of the institution.

But the example raises another problem. Accountability is not only individual; but it does not take place in Washington either. It takes place at the other end of the line—at home. If "home" is the place where legislators interpret the Congress to their constituents, and if "home" is the place where they make themselves individually accountable to their constituents, those of us who want to impress their representational responsibilities upon them will have to turn away from Washington. We shall have to monitor the home relationship.

But we are ill equipped and ill inclined to do so. The national media is both Washington-oriented and president-oriented. Some national television commentators do not pay members of Congress the barest courtesy of learning their names or where they come from. Walter Cronkite pronounces the name of CBS's own Manhattan Congressman Edward Koch as "Kock." He calls New York Congressman James Scheuer, "Shuwer." He identifies the leader of the recent congressional fact-finding mission to Vietnam as Congressman John Flynt of "Florida," instead of Georgia. Apparently, a lot less effort goes into pronouncing and locating United States congressmen than went into pronouncing and locating hamlets in Indochina. When compelled to focus on the Congress during the impeachment inquiry, television commentary was encrusted with the clichés of the trade—betraying, again, the lack of attentiveness to Congress. Haynes Johnson (who is attentive) wrote:

> The only blemish on the hearings to date has come not from the congressmen but from some of the TV commentators. On the opening night of the hearings, telecast by ABC, the commentators, as is their right, offered a number of disparaging remarks. The pace was too slow, the members needed a TV director, how could anyone suffer through 365 days of hearings. At one point, Mark Twain's cynical remark about looking toward the Congress to discover the common class of criminals was paraphrased. Yesterday morning, on NBC's "Today" program, a network correspondent described the hearings as "boring." [3]

When impeachment struck, the national media suddenly discovered that we have a representative form of government in the United States. And for a few weeks, in December 1973 and January 1974, national television, newspapers, and magazines dispatched their reporters from Washington to monitor the home relationships of a newfound species—members of the House. The reportage brought a breath of fresh air and a touch of political reality to the news about Congress. But many newsgatherers, accustomed to a president-Washington diet, missed the complex process by which each House member interpreted the impeachment issue to his constituents and worked to legitimize his position in their eyes. Too often, what we got was simple box-score reporting, a prediction of a vote—in Washington, pro- or antipresident, of course. We cannot criticize the Washington press and TV corps too harshly, however, for their inadequate "home" coverage. They had, after all, been hastily summoned to undertake a most novel assignment—to portray the workings of representative democracy in America.

We should not remain strangers to the representational roots of our political system—not for our own good and not if we are to keep closer tabs on the members of Congress. But there is no easy remedy.

Mine is simply to ask the national media to do better. And my pet proposal is this: the nightly TV news shows should devote five to seven minutes regularly—say, every two weeks—to featuring the home activity of a member of the Senate or House. The series would be done by people who know the area they are talking about as well as Washington. It would have two themes. One would be to educate us in the incredible diversity of this country—as that diversity is reflected in the diversity of constituencies and the diverse constellations of views in each. Over time, the viewing public might come to appreciate the representative virtues of Congress, understand the roots of its slowness in action, and, perhaps, become more disposed to view its outcomes as fair.

A second theme would be to teach us to discriminate between legislators who accept their representational responsibilities and those who do not, to detect the proportions of reasoned explanation and demagoguery in each home relationship. For example, a senator or congressman who never has to explain to his constituents why some action of his might not bring them short-term benefits, who never has to explain why their interests might have to be compromised with certain other interests, who never has to explain to them why he thinks their views are wrong—that legislator is simply not doing his educational job. A series of this sort might enlighten not only us, but the Washington-president-oriented news groups themselves. It might also serve as a model for local TV or other mass media. My own research has taken me to many congressional districts, and I am convinced that such a series could be entertaining as well as enlightening.

Ralph Nader grasped a profoundly important idea when he launched his "Profiles" project—the idea that the behavior and the character of each senator and representative could usefully be interpreted to his constituents. Nader's project was sloppily executed; it had a sectarian appeal; it rewarded irresponsibility; and it demeaned the political art. It seems to have suffocated to death beneath the pile of Nader's enthusiasms. That is a pity, because his idea is too good to lose. My proposal follows in the basic spirit of Nader. Unlike him, however, I believe that if we show the represented what their representatives are doing, they will like most of what they see. Nonetheless, we shall doubtless find some legislators who are shirking their responsibilities at home.

I can think of three such types that ought to be flagged. One is the status-oriented legislator, for whom being in Congress is an end in itself, requiring that he make little contribution to the collective legislative performance, and leaving him free to criticize Congress because he takes no part in it. His relationship with his constituents is exhausted by his efforts to remain popular with them. Second is the single-issue legislator, who restricts his knowledge, interest, and conversation to one constituency-based issue. His refusal to balance the interests he champions against the competing claims of others keeps him from legislative compromise or from a broader view of the world, thereby severely limiting his contribution to the collective performance. But he continues to talk his constituents into believing that his narrow focus and legislative rigidity are protective of their best interests. Third is the higher-office-seeking legislator, who uses his present Senate position to seek the presidency or his House position to run for the Senate. No one who has ever been around the office of a presidential or senatorial hopeful can overlook the wholesale diversion of personal, institutional, and public resources from the legislator's performance inside his chamber and from his relationships at home. Individual ambition makes the political system go, but it also imposes costs on the congressional collectivity and on numerous constituencies. Legislators using one office to run for another should, at least, explain the costs and benefits of their candidacy to the people they represent. Better still, they should resign and bear the costs of their ambition themselves.

The representational character of Congress is one of its greatest institutional strengths. And we have followed the flow of at least two streams of internal reform by urging its further strengthening. Our emphasis has been to ask individual legislators to work harder at their representational responsibilities—by explaining (to those they represent) their individual acts and the likely consequences of those acts for the collective performance of Congress. We have asked Congress-watchers to hold legislators to these prescriptions by attending less to their activity in Washington and more to their activity at home. Were these altered responsibilities to be assumed by all concerned, the representative strengths of Congress would be immeasurably strengthened.

But we should not conclude this essay on a note implying that no other responsibilities exist in the area. There still remains the classic problem of adequate representation in Congress—especially for people whose interests lie at the core of the country's most deep-seated social problems. Different observers will have different preferences in this regard. In my view, the most serious existing flaw is the representation of our 10 percent black population by 2 percent of the members of Congress. Surely the presence of thirty more black legislators in Congress would strengthen its representational strength. Should such a change come, it will doubtless enhance the reputation Congress most wants to live down, as our slow institution; but it will also enhance the reputation Congress most needs to live up to, as our fair institution.

NOTES

1. For examples, Taylor Branch, "Profiles in Caution: The Senate's Bad Advice and Grudging Consent," *Harpers*, July 1973; Elizabeth Drew, "Why Congress Won't Fight," *New York Times Magazine*, September 23, 1973; Russell Baker, "Moods of Washington," *New York Times Magazine*, March 24, 1974.

2. For example, Joseph Alsop, who wrote: "Indeed the worst proof of the incompetence of Congress is the way the affair of the President's impeachment is being permitted to drag on and on—thereby prolonging the paralysis. It is time to get it over with. We have had enough congressional antigovernment." Joseph Alsop, "A Congressional Government?" *Washington Post*, June 7, 1974.

3. Haynes Johnson, "Judiciary Members Rising Splendidly to History," *Washington Post*, July 24, 1974.

14. Congress and the Quest for Power

Lawrence C. Dodd

The postwar years have taught students of Congress a very fundamental lesson: Congress is a dynamic institution. The recent congressional changes picture an institution that is much like a kaleidoscope. At first glance the visual images and structural patterns appear frozen in a simple and comprehensible mosaic. Upon closer and longer inspection the realization dawns that the picture is subject to constant transformations. These transformations seem to flow naturally from the prior observations, yet the resulting mosaic is quite different and is not ordered by the same static principles used to interpret and understand the earlier one. The appreciation and understanding of the moving image requires not only comprehending the role of each colorful geometric object in a specific picture, nor developing a satisfactory interpretation of the principles underlying a specific picture or change in specific aspects of the picture, but grasping the dynamics underlying the structural transformations themselves. So it is with Congress. To understand and appreciate it as an institution we must focus not only on particular aspects of internal

AUTHOR'S NOTE: For critical assistance at various stages in the writing of this essay, I would like to thank Arnold Fleischmann, Michael N. Green, Bruce I. Oppenheimer, Diana Phillips, Russ Renka, Terry Sullivan, and numerous graduate and undergraduate students who shared with me their questions and insights.

269

congressional structure and process, nor on changes in particular patterns. We must seek to understand the more fundamental dynamics
that produce the transformations in the congressional mosaic.

This essay represents an attempt to explain the dynamics of congressional structure.[1] Part I presents a general interpretation of the
motives that lead members to organize Congress along particular lines,
and attempts to specify the type of institutional structure and behavior
that should flow from these motives. The model generated in Part I fits
roughly with (and derives from a study of) congressional structure and
behavior as represented by scholars of the era from the mid-1950s to
the mid-1960s. That time period is treated as one observation point—
much like one glance through a kaleidoscope. Part II argues that there
is an inherent paradox within the motivational principles uncovered
in Part I: to the extent that members of Congress try to maximize their
personal goals in the short run, they create a congressional structure
that undermines their ability to realize the personal goals over the
long run. Members of Congress come to realize this fact in periods of
institutional crisis and produce the type of structural reforms witnessed in the 1973–75 period. This tension between the short-term and
long-term goal maximization generates the basic organizational dynamics of Congress. Part III argues that the pattern of change identified in Part II, a pattern that is cyclical in nature, does in fact characterize congressional organization and American politics generally,
particularly in the twentieth century. Part IV argues that this cyclical
theory allows us to predict the general fate of current congressional
reforms. Part V considers the extent to which the overall cyclical pattern conforms to a Madisonian vision of American politics and the
consequent implications for the future of Congress and American politics.

I

As with politicians generally, members of Congress enter politics
in a quest for personal power. This quest may derive from any
number of deeper motives: a desire for ego gratification or for prestige, a search for personal salvation through good works, a hope to
construct a better world or to dominate the present one, or a preoccupation with status and self-love. Whatever the source, most
members of Congress seek to attain the power to control policy decisions that impose the authority of the state on the citizenry at large.

The most basic lesson that any member of Congress learns on en-
tering the institution is that the quest for power by service within

Congress requires reelection. First, reelection is necessary in order to remain in the struggle within Congress for "power positions." [2] Staying in the struggle is important not only in that it provides the formal status as an elected representative without which an individual's influence on national legislative policy lacks legal authority; the quest for power through election and reelection also signals one's acceptance of the myth of democratic rule and thus one's acceptability as a power seeker who honors the society's traditional values. Second, reelection, particularly by large margins, helps create an aura of personal legitimacy. It indicates that one has a special mandate from the people, that one's position is fairly secure, that one will have to be "reckoned with." Third, long-term electoral success bestows on a member of Congress the opportunity to gain the experience and expertise, and to demonstrate the legislative skill and political prescience, that can serve to justify the exercise of power.

Because reelection is so important, and because it may be so difficult to ensure, its pursuit can become all-consuming. The constitutional system, electoral laws, and social system together have created political parties that are weak coalitions. A candidate for Congress normally must create a personal organization rather than rely on her or his political party. The "electoral connection" that intervenes between the desire for power and the realization of power may lead members to emphasize form over substance, position taking, advertising, and credit claiming rather than problem solving. In an effort to sustain electoral success, members of Congress may fail to take controversial and clear positions, fail to make hard choices, fail to exercise power itself.[3] Yet members of Congress generally are not solely preoccupied with reelection. Most members have relatively secure electoral margins. This security stems partially from the fact that members of Congress *are* independent of political parties and are independent from responsibility for selecting the executive, and thus can be judged more on personal qualities than on partisan or executive affiliations. Electoral security is further reinforced because members of Congress personally control financial and casework resources that can help them build a loyalty from their constituents independent of policy or ideological considerations. The existence of secure electoral margins thus allows members to devote considerable effort toward capturing a "power position" within Congress and generating a mystique of special authority that is necessary to legitimize a select decision-making role for them in the eyes of their nominal peers.

The concern of members of Congress with gaining congressional power, rather than just securing reelection, has had a considerable influence on the structure and life of Congress. Were members solely preoccupied with reelection, we would expect them to spend little

Might not this description be accurate!!?

time in Washington and devote their personal efforts to constituent speeches and district casework. One would expect Congress to be run by a centralized, efficient staff who, in league with policy-oriented interest groups, would draft legislation, investigate the issues, frame palatable solutions, and present the members with the least controversial bills possible. Members of Congress would give little attention to committee work, and then only to committees that clearly served reelection interests. The primary activity of congresspeople in Congress, rather, would be extended, televised floor debates and symbolic roll call votes, all for show. Such a system would allow the appearance of work while providing ample opportunity for the mending of home fences. Alternatively, were only a few members of Congress concerned about power, with others concerned with reelection, personal finances, or private lives, one might expect a centralized system with a few leaders exercising power and all others spending their time on personal or electoral matters.

Virtually all members of the U.S. Congress are preoccupied with power considerations. They are unwilling—unless forced by external events—to leave the major decisions in either a centralized, autonomous staff system or a central leadership. Each member wants to exercise power—to make the key policy decisions. This motive places every member in a personal conflict with every other member: to the extent that one member realizes her or his goal personally to control all key decisions, all others must lose. Given this widespread power motive, an obvious way to resolve the conflict is to disperse power—or at least power positions—as widely as possible. One logical solution, in other words, is to place basic policy-making responsibility in a series of discrete and relatively autonomous committees and subcommittees, each having control over the decisions in a specified jurisdictional area. Each member can belong to a small number of committees and, within them, have a significant and perhaps dominant influence on policy. Although such a system denies every member the opportunity to control all policy decisions, it ensures that most members, particularly if they stay in Congress long enough to obtain a subcommittee or committee chair, and if they generate the mystique of special authority necessary to allow them to activate the power potential of their select position, can satisfy a portion of their power drive.

Within Congress, as one would expect in light of the power motive, the fundamental structure of organization is a committee system. Most members spend most of their time not in their district but in Washington, and most of their Washington time not on the floor in symbolic televised debate but rather in the committee or subcommittee rooms, in caucus meetings, or in office work devoted to legislation.[4] While the staff, particularly the personal staff, may be relegated

Context with favorite legis. Facilitator?

to casework for constituents, the members of Congress sit through hearing after hearing, debate after debate, vote after vote seeking to shape in subcommittee, committee, and floor votes the contours of legislation. This is not to suggest, of course, that members of Congress do not engage in symbolic action or personal casework and do not spend much time in the home district; they do, in their effort at reelection. Likewise, staff do draft legislation, play a strong role in committee investigations, and influence the direction of public policy; they do this, however, largely because members of Congress just do not have enough time in the day to fulfill their numerous obligations. Seen in this perspective, Congress is not solely, simply, or primarily a stage on which individuals intentionally and exclusively engage in meaningless charades. Whatever the end product of their effort may be, members of Congress have actively sought to design a congressional structure and process that would maximize their ability to exercise personal power within Congress and, through Congress, within the nation at large.

The congressional committee structure reflects rather naturally the various dimensions that characterize the making of public policy. There are *authorization* committees that create policies and programs, specify their duties and powers, and establish absolute funding levels. There are *appropriations* committees that specify the actual funding level for a particular fiscal year. There are *revenue* committees that raise the funds to pay for the appropriations necessary to sustain the authorized programs. In addition, since Congress itself is an elaborate institution that must be serviced, there are *housekeeping* committees— those that provide for the day-to-day operation of Congress. In the House of Representatives there is also an *internal regulation* committee, the House Rules Committee, that schedules debate and specifies the rules for deliberation on specific bills.

These committees vary greatly in the nature and comprehensiveness of their impact on national policy making. The housekeeping committees tend to be *service* committees and carry little national weight except through indirect influence obtained from manipulating office and staff resources that other members may want so desperately as to modify their policy stances on other committees. A second set of committees, authorization committees such as Interior or Post Office, have jurisdictions that limit them to the concerns of fairly narrow constituencies; these are *reelection* committees that allow members to serve their constituencies' parochial interests but offer only limited potential to effect broad-scale public policy. A third group of committees are *policy* committees, such as Education and Labor or International Relations, that consider fairly broad policy questions, though questions that have fairly clear and circumscribed jurisdictional limits.

A fourth set of committees are the *"power"* committees, which make decisions on issues such as the scheduling of rules (the House Rules Committee), appropriations (House and Senate Appropriations committees), or revenues (House Ways and Means or Senate Finance) that allow them to affect most or all policy areas.[5] Within a pure system of committee government, power committees are limited in the comprehensiveness of their control over the general policy-making process. No overarching control committee exists to coordinate the authorization, appropriations, or revenue process.

Because an essential type of legislative authority is associated with each congressional committee, members find that service on any committee can offer some satisfaction of their power drive. There are, nevertheless, inherent differences in the power potential associated with committees, differences that are tied to the variation in legislative function and in the comprehensiveness of a committee's decisional jurisdiction. This variation between committees is sufficient to make some committees more attractive as a place to gain power. Because members are in a quest for power, not simply reelection, they generally will seek to serve on committees whose function and policy focus allow the broadest personal impact on policy.

Maneuvering for membership on the more attractive committees is constrained by two fundamental factors. First, there are a limited number of attractive committee slots, and much competition will exist for these vacancies. Most members cannot realize their goal to serve on and gain control of these committees. For this reason, much pressure exists to establish norms by which members "prove" themselves deserving of membership on an attractive committee. Such norms include courtesy to fellow members, specialization in limited areas of public policy, a willingness to work hard on legislation, a commitment to the institution, adherence to the general policy parameters seen as desirable by senior members of Congress who will dominate the committee nominations process, and a willingness to reciprocate favors and abide by the division of policy domains into the set of relatively independent policy-making entities. Members who observe these norms faithfully will advance to the more desirable committees because they will have shown themselves worthy of special privilege, particularly if they also possess sufficient congressional seniority.[6]

Seniority is particularly important because of the second constraint on the process—the fact that service on the more powerful committees may limit one's ability to mend electoral fences. On the more comprehensive committees, issues often can be more complex and difficult to understand, necessitating much time and concentration on committee work; members may not be able to get home as often or as easily. Issues will be more controversial and will face members with difficult and often unpopular policy choices; members will be less able to engage in the politics of form over substance. The national visibility of the members will be greater, transforming them into public figures whose personal lives may receive considerable attention. Indiscretions that normally might go unreported will become open game for the press and can destroy careers. Thus, although it is undoubtedly true that service on the more comprehensive committees may bring with it certain attributes that can help reelection (campaign contributions from interest groups, name identification and status, a reputation for power that may convince constituents that "our member can deliver"), service on the more attractive committees does thrust members into a more unpredictable world. Although members generally will want to serve on the most powerful committees, it will normally be best for them to put off such service until they have a secure electoral base and to approach their quest for power in sequential steps.

Because of the constraints operating within a system of committee government, congressional careers reflect a set of stages. The first stage entails an emphasis on shoring up the electoral base through casework, service on constituent-oriented reelection committees, and gaining favor within Congress by serving on the housekeeping committees. Of course, the first stage is never fully "completed": there is never a time at which a member of Congress is "guaranteed" long-term reelection or total acceptance within Congress, so both constituent and congressional service are a recurring necessity. But a point is normally reached—a point defined by the circumstances of the member's constituency, the opportunities present in Congress, and the personality and competence of the member—when he or she will feel secure enough, or perhaps unhappy enough, to attempt a move to a second stage. In the second stage members broaden their horizons and seek service on key policy committees that draft important legislation regulating such national policy dimensions as interstate commerce, education, or labor. In this stage, representatives begin to be "legislators," to preoccupy themselves with national policy matters. Because of the limited number of positions on power committees, many members will spend most, perhaps the rest, of their career in this stage, moving up by committee seniority to subcommittee and committee chairs on the policy committees. As they gain expertise in the specific policy area, and create a myth of special personal authority, they will gain power in some important but circumscribed area of national policy. For members who persist, however, and/or possess the right attributes of electoral security and personal attributes, a third stage exists: service on a power committee—Rules, Ways and Means, or Finance, Appropriations, and, in the Senate, Foreign Relations. Service on these committees is superseded, if at all, only by involvement in a fourth stage: service in the party leadership as a floor leader or Speaker. Few individuals ever have the opportunity to realize this fourth and climactic step; in a system of committee government, in fact, this step will be less sought and the battles less bitter than one might expect,[7] considering the status associated with them, because power will rest primarily in committees rather than in the party. Although party leadership positions in a system of committee government do carry with them a degree of responsibility, particularly the obligation to mediate conflicts between committees and to influence the success of marginal legislation on the house floor, members will generally be content to stay on a power committee and advance to subcommittee and committee chair positions rather than engage in an all-out effort to attain party leadership positions.

This career path, presented here in an idealized and simplified fashion, is a general "power ladder" that members attempt to climb in their quest for power within Congress. Some members leave the path voluntarily to run for the Senate (if in the House), to run for governor, to serve as a judge, or to serve as president. Some for special reasons bypass one or another stage, choose to stay at a lower rung, are defeated, or retire. Despite exceptions, the set of stages is a very real guide to the long-term career path that members seek to follow. Implicit within this pattern is the very real dilemma discussed earlier: progress up the career ladder brings with it a greater opportunity for significant personal power, but also greater responsibility. As members move up the power ladder, they move away from a secure world in which reelection interest can be their dominant concern and into a world in which concerns with power and public policy predominate. They take their chance and leave the security of the reelection stage because of their personal quest for power, without which reelection is a largely meaningless victory.

The attempt to prove oneself and move up the career ladder requires enormous effort. Even after one succeeds and gains a power position, this attainment is not in itself sufficient to guarantee the personal exercise of power. To utilize fully the power prerogatives that are implicit in specific power positions, a member must maintain the respect, awe, trust, and confidence of committee and house colleagues; he or she must sustain the aura of personal authority that is necessary to legitimize the exercise of power. Although the norm of seniority under a system of pure committee government will protect a member's possession of a power position, seniority is not sufficient to guard personal authority. In order to pass legislation and dominate policy decisions in a committee's jurisdictional area, a committee chair must radiate an appearance of special authority. The member must abide by the norms of the house and the committee, demonstrate legislative competence, and generate policy decisions that appear to stay within the general policy parameters recognized as acceptable by the member's colleagues. Among reelection efforts, efforts to advance in Congress to power positions, efforts to sustain and nurture personal authority, and efforts to exercise power, the members of Congress confront an incredible array of crosscutting pressures and internal dilemmas—decisions about how to balance external reelection interests with the internal institutional career, how to maximize the possibility of power within Congress by service on particular committees, how to gain and nurture authority within committees by specific legislative actions. The world of the congressman or congresswoman is complicated further, however, by a very special irony.

II

As a form of institutional organization, committee government possesses certain attributes that recommend it. By dividing policy concerns among a variety of committees it allows members to specialize in particular policy areas; this division provides a congressional structure through which the members can be their own expert advisers and maintain a degree of independence from lobbyists or outside specialists. Specialization also provides a procedure whereby members can become acquainted with particular programs and agencies and follow their behavior over a period of years, thus allowing informed oversight of the implementation of public policy. The dispersion of power implicit in committee government is important, furthermore, because it brings a greater number of individuals into the policy-making process and thus allows a greater range of policy innovation. In addition, as stressed above, committee government also serves the immediate power motive of congresspeople by creating so many power positions that all members can seek to gain power in particular policy domains.

Despite its assets, committee government does have severe liabilities, flaws that undermine the ability of Congress to fulfill its constitutional responsibilities to make legislative policy and oversee the implementation of that policy. First, committee government by its very nature lacks strong, centralized leadership, thereby undermining its internal decision-making capacity and external authority. Internally, Congress needs central leadership because most major questions of public policy (such as economic or energy policy) cut across individual committee jurisdictions. Since each committee and subcommittee may differ in its policy orientation from all others, and since the support of all relevant committees will be essential to an overall program, it is difficult, if not impossible, to enact a coherent general approach to broad policy questions. A central party leader or central congressional steering committee with extensive control over the standing committees could provide the leadership necessary to assist the development and passage of a coherent policy across the various committees, but committee government rejects the existence of strong centralized power. The resulting dispersion of power within Congress, and the refusal to allow strong centralized leadership, ensures that congressional decisions on major policy matters (unless aided and pushed by an outside leader) will be incremental at best, immobilized and incoherent as a norm. And to the extent that a Congress governed by committees can generate public policy, it faces the external problem of leadership, the inability of outside political actors, the press, or the public to identify a legitimate spokesperson for Congress on any general policy question. The wide dispersion of power positions allows numerous members to gain a degree of dominance over specific dimensions of a policy domain; all of these members can speak with some authority on a policy question, presenting conflicting and confusing approaches and interpretations. In cases where Congress does attempt to act, Congress lacks a viable mechanism through which to publicize and justify its position in an authoritative manner. Should Congress be in a conflict with the president, who can more easily present a straightforward and publicized position, Congress almost certainly will lose out in the eyes of public opinion. Lacking a clearly identifiable legislative leader in its midst, Congress is unable to provide the nation with unified, comprehensible, or persuasive policy leadership.

Closely related to the lack of leadership is a lack of *fiscal coordination*. Nowhere within a system of committee government is there a mechanism to ensure that the decisions of authorization, appropriations, and revenue committees have some reasonable relationship to one another. The authorization committees make their decisions about the programs to authorize largely independent of appropriations committee decisions about how much money the government will spend. The appropriations committees decide on spending levels largely independent of revenue committee decisions on taxation. Since it is always easier to promise (or authorize) than to deliver (or spend), program goals invariably exceed the actual financial outlays and thus the actual delivery of services. And since it is easier to spend money than to make or tax money, particularly for politicians, expenditures will exceed the revenues to pay the bills. Moves to coordinate the authorization, appropriations, and revenue processes are inconsistent with committee government, since such an effort would necessarily create a central mechanism with considerable say over all public policy and thus centralize power in a relatively small number of individuals. Committee government thus by its very nature is consigned to frustration: the policies that it does produce will invariably produce higher expectations than they can deliver; its budgets, particularly in periods of liberal, activist Congresses, will produce sizable and unplanned deficits in which expenditures far exceed revenues. The inability of committee government to provide realistic program goals and fiscal discipline will invite the executive to intervene in the budget process in order to provide fiscal responsibility and coordination. The result, of course, will be a concomitant loss of the congressional control over the nation's purse strings.

A third detriment associated with committee government, and one that is exacerbated by the absence of leadership and committee coordination, is the lack of *accountability* and *responsibility*. A fundamental justification of congressional government is that it allows political decision making to be responsive to the will of a national majority. Committee government distributes this decision-making authority among a largely autonomous set of committees. Since seniority protects each committee's membership from removal and determines who will chair each committee, a committee's members can feel free to follow their personal policy predilections and stop any legislation they wish that falls within their committee's jurisdiction, or propose any that they wish. Within a system of committee government, resting as it does on the norm of seniority, no serious way exists to hold a specific committee or committee chair accountable to the majority views of Congress or the American people, should those views differ from the views held within a particular committee. Because of the process whereby members are selected to serve on major committees—a process that emphasizes not their compatibility with the majority's policy sentiment but rather their adherence to congressional norms, general agreement with the policy views of senior congresspeople, and possession of seniority—the top committees (especially at the senior ranks) are quite likely to be out of step with a congressional or national majority. This lack of representativeness is particularly likely if patterns of electoral security nationwide provide safe seats (and thus seniority) to regions or localities that are unrepresentative of the dominant policy perspectives of the country. Responsiveness is further undermined because the absence of strong central leaders, and a widespread desire among members for procedural protection of their personal prerogatives, require reliance on rigid rules and regulations to govern the flow of legislation and debate, rules such as the Senate's cloture rule that allows the existence of filibusters. Under a system of party government, where limiting rules may exist on the books, strong party leaders can mitigate their effects. In a system of committee government, rules become serious hurdles that can block the easy flow of legislation, particularly major, controversial legislation, thereby decreasing the ability of Congress to respond rapidly to national problems. Committee government thus undermines the justification of Congress as an institution that provides responsive, representative government. Since institutions derive their power not solely from constitutional legalisms but from their own mystique of special authority that comes from their legitimizing myths, committee government undercuts not only Congress's ability to exercise power but also the popular support that is necessary to maintain its power potential.

The lack of accountability and the damage to Congress's popular support are augmented by a fourth characteristic of committee government—a tendency toward *insulation* of congressional decision making. This insulation derives from three factors. First, members of committees naturally try to close committee sessions from public purview, limiting thereby the intrusion of external actors such as interest groups or executive agencies and thus protecting committee members' independent exercise of power within committees. Second, the creation of a multiplicity of committees makes it difficult for the public or the press to follow policy deliberations even if they are open. Third, it is difficult if not impossible to create clear jurisdictional boundaries between committees. The consequent ambiguity that exists between jurisdictional boundaries will often involve committees themselves in extensive disputes over the control of particular policy domains, further confusing observers who are concerned with policy deliberations. By closing its committee doors, creating a multiplicity of committees, and allowing jurisdictional ambiguities, a system of committee government isolates Congress from the nation at large. Out of sight and out of mind, Congress loses the attention, respect, and understanding of the nation and becomes an object of scorn and derision, thus further undermining the authority or legitimacy of its pronouncements and itself as an institution.

Finally, committee government undermines the ability of Congress to perform that one function for which committee government would seem most suited—aggressive oversight of administration. According to the classic argument, the saving grace of committee government is that the dispersion of power and the creation of numerous policy experts ensure congressional surveillance of the bureaucracy. Unfortunately, this argument ignores the fact that the individuals on the committees that pass legislation will be the very people least likely to investigate policy implementation. They will be committed to the program, as its authors or most visible supporters, and will not want to take actions that might lead to a destruction of the program. The impact of publicity and a disclosure of agency or program shortcomings, after all, is very unpredictable and difficult to control and may create a public furor against the program. The better part of discretion is to leave the agency largely to its own devices and rely on informal contacts and special personal arrangements, lest the glare of publicity and the discovery of shortcomings force Congress to deauthorize a pet program, casting aspersions on those who originally drafted the legislation. Members of Congress are unwilling to resolve this problem by creating permanent and powerful oversight committees because such committees, by their ability to focus attention on problems of specific agencies and programs, would threaten the authority of legislative committees to control and direct policy in their allotted policy area. Committee government thus allows a *failure of executive oversight*.

In the light of these five problems, the irony of committee government is that it attempts to satisfy members' individual desires for personal power by dispersing internal congressional authority so widely that the resulting institutional impotence cripples the ability of Congress to perform its constitutional roles, thereby dissipating the value of internal congressional power. Members of Congress thus are not only faced with the daily dilemma of balancing reelection interests with their efforts at upward power mobility within Congress; their lives are also complicated by a cruel paradox, the ultimate incompatibility of widely dispersed power within Congress, on the one hand, and a strong role for Congress in national decision making, on the other. This inherent tension generates an explosive dynamic within Congress as an organization and between Congress and the executive.

In the short run, as members of Congress follow the immediate dictates of the personal power motive, they are unaware of, or at least unconcerned with, the long-term consequences of decentralized power; they support the creation of committee government. The longer committee government operates, the more unhappy political analysts and the people generally become with the inability of Congress to make national policy or ensure policy implementation. With Congress deadlocked by immobilism, political activists within Congress and the nation at large turn to the president (as the one alternative political figure who is popularly elected and thus should be responsive to popular sentiments) and encourage him (or her, if we ever break the sex barrier) to provide policy leadership and fiscal coordination, to open up congressional decision making to national political forces and ensure congressional responsiveness, and to oversee the bureaucracy. Presidents, particularly those committed to activist legislation, welcome the calls for intervention and will see their forthright role as an absolute necessity to the well-being of the Republic. Slowly

at first, presidents take over the roles of chief legislator, chief budgetary officer, overseer of the bureaucracy, chief tribune, and protector
of the people.[8] Eventually the president's role in these regards becomes so central that he feels free to ignore the wishes of members of
Congress, even those who chair very important committees, and impose presidential policy on Congress and the nation at large.

The coming of a strong, domineering, imperial president who ignores Congress mobilizes its members into action. They see that their
individual positions of power within Congress are meaningless unless
the institution can impose its legislative will on the nation. They
search for ways to regain legislative preeminence and constrain the executive. Not being fools, members identify part of the problem as an
internal institutional one and seek to reform Congress. Such reform efforts come during or immediately following crises in which presidents
clearly and visibly threaten fundamental power prerogatives of Congress. The reforms will include attempts to provide for more centralized congressional leadership, fiscal coordination, congressional openness, better oversight mechanisms, clarification of committee
jurisdictions, procedures for policy coordination, and procedures to
encourage committee accountability. Because the quest for personal
power continues as the underlying motivation of individual members,
the reforms are basically attempts to strengthen the value of internal
congressional power by increasing the power of Congress vis-à-vis the
executive. The reform efforts, however, are constrained by consideration of personal power prerogatives of members of Congress. The attempt to protect personal prerogatives while centralizing power builds
structural flaws into the centralization mechanisms, flaws that would
not be present were the significance of congressional structure for the
national power of Congress itself the only motive. The existence of
these flaws provides the openings through which centralization procedures are destroyed when institutional crises pass and members again
feel free to emphasize personal power and personal careers. In addition, because policy inaction within Congress often will be identified
as the immediate cause of presidential power aggrandizement, and
because policy immobilism may become identified with key individuals or committees that have obstructed particular legislation, reform
efforts also may be directed toward breaking up the authority of these
individuals or committees and dispersing it among individuals and
committees who seem more amenable to activist policies. This short-
term dispersal of power, designed to break a legislative logjam (and,
simultaneously, to give power to additional individuals), will serve to
exacerbate immobilism in the long run when the new mechanisms of
centralization are destroyed.

Viewed in a broad historical perspective, organizational dynamics within Congress, and external relations of Congress to the president, have a "cyclical" pattern. At the outset, when politicians in a quest for national power first enter Congress, they decentralize power and create committee government. Decentralization is followed by severe problems of congressional decision making, presidential assumption of legislative prerogatives, and an eventual presidential assault on Congress itself. Congress reacts by reforming its internal structure: some reform efforts will involve legislation that attempts to circumscribe presidential action; other reforms will attempt to break specific points of deadlock by further decentralization and dispersal of congressional authority; eventually, however, problems of internal congressional leadership and coordination will become so severe that Congress will be forced to undertake centralizing reforms. As Congress moves to resolve internal structural problems and circumscribe presidential power, presidents begin to cooperate so as to defuse the congressional counterattack; to do otherwise would open a president to serious personal attack as anticongressional and thus antidemocratic, destroying the presidency's legitimizing myth as a democratic institution and identifying presidential motivations as power aggrandizement rather than protection of the Republic. As the immediate threat to congressional prerogatives recedes, members of Congress (many of whom will not have served in Congress during the era of institutional crisis) become preoccupied with their immediate careers and press once again for greater power dispersal within Congress and removal of centralizing mechanisms that inhibit committee and subcommittee autonomy. Decentralization reasserts itself and Congress becomes increasingly leaderless, uncoordinated, insulated, unresponsive, unable to control executive agencies. Tempted by congressional weakness and hounded by cries to "get the country moving," the executive again reasserts itself and a new institutional crisis eventually arises. A review of American history demonstrates the existence of this cycle rather clearly, particularly during the twentieth century.

III

Throughout the nineteenth century, the national government was not immensely powerful. Most politicians were not drawn to long-term careers in Congress. Those who were drawn to Congress and were concerned with congressional power did struggle for power positions, a struggle that initially served to create a fledgling committee system.[9] The committee system was balanced by and guided by strong central leadership, particularly in the House of Representatives, where the Speakership offered a clear mechanism for legislative leadership. The central leaders were able to maintain considerable authority because they offered services—such as selection of committee members and chairpeople, policy development and guidance, mediation of parliamentary conflicts, scheduling of legislation—that were necessary to avoid the chaos implicit in the high turnover of members throughout most of the nineteenth century. The leaders' authority was challenged occasionally by other members who wanted greater independence and more autonomy for themselves and their committees. These challenges led to a "minicycle" in which forces of decentralization occasionally would assert themselves within Congress and attempt to disperse power.[10] Supporters of decentralization during the nineteenth century were never numerous enough to break the power of central leaders permanently, however, since the number of congresspeople committed to congressional careers of any significant duration was quite low.

Events of the late nineteenth century altered dramatically the nature of national power. The Civil War ended the ambiguities about the supremacy of the national government over the states and clearly established the hegemony of the national government in political affairs. The industrial revolution, whose effects began to multiply in the late nineteenth century, helped create an interdependent economy based on interstate commerce, thus expanding the power potential of the national government by confronting it with social and economic decisions of considerable magnitude that lay within its constitutional mandate. The industrial revolution also provided America (as well as other nations) with the technical means to span the oceans, conquer far-off lands, and gain international markets for American goods. America thus discovered the world, the world rediscovered America, and the national government discovered anew its constitutional responsibility for foreign policy and the regulation of American involvement in foreign commerce.

As these responsibilities served to strengthen the power of the national government over the lives of individual citizens, Congress became a center of national decision making. The Constitution gave to it the delegated powers to regulate interstate and foreign commerce, give advice and consent (on the part of the Senate) to treaties and ambassadorial nominations, control defense authorizations and appropriations, and declare war. Politicians who wanted to exercise these prerogatives had to go to Congress and stay there, which they did in ever-increasing numbers.[11] In the late nineteenth century congressmen attracted to long-term careers found power in the House centralized in the hands of a Speaker and power in the Senate centralized in the majority party leadership and majority caucus.[12] The centralized conduct of congressional operations denied the rank-and-file members the personal congressional power that growing numbers of them sought. Between 1910 and 1915 their numbers were sufficient so that these disaffected members successfully attacked the foundations of party government in both chambers, overthrowing both the Speakership and the party caucus and dispersing congressional power to the standing committees.[13] The system of committee government that emerged was held together by the institutional norms and rules that had been growing up over the preceding decades as congressional turnover had decreased, particularly the norm of seniority. As Congress moved to a system of committee government, the inherent problems began to emerge.[14] The presidency, which had benefited as an institution from the growth of an administrative state that it partially headed, from the visibility given it by the new nationwide system of mass communications, and from the rise of international relations, became increasingly free from congressional constraints and able to assert national dominance.[15]

From around 1910 to 1945 the presidency grew enormously in power, while Congress floundered. In 1921, in an act that recognized the inability of a decentralized Congress to provide policy coordination and a coherent budget, Congress created the Bureau of the Budget (BOB) and placed it in the executive branch. In the 1930s Roosevelt asserted strongly the role of chief legislator, with major laws drafted in the White House or executive agencies. Roosevelt also seized BOB—which was moved directly under his control—as a tool of presidential decision making. In addition, Roosevelt gained the authority to reorganize the executive branch and thus gained more direct control of the bureaucracy. By the early 1940s many congressional committees were overwhelmed by the executive: their staff work was conducted by staffs from the agencies; their legislation came from the president and the agencies; many committees would not consider legislation that was not approved by BOB; and the legislation that did pass Congress provided the executive broad rule-making authority.[16]

The Roosevelt presidency constituted such a direct threat to Congress—to its control over legislative decision making, the budget, and the bureaucracy—that its members moved to put their own houses in order by passing, in modified form, the 1946 Legislative Reorganization Act. In an attempt to resolve the problems of *leadership* and *accountability*, the act proposed the creation of party policy committees for each party in each house.[17] The House defeated this proposal and it was knocked out of the final act. As a means of providing for *fiscal coordination*, the act proposed and Congress approved the creation of a Joint Committee on the Budget to be composed of all members of the House and Senate Appropriations committees, the

House Ways and Means Committee, and the Senate Finance Committee. A third provision of the act, passed by Congress, involved the reduction of the number of standing committees from 33 to 15 in the Senate and from 48 to 19 in the House, as well as a reduction in subcommittees. As part of this process, Congress tried to clarify jurisdictional boundaries between committees. These efforts were designed to reduce the degree of committee *insulation*, as well as to make leadership and coordination easier. Fourth, in an attempt to provide for greater *oversight* of the executive, the act directed the standing committees to exercise "continuous watchfulness" over the agencies under each committee's jurisdiction, thereby removing any doubt as to their role in bureaucratic surveillance, and also authorized each standing committee to hire professional staff members, setting a limit of four on all except Appropriations.

The 1946 Legislative Reorganization Act served to bring to a close the first twentieth-century cycle of organizational change within Congress and external struggle between Congress and the presidency. With the passage of the act, Congress was able to assert a greater degree of autonomy from the agencies and the president, particularly because of its increased staff resources. The greater congressional autonomy was assisted, however, by the fact that eight of the fourteen years following the passage of the act witnessed a divided government in which the majority party in Congress failed to control the presidency. The act itself actually did little to resolve the fundamental problems of Congress. In their attempt to protect fundamental personal prerogatives, members of Congress failed to take the really difficult steps that might have helped resolve structural problems within Congress. They left party leadership as weak after the act as before, ensuring that central party leaders would offer no threat to committee autonomy; congressional leadership and accountability remained weak. The members of Congress created a joint budget committee whose size was so large (over 100 members) that it was unworkable, whose membership had vested interests (as members of the appropriations and revenue committees) in protecting the power of outside committees, whose powers were nonexistent, and whose legislative timetable (a budget by the second month of a congressional session) was totally unrealistic. Within four years the new budget process had ceased to operate and the problems of fiscal coordination were free to reign. Third, the act did nothing to open committee meetings, to stop long-run proliferation of subcommittees, or to provide sure-fire centralized mechanisms that could enforce committee jurisdictions; the act did not defuse the problems of insulation. And the primary direct effort toward guaranteeing oversight, a provision encouraging its conduct, was a pathetic attempt at problem avoidance that left responsibility for oversight once again in the hands of those least likely to conduct it.

In the final analysis, the 1946 Reorganization Act did not replace the old order of committee government with a new order of congressional rule; the reorganization refurbished the old order and removed some of its most glaring shortcomings but in the end left committee government intact and strengthened. The new committees, by virtue of broader jurisdictions and increased staff resources, were actually stronger and more potent forces than before. Because the new committees were stronger entities, the committee chairpeople—whose prerogatives had not been reduced—emerged as even more powerful figures. The postwar system of committee government thus possessed all of the fundamental problems of the prior era. The 1946 act, moreover, contributed to the *isolation* of most members from congressional power. In streamlining the committee system the act left a relatively small number of autonomous positions that carried with them real power and status. The reform effort thus provided neither the benefits of decentralization (widespread expertise and policy innovation) nor the benefits of centralization (leadership and coordination).

Throughout the 1950s and 1960s, congressional policy making evidenced considerable deadlock. Part of the deadlock, no doubt, was due to the conservative orientation of its members. But part was clearly due to the nature of the postwar committee government, the most apparent attribute of which was the dominance of conservative committee chairpeople. Liberal Democratic activists, particularly in the House, organized to break this deadlock by breaking up the power of committee chairs and dispersing it to subcommittees and subcommittee chairs, thereby also increasing their potential ability to gain power positions. On a committee-by-committee basis they succeeded until the point that, in the early 1970s, they were strong enough to institutionalize a system of subcommittee government by altering the congressional rules. A similar breakthrough had come more informally and earlier in the Senate, so that by the 1970s power within Congress was far more decentralized than it had ever been in the period before World War II.

As liberal activists within Congress moved to decentralize its internal authority, the presidency again came to the fore as the dominant national institution. In the postwar era, under the rubric of national security, presidents gained control of a "secrecy system" in which they dominated (to the extent that any external institution did) the nation's intelligence community. Congress itself was so pluralistic—and its pluralism was increasing so steadily—that presidents and the agencies could easily "justify" ignoring Congress lest congressional leaks expose national "secrets." In foreign policy, "by the 1960s and 1970s, Presidents began to claim the power to send troops at will around the world as a sacred and exclusive presidential right," a right derived from the greater capacity of the executive branch to respond rapidly to international events and to create a coherent and rational foreign policy.[18] Domestically, Kennedy and Johnson asserted in Rooseveltian tradition the primacy of the president as chief legislator and chief budgetary officer, a role reinforced by the increasing desire of the country for a planned and prosperous economy. By the 1970s the presidency was again ascendant in American politics and undertaking political actions far in excess of its legitimate constitutional role. In Schlesinger's term, "constitutional comity" between Congress and the president had broken down. Vietnam, Cambodia, and Watergate were obvious symbols of this breakdown. But the most serious direct assault on Congress came with the attempts by Richard Nixon to impound duly appropriated funds.

The lack of fiscal coordination within Congress meant that in an age of activist legislators, and without external coordination by the executive branch, Congress would generate huge and unplanned deficits, these deficits being the result of dispersed and incremental decision making. With the coming of the Nixon years, both of these conditions were met: a liberal Congress and a divided government in which the liberal Congress faced a conservative president on whom Congress could not rely to provide a budget geared to liberal priorities. The result was huge budgetary deficits. Nixon's response was not to veto the appropriations, which for a variety of reasons seemed politically untenable and unwise, but to impound specific funds and refuse to spend them. He concentrated his efforts on the social legislation that he opposed, and "from 1969 to 1972 . . . impounded 17 to 20 percent of controllable expenditures. . . ." [19] A final straw in the impoundment controversy was Nixon's assertion that impoundment was a constitutional right of the president. Nixon lost this argument in court battle after battle, but in the process he won his policy goals because his unconstitutional impoundments nevertheless succeeded in destroying or crippling the programs he opposed. And, politically, Congress could not move to impeach Nixon for his unconstitutional acts because he had the political trump card: his unconstitutional acts, so he could argue, were necessary to save the Republic from the economic disaster inherent in the budgetary deficits produced by the fiscal irresponsibility of the decentralized, leaderless, uncoordinated, unresponsive, insulated Congress.

Nixon's impoundment of duly appropriated funds confronted members of Congress with the ultimate dilemma implicit within a system of committee government in the twentieth century. The members of Congress could disperse power internally, play their power game, give half the members of each house a power position. The dispersion of power, however, created policies and budgets that the members of Congress could not defend rationally. The president was free ultimately to ignore congressional decisions if he so wished. He could not be threatened by impeachment because of unconstitutional impoundments, since impeachment is ultimately a political undertaking and the president had the political upper hand as a result of the irresponsible behavior on the part of Congress. Nixon thus presented members of Congress with the clearest message yet that the value of power within Congress depended on its ability to ensure the implementation of the policy results generated by internal congressional decision making. Nixon's actions, however, were "not an aberration but a culmination" [20] of forces at work in twentieth-century society, particularly the internal dynamics of Congress as an institution.

The response of Congress to the external threat that had been growing from the 1960s to the early 1970s, and that materialized most dramatically in the impoundment controversy, was to reform its internal organization and procedures once again. The move toward reform came largely in the Democratic party, which, as the congressional majority party, had the most to lose in a shift of power from Congress to a Republican president. Because the lower national status and visibility of House members made their personal power more dependent on the national power of their institution, and because the size of the House meant that problems of leadership, coordination, insulation, and responsiveness undermined more critically its internal decision-making capacity and consequent external authority, the House of Representatives led the reforms.

These reform efforts—from increased leadership power and fiscal coordination to alterations in oversight procedures—seem to have brought an end to a second cycle of internal organizational change and external congressional struggle with the executive branch. Few calls remain within Congress for further centralization of power. The internal struggle has shifted from planning centralized reforms such as the new budgetary process to an effort to implement and institutionalize them. Externally, the president seems less arrogant and aggrandizing in behavior than did Nixon or Johnson. As a result of these reform efforts, and the Watergate incident, the Congress appears resurgent. Is this true? Will it last?

IV

Congressional history during the era of strong national government can be characterized as cyclical in nature. The cyclical pattern derives from the implicit tension between the quest for power by individuals within Congress and the necessity of maintaining the external authority of the institution. The power motive is a very delicate phenomenon, resting as it does in the psyche of politicians who face incredible obstacles and personal demands in any attempt to realize their power drive. For several reasons, however, it seems unlikely that a significant and permanent decline will occur soon in the interest that politicians demonstrate toward congressional service. First, it seems unlikely that individuals preoccupied with political power can look outside of the nation-state for a realization of their quest. Within the nation-state all tendencies seem to indicate a continuing flow of authority away from local and state levels and toward a national level. Individuals preoccupied with attaining political power have no place to look but at the national level. Second, the recent reforms are the most dramatic alterations of internal congressional power relations since the overthrow of Cannon and have been hailed by James Sundquist as restoring the imbalance between congressional and executive power.[21] Politicians have even more reason than Sundquist to find these reforms successful, since this conclusion serves to convince them that service is worth it after all, and offers a means to attain their power goal. Third, electoral security of members of Congress has been increasing dramatically over the past decade or so. The demands of reelection should not be so great that members of Congress will feel that their reelection efforts will of necessity deny them the opportunity and time to seek and exercise congressional power. Finally, underneath the centralizing reforms, which might seem to make Congress less attractive for particular individuals, the dispersion of power of the 1947 to 1973 era remains, institutionalized by a Subcommittee Bill of Rights and augmented by further decentralization decisions that occurred as part of the 1973–75 era. Numerous subcommittee chairs and the resources that go with them, as well as an appearance of power and status, all exist to draw members back to Congress.

The thrust of these arguments is that no changes have occurred that alter the power motive underlying the internal congressional cycle. Can we therefore expect the cycle to continue to operate and the centralizing reform efforts to be undercut in the coming years? The answer to this question would seem to depend largely on the extent to which the reforms really did strengthen central policy organs. It could be that the recent institutional crisis was so severe that members did create central mechanisms so strong that those mechanisms cannot be easily undermined. Alternatively, members may have continued their preoccupation with personal prerogatives, even in the midst of external institutional decay. In the latter case, we would expect an examination of the reform attempt to demonstrate failure of action and, in situations in which reforms actually did pass, evidence of built-in structural flaws that will deflate the renewed congressional resurgence and aid the move toward decentralization. As selected illustrations will indicate, this latter interpretation is the more plausible one.

With regard to *leadership*, the Senate made no effort to restructure the institutional authority or roles of its party leaders. In the House, where serious attempts were made, the Democratic party leader's power (that is, the power of the Speaker in periods of majority party status) is still quite problematic. First, the rise of the caucus and the caucus chairperson, and the lack of a central role of the Speaker in the caucus, has served to dichotomize the power of the Democratic party leadership and has created a situation in which the Speaker may be opposed by a strong caucus chairperson, who can manuever the caucus against the Speaker. The inability of the Speaker to gain central authority in the caucus (for example, as its automatic chair) undercuts severely the authority of the Speaker and his ability to speak for and guide the party. This fragmentation within the leadership ranks continues in the Steering and Policy Committee where the Speaker (who chairs the meeting) and the caucus chairperson both sit, along with 22 other members. While the Speaker has the authority to select 9 of the 22, 12 are chosen by regional caucuses, not by the party caucus as a whole. The emphasis on regional selection of half of the Steering and Policy membership activates not the majority sentiments that might tie the Steering Committee and the party caucus together, but differences that can tear them apart. This is particularly true in light of the *juniority* rule in which Steering and Policy positions within each region must be rotated from Congress to Congress between junior and senior members of the region, even if only one junior member or senior member exists to be chosen. Under such decision rules it is quite possible to generate 12 members who—chosen because of regional affiliations and degree of congressional service rather than policy sentiments—are out of step with the majority of the party and can immobilize the Steering and Policy Committee. The Speaker's authority is also weak because the recent reforms have not given him greater procedural authority on the floor, or personal incentives that the Speaker can use to bargain and cajole with. In addition, in the summer of 1976 the House Democratic caucus defeated the most serious attempt to provide the Speaker with incentives he could use as inducements to party loyalty—the power to select Democratic members of the House Administration Committee and through them control resources such as office space.

The move toward greater *fiscal coordination*—the creation of the new budget committees and a new budget process—has been limited and perhaps crippled fatally by two efforts at protecting the power of existing House committees. First, 10 of the 25 members of the House Budget Committee must come from the House Appropriations and

House Ways and Means committees, 5 from each. Second, all members of the House Budget Committee maintain membership on other committees (including Appropriations and Ways and Means) and are limited in service on the Budget Committee (though not on the other committees) to four years out of every ten. These two rules were the price that had to be paid in the House to gain passage of the Budget Act. Together, they help guarantee that the loyalty of House Budget Committee members is not to the Budget Committee, and thus to a centralized coordination of fiscal policy, but to their other committee assignments (particularly to the two committees, Appropriations and Ways and Means, whose fiscal authority and general status is most threatened by the Budget Committee), and thus to the protection of the autonomy and authority of the other committees. It is, after all, the other committees to which they must look for their long-term power, not the Budget Committee (because of the four-year service limit). It would be hard enough to make the new process work even with a united and cohesive Budget Committee; the internal divisions and weakness built into the House committee seem destined to destroy the process altogether.

The moves to increase *accountability* and *responsibility* did produce a mild change in the Senate cloture rule. Unfortunately, the other reforms—those that have focused on the ability of the caucuses (particularly the House Democratic caucus) to discipline committee chairpeople and select chairs more in line with the policy sentiments of the caucus majority—have suffered from a severe irony. Committee power, and to a large extent congressional power, now rests with subcommittees and subcommittee chairs, not committees and committee chairs. The only subcommittee chair nominations that will be reviewed and ratified or rejected by the House Democratic party caucus are those on the Appropriations Committee. Selection of all other subcommittee chairs is left to the party caucus within the parent standing committee. The majority party caucus thus has gained the real power to hold committee chairs accountable at precisely the time that they matter least. The party caucus does not have a direct procedure to hold most subcommittee chairs accountable; there are, in fact, so many subcommittee chairs now that it would be practically impossible for the full caucus, or even the Steering and Policy Committee, to maintain even a cursory knowledge of their behavior. Since it is the committee caucuses that must constrain and guide subcommittee chairs, and ensure that they reflect the dominant sentiments of the House majority, it is increasingly important that committee caucuses be representative of the party at large and reflect its dominant sentiments in their policy jurisdiction. The representativeness of committees, and the accountability that would come from it, will be much harder for the party to ensure and maintain than the discipline of a small number of powerful committee chairs, if only because of the large numbers of members involved. Considering how hard it has been, and how long it has taken, for the party to evolve a system that would allow the disciplining of committee chairs, it may be a much harder and longer process to move to a system that would ensure a representative selection of committee members who could be trusted to reflect dominant party sentiments and discipline subcommittee chairs accordingly. The alternative, to centralize power within committee chairs who would then be held accountable by the new caucus rules, seems politically impossible in the near future, given the power motive that generated—and continues to generate—subcommittee power; such a move seems probable only if a new institutional crisis forces it (or an analogous move) on the members of the House and on Congress generally.

The effort to reduce congressional *insulation* has hardly fared any better. It has produced one victory of sorts—the sunshine rules that have opened virtually all committee meetings. The open hearings, and the widespread publicity of some meetings, may well have increased somewhat the public's respect for Congress, as in the Senate Watergate hearings or the House Judiciary proceeding on impeachment. Even this victory has had its price, in making committees more susceptible to intrusion by powerful external groups, particularly executive agencies, intrusion that may undermine congressional autonomy; but the sunshine has seemed worth it. Elsewhere, unfortunately, the moves against insulation have been far less successful in their initial passage, much less so in their final impact. The plan of the Bolling Committee to provide for clearer and more rational committee jurisdictions had the misfortune to come to the House floor only after years of power dispersion to subcommittees and the institutionalization of the power of subcommittee chairs. The Bolling plan would have undermined many of these new domains and cast uncertainty into the future of others. Most important, the Bolling plan hurt liberals as well as conservatives, throwing the former (who had supported many of the other reforms) into the arms of the latter, thereby producing a majority against the plan. The Bolling plan was defeated miserably. The cause of its defeat lay with the power motive and the desire of members of Congress, even under the greatest assault on the power of Congress in American history, to protect their personal power prerogatives. This concern for personal power prerogatives, and a widespread willingness to create even more power positions, also meant that no reform was proposed successfully to reduce the multiplicity of subcommittees. Instead, the desire to break up the power of committee chairs that had remained strong, particularly Wilbur Mills's power as chair of Ways and Means, led to a rule requiring all committees of more than 15 members to have subcommittees. The move to increase the number of subcommittees also was exacerbated by a provision of the Hansen plan that encouraged the creation of oversight subcommittees. Overall, to the extent that a multiplicity of committees and subcommittees contributes to congressional insulation, that insulation was increased rather than decreased.

Finally, there were the attempts to increase congressional *surveillance* or *oversight* of executive branch behavior. Once again Congress was unable to undertake strong action. This failure was painfully evident in the oversight hearings into intelligence activity of the federal government; Congress, particularly the House, became so bogged down in attempts by each member to assert her or his own policy perspectives that no overarching legislation or powerful oversight mechanism was produced. Less evident, but no less indicative, were congressional mistakes in the War Powers Act. With the War Powers Act, members of Congress wanted a procedure that would leave them each in control of a piece of the congressional decision; at the same time, they wanted a decision procedure that would leave open their option to exercise power, but a procedure that would not force them to do so if that exercise might prove costly in political terms. The desire of each member for a piece of the war power prerogative kept members from establishing a central Congressional Security Council, analogous to the National Security Council, that they could have mandated to exercise congressional prerogatives in a time of imminent emergency. Rather, they left the president free to act for up to sixty days on his own. In so doing, they also left themselves the protection of facing a decision only after public reaction to the president had become established. Although this might seem an astute move on the part of Congress, in effect it gave congressional war-making powers to the president for sixty days *unless* Congress chose to enforce them. Within sixty days, as any student of the modern presidency should know, a president can maneuver the country into a situation in which it is politically impossible for Congress to fail to support the president. And it is simply not the case that international relations are so complex, and events so fast-moving, that Congress had no alternative. If Congress can invest its war-making powers in a president, it can likewise delegate them to a small number of its own members whose advice and consent a president could be required to receive. After all, all modern presidents have had time to consult the National Security Council and key advisers before acting. Short of imminent nuclear attack, an extreme case whose possibility cannot be used to dictate the norm, a Congressional Security Council would be just as feasible as, and far more necessary for government in a democratic society than, the National Security Council. Members of Congress have failed to establish such a council, which could oversee presidential war making and defend congressional prerogatives, because members of Congress do not want to centralize congressional power. The continuing irony, an irony they truly fail to grasp, is that the unwillingness to structure congressional power in a manner that adjusts to the twentieth-century realities of foreign policy ultimately abrogates the war-making authority of Congress.

A concluding illustration of Congress's dilemma is its attempt to encourage oversight of the bureaucracy. The Senate essentially failed to act. The House, in attempting to act, stripped the most meaningful elements out of the Bolling Committee's oversight recommendations. In order to have serious oversight of the bureaucracy, that authority must be taken from the legislative committees and placed in an oversight committee in each house that has real authority and power to investigate and to force Congress to react to the results of its investigation. The Bolling Committee recommended that the House strengthen the ability of the Government Operations Committee to be a real oversight committee by giving it privileged status to offer amendments to authorizing legislation, amendments that would result from its oversight investigations and present the House with the clear opportunity to incorporate the recommendations in the authorizing legislation. This recommendation was the test case of congressional willingness to have oversight activity. The move was defeated; it was a threat to the authority of the other standing committees. Instead, the Government Operations Committee was authorized to make a report on the planned oversight activities of the other committees. The attempt to create independent oversight activity turned to the creation of oversight subcommittees within existing legislative committees. Even this was defeated as a mandatory move and committees were merely told that they had the option of either creating such subcommittees or instructing the existing subcommittees to undertake oversight action. Less than half of the committees have turned to oversight subcommittees. The moral should be clear: Congress fails to conduct oversight of the bureaucracy not because there are no incentives to it (there are, power and publicity for those who conduct it) nor because it fails to help reelection (being a member of a powerful oversight committee would be a sure-fire method of ensuring widespread publicity). Congress fails to conduct oversight because most members of Congress *fear* its impact on the authority of their existing committee assignments and *fear* the power that a strong oversight committee would have in Congress and in national policy making. Because of the underlying power motive, Congress has failed, and continues to fail, to structure itself in a manner conducive to oversight of the bureaucracy.

As this review should demonstrate, Congress in the 1970s has attempted to act on the problems of leadership, coordination, accountability, insulation, and oversight; its actions in each area have been constrained by and ultimately crippled by a preoccupation of its members with personal power prerogatives. In light of this overview, it is quite sensible to expect the reform efforts of the 1973–75 period, the centralizing era, to be slowly but surely undermined as members reassert the exercise of their power prerogatives, thrusting the country into a new cycle. Much depends on the presidency and the willingness of presidents to show a greater sensitivity to Congress. In all probability, given the extensiveness of congressional reaction in the preceding few years, and the impeachment proceedings against Nixon, the high point of presidential aggressiveness during the postwar cycle was reached with Nixon in 1973. In the years immediately ahead, the country should witness a more cooperative presidency as presidents attempt to defuse the congressional resurgence, a phenomenon already witnessed partially in the Ford presidency. The seduction of Congress is most likely, of course, if an era of united government should dawn in which the individual in the White House is an ideological and partisan compatriot of members of Congress. With a less threatening presidency, the internal dynamics within Congress should lead once again to a push toward decentralization, with a maintenance and strengthening of the 1970–73 era reforms. With Congress not being confronted by apparent institutional crisis, the entity that would be the most probable and immediate victim of this move toward decentralization would be the congressional budget system, since it is the entity that can most severely constrain the autonomous decision-making authority of individual committees and subcommittees. The short-term survival of the budget process in its current form, and as an *autonomous* mechanism of congressional decision making, would seem probable only with the election of a president or a series of presidents who continued attacks on Congress analogous to those made by Nixon and would probably be most likely in an era of divided government.

When a period of quiescence does come, and as the personal power motives of congresspeople produce a move within Congress toward decentralized decision making, it is realistic to assume that the problems inherent in congressional decentralization will lead the nation to demand yet another resurgence of presidential power, unleashing again the momentum toward an institutional crisis in which a president or a series of presidents will overstep dramatically the bounds of political and constitutional comity. The resurgence of presidential power may even come through the centralized congressional mechanisms themselves. For example, the internal moves by self-interested members of Congress against centralized policy organs or against the decisions of those organs (such as the new budget process, the Speakership, or the Steering and Policy Committee) would provide a president with the opportunity to intervene forcefully in the congressional process and throw his weight behind the central policy mechanisms. In such a case we should expect Congress to pay a high price for its "salvation," with the president using and altering such mechanisms to meet the policy ends and power advantage of the president. A majority party president with strong policy commitments could begin the manipulation of the central policy mechanisms by use of a strong presidential liaison team to exert executive influence on the budget committees and budget resolution votes, through agency "cooperation" with and "assistance" to the Congressional Budget Office, and by presidential cooptation of congressional party leaders. We would eventually expect formal alterations in the congressional budget process that would institutionalize executive control of it (perhaps through "coordination" of the CBO with the OMB), thus allowing and formalizing an executive branch penetration of the congressional decision-making process far greater than ever before. Alternatively, Congress may overthrow the new centralizing mechanisms in form as well as reality, leaving in their stead a system totally based on subcommittee government and leaving the executive free to develop other means by which to more strongly coordinate and dominate congressional decision making.

Whatever the precise form of behavior, the logic of the power motive suggests another cycle involving internal moves toward decentralized policy making in Congress, presidential usurpation of congressional authority, and eventual warfare between Congress and presidents over public policy and institutional prerogatives. The immediate question, within the context of this perspective, is not whether a surge toward decentralization and institutional crisis is likely, but rather what such an occurrence will mean when it comes, and what the general cycle tells us about Congress and American politics generally.

V

In order to interpret the significance of the cyclical pattern of internal congressional change for the external struggle between Congress and the executive, we must return to the *Federalist Papers* and James

Madison. Madison's analysis of the U.S. Constitution provides us with the most convincing justification of the Constitution and the most prescient projection of the behavioral patterns expected to flow from its institutional structure. The classic summary of his stance is in Federalist #51:

> In order to lay a due foundation for that separate and distinct exercise of the different powers of government, which to a certain extent is admitted on all hands to be essential to the preservation of liberty, it is evident that each department should have a will of its own. . . .
>
> [T]he great security against a gradual concentration of the several powers in the same department consists in giving to those who administer each department the necessary constitutional means and personal motives to resist encroachment of the others. The provision for defense must in this, as in all other cases, be made commensurate to the danger of attack. Ambition must be made to counteract ambition. The interest of the man must be connected with the constitutional rights of the place.[22]

The devices to which Madison refers here are a separation of powers among the legislative, executive, and judicial branches or departments and a system of checks and balances between these branches. Explicit in the Madisonian conception is an assumption that tension will exist between the branches of government, a tension deriving from the natural ambitions of the politicians within each institution. Ambition will naturally lead these politicians to aggrandize power for themselves by asserting a broad political role for their institution. Inherent in this conception of interbranch tension is the expectation of thrust and counterthrust between the institutions, particularly Congress and the presidency, with one branch asserting itself only to be constrained by the other.

From a Madisonian perspective, Congress should have no problem in asserting its "will" and checking executive aggrandizement. This ability will exist, in large part, because a "few of the members, as happens in all such assemblies, will possess superior talents; will, by frequent re-election, become members of long standing; will be thoroughly masters of the public business. . . ." This tendency toward a few involved legislators would be reinforced in the U.S. Congress by the problems of service, "the distances which many of the representatives will be obliged to travel and the arrangements rendered necessary by that service. . . ."[23] In fact, Madison saw the real problem of Congress not in a weakness of will but in a tendency toward too great an internal concentration of authority and too strong a congressional will. For this reason, Madison feared Congress as the primary threat to the Republic and directed the most attention to constitutional constraint on Congress, not on the executive.[24]

In a Madisonian interpretation, the congressional cycle is one additional element that helps the system of separation of powers and checks and balances work. It ensures that the health and vibrancy of the presidency is maintained in the face of the more threatening legislature, and that there will be struggle and compromise between the Congress and the presidency. Because each institution thus can maintain its autonomy and will, and because Congress is sufficiently restrained by both the external checks and its internal dynamics, the power shift between Congress and the presidency revolves around a constant center or balance point, and the parameters of the cycle are relatively constant, with neither institution ever allowing the other to proceed too far in power aggrandizement. When each cycle is complete, the constitutional powers of the two institutions are once again intact and in balance, a balance specified by the Constitution. During each cycle the rise of one institution and the decline of the other is maintained within clearly defined boundaries that are relatively similar from cycle to cycle. No tendency exists for the institutional excesses to increase in extensiveness or severity from cycle to cycle. The cycle thus can last indefinitely and is, in fact, a "good" thing. The current resurgence of Congress demonstrates its resilience as an institution, its ability to rise to the demands of the day. The failure of the centralizing reforms over the coming years will not be a "bad" thing but merely a natural process that is essential to the dynamics of the Madisonian system of government.

Throughout the nineteenth century, American politics probably did conform fairly closely to the Madisonian interpretation, with the minicycles discussed earlier a constraint on internal congressional ambitions and external aggrandizement. Congress probably was the greatest threat (from a Madisonian perspective) to the constitutional system and to property, and the dominant force in American politics. After a review of twentieth-century congressional behavior, there is good reason to suspect that the Madisonian interpretation no longer applies.

Madison assumed that each institution would sustain sufficient internal integrity that it could have an "institutional will" and would have the institutional capacity to exert that will and counteract the aggrandizing tendencies of other institutions. That assumption was central to Madison's argument and, in the case of Congress, rested on supporting assumptions of high turnover and unpleasant working conditions that would lead Congress naturally to invest its authority in a few select individuals. The alterations in American society and politics in the late nineteenth century that made Congress a more attractive place in which to serve (owing to the growth of national power) and an easier place in which to serve (owing to greater ease of travel and the existence of professional occupations that would mesh well with congressional service) undermined Madison's supporting assumptions, creating internal problems for Congress as an institution that were of a magnitude Madison never envisioned. These problems—of leadership, coordination, insulation, accountability, oversight—have crippled both the ability of Congress to know its "will" and its ability to assert its will. Simultaneously, the growth in societal complexity and international interdependence put a greater emphasis on the speed and efficiency of national decision making. The standard for congressional performance thus was raised at precisely the time that its capacity to perform was being undercut. Unfortunately for Congress, these same changes that hurt it served to highlight the attributes of the presidency—its ability to act quickly, coherently, and decisively; in fact, the coming of the mass media increased the capacity of the president to publicize his will and project a mystique of special authority that is essential to the exercise of power.

It is unrealistic to expect that this shift to presidential ascendancy can or will be altered by the Supreme Court. The power alterations result from inherent constitutional and institutional problems that the Court largely is unable to address. In addition, the judicial appointive process in the Constitution created an informal alliance between the Court and the presidency,[25] an alliance that should constrain the Court from serious innovative efforts to create conditions and interpretations that might subtly alter the formal Constitution so as to strengthen Congress.[26]

The institutional power struggles of the twentieth century thus are operating by a different set of principles, and toward a different end, than the dynamics of Madisonian government suggest. First, the presidency and the executive branch generally gain more authority or power with each cycle than they are forced to give up. During the cycle from 1910 to 1945, for example, the presidency gained dominance over the bureaucracy (that is, to the degree that any external institution dominates the bureaucracy), gained the legitimate role as the nation's chief legislator, and gained legitimacy as chief budgetary officer. With the resurgence of Congress in the postwar years, the presidency still maintained all of the roles—if not as strongly as in Roosevelt's case, certainly more strongly than before the Roosevelt era. At what appears to be the end of a 1945–73 cycle, the presidency has added to its earlier roles (1) a new and legitimized role as the nation's independent agent in war (as a result of the sixty-day provision of the War Powers Act); (2) a wider range of options with regard to control of the budget and the spending of funds (as a result of the Impoundment Act, which, while trying to limit presidential impoundments, succeeded in giving the president a political weapon, impoundment recommendations, to use against Congress and in legitimizing the president's prerogatives to propose a delay or rescission in spending for reasons other than financial efficiency); and (3) retained central authority over the intelligence community and the bureaucracy generally. At the same time that the balance of power seems to be shifting toward the presidency, a second trend seems also to be occurring: an overall increase with each cycle in the extremity of presidential transgressions. Recent presidents' illegal use of the nation's intelligence community, the expanding misuse of presidential war-making powers, and Nixon's unconstitutional impoundments are cases in point.

Existing factors suggest that these trends will continue and worsen. First, the domestic and international problems appear to be increasing in severity, rather than decreasing. The existence of these problems, and the necessity of national action to resolve them, will continue to draw politicians to Congress and sustain the power cycle. The severity of the problems, however, and the existence of congressional immobilism, will justify a continuing and increasing reliance on the executive. This move toward executive power will be reinforced by a second trend: the electoral difficulties of becoming president are so great, and are increasing so significantly with well-intentioned reforms designed to purify presidential politics, that there is an inherent self-selection and weeding process such that the people who rise to that office are, and increasingly will be, immensely power-driven individuals, a phenomenon reinforced by the pressures on and isolation of presidents. In addition, should presidents attempt to forsake proffered power, the structure of American politics and the presidential office probably will offer them no eventual alternative but to accept the expanded authority: with policy immobilism and a resultant economic and social crisis, it would actually be an act of immediate and contextual irresponsibility for presidents not to act in particular and desperate situations.

A final factor which suggests that the momentum toward presidential power will continue and increase is the internal power structure of the current Congress. Underlying the reforms of the 1973–75 era are the reforms of 1970–73. These earlier reforms created a dispersion of power within Congress that is truly unprecedented in American history. As the centralizing mechanisms of the 1973–75 era falter, congressional decision making (as an autonomous process) will depend on an institutionalized system of subcommittee government. Given the greater dispersion of power in that system, the problems of leadership, coordination, insulation, accountability, and oversight that face Congress will be of a magnitude beyond any we have witnessed thus far. The political immobilism implicit in this situation will be intolerable without a strong president. Presidents seeking to assert authority will not face relatively strong committee chairs like Wilbur

Mills, who have authority over a moderate range of policy areas, but relatively weak and isolated subcommittee chairs who can at best dominate a small policy domain and thus will have less maneuverability and fewer resources to use in a congressional-executive struggle. Congress increasingly will be a primary justification for a strong presidency and increasingly an ineffective agent in the constraint of presidential imperialism.

The thrust of my argument, then, is that the Madisonian system is self-destructing. An age of strong national government magnifies the power motive underlying politics generally and sets in motion organizational dynamics within Congress that undermine its ability to perform its constitutional roles. These governmental roles are undertaken by a strong presidency whose institutional integrity and external authority are not decreased but actually increased by the complexities and technology of modern society. In light of human nature and the rules of the political struggle specified in the U.S. Constitution, this alteration in the conduct of governmental roles is a natural reaction of the relevant actors and institutions to the growth of the power of the national government. Seen in this context, the ongoing and continuing destruction of the constitutional system does not stem necessarily from evil motives or evil people. Politicians' quest for power within Congress can derive from the most noble of desires to serve humanity. Power aggrandizement on the part of presidents may be forced on them by the very nature of the political immobilism within Congress and the severity of social and economic crises in the country.

The source of constitutional destruction, and the decline of Congress, lies in the Constitution itself and its inappropriateness today as a guide to representative government. The separation-of-power system provides Congress with an autonomy, as is desirable, that allows it an internal organizational life independent of the executive branch. It also properly invests Congress with legislative authority, delegating it in clear and unmistakable terms. Yet legislative authority is a type of responsibility that can be decentralized and thus afflicted by the problems evident in a system of pure committee government. The Constitution provides no function or structure to Congress that would create internal congressional incentives supportive of power centralization, coordination, and institutional integrity. It merely assumes that these will be maintained by the natural operation of political life in a simple, agrarian society. When the latter assumption is no longer valid, when it is no longer true that policy problems will be simple and congressional life will draw only a few legislators committed to long-term congressional careers and power, there is no provision within the constitutional system—no incentive system—that will lead members naturally to sustain mechanisms of institutional centralization.

As a Congress composed of members who are concerned about public policy becomes increasingly and necessarily enmeshed in institutional immobilism—an immobilism that may result from the very genuineness of members' policy concerns—Congress faces the external checks and balances built into the Constitution. Ironically, since the Founding Fathers thought that Congress was the most dangerous branch, the really powerful checks, such as veto and judicial review, were given to the president and the Court to use against Congress. The inability of the legislature to know its will thus is exacerbated by the ability of the president and the Court, separately or in alliance, to debilitate any congressional will that may exist by throwing in front of Congress the requirement that it make legislative policy not by majority vote but by two-thirds vote.

In light of these considerations, a successful end to the debilitating cycles of the twentieth century requires that we direct attention not to internal congressional reform but to fundamental alterations of the constitutional system itself. We must create an incentive system within the Constitution that, while sustaining a degree of congressional decentralization that will allow for innovation and expertise, will lead members of Congress naturally to support centralizing mechanisms that can sustain institutional integrity. We also must reconsider the nature of the checks-and-balances system with the intent of strengthening the position of Congress. Simultaneously, we can redirect the values by which we wish institutional politics to be conducted, shifting from a politics of minority veto and policy inaction toward majority government and social justice.

It may be that changes within the confines of the current Constitution will be sufficient for our ends.[27] Perhaps constitutional specifications of certain electoral laws could ensure a more competitive electoral system at the congressional level which, by generating higher turnover and more internal institutional need for leadership by individual members, would force a greater degree of centralization. Constitutional provisions giving real authority to the Speaker of the House or the president pro tem of the Senate could give them real incentives to use in the creation and long-term maintenance of significant centralized policy organs in each house. The creation at a constitutional level of a Congressional Security Council that could exercise congressional authority under specific emergency conditions might help Congress regain constitutional control of war making. Finally, a revision of the veto provision (making overrides easier or vetoes harder) might help sustain congressional policy making by holding out the hope that congressional decisions eventually could become the law of the land. While some of the above perhaps could be handled legislatively, it is critical that the changes come at the constitutional level, the level most difficult for members of Congress to manipulate and undermine for personal advantage.

Finally, we must realize that the complex and demanding nature of contemporary life raises serious and fundamental questions as to the viability of Congress within a system of separation of powers and checks and balances. We should reconsider, therefore, our constitutional system itself and direct some attention toward assessing the viability of a new constitutional structure less geared to policy immobilism and institutional conflict. As we consider movement toward alternative constitutions we must realize that constitution making is serious and difficult business. It requires realistic and hard-headed assessment of human nature, of the implications of different institutional arrangements, of the social conditions within which politics is to be conducted, and of the consequences that will derive from the interaction of these three elements of political life. In many ways Madison's performance in the *Federalist Papers* is still the best guide to this type of undertaking. A proper respect for his intellect is always advisable. Yet we also must unlock ourselves from the infatuating clarity and logic of Madison's arguments that continue to exert a seductive hold on our imaginations long after the supporting conditions assumed by them have passed. The transformations of our society in the last century undercut the accuracy of his forecasts. The changes in our values, and hopefully the growth of a greater commitment to majoritarian government and popular justice, alter the goals to which a new or modified constitutional arrangement should be committed. The quest for democratic government demands that we throw off the Sisyphean preoccupation with internal congressional reform and reconsider the constitutional structure that today necessarily consigns Congress— our most democratic institution—to an increasingly weakened political role in an ever more powerful national government.

NOTES

1. The approach presented here has been influenced particularly by the work of Fenno, Huntington, and Mayhew. See Richard F. Fenno, Jr., *Congressmen in Committees* (Boston: Little, Brown, 1973); Samuel P. Huntington, "Congressional Responses to the Twentieth Century," in David B. Truman, ed., *The Congress and America's Future* (Englewood Cliffs, N.J.: Prentice-Hall, 1965); David Mayhew, *Congress: The Electoral Connection* (New Haven, Conn.: Yale University Press, 1974).

2. By the power positions I mean those formal positions within the

congressional institution that carry with them the legal authority over such prerogatives as parliamentary procedure, financial and staff resources, information collection and dispersal, and agenda setting, that are amenable to the control of policy making in a legislative assembly.

3. See Mayhew, op. cit., pp. 32–77.

4. A survey conducted during the 89th Congress under the auspices of the American Political Science Association's Study of Congress found that the average congressperson spent only 5.6 days per month in the home district while Congress was in session (a phenomenon that increasingly covers the calendar year). Although the figure demonstrates that members do take care to return home (a fact that Fenno's research shows is partially related to the location of the family home), members clearly devote *most* of their time to work in Washington. While in Washington, the average member's work week stretches to 59.3 hours per week and has a clear legislative cast to it, with 22.5 hours devoted to work related to legislative research or committee activity, or to party and leadership activities; an additional 15.3 hours are spent on the floor; 7.2 hours are spent answering mail; 5.1 hours handling constituent problems and 4.4 hours visiting with constituents in Washington; 2.7 hours on writing chores, speeches, and magazine articles; 2.3 hours with lobbyists; 2.1 hours on press work, radio and TV appearances. See Donald G. Tacheron and Morris K. Udall, *The Job of the Congressman* (Indianapolis: Bobbs-Merrill, 1970), pp. 303–4; see also Richard F. Fenno, Jr., "U.S. House Members in Their Constituencies," *American Political Science Review*, forthcoming in September 1977.

5. This breakdown of committee types, and the idea of a set of career stages, derive from a very liberal reading of Fenno, *Congressmen in Committees*, together with the literature on committee attractiveness and mobility between committees. For a good summary discussion of this latter literature, see Leroy Rieselbach, *Congressional Politics* (New York: McGraw-Hill, 1973), p. 30.

6. On the existence of congressional norms or folkways, see Donald Matthews, *U.S. Senators and Their World* (New York: Vintage, 1960); and Herbert Asher, "The Learning of Legislative Norms," *APSR* 67 (1967): 501. On the committee selection process, see Nicholas Masters, "Committee Assignments in the House of Representatives," *APSR* (1961): 345–57; and David W. Rohde and Kenneth A. Shepsle, "Democratic Committee Assignments in the U.S. House of Representatives," *APSR* 67 (1973): 889–905.

7. See Robert L. Peabody, *Leadership in Congress* (Boston: Little, Brown, 1976). I am struck in Peabody's discussion by the small

number of leadership challenges, the lack of really bitter struggles, and the short amount of time and small amount of resources put into leadership battles.

8. Some of the major academic works that reflect these calls for presidential assertion are Richard Neustadt, *Presidential Power* (New York: Wiley, 1960); Joseph Harris, *Congressional Control of Administration* (Washington, D.C.: Brookings Institution, 1964); James MacGregor Burns, *The Deadlock of Democracy* (Englewood Cliffs, N.J.: Prentice-Hall, 1963). The classic glorification of the twentieth-century presidency is Clinton Rossiter, *The American Presidency* (New York: New American Library, 1956).

9. Joseph Cooper, "The Origins of the Standing Committees and the Development of the Modern House," *Rice University Studies* 56 (1970); Lauros G. McConachie, *Congressional Committees* (New York: Crowell, 1898).

10. The assertion as to a minicycle is based on a reading of George R. Brown, *The Leadership of Congress* (Indianapolis: Bobbs-Merrill, 1922); and Richard Bolling, *Power in the House* (New York: Capricorn, 1968).

11. The literature demonstrating the decline in turnover includes H. Douglas Price, "Congress and the Evolution of Legislative 'Professionalism'," and Morris P. Fiorina, David W. Rohde, and Peter Wissel, "Historical Change in House Turnover," both in Norman J. Ornstein, ed., *Congress in Change* (New York: Praeger, 1975); Nelson Polsby, "The Institutionalization of the House of Representatives," *APSR* 62 (1968): 144–69.

12. On the House, see Brown, op. cit.; on the Senate, see David J. Rothman, *Politics and Power* (New York: Atheneum, 1969).

13. See Kenneth W. Hechler, *Insurgency: Personalities and Politics of the Taft Era* (New York: Columbia University Press, 1940).

14. Discussions of these problems in the 1920s are contained in Brown, op. cit., and Lindsay Rogers, *The American Senate* (New York: Knopf, 1926).

15. For a more general discussion of the rise of the presidency, see James MacGregor Burns, *Presidential Government* (Boston: Houghton Mifflin, 1965); and Arthur M. Schlesinger, Jr., *The Imperial Presidency* (New York: Popular Library, 1973).

16. See George B. Galloway, *Congress at the Crossroads* (New York: Crowell, 1946), pp. 7–8, 53, 242–54.

17. George B. Galloway, "The Operation of the Legislative Reorganization Act of 1946," *APSR* 45 (1951): 51.

18. Schlesinger, op. cit., p. 298.

19. James P. Pfiffner, "Congressional Budget Reform, 1974: Initiation and Reaction," 1975 APSA convention paper, pp. 4–5; see also

Louis Fisher, *Presidential Spending Power* (Princeton, N.J.: Princeton University Press, 1975), pp. 147–201.

20. Schlesinger, op. cit., p. 395.

21. James L. Sundquist, "Congress and the President: Enemies or Partners?" in this volume. Sundquist writes: "Viewed in the perspective of history, the changes in the executive-legislative power balance wrought by a single Congress—the 93rd—are truly momentous. Ever since the era of congressional government at the close of the Civil War . . . , the flow of power had been all one-way, in the direction of the president. In just two years, the trend of a hundred years was dramatically reversed. An extraordinary abuse of presidential power triggered a counteraction equally extraordinary, and the ponderous processes of institutional change were expedited." Sundquist seems to reflect an essentially Madisonian conception of the recent changes in congressional structure.

22. James Madison, Federalist No. 51, in Alexander Hamilton, James Madison, and John Jay, *The Federalist Papers*, edited by Clinton Rossiter (New York: New American Library), pp. 321–22.

23. Madison, Federalist No. 53, pp. 334–35.

24. Madison, Federalist No. 48, p. 309.

25. Robert Scigliano, *The Supreme Court and the Presidency* (New York: Free Press, 1971), p. 197.

26. Ibid., pp. 200–201.

27. For an intriguing dialogue on the Constitution and current problems, see Bob Eckhardt and Charles L. Black, Jr., *The Tides of Power: Conversations on the American Constitution* (New Haven, Conn.: Yale University Press, 1976).

Bibliography

Bauer, Raymond A., Ithiel de Sola Pool, and Lewis A. Dexter. *American Business and Public Policy*. New York: Atherton, 1963.

Bibby, John F., and Roger H. Davidson. *On Capitol Hill*. 2nd ed. Hinsdale, Ill.: Dryden, 1972.

Bolling, Richard. *House Out of Order*. New York: Dutton, 1965.

———. *Power in the House*. New York: Dutton, 1968.

Bowler, M. Kenneth. *The Nixon Guaranteed Income Proposal: Substance and Process in Policy Change*. Cambridge, Mass.: Ballinger, 1974.

Brown, George R. *The Leadership of Congress*. Indianapolis: Bobbs-Merrill, 1922.

Bullock, Charles S., III. "House Careerists: Changing Patterns of Longevity and Attrition." *American Political Science Review* 66 (1972).

Burns, James MacGregor. *The Deadlock of Democracy*. Englewood Cliffs, N.J.: Prentice-Hall, 1963.

Clausen, Aage R. *How Congressmen Decide*. New York: St. Martin's, 1973.

Clem, Alan L., ed. *The Making of Congressmen: Seven Campaigns of 1974*. North Scituate, Mass.: Duxbury, 1976.

Cooper, Joseph. *The Origins of the Standing Committees and the Development of the Modern House*. Houston, Tex.: William Marsh Rice University, 1971.

Davidson, Roger H., David M. Kovenock, and Michael K. O'Leary.

Congress in Crisis: Politics and Congressional Reform. Belmont, Calif.: Wadsworth, 1966.

Davidson, Roger H., and Walter J. Oleszek. "Adaptation and Consolidation: Structural Innovation in the U.S. House of Representatives." *Legislative Studies Quarterly* 1 (1976): 37–65.

Dexter, Lewis A. *The Sociology and Politics of Congress.* Chicago: Rand McNally, 1969.

———. *How Organizations Are Represented in Washington.* Indianapolis: Bobbs-Merrill, 1969.

Dodd, Lawrence C. *Congress and Public Policy.* Morristown, N.J.: General Learning Press, 1975.

Eckhardt, Bob, and Charles L. Black, Jr. *The Tides of Power: Conversations on the American Constitution.* New Haven, Conn.: Yale University Press, 1976.

Erikson, Robert. "The Advantage of Incumbency in Congressional Elections." *Polity* 3 (1971).

Evans, Rowland, and Robert Novak. *Lyndon B. Johnson: The Exercise of Power.* New York: New American Library, 1966.

Fenno, Richard F., Jr. *Congressmen in Committees.* Boston: Little, Brown, 1973.

———. "The Internal Distribution of Influence: The House." In *The Congress and America's Future,* edited by David B. Truman. Englewood Cliffs, N.J.: Prentice-Hall, 1965.

———. *The Power of the Purse.* Boston: Little, Brown, 1966.

Ferejohn, John. *Pork Barrel Politics.* Stanford, Calif.: Stanford University Press, 1974.

Fiorina, Morris, P., David W. Rohde, and Peter Wissel. "Historical Change in House Turnover." In *Congress in Change,* edited by Norman J. Ornstein. New York: Praeger, 1975.

Fishel, Jeff. *Party and Opposition.* New York: McKay, 1973.

Froman, Lewis A., Jr. *The Congressional Process: Strategies, Rules and Procedures.* Boston: Little, Brown, 1967.

Galloway, George B. *Congress at the Crossroads.* New York: Crowell, 1946.

Goodwin, George, Jr. *The Little Legislatures.* Amherst: University of Massachusetts Press, 1970.

Harris, Joseph. *Congressional Control of Administration.* Washington, D.C.: Brookings Institution, 1964.

Hechler, Kenneth W. *Insurgency: Personalities and Politics of the Taft Era.* New York: Columbia University Press, 1940.

Hinckley, Barbara. *The Seniority System in Congress.* Bloomington: Indiana University Press, 1971.

———. *Stability and Change in Congress.* New York: Harper & Row, 1971.

Holtzman, Abraham. *Legislative Liaison.* Chicago: Rand McNally, 1970.

Huitt, Ralph K., and Robert L. Peabody. *Congress: Two Decades of Analysis.* New York: Harper & Row, 1969.

Huntington, Samuel P. "Congressional Responses to the Twentieth Century." In *The Congress and America's Future,* edited by David B. Truman. 2nd ed. Englewood Cliffs, N.J.: Prentice-Hall, 1973.

Jewell, Malcolm. *Senatorial Politics and Foreign Policy.* Lexington: University of Kentucky Press, 1962.

Jones, Charles O. *The Minority Party in Congress.* Boston: Little, Brown, 1970.

Kernell, Sam. "Is the Senate More Liberal Than the House?" *Journal of Politics* 35 (May 1973): 332–63.

Kingdon, John W. *Congressmen's Voting Decisions.* New York: Harper & Row, 1973.

MacNeil, Neil. *Dirksen: Portrait of a Public Man.* New York: World, 1970.

McPherson, Harry. *A Political Education.* Boston: Little, Brown, 1972.

Manley, John F. *The Politics of Finance.* Boston: Little, Brown, 1970.

Matthews, Donald R. *U.S. Senators and Their World.* New York: Vintage, 1960.

Matthews, Donald R., and James Stimson. "Decision-Making by U.S. Representatives: A Preliminary Model." In *Political Decision-Making,* edited by S. Sidney Ulmer. Cincinnati: Van Nostrand, 1970.

Mayhew, David R. *Congress: The Electoral Connection.* New Haven, Conn.: Yale University Press, 1974.

———. *Party Loyalty among Congressmen.* Cambridge, Mass.: Harvard University Press, 1966.

Miller, Clem. *Member of the House.* New York: Scribners, 1962.

Moe, Ronald C., and Steven C. Teel. "Congress as Policy-Maker: A Necessary Reappraisal." *Political Science Quarterly* 85 (1970): 443–70.

Ogul, Morris S. *Congress Oversees the Bureaucracy.* Pittsburgh: University of Pittsburgh Press, 1976.

Oppenheimer, Bruce I. *Oil and the Congressional Process: The Limits of Symbolic Politics.* Lexington, Mass.: Lexington Books, 1974.

Orfield, Gary. *Congressional Power: Congress and Social Change.* New York: Harcourt Brace Jovanovich, 1975.

Ornstein, Norman J. "Causes and Consequences of Congressional Change: Subcommittee Reforms in the House of Representatives, 1970–1973." In *Congress in Change,* edited by Norman J. Ornstein.

———, ed. *Congress in Change.* New York: Praeger, 1975.

Patterson, Samuel C. "Congressional Committee Professional Staffing: Capabilities and Constraints." In *Legislatures in Developmental Per-*

spective, edited by Allan Kornberg and Lloyd Musolf. Durham, N.C.: Duke University Press, 1970.

Peabody, Robert L. *Leadership in Congress: Stability, Succession and Change.* Boston: Little, Brown, 1976.

Peabody, Robert L., and Nelson W. Polsby, eds. *New Perspectives on the House of Representatives.* Chicago: Rand McNally, 1963.

Polsby, Nelson W. *Congress and the Presidency.* 3rd ed. Englewood Cliffs, N.J.: Prentice-Hall, 1976.

――――. "Institutionalization in the U.S. House of Representatives." *American Political Science Review* 62 (1968): 144–68.

Polsby, Nelson W., Miriam Gallagher, and Barry Rundquist. "The Growth of the Seniority System in the House of Representatives." *American Political Science Review* 63 (1969): 787–807.

Pressman, Jeffrey. *House vs. Senate.* New Haven, Conn.: Yale University Press, 1966.

Price, David E. *Who Makes the Laws?* Cambridge, Mass.: Schenkman, 1972.

Price, H. Douglas. "Congress and the Evolution of Legislative Professionalism." In *Congress in Change,* edited by N. J. Ornstein. New York: Praeger, 1975.

Rieselbach, Leroy. *Congressional Politics.* New York: McGraw-Hill, 1973.

Ripley, Randall B. *Majority Party Leadership in Congress.* Boston: Little, Brown, 1969.

――――. *Party Leaders in the House of Representatives.* Washington, D.C.: Brookings Institution, 1967.

――――. *Power in the Senate.* New York: St. Martin's, 1969.

Robinson, James A. *The House Rules Committee.* Indianapolis: Bobbs-Merrill, 1963.

Rohde, David W. "Committee Reform in the House of Representatives and the Subcommittee Bill of Rights." *The Annals* 411 (January 1974): 39–47.

Rohde, David W., and Kenneth A. Shepsle. "Democratic Committee Assignments in the U.S. House of Representatives." *American Political Science Review* 67 (1973): 889–905.

Rothman, David J. *Politics and Power.* New York: Atheneum, 1969.

Saloma, John S., III. *Congress and the New Politics.* Boston: Little, Brown, 1969.

Schwarz, John E., and L. Earl Shaw. *The United States Congress in Comparative Perspective.* Hinsdale, Ill.: Dryden Press, 1976.

Seidman, Harold. *Politics, Position, and Power.* 2nd ed. London: Oxford University Press, 1975.

Stewart, John G. "Two Strategies of Leadership: Johnson and Mansfield." In *Congressional Behavior,* edited by Nelson W. Polsby. New York: Random House, 1971.

Sundquist, James L. *Politics and Policy.* Washington, D.C.: Brookings Institution, 1968.

Tacheron, Donald G., and Morris K. Udall. *The Job of the Congressman.* Indianapolis: Bobbs-Merrill, 1970.

Truman, David B. *The Governmental Process.* New York: Knopf, 1951.

Turner, Julius. *Party and Constituency: Pressures on Congress.* Rev. ed. by Edward V. Schneier, Jr. Baltimore: Johns Hopkins Press, 1970.

Vogler, David J. *The Politics of Congress.* Boston: Allyn & Bacon, 1974.

———. *The Third House.* Evanston, Ill.: Northwestern University Press, 1971.

Wildavsky, Aaron. *The Politics of the Budgetary Process.* Boston: Little, Brown, 1964.

Wilson, Woodrow. *Congressional Government.* Gloucester, Mass.: Peter Smith, 1885, 1973.

Wolfinger, Raymond E., and Joan Heifetz Hollinger. "Safe Seats, Seniority, and Power in Congress." *American Political Science Review* 59 (1965): 337–49.

Young, James S. *The Washington Community, 1880–1828.* New York: Columbia University Press, 1966.

The Contributors

LAWRENCE C. DODD is Assistant Professor of Government at the University of
Texas in Austin. He received his B.A. at Midwestern University (Wichita
Falls, Texas) in 1968, conducted graduate work at Tulane University, and
received his Ph.D. from the University of Minnesota in 1972. He has
served as an NDEA Fellow (1968–69), a Ford Fellow (1971–72), and a Congressional Fellow (1974–75). He is the author of *Congress and Public Policy*
(1975) and *Coalitions in Parliamentary Government* (1976), as well as articles
that have appeared in several scholarly journals.

BRUCE I. OPPENHEIMER, Assistant Professor of Politics at Brandeis University,
received his B.A. from Tufts University and his Ph.D. from the University
of Wisconsin. In 1970–71 he was a Governmental Studies Fellow at the
Brookings Institution, and in 1974–75 he was an American Political
Science Association Congressional Fellow. Among his publications is *Oil
and the Congressional Process—the Limits of Symbolic Politics* (1974).

NORMAN J. ORNSTEIN is Associate Professor of Politics at Catholic University.
Most recently he has worked on the staff of the Temporary Select Committee to Study the Senate Committee System. Among his publications is
Congress in Change: Evolution and Reform (1975). He was an American Political Science Association Congressional Fellow in 1969–70. Currently he
is working with Robert Peabody and David Rohde on a book on the U.S.
Senate.

DAVID W. ROHDE, Associate Professor of Political Science at Michigan State
University, received his B.S. from Canisus College and his Ph.D. from the

313

University of Rochester. He is coauthor of *Supreme Court Decision Making* (1976). He is currently working with Norman Ornstein and Robert Peabody on a book on the U.S. Senate.

ROBERT L. PEABODY is Professor of Political Science at The Johns Hopkins University. He has served as Associate Director of the A.P.S.A. Study of Congress and recently as staff assistant to former House Speaker Carl Albert. He is the author of a number of books on Congress including *Leadership in Congress: Stability, Succession and Change* (1976); editor of *Education of a Congressman* (1972); coauthor of *To Enact a Law: Congress and Campaign Finance* (1972); coauthor of *Congress: Two Decades of Analysis* (1969); and coeditor of *New Perspectives on the House of Representatives*. He is currently working with Norman Ornstein and David Rohde on a book on the U.S. Senate.

ALBERT D. COVER is Assistant Professor of Political Science at The University of Michigan. He received his Ph.D. from Yale University, where he had previously taught. In 1973–74 he was an American Political Science Association Congressional Fellow.

DAVID R. MAYHEW is Associate Professor of Political Science at Yale University and Acting Chairman of the Yale Department in 1976–1977. He received his Ph.D. from Harvard University and was an American Political Science Association Congressional Fellow in 1967–68. His publications include *Party Loyalty Among Congressmen* (1966) and *Congress: The Electoral Connection* (1974).

JOHN F. MANLEY, Professor of Political Science at Stanford University, is currently on leave at the Center for Advanced Study in Behavioral Sciences. Among his publications are *The Politics of Finance* (1970) and *American Government and Public Policy* (1976). He is a recent Guggenheim Fellow.

CATHERINE RUDDER, Assistant Professor of Political Science at the University of Georgia, received her doctorate from Ohio State University. She served as an American Political Science Association Congressional Fellow in 1974–75, being assigned to the staffs of Senator Dick Clark of Iowa and Representative Abner Mikva of Illinois, a member of the Committee on Ways and Means.

JOSEPH COOPER is currently on leave from his position as Professor of Political Science at Rice University, serving as staff director of the U.S. House of Representatives Commission on Administrative Review. He is the author of a monograph on the origins and development of the committee system in the House of Representatives as well as various articles on Congress and the presidency. He is coeditor of the Sage Yearbook on Electoral Studies and received his Ph.D. from Harvard University in 1961.

JOHN W. ELLWOOD holds a Ph.D. in political science from The Johns Hopkins University and has taught at the State University of New York's College at Fredonia and the University of Virginia. As a Congressional Fellow during the 1974–75 academic year he had assignments with the Senate Budget Committee and the Congressional Budget Office, and he is currently Special Assistant to the Deputy Director of CBO.

JAMES A. THURBER is Associate Professor in the School of Government and Public Administration at the American University. He has also taught at the University of Maryland, George Washington University, and Washington State University. Professor Thurber, who received his Ph.D. at Indiana University, has worked for the Temporary Select Committee to Study the Senate Committee System, Senator Hubert H. Humphrey, and Congressman James G. O'Hara. He has published articles on various aspects of American politics, but his most recent work has focused on congressional budget reform.

JOHN T. ELLIFF is Associate Professor of Politics at Brandeis University, having taught previously at Barnard College and Harvard and Columbia Universities. He served as Domestic Intelligence Task Force Leader for the Senate Select Committee on Intelligence Activities in 1975–76 and was a principal author and editor of its final report on *Intelligence Activities and the Rights of Americans*. He is the author of *Crime, Dissent, and the Attorney General: The Justice Department in the 1960s* (1971) and numerous articles on the FBI.

MORRIS S. OGUL is Professor of Political Science at the University of Pittsburgh. He received his Ph.D. from the University of Michigan. He is the author of *Congress Oversees the Bureaucracy* (1976) and is coauthor with William J. Keefe of *The American Legislative Process*, 4th ed. (1977).

JAMES L. SUNDQUIST, a senior fellow at the Brookings Institution, has worked in both the legislative branch (as a Senate administrative assistant) and the executive branch (in the Executive Office of the President). He is author of several books, including *Politics and Policy: The Eisenhower, Kennedy, and Johnson Years*. His essay in this volume is condensed from a chapter in his *Setting National Priorities: the Next Ten Years* (1976).

CHARLES O. JONES, Maurice Falk Professor of Politics at the University of Pittsburgh, has written articles and books on Congress, political parties, and public policy. His most recent work is *Clean Air: The Policies and Politics of Pollution Control* (1975). Professor Jones is managing editor of the *American Political Science Review*.

RICHARD F. FENNO, JR., Professor of Political Science at the University of Rochester, received his B.A. from Amherst College and his Ph.D. from Harvard University. He is author of *The President's Cabinet* (1959), *The Power of the Purse: Appropriations Politics in Congress* (1966), *Congressmen in Committees* (1973), and coauthor of *National Politics and Federal Aid to Education* (1962). Currently he is writing a book on the activities of U.S. House members in their constituencies.